"As a Thief in the Night"

"As a Thief in the Night"

THE MORMON QUEST
FOR MILLENNIAL DELIVERANCE

Dan Erickson

Signature Books
Salt Lake City

To my wife,

Jennifer K. Erickson

JACKET DESIGN: RON STUCKI

∞ *"As a Thief in the Night": The Mormon Quest for Millennial Deliverance* was printed on acid-free paper.
It was printed in the United States of America.

2002   2001   00   99   98   6   5   4   3   2   1

LIBRARY OF CONGRESS CATALOGING-IN-PUBLICATION DATA
Erickson, Dan
      As a thief in the night : the Mormon quest for
   millennial deliverance / by Dan Erickson.
         p.   cm.
      Includes bibliographical references and index.
      ISBN 1-56085-100-7
      1. Millennialism—United States—History of doctrines—
   19th century.   2. Church of Jesus Christ of Latter-day
   Saints—History of doctrines—19th century.   3. Mormon
   Church—History—19th century.
   I. Title.
   BX8643.M54E75   1998
   236'.9—dc21   98-15272
                                                CIP

CONTENTS

CHAPTER ONE.   Introduction   1

CHAPTER TWO.   American Millennialism   13

CHAPTER THREE.   Modern Revelation: 33
                 Origins of a Separatist Theology

CHAPTER FOUR.   Early Mormon Millennialism   65

CHAPTER FIVE.   The Gathering: 93
                 Separatism Shapes a Society

CHAPTER SIX.   Mormon Nauvoo: 123
                 Separatism Defines a City

CHAPTER SEVEN.   Mormons versus the United States: 149
                 The Utah War and Civil War Periods

CHAPTER EIGHT.   Millennialism and the   179
                 Anti-Polygamy Campaign

CHAPTER NINE.   The Decline of Millennialism   213

CHAPTER TEN.   Conclusion   223

                 Bibliography   231

                 Index   267

CHAPTER ONE

INTRODUCTION

In 1952 Ira Brown lamented America's millennial past as being "among the most neglected ... themes in the history of American thought."[1] Over the past forty years religious, social, and intellectual historians of the American experience have moved to rectify this omission and an explosion of new scholarship has developed a depth of millennial historiography.[2] Commenting on this phenomenon, James Moorhead contends scholars now find millennialism everywhere and it has "proven to be one of the most fertile areas of investigation in American religious history."[3] Leonard Sweet declares: "[T]he word millennialism has become almost synonymous in recent years with American religious history."[4] This outpouring of

1. Ira V. Brown, "Watchers for the Second Coming: The Millenarian Tradition in America," *Mississippi Valley Historical Review* 39 (Dec. 1952): 441.

2. See David E. Smith, "Millenarian Scholarship in America," *American Quarterly* 17 (Fall 1965): 535-49; Hillel Schwartz, "The End of the Beginning: Millenarian Studies, 1967-1975," *Religious Studies Review* 2 (July 1976): 1-15; Leonard I. Sweet, "Millennialism in America: Recent Studies," *Theological Studies* 40 (Sept. 1979): 510-31; Dietrich G. Buss, "Meeting of Heaven and Earth: A Survey and Analysis of the Literature on Millennialism in America, 1965-1985," *Fides et Historia* 20 (Jan. 1988): 5-28.

3. James H. Moorhead, "Searching for the Millennium in America," *Princeton Seminary Bulletin* 8 (1987): 17.

4. Leonard I. Sweet, "The Evangelical Tradition in America," in *The Evangelical Tradition in America*, ed. Leonard I. Sweet (Macon, GA: Mercer University Press, 1984), 23.

new knowledge has coincided with an equal intensity of scholarship regarding Mormonism.[5] Yet the combining of these two elements remains in its infancy, and Mormon millennial historian Grant Underwood has asserted the meaning and force of millennialism in Mormon thought "is just beginning to be plumbed."[6]

For many religious historians of this period, Mormon millennialism has been difficult to classify. Ernest Tuveson admitted that he had trouble categorizing Mormon eschatology. Although he contends they "maintain a millenarian doctrine" (premillennialists), he later argues "they certainly do not think that the course of history is one of increasing decline, which can only be ended by the personal intervention of the Lord."[7] Gordon Wood concurs that Mormon belief regarding the Second Coming "cannot be easily fit into any single pattern of millennialism."[8] John F. C. Harrison identifies Mormonism as a unique form of millenarianism emphasizing "Zion was to be built in the American West, and that in the near future."[9]

In placing Mormon eschatology within the greater context of nineteenth-century American millennialism, the historiography of Mormonism has focused primarily on the pre-1850 period or has stressed that millennialism was but part of the continuity of Mormon thought from the early days to the present.[10] This study approaches

---

5. A starting point is the 62-page bibliography in James B. Allen and Glen M. Leonard, *The Story of the Latter-day Saints* (Salt Lake City: Deseret Book Co., 1976), 639-700.

6. Grant Underwood, "Seminal Versus Sesquicentennial Saints: A Look at Mormon Millennialism," *Dialogue: A Journal of Mormon Thought* 14 (Spring 1981): 41.

7. Ernest Lee Tuveson, *Redeemer Nation: The Idea of America's Millennial Role* (Chicago: University of Chicago Press, 1968), 34n11, 175-76.

8. Gordon S. Wood, "Evangelical America and Early Mormonism," *New York History* 61 (Oct. 1980): 385.

9. J[ohn]. F. C. Harrison, *The Second Coming: Popular Millenarianism 1780-1850* (New Brunswick, NJ: Rutgers University Press, 1979), 176-92, 181.

10. See Marvin S. Hill, "The Role of Christian Primitivism in the Origin and Development of the Mormon Kingdom, 1830-1844," Ph.D. diss., University of Chicago, 1968; Hill, *Quest for Refuge: The Mormon Flight from*

Mormon millennialism from the point of view of its separatist tendencies, a perspective initiated with Joseph Smith's first religious

---

American Pluralism (Salt Lake City: Signature Books, 1989); Hill, "Quest for
Refuge: An Hypothesis as to the Social Origins and Nature of the Mormon
Political Kingdom," Journal of Mormon History 2 (1975): 3-20; Hill, "The
Shaping of the Mormon Mind in New England and New York," Brigham
Young University Studies 9 (Spring 1969): 351-72; and Gordon D.
Pollock, In
Search of Security: The Mormons and the Kingdom of God on Earth, 1830-1844
(New York: Garland Publishing, 1989). Grant Underwood's studies,
centering primarily on early Mormon millennialism, are found in his "Early
Mormon Millennialism: Another Look," M.A. thesis, Brigham Young
University, 1981; Underwood, "Seminal Versus Sesquicentennial Saints";
Underwood, "Millenarianism and the Early Mormon Mind," Journal of
Mormon History 9 (1982): 41-51; Underwood, "Early Mormon Millennialism:
Another Look," Church History (June 1985): 215-29; Underwood,
"Re-Visioning Mormon History," Pacific Historical Review 55 (Aug. 1986):
403-26; Underwood, "Apocalyptic Adversaries: Mormonism Meets
Millerism," John Whitmer Historical Association Journal 7 (1987): 53-61;
Underwood, "The Religious Milieu of English Mormonism," in Mormons in
Early Victorian Britain, eds. Richard L. Jensen and Malcolm R. Thorp (Salt
Lake City: University of Utah Press, 1989), 31-48; Underwood, The
Millenarian World of Early Mormonism (Urbana: University of Illinois Press),
1993. A noted exception is Louis G. Reinwand's study of Mormon
millennialism in Utah in the nineteenth century and, to a lesser extent,
emphasized millennialism as one of many important doctrines to the early
Saints. See Reinwand, "An Interpretive Study of Mormon Millennialism
During the Nineteenth Century with Emphasis on Millennial Developments
in Utah," M.A. thesis, Brigham Young University, 1971. Klaus J. Hansen ties
Mormon millennialism to the Mormon Council of Fifty. See Hansen, Quest
for Empire: The Political Kingdom of God and the Council of Fifty in Mormon
History (Lansing: Michigan State University Press, 1970), 1-23; see also
Hansen, "The Metamorphosis of the Kingdom of God: Toward a
Reinterpretation of Mormon History," Dialogue: A Journal of Mormon Thought
1 (Autumn 1966): 63-83; Hansen, "Mormonism and American Culture: Some
Tentative Hypotheses," in The Restoration Movement: Essays in Mormon History,
rev. ed., eds. F. Mark McKiernan, Alma R. Blair, and Paul M. Edwards
(Independence, MO: Herald Publishing House, 1992), 1-25; and Hansen,
Mormonism and the American Experience (Chicago: University of Chicago Press,
1981).

experience and which continued to the end of the nineteenth century.[11]

Since the LDS church's organization in 1830, Mormons and other members of American society have experienced varying levels of contention. The backlash of Mormon-non-Mormon friction initially led the Latter-day Saints to move from New York, seeking refuge by "gathering" in Kirtland, Ohio, in 1831, then in Jackson County, Missouri. This trek was initiated by prophetic revelation and a belief that a righteous people should be gathered at the city of "Zion" to receive Jesus Christ at his coming. The Saints eventually fled both locales to settle in Far West, Missouri. Driven out of Missouri in 1838-39 by Missouri governor Lilburn Boggs's well-known Extermination Order, they crossed the Mississippi to found the city of Nauvoo, Illinois.[12]

---

11. Thomas G. Alexander concedes that up until 1890 premillennialism and the imminence of the prophesied apocalypse played a central role in Mormon thought. Nevertheless he contends that emphasis must be placed, particularly during Mormon church president Wilford Woodruff's administration, on shifting the church's organizational focus from millennialism to temples and salvation of the dead as the means of preparing for Christ's return to establish his kingdom on earth. See Alexander, "Wilford Woodruff and the Changing Nature of Mormon Religious Experience," *Church History* 45 (Mar. 1976): 69; see also Alexander, *Mormonism in Transition: A History of the Latter-day Saints, 1890-1930* (Urbana: University of Illinois Press, 1986), 1-15; Alexander, *Things in Heaven and Earth: The Life and Times of Wilford Woodruff, a Mormon Prophet* (Salt Lake City: Signature Books, 1991); Alexander, "'To Maintain Harmony': Adjusting to External and Internal Stress, 1890-1930," *Dialogue: A Journal of Mormon Thought* 15 (Winter 1982): 44-58; and Alexander, "The Odyssey of a Latter-day Prophet: Wilford Woodruff and the Manifesto of 1890," *Journal of Mormon History* 17 (1991): 169-206.

12. Richard Lloyd Anderson, "Atchison's Letters and the Causes of Mormon Expulsion from Missouri," *Brigham Young University Studies* 26 (Summer 1986): 3-47; Stephen C. LeSueur, *The 1838 Mormon War in Missouri* (Columbia: University of Missouri Press, 1987); Leland H. Gentry, "A History of the Latter-day Saints in Northern Missouri from 1836-1839," Ph.D. diss., Brigham Young University, 1965.

Motivated by their experience in Ohio and Missouri, and their lack of political power in each location, the Mormons in Nauvoo established a virtual independent city-state.[13] Within its charter Nauvoo was granted a municipal court with the power to issue writs of habeas corpus and the authority to create its own military establishment, the Nauvoo Legion. Mormon interpretation of Nauvoo's charter and the new-found Mormon sense of political power further alienated non-Mormons who viewed the Mormon stronghold as a bastion of lawlessness and the Nauvoo Legion as a potential armed aggressor.[14] The murders of the prophet Joseph Smith and his brother Hyrum in 1844 precipitated the Mormons' expulsion from Illinois and United States territory, initiating their migration to the Great Basin.

The contentious relationship between the Mormon church and American society continued in the West. Although much of the conflict may be viewed as resentment by non-Mormons in Utah toward the church's theocratic control of Utah Territory, the main impetus for opposition was the practice of plural marriage or polygamy.[15] All of this culminated in the anti-polygamy campaign. Resisting the federal government's outlawing of both polygamy and cohabi-

---

13. Robert Flanders, *Nauvoo: Kingdom on the Mississippi* (Urbana: University of Illinois Press, 1965), 104; James L. Kimball, Jr., "The Nauvoo Charter: A Reinterpretation," *Journal of the Illinois State Historical Society* 64 (Spring 1971): 66-78; James L. Kimball, Jr., "A Wall to Defend Zion: The Nauvoo Charter," *Brigham Young University Studies* 15 (Summer 1975): 499-526.

14. Kenneth H. Winn, *Exiles in a Land of Liberty: Mormons in America, 1830-1846* (Chapel Hill: University of North Carolina Press, 1989), 162.

15. Works advocating political domination factors for Mormon-non-Mormon conflict include Gustive O. Larson, *The "Americanization" of Utah for Statehood* (San Marino, CA: Huntington Library, 1971), viii; and Hansen, *Quest for Empire*, 171. Works whose position supports the primacy of polygamy as the catalyst for conflict include Edward Leo Lyman, *Political Deliverance: The Mormon Quest for Utah Statehood* (Urbana: University of Illinois Press, 1986), 2; B. Carmon Hardy, *Solemn Covenant: The Mormon Polygamous Passage* (Urbana: University of Illinois Press, 1992), 58-59; and Alexander, *Things in Heaven and Earth*, xiii.

tation, and considering polygamy a vital tenet of their faith, church leaders refused to succumb to the pressure to assimilate into mainstream America.

Mormons viewed the federal anti-polygamy campaign as a "last-days" persecution leading to the anticipated Millennium, and the Saints, under the leadership of church president John Taylor, sought to evade assimilation. In a final attempt to preserve the institution of polygamy, Taylor's separatist strategy included church leaders going "underground," authorizing establishment of a polygamist bastion in Mexico outside the United States, and initiating a potential polygamous retreat in Canada. But the national government's anti-polygamy campaign proved successful, ending with Mormon church president Wilford Woodruff's 1890 Manifesto admonishing church members to obey the law of the land.

The attempt to maintain the institution of polygamy in the face of U.S. government pressure followed earlier Mormon separatist actions and was based on the Mormon millennial world view. Over its first sixty-year history, much of the LDS-gentile conflict was influenced by expectation that the Second Coming was imminent, an event that would transform the earth and deliver the Mormons from their enemies. The short-term nature of their millennial anticipation, particularly during the Ohio-Missouri-Illinois period, kept an us-versus-them mentality in the forefront of their consciousness. But Mormonism was repeatedly forced to accept a delay of the promised "winding-up scene." In the 1830s Zion (in Missouri) went unredeemed, and the 1840s saw Joseph Smith murdered and the Saints expelled from Illinois. The 1850s-1860s witnessed the proposed State of Deseret become Utah Territory under U.S. government control rather than the desired Mormon theocracy. And then the "official" abandonment of polygamy in the 1890s "turned out to be a prologue to modern Mormonism" rather than the Saints' apocalyptic triumph.[16]

---

16. Jan Shipps, *Mormonism: The Story of a New Religious Tradition* (Urbana: University of Illinois Press, 1985), 148. See also Harold Bloom, *The American Religion: The Emergence of a Post-Christian Nation* (New York: Simon

Despite its claim to Americanism, Mormonism was "consistently seen as un- and anti-American."[17] Political solidarity, block voting, and economic communitarianism offended Jacksonian republicanism. Joseph Smith's desire to establish a political kingdom, including his candidacy for the U.S. presidency, demonstrated to outsiders that Mormons were not "Americans" in the true definition of the term.[18] Polygamy, first made public in Utah, further offended non-Mormons and resulted in a new round of Mormon-American confrontation. Unwilling to live with and among "gentiles," Mormons were convinced that only in maintaining their separateness from pluralistic America could they prepare a people for the coming of the Lord. As such, conflict persisted between some aspect of American society and the Mormons for over fifty years.[19]

The nineteenth century ended with the Mormon church forced to conform with American values. In viewing this transformation, Klaus Hansen contends that Mormons initially were dissenters who by the twentieth century had become "active and approving participants in modern America."[20] Anthropologist Mark Leone asserts Mormon church accommodation replicates social reality and change "creating and recreating Mormonism."[21] Yet in examining this adaptation process much of the intensity of early Mormon millennialism has been neglected. Nathan Hatch contends the tendency to overlook this aspect of early Mormonism is due to modern elitist frameworks based on current value systems. "We are scandalized by the reality that most popular religion is vulgar religion," and certainly primitive

---

and Schuster, 1992), 70.

17. Martin E. Marty, foreword to Klaus J. Hansen, *Mormonism and the American Experience* (Chicago: University of Chicago Press, 1981), xiii.

18. Winn, *Exiles in a Land of Liberty*, 203-207.

19. Larry M. Logue, *A Sermon in the Desert: Belief and Behavior in Early St. George, Utah* (Urbana: University of Illinois Press, 1988), 1.

20. Hansen, *Mormonism and the American Experience*, xvi. See also Philip L. Barlow, *Mormons and the Bible: The Place of the Latter-day Saints in American Religion* (New York: Oxford University Press, 1991), viii.

21. Mark P. Leone, *Roots of Modern Mormonism* (Cambridge, MA: Harvard University Press, 1979), 192-93.

Mormonism remained "radical, apocalyptic, absolutist, [and] extreme."[22]

Focusing on millennialism as the impetus for Mormon separatist behavior, this study examines the near unanimity of Mormon belief in the establishment of God's separate kingdom on earth, with his righteous servants awaiting deliverance from their enemies at Christ's return. This Mormon millennial world view, with its goal of separating the Saints from non-Mormon Babylon, continued until the church's capitulation near the beginning of the twentieth century.

The Mormon view of history, like that of ancient Hebrews, is teleological, linear, proceeding in a straight line toward a predetermined, divinely intended culmination (the coming of the Messiah).[23] Yet an historical study of the Latter-day Saints entails unique challenges. In examining Mormonism within the context of nineteenth-century American religious experience, Jan Shipps argues Mormonism's differences with mainstream Christianity are so profound it must be classified as a new religious tradition like Islam or Christianity.[24] Sydney Ahlstrom demonstrates his difficulty in categorizing Mormonism when declaring, "One cannot even be sure if the object of our consideration is a sect, a mystery cult, a new religion, a church, a people, a nation, or an American subculture; indeed, at different times and places it is all of these."[25]

Additionally, Mormon belief in modern revelation amplifies the problem, particularly in determining the tenacity and permanence of theological tenets. Ascertaining what is revelation or scripture com-

---

22. Nathan O. Hatch, "Mormon and Methodist: Popular Religion in the Crucible of the Free Market," *Journal of Mormon History* 20 (Spring 1994): 39, 38.

23. Allan J. Lichtman and Valeri French, *Historians and the Living Past* (Arlington Heights, IL: Harlan Davidson, 1978), 86-87; Roger D. Launius, "Mormon Memory, Mormon Myth, and Mormon History," *Journal of Mormon History* 21 (Spring 1995): 12.

24. Jan Shipps, *Mormonism*, 85. See also Bloom, *The American Religion*, 81-83, 87-89, 96.

25. Sydney E. Ahlstrom, *A Religious History of the American People* (New Haven: Yale University Press, 1972), 508.

plicates the process. One must unravel and decipher both ancient and modern scripture, oracles from the church hierarchy, private revelation (including personal inspiration and patriarchal blessings), non-canonized scripture, temporary (and sometimes changing) scripture, and other revelatory forms of the Mormon religious creed.[26]

Historians faced with the task of dealing with studies focusing on religion must also confront methodological ramifications. Recent discussion of the objectivity question has left many believing that any quest for objectivity is futile. Eugen Weber has declared that "all that the historian may hope to do is to record a *passing point of view* as honestly and as thoughtfully as he knows how."[27] While accepting the notion that absolute objectivity is impossible, a position may be argued that somewhere between the great divide of absolute objectivity and inevitable subjectivity falls the realm of appropriate scholarly pursuit. What an historian must attempt to do when confronting religious history is to perform the task, to the fullest degree possible, of understanding and explaining the forces which give rise to the thoughts and actions of the players within the historic drama.[28] And although religious history is a process that must appeal to factors that are subject to public inspection and scrutiny, this does not preclude "the possibility that the projected meanings may have an ultimate status independent of man."[29]

Yet in examining evidence and motivation how must religious experience be evaluated? Philip Barlow asks: "Should scripture and religion be viewed from the perspective of culture, or should

---

26. Barlow, *Mormons and the Bible*, x.

27. Eugen Weber, *A Modern History of Europe* (New York: W.W. Norton and Co., 1971), 1125 (emphasis mine). For a discussion of the abandonment of objectivity, see Peter Novick, *That Noble Dream: The "Objectivity Question" and the American Historical Profession* (Cambridge, Eng.: Cambridge University Press, 1988), 522-629.

28. John G. Gager, "Early Mormonism and Early Christianity: Some Parallels and Their Consequences for the Study of New Religions," *Journal of Mormon History* 9 (1982): 55.

29. Peter L. Berger, *The Sacred Canopy: Elements of a Sociological Theory of Religion* (Garden City, NY: Doubleday and Co., 1967), 181.

culture be viewed through the lens of scripture and religious faith?"[30] If God exists, and, acting through men and women, influences historical circumstances and outcomes, mere mortals still must interpret such divine intervention through the lens of human experience. Whether or not one believes, or whether or not revelations and spiritual manifestations are authentic, their interpretations still must be analyzed and examined in terms of cultural and environmental forces.[31] Kenelm Burridge describes the dilemma: "If we are confronted with evidence of a divine revelation, we cannot declare it irrelevant or irrational or fantasy or wishful thinking. We must take it seriously and try to account for what actually occurs. Even if our own private assumptions do not admit of such a thing as divine revelation, we must admit that for others it does exist."[32]

Historians of the Mormon experience have acknowledged and attempted to breach the objectivity divide in a variety of ways.[33] The methodology used in this study approaches the search for historical understanding of sacred causes and consequences by relating "events as participants experienced them."[34] Insofar as religious experiences and revelations were authentic to those who acted on those beliefs, they will be treated as such in the discussion that follows, since a good-faith attempt to relay to the modern observer the motivation

---

30. Barlow, *Mormons and the Bible*, xviii.

31. Ibid., xvii-xviii. See also Mircea Eliade, "The Sacred in the Secular World," *Cultural Hermeneutics* 1 (1973): 101-13.

32. Kenelm Burridge, *New Heaven, New Earth: A Study of Millenarian Activities* (New York: Schocken Books, 1969), 117-18.

33. Marvin S. Hill, "Positivism or Subjectivism? Some Reflections on a Mormon Historical Dilemma," *Journal of Mormon History* 20 (Spring 1994): 21.

34. See Richard L. Bushman, *Joseph Smith and the Beginnings of Mormonism* (Urbana: University of Illinois Press), 3. Bushman's approach to Mormon history, which attempts to reconstruct the past from Joseph Smith and his followers' perspective and world view, is criticized by Nathan Hatch as "one-dimensional scholarship." See Hatch, "Mormon and Methodist," 36-37.

and perceived reality of these historical actors is always a worthwhile endeavor.

Weighing these sometimes conflicting elements, this study aspires to evaluate critically the importance early Mormon millennial enthusiasm played in nineteenth-century Mormon history. Hopefully, the result will share William McNeill's vision of what historians can achieve when they "bend their minds as critically and carefully as they can to the task of making their account of public affairs credible as well as intelligible to an audience that shares enough of their particular outlook and assumptions to accept what they say."[35]

Approaching Mormon history within a framework of millennial aspirations, the present analysis argues that for their first sixty-year history the Latter-day Saints were apocalyptic premillennialists—but with a difference. From this difference emerged a new religious group embracing modern scripture and revering modern prophets who received divine communication, a people commissioned to build a literal kingdom of God on the American continent to prepare for the imminent return of the promised Messiah. Their millennial passage, ambiguous, evolving, always waiting, anticipating, and eventually capitulating to the dominant American society, is the essence of this study.

---

35. William H. McNeill, *Mythhistory and Other Essays* (Chicago: University of Chicago Press, 1986), 19.

CHAPTER TWO

AMERICAN MILLENNIALISM

To understand the context and intensity of early Mormon millennialism, one must consider both the history of millennialism in the American tradition and the transformation of mainstream American Protestant thought from premillennialism to postmillennialism near the beginning of the nineteenth century. This postmillennial search for personal and community righteousness led to the great era of religious revivals from which Mormonism traces its origins.[1]

One's search for meaning usually leads to eschatological inquiry. More than mere theology, millennialism is a way of looking at the world, human history, and the destiny of humankind.[2] Leonard Sweet describes millennialism's impact on a social structure as a "force that can exert formative influence over all strata [of] society."[3] At Mormonism's inception two rival world views, premillennial and postmillennial, anticipated differing future millennial kingdoms. These differences included determining what type of supernatural

---

1. Marvin S. Hill, "The Rise of Mormonism in the Burned-over District: Another View," *New York History* 61 (Oct. 1980): 419. William Warren Sweet calls Mormonism the "most completely indigenous" movement rising from the revivalist setting; see his *Religion in the Development of American Culture, 1765-1840* (1952; reprint, Gloucester, MA: Peter Smith, 1963), 285.

2. J[ohn]. F. C. Harrison, *The Second Coming: Popular Millenarianism, 1780-1850* (New Brunswick, NJ: Rutgers University Press, 1979), 228.

3. Leonard I. Sweet, "Millennialism in America: Recent Studies," *Theological Studies* 40 (Sept. 1979): 153.

intervention was expected (or lack thereof) and deciding what humanity's role in the winding-up scene would be.[4]

The earliest apocalyptic tradition stems from the Jews who saw themselves as God's chosen, and their history as sacred history. Jews, aided by a sense of their own chosen condition, understood oppression and hardship as a sign that their deliverance was nigh. Inherent in this position is the view of an evil force which becomes increasingly wicked until it is suddenly overthrown by divine power. God then rewards the righteous who inherit his kingdom. Like the Jews, early Christians developed an apocalyptic tradition that salvation was imminent and their enemies would soon be destroyed.[5] First-century Christianity is the background used to understand American millennialism because, as James West Davidson concedes, "eight- eenth-century New England is closer to the first century than to the twentieth."[6]

Although small in verse, the biblical account of a future millennium, contained primarily in the books of Daniel and Revelation, has proven to hold a profound effect on humanity's concept of history. In describing the force of these accounts, Ernest Tuveson contends that "no other passage of comparable length has ever had such great and long-lasting influence on human attitudes and beliefs."[7] As described in the book of Revelation, millennialism predicts a linear view of time. God acts in history and uses humankind, yet he is not determinative and his influence is only made use of by free individuals. Imbedded in Christian mil-

---

4. James H. Moorhead, "Searching for the Millennium in America," *Princeton Seminary Bulletin* 8 (1987): 23; Sacvan Bercovitch, *The American Jeremiad* (Madison: University of Wisconsin Press, 1978), 94.

5. Walter Schmithals, *The Apocalyptic Movement: Introduction and Interpretation*, trans. John E. Steely (Nashville: Abingdon Press, 1975), 13-150; Norman Cohn, *The Pursuit of the Millennium* rev. ed. (New York: Oxford University Press, 1970), 19-24.

6. James West Davidson, *The Logic of Millennial Thought: Eighteenth-Century New England* (New Haven, CT: Yale University Press, 1977), 12.

7. Ernest Lee Tuveson, *Redeemer Nation: The Idea of America's Millennial Role* (Chicago: University of Chicago Press, 1968), 9.

lennialism is a deeply held belief that the Bible contained prophecies about the future including the return of Jesus Christ and
his establishing a thousand-year reign of peace. Viewing all history as religious chiliasm, where the world is moving toward its
imminent consummation, the Millennium becomes history's last
stage, offering the great reversal where God finally exalts the
heretofore persecuted righteous saints. God's plan from the beginning was to end the world with the return of Christ, and the
daily events men and women participate in are merely an ele-
ment of the Apocalypse. The book of Revelation concludes with
John assured that the end is near and history will end with the
righteous victorious.[8]

The biblical narrative cites the Millennium as but part of a
world view that anticipates an overthrow of the current world order as it exists. Millennialism is a way for ordinary people to confront the changes facing them and their society, and make sense
of new and bewildering experiences by providing hope and vision
of the future as it should be. Millennial thought seeks to give
meaning to the suffering of the innocent and righteous, and rep-
resents a moral order where vindication will prevail.[9] Crisis, judgement, the resurrection of the dead, and eternal reward or damna-
tion is humankind's destiny.

After the death of Christ, the Christian tradition continued to
view a chosen people, now the Christians, who would prepare and
inherit the kingdom of God during the Millennium. Christ first came
as a meek lamb, but when he returns it will be as a warrior (Rev. 18-19,
20:4-6). Christians, constantly on the watch for the "signs of the
times," viewed chaos, wars, plagues, famines, and droughts as signals
that the end was near. Scripture emphasized the suddenness of
Christ's return, that he would come "as a thief in the night," and the

8. Joseph M. Hallman, "God and the End of Civilization," *American
Journal of Theology and Philosophy* 4 (Sept. 1983): 114.

9. Moorhead, "Searching for the Millennium in America," 23-25;
Michael Barkun, *Crucible of the Millennium: The Burned-Over District of New
York in the 1840s* (Syracuse: Syracuse University Press, 1986), 9-10.

troubles of the world would be replaced by a new heaven and a new earth.[10]

An early dualism in Christian thought drew the line between good and evil sustaining the first believers. History was seen as the continuous struggle of God against Satan: "it is [therefore] natural for adherents of the kingdom to perceive a coherent, sinister intelligence animating the various problems they encounter."[11] The book of Revelation is a great drama of angels and God's people versus demons and the armies of Satan. As forces line up heading for either condemnation or redemption, there is no neutral ground. Yet human suffering is temporary, and ultimately good must overcome evil. When the Messiah returns, he will set things right. Millennial history is parallel in nature, where God redeems society and individual souls simultaneously.[12] The apocalyptic model of history moves from crisis to judgement to vindication, mirroring "the evangelical conception of [an] individual soul's pilgrimage from sin, through the storm to conversion, to new life."[13] Although the notion of the Millennium would bring different images and meanings to different people, all would see a vision of "a new heaven and a new earth," a perfect environment where humans would live without sin or suffering.[14]

In analyzing the history of early Christian eschatology, Medieval historian Norman Cohn created a model for classifying the unique eschatological characteristics defined as "millenarian."[15] For the pur-

---

10. Cohn, *The Pursuit of the Millennium*, 30, 35.

11. James H. Moorhead, *American Apocalypse: Yankee Protestants and the Civil War 1860-1869* (New Haven, CT: Yale University Press, 1978), 7.

12. Tuveson, *Redeemer Nation*, 4-12.

13. Moorhead, "Searching for the Millennium in America," 30-31; Davidson, *The Logic of Millennial Thought*, 122-75; Jerald C. Brauer, "Revivalism and Millenarianism in America," in *In the Great Tradition: In Honor of Winthrop S. Hudson, Essays on Pluralism, Voluntarism, and Revivalism*, eds. Joseph D. Ban and Paul R. Dekar (Valley Forge, PA: Judson Press, 1982), 147-59.

14. Harrison, *The Second Coming*, 9-10; Barkun, *Crucible of the Millennium*, 11-12.

15. J. F. C. Harrison has suggested that "millenarian" be used for

pose of this study, the terms millenarian and premillennial will be used interchangeably. As a starting point, Cohn's model is "simply a convenient label for a particular type of salvationism" but remains a useful tool for understanding the distinctive millenarian world view. Millenarian salvation is pictured as

a.   collective, in the sense that it is to be enjoyed by the faithful as a collectivity;

b.   terrestrial, in the sense that it is to be realized on this earth and not in some other-worldly heaven;

c.   imminent, in the sense that it is to come both soon and suddenly;

d.   total, in the sense that it is utterly to transform life on earth, so that the new dispensation will be no mere improvement on the present but perfection itself;

e.   miraculous, in the sense that it is to be accomplished by, or with the help of, supernatural agencies.[16]

---

groups made up of popular, unlettered religious movements, and millennialists for more intellectual end-time arguments, i.e., based on biblical, chronological calculations; see his *The Second Coming*, 5-7. Michael Barkun disagrees since "the scholarly musings of one generation had a way of emerging in the popular religiosity of another"; see his *Crucible of the Millennium*, 11.

16. Cohn's model was presented at a conference held at the University of Chicago, 8-9 April 1960, and originally published in a volume based on that conference. See Norman Cohn, "Medieval Millenarianism: Its Bearing on the Comparative Study of Millenarian Movements," in *Millennial Dreams in Action*, ed. Sylvia L. Thrupp (The Hague: Mouton and Co., 1962), 31-43. See also Cohn, *The Pursuit of the Millennium*, 15-18. A sampling of other works which use Cohn's model include Barkun, *Crucible of the Millennium*, 18; Harrison, *The Second Coming*, 8-9; David E. Smith, "Millennial Scholarship in America," *American Quarterly* 17 (Fall 1965): 538-39. Grant Underwood used this model in classifying early-nineteenth-century Mormons as millenarian. See Underwood, "Millenarianism and the Early Mormon Mind," *Journal of Mormon History* 9 (1982): 41-42; and Underwood, *The Millenarian World of Early Mormonism* (Urbana: University of Illinois Press, 1993), 5-6, 24-41. A model similar to Cohn's can be found in Moorhead, "Searching for the Millennium in America," 29. Also useful is Bryan R. Wilson's "response model" which analyzes how new religious movements respond to the outside

In one sense the hoped-for millennium must be considered a "fantasy" in that its imminence has proven false, particularly when political and/or military battles with established authorities have failed.[17]

Millenarian strength was usually in rural areas, and in most instances has required a prophet to give a millenarian movement meaning and coherence. When social unrest occurred, the poor would seek improved conditions through divine intervention and by receiving prophets or would-be messiahs. They anticipated the final battle between the righteous and the wicked was about to transpire, after which Christ's kingdom would be established.[18] Norman Cohn summarizes the social setting for millenarian movements as an environment where people "living in a state of chronic frustration and anxiety [that frustration would] suddenly discharge ... itself in a frantic urge to smite the ungodly—and by doing so to bring into being ... that final kingdom where the Saints ... were to enjoy ease and riches, security and power for all eternity."[19]

The idea of imminence delivered the great reversal to the here and now, bringing judgement to the present as the Millennium "hastens the process of retribution and vindication."[20] Hillel Schwartz labels waiting for the destruction of the wicked the "ethos of judgement," and by definition the Millennium is "a time when judgement future [comes] down to earth," elevates the saints, and destroys the anti-Christ.[21] The supernatural aspect of the great reversal guaranteed that the wicked's present triumph was temporary and

culture. See Wilson, *Magic and the Millennium: A Sociological Study of Religious Movements of Protest Among Tribal and Third-World Peoples* (London: Heineman Education Books, 1973), 18-30.

17. Barkun, *Crucible of the Millennium*, 19.

18. Max Weber, *The Sociology of Religion*, trans. Ephraim Fischoff (Boston: Beacon Press, 1963), 46; Wilson, *Magic and the Millennium*, 499; Harrison, *The Second Coming*, 11; Cohn, *The Pursuit of the Millennium*, 16.

19. Cohn, *The Pursuit of the Millennium*, 59-60.

20. Davidson, *The Logic of Millennial Thought*, 294.

21. Hillel Schwartz, *The French Prophets: The History of a Millenarian Group in Eighteenth Century England* (Berkeley: University of California Press, 1980), 3-4; Davidson, *The Logic of Millennial Thought*, 295.

that God would "soon set the scales of justice aright at the Day of Judgement."[22]

In summary premillennialists held that the Millennium was to be preceded by Christ's advent followed by a thousand years of peace. God would not convert the masses; on the contrary, the world was moving steadily downward, declining both morally and physically. When the earth becomes ripe for destruction, God will unleash unprecedented destruction, taking vengeance on the wicked. This transformation would be both total and sudden, abruptly abolishing evil and sin and restoring peace. With the inauguration of his divine wrath, God would destroy and remove all corruption. For only after the wicked are destroyed can Christ abide on earth. Premillennialist thought could influence one's outlook on life, and millenarians were seen as anxious, pessimistic, gloomy, less active, anti-progressive, and socially conservative, expecting cataclysmic solutions to solve current problems. Dualist in nature, premillennialism viewed the overturn of the wicked as the defeat of a superhuman enemy, restoring to human-kind its divine inheritance at the apex of history.[23]

From the earliest days of Christianity, the apocalyptic tradition adapted to changing circumstances as disciples looked for Christ's imminent return without obtaining a fulfillment. Although affliction was seen as an essential part of persecution, early Christians were faced with the fact that Christ did not return quickly and had allowed his Saints to suffer.[24] In the third century a step towards a progressive millennium was initiated by the influential theologian Origen who interpreted millennial prophecies and predictions metaphorically, and a philosophical shift began to identify the Kingdom of God, not in time and space, but as something that would take place in the hearts and souls of believing men and women. In the fifth century

---

22. Davidson, *The Logic of Millennial Thought*, 83.

23. Barkun, *Crucible of the Millennium*, 24-25; Tuveson, *Redeemer Nation*, 34-35, 76-78; Davidson, *The Logic of Millennial Thought*, 28-33; Smith, "Millennial Scholarship in America," 535-49.

24. Theodore Olson, *Millennialism, Utopianism, and Progress* (Toronto: University of Toronto Press, 1982), 84-92; Harrison, *The Second Coming*, xv-xvi, 4; Davidson, *The Logic of Millennial Thought*, 114-21.

Augustine's *The City of God* saw the Millennium as a spiritual allegory, already begun at Christ's birth, now realized in the form of the church. Therefore the second coming of Christ would occur *after* the thousand-year period of bliss prophesied in the twentieth chapter of the book of Revelation.[25] Millennialism gradually changed, solidified by Augustine's emphasis on the "allegoric rather than the literal fulfillment of prophecies," believing that hope in the church was the answer to eschatological desires.[26]

Yet through the Middle Ages a literal interpretation of the Millennium refused to die and the Christian apocalyptic tradition continued, particularly in the form of popular religion. Sixteenth-century papal Rome became identified with the "Church of the Devil," and a re-emergence of premillennialism began to take place.[27] Reformation millenarian doctrine rejected the Augustinian Christian belief that the Second Advent would occur after the Millennium.[28]

In America seventeenth-century New Englanders believed their new home was the place where the Reformation would be carried to its next level. They considered their "errand into this wilderness" was

---

25. W. Stanford Reid, "The Kingdom of God: The Key to History," *Fides et Historia* 13 (Spring-Summer 1981): 7; Robert G. Clouse, ed., *The Meaning of the Millennium: Four Views* (Downers Grove, IL: InterVarsity Press, 1977), 9-10; Cohn, *The Pursuit of the Millennium*, 29. Earnest Tuveson expressed an aversion to the standard pre- vs. postmillennialist dichotomy, believing that Augustine would fall into a third category. Although technically postmillennial (the Millennium precedes the Parousia), there remain significant differences between Augustinians who saw the hoped for "City of God" as separate from the evil world and traditional post-millennialists. See Tuveson, *Redeemer Nation*, 34n11.

26. Ernest R. Sandeen, *The Roots of Fundamentalism: British and American Millenarianism, 1800-1930* (Chicago: University of Chicago Press, 1970), 4.

27. Wilber B. Wallis, "Reflections on the History of Premillennial Thought," in *Interpretation and History*, eds. R. Laird Harris, Swee-Hwa Quek, and J. Robert Vannoy (Singapore: Christian Life Publishers, 1986), 228.

28. Katherine R. Firth, *The Apocalyptic Tradition in Reformation Britain, 1530-1645* (Oxford: Oxford University Press, 1979), 1-27; Sandeen, *The Roots of Fundamentalism*, 8-31.

a prelude to the world's redemption. Many times calling themselves "Israel," the Puritans saw providence separating them from the motherland, leading religious exiles to America as part of God's plan to create a society prepared for the Millennium. Why else would the Almighty hold in abeyance the discovery of such a vast land as America until the earth was ready for the end of Babylon?[29]

Early Puritans developed a religious philosophy with America as the focus of their millennial hope. American theologians such as Increase and Cotton Mather and John Elliot expected that God would gather the elect and locate the new Jerusalem on American soil. Both Increase and Cotton Mather were premillennialists who believed in the supernatural and imminent return of Christ, and told parishioners they were living in the "last days." Much of Cotton Mather's theology focussed on biblical prophecies, believing that the seventh "day" of history, or the Millennium, like the day of creation, would be a time of rest, and he kept a close eye on the Jews since prophecy foretold their conversion prior to the winding up scene. Mather's publications affirmed that the end was near and he died believing the Millennium was imminent.[30]

---

29. For background on Puritan millennialism, see Peter Toon, *Puritans, the Millennium and Future Israel: Puritan Eschatology, 1600-1660* (Cambridge, Eng.: James Clark, 1970); Sacvan Bercovitch, *The Puritan Origins of American Self* (New Haven, CT: Yale University Press, 1975); J. F. Maclear, "New England and the Fifth Monarchy: The Quest for the Millennium in Early American Puritanism," *William and Mary Quarterly* 32 (Apr. 1975), 222-60; Alfred Cohen and Vavasor Powell, "Two Roads to the Puritan Millennium," *Church History* 32 (Sept. 1963): 322-38; John F. Wilson, "Comment on 'Two Roads to the Millennium,'" *Church History* 32 (Sept. 1963): 339-43; Tuveson, *Redeemer Nation*, 24-25, 97-99, 128.

30. Robert Middlekauff, *The Mathers: Three Generations of Puritan Intellectuals, 1596-1728* (New York: Oxford University Press, 1971), 20-24; Moorhead, "Searching for the Millennium in America," 23-25; Davidson, *The Logic of Millennial Thought*, 36. Most early theories identifying American Indians as part of the lost tribes of Israel were associated with a millennial view of history. John Elliot, Samuel Sewel, and Cotton Mather believed the Indians descended from Israel's lost tribes and that by converting them they could help usher in the Millennium. Joseph Mede speculated they may be

In the late seventeenth century Puritan theologians continued to emphasize the premillennial belief that the righteous would reign with Christ for a thousand years prior to the final judgement and destruction.[31] But gradually a disagreement developed over humankind's role in the final scene, and to what exactly an individual should aspire. Must one wait patiently or should an activist role be taken? Those who hoped for a more gradual millennium supposed God was relying on them to speed the cause. Some contended that not all supernatural prophecy should be taken literally, literal meanings could be put aside provided sufficient justification existed. Those who leaned toward literalism preferred a supernatural reading of biblical prophecy, those who opted for metaphorical interpretations adopted a natural millennial process. Philosophically the great reversal troubled many, for if Satan had his way until the final hour, "earth's history is but a long series of Satan's acts frustrating God's plan, until God is forced to use miraculous intervention to end the struggle."[32] Even premillennialist Cotton Mather feared that Christians who believed in a supernatural necessity would become lackadaisical.[33]

Revived in the eighteenth century, the American version of postmillennialism began as an increasingly secular vision of the transformation process which could occur by human effort. American colonists identified themselves with chosen Israel, and progress and America's destiny became inseparable as Americanism and religion melded together in millennial terms. A new vision of the future saw the advancement of science and democracy as a sign the Millennium may be a period of peace, where large numbers of people could be saved ver-

used as part of Satan's final army in the battle of Armageddon. See Dietrich G. Buss, "Meeting of Heaven and Earth: A Survey and Analysis of the Literature on Millennialism in America, 1965-1985," *Fides et Historia* 20 (Jan. 1988): 5-6; Timothy Sehr, "John Elliott: Millennialist Missionary," *Historian* 46 (Feb. 1984): 187-203; Davidson, *The Logic of Millennial Thought*, 54-67; Smith, "Millennial Scholarship in America," 539-40.

31. Davidson, *The Logic of Millennial Thought*, 37-44.

32. Tuveson, *Redeemer Nation*, 32.

33. Davidson, *The Logic of Millennial Thought*, 83-101.

sus premillennialist notions of a minor elect group redeemed at Christ's coming. As such, American postmillennialism's birth did not initiate with Jonathan Edwards but surfaced almost a century earlier in the hopeful expectations of Samuel Sewel, Cotton Mather, and Joseph Morgan, carried forward by John Owen and John Cotton.[34]

Postmillennialism was more than placing Christ's return at the end of the thousand years of millennial bliss, it was a way of viewing progress and the world, an understanding that improvement would follow rational law which humans could master for their own betterment. Postmillennial philosophy was a compromise between an apocalyptic sense of the end based on the book of Revelation and a progressive view of humanity's future. With the return of Christ placed at the end of the Millennium, there was now time for the gradual perfection of people and society, human effort counted, and evangelicalism could combine with American citizenry to create heaven on earth.[35]

Postmillennialists saw no need for divine intervention to overcome evil, human progress would gradually change society. The Millennium was no longer fixed in time but a gradual step of events realized by degrees. If Christ was not to inaugurate the Millennium, then human action could matter and there would be no need to wait. One must not abandon a quest for righteousness to await divine intervention but should continue to attempt to reform society. Postmillennial emphasis on human effort redefined the struggle between good and evil into thousands of small contests rather than one climatic battle, thus allowing for the weathering of disappointment by pushing the final victory far into the distant future. Postmillennialism did not remove God from humankind's perfection; he became a co-participant. Down-playing millenarian godly intervention, the world's perfection would occur by divinely

---

34. Barkun, *Crucible of the Millennium*, 17; Buss, "Meeting of Heaven and Earth," 7-8; Smith, "Millennial Scholarship in America," 541-49.

35. James H. Moorhead, "Between Progress and Apocalypse: A Reassessment of Millennialism in American Religious Thought, 1800-1880," *Journal of American History* 71 (Dec. 1984): 526-41.

inspired mortals assuming a leading role in society. Saved souls would become more virtuous, political ethics would further evolve, and virtuous individuals would enthusiastically support religious and upright causes creating a heaven-bound spiral of upward achievement.[36]

In the Great Awakening God's spirit appeared to be breaking out everywhere confirming that a renewal could take place without the direct appearance of Christ. Ministers identified the spiritual awakening with the bursting forth of the Holy Spirit that they anticipated would take place in the last days.[37] Through his dissemination and streamlining of postmillennial thought into a consistent theology, Jonathan Edwards became the first American postmillennialist of stature.[38] Edwards's eschatology, which departed significantly from existing premillennial thought, believed that the redemption of humanity entailed subduing God's enemies in the world as we know it.[39] Edwards encouraged the practice and

---

36. Davidson, *The Logic of Millennial Thought*, 28-29; Barkun, *Crucible of the Millennium*, 25-28.

37. Davidson, *The Logic of Millennial Thought*, 32, 122-25.

38. C. C. Goen, "Jonathan Edwards: A New Departure in Eschatology," *Church History* 28 (Mar. 1959): 25-40; Stephen J. Stein, "A Notebook on the Apocalypse by Jonathan Edwards," *William and Mary Quarterly* 29 (Oct. 1972): 623-34; Perry Miller, "The End of the World," *William and Mary Quarterly* 8 (Apr. 1951): 171-91; Bercovitch, *The American Jeremiad*, 94-95, 98; Smith, "Millennial Scholarship in America," 538-39; Moorhead, "Between Progress and Apocalypse," 526-27.

39. Alan Heimert, *Religion and the American Mind: From the Great Awakening to the Revolution* (Cambridge, MA: Harvard University Press, 1966), 66; Tuveson, *Redeemer Nation*, 28-31. Neither pre- nor postmillennialists fit given stereotypes and scholars question whether the line can be drawn so cleanly between the two. James Moorhead cautions against "simplistic caricatures," showing that premillennialism sometimes included activism; see his "Searching for the Millennium in America," 21-22, and "Between Progress and Apocalypse," 525. Other works which call for a greater understanding of millennialism's ambiguities include Davidson, *The Logic of Millennial Thought*, 28-36, 274-77; John M. Butler, "Adventism and the American Experience," in *Rise of Adventism: Religion and Society in*

spread of prayer meetings, hoping to augment the Holy Spirit's influence. To Edwards the road to the Millennium all but by-passed Armageddon by occurring in a series of natural steps. Small events led to the grand vision of redemption as each believer placed "his own pilgrimage within an immensely larger and more important context."[40]

Subsequent to the French and Indian War, many American colonists saw themselves following in the steps of the Reformation to become the new chosen people of God.[41] Where millennialism was used in revolutioary ideology, it was tied to postmillennial notions of self-determination as the next step in human progress, a prelude to the commencement of a future world of righteousness.[42] Terms such as "patriotic millennialism," "civil millennialism," and "republican millennialism" all described the merging of biblical millennial aspirations and American revolutionary ideology.[43] Alexis de Toqueville would later describe the United States

---

Mid-Nineteenth-Century America, ed. Edwin S. Gaustad (New York: Harper and Row, 1974), 173-206; and Ernest R. Sandeen, "The 'Little Tradition' and the Form of Modern Millenarianism," *Annual Review of the Social Sciences of Religion* 4 (1980): 165-80.

40. Davidson, *The Logic of Millennial Thought*, 32, 152, 168; Heimert, *Religion and the American Mind*, 66.

41. Tuveson, *Redeemer Nation*, 101-102; Nathan O. Hatch, *The Sacred Cause of Liberty: Republican Thought and the Millennium in Revolutionary New England* (New Haven, CT: Yale University Press, 1977), 9-10; Davidson, *The Logic of Millennial Thought*, 28. See also Mark A. Noll, "From the Great Awakening to the War for Independence: Christian Values in the American Revolution," *Christian Scholar's Review* 12 (1983): 99-110; Bernard Bailyn, "Religion and Revolution: Three Biographical Studies," *Perspectives in American History* 4 (1970): 85-169.

42. Buss, "Meeting of Heaven and Earth," 10; Davidson, *The Logic of Millennial Thought*, 213; Melvin B. Endy, Jr., "Just War, Holy War, and Millennialism in Revolutionary America," *William and Mary Quarterly* 42 (Jan. 1985): 3-25.

43. Ruth Block titles her chapter on this topic "revolutionary millennialism." See her *Visionary Republic: Millennial Themes in American Thought, 1756-1800* (Cambridge, Eng.: Cambridge University Press, 1985), 75-93; and

as the most thoroughly Christian nation in the world. This assurance of America's divine mission ingrained into the new nation's self-identity a "civil religion" where sacred symbols took on political meanings. Here American Protestantism and nationalism joined to form a unity between citizenry and evangelicalism creating what Sidney Mead calls "a nation with the soul of a church" where "every patriot is a Christian and every Christian a patriot."[44] American millennialism's vocabulary and ideas became entrenched, and by blending millennialism with nationalism the myth of America as a chosen land and a redeemer nation became "so common as to be almost canonical."[45]

By the beginning of the nineteenth century postmillennialism was in full bloom. Characterizing Americans at the turn of the cen-

---

Barkun, *Crucible of the Millennium*, 22.

44. Alexis De Toqueville, *Democracy in America*, 2 vols., ed. Phillip Bradley (1835; reprint, New York: Vintage Books, 1945), 1:314; Sidney E. Mead, "The Nation with the Soul of a Church," *Church History* 36 (Sept. 1967): 262-83; Sidney E. Mead, *The Nation with the Soul of a Church* (New York: Harper and Row, 1975); William G. McLoughlin, *Revivals, Awakenings, and Reform* (Chicago: University of Chicago Press, 1978), 105-106. On America's civil religion, see Robert N. Bellah, "Civil Religion in America," *Daedalus* 96 (Winter 1967): 9-21; Catherine L. Albanese, "Dominant and Public Center: Reflections on the 'One' Religion of the United States," *American Journal of Theology and Philosophy* 4 (Sept. 1983): 83-96; Robert Bellah and Philip E. Hammond, eds., *Varieties of Civil Religion* (San Francisco: Harper and Row, 1980); Robert D. Linder and Richard Pierard, *Twilight of the Saints: Biblical Christianity and Civil Religion in America* (Downers Grove, IL: Inter-varsity Press, 1978); John F. Wilson, "The Status of Civil Religion in America," in *The Religion of the Republic*, ed. Elwyn Smith (Philadelphia: Fortress Press, 1971); and Sidney E. Mead, *The Old Religion in the Brave New World: Reflections on the Relation Between Christendom and the Republic* (Berkeley: University of California Press, 1977).

45. Moorhead, "Between Progress and Apocalypse," 531; J. F. Maclear, "The Republic and the Millennium, in *The Religion of the Republic*, ed. Elwyn A. Smith (Philadelphia: Fortress Press, 1971), 184-216; William A. Clebsch, "America's 'Mythique' as Redeemer Nation," *Prospects* 4 (1979): 79-94; Conrad Cherry, *God's New Israel: Religious Interpretations of American Destiny* (Englewood Cliffs, NJ: Prentice-Hall, 1971).

tury as living in the "shadow of Christ's second coming more intensely than any generation," scholars have described the United States during this period as "drunk on the millennium."[46] The power of the Second Great Awakening lay in its popular enthusiasm from below, and crucial to understanding postmillennialism's influence on American society is the revival movement. Revivals were both a sign that a new religious age had occurred as well as demonstrating that people could influence a change for good, a taste of future bliss. Postmillennial revivalism shifted the emphasis from the world's cosmic battle between Christ and Satan to the struggle between good and evil within the individual soul, and the conversion process became as important as theology.[47] Religious revivals, missions, Bible societies, and social reform movements would mobilize people individually and in concert, and step-by-step humanity's advance would lead to future triumphs.[48]

---

46. Nathan O. Hatch, *The Democratization of American Christianity* (New Haven, CT: Yale University Press, 1989), 184; Sandeen, *The Roots of Fundamentalism*, 42.

47. William G. McLoughlin, "Religious Freedom and Popular Sovereignty: A Change in the Flow of God's Power, 1730-1830," in *In the Great Tradition*, 173-92; Gordon S. Wood, "Evangelical America and Early Mormonism," *New York History* 61 (Oct. 1980): 372; Barkun, *Crucible of the Millennium*, 58; Davidson, *The Logic of Millennial Thought*, 129-31, 175; Moorhead, "Between Progress and Apocalypse," 536-41.

48. Jerald C. Brauer, "Revivalism and Millenarianism in America," in *In the Great Tradition*, 152-53; Barkun, *Crucible of the Millennium*, 147-48. On American revivalism, see William Warren Sweet, *Revivalism in America: Its Origin, Growth and Decline* (1944; reprint, Gloucester, MA: Peter Smith, 1965); William Warren Sweet, *Religion in the Development of American Culture 1765-1840* (1952; reprint, Gloucester, MA: Peter Smith, 1963); Timothy L. Smith, *Revivalism and Social Reform: Protestantism on the Eve of the Civil War* (New York: Abingdon Press, 1957); Sidney E. Mead, *The Lively Experiment: The Shaping of American Christianity in America* (New York: Harper and Row, 1963); Perry Miller, *The Life of the Mind in America: From the Revolution to the Civil War* (New York: Harcourt, Brace and World, 1965); Martin E. Marty, *Righteous Empire: The Protestant Experience in America* (New York: Dial Press, 1970); and Robert T. Handy, *A Christian America: Protestant Hope and*

The revival movement peaked in New York's "burned-over district" and in northern Ohio. Here the "yearnings of people simply overwhelmed the traditional religious institutions," and religious restlessness following the Revolution allowed seekers to move from denomination to denomination as never before. Francis Asbury's description of a four-day revival meeting where over 3,000 seekers attended to hear 100 preachers typified the religious environment. The great revivalist Charles G. Finney stormed western New York and in 1830 spent six months in Rochester preaching revivalist salvation. Ordinary people, farmers, bricklayers, millers, carpenters, businessmen, mothers, wives, all sought certitude in this new-found way of viewing traditional conventional society.[49] Yet with an air of optimism postmillennialists still felt anxiety about the unknown future and were not immune to paranoia and conspiratorial urgings. The dualistic struggle between good and evil still fell into apocalyptic images. And within this context Protestants saw God's enemies in Mormonism, Catholicism, and freemasonry.[50]

The paradox of postmillennial-driven revivalism was that the more it was accepted and emphasized the distant future, the more secularized and less truly millennial it became, and the farther away the final goal seemed. If thousands of small steps led to perfection, this far-off millennium would never be achieved in one's lifetime. For many postmillennialism became less useful as a way of ordering society in the more complex world of social and economic distress

---

Historical Realities (New York: Oxford University Press, 1971).

49. Wood, "Evangelical America and Early Mormonism," 372-73; Hatch, *The Democratization of American Christianity*, 49-64; Whitney R. Cross, *The Burned-over District: The Social and Intellectual History of Enthusiastic Religion in Western New York, 1800-1850* (Ithaca, NY: Cornell University Press, 1950), 3-109.

50. David Brion Davis, "Some Themes of Counter-Subversion: An Analysis of Anti-Masonic, Anti-Catholic, and Anti-Mormon Literature," *Mississippi Valley Historical Review* 47 (Sept. 1960): 205-24. Anti-Catholic themes increased in the 1820s with increased Catholic immigration merging both social and economic American nationalist resentment. See Barkun, *Crucible of the Millennium*, 54-56.

and dislocation.[51] With traditions of the past now breaking apart, ordinary people sought answers to new convulsions in the scriptures and biblical prophecy, and in the early nineteenth century a renewed premillennialism developed.[52]

A product of the Second Great Awakening's bringing of religion to the outposts of an expanding American society was a more democratic, more personal, more evangelical religion where a new generation of common people became freer and more independent.[53] Here rural New Englanders attempted to make sense of a changing environment and create social patterns capable of commanding allegiance. In this age of displacement and uncertainty, thousands became "seekers," looking for heavenly manifestations and signs of God's place in their lives, willing to accept new-found prophets who could explain and confront social tensions.[54] By implementing their own brand of individualism, new millenarian and utopian movements challenged previously rigid church structures and became avenues for hope in a radically changed world.[55] The capacity to embrace change enabled groups such as the Mormons, Shakers, and the Oneida community to form societies which dramatically altered existing norms.[56]

---

51. Barkun, *Crucible of the Millennium*, 8-29.

52. Sandeen, *The Roots of Fundamentalism*, 22-27; Hatch, *The Democratization of American Christianity*, 6.

53. Wood, "Evangelical America and Early Mormonism," 361.

54. Ralph H. Gabriel, "Evangelical Religion and Popular Romanticism in Nineteenth Century America," *Church History* 19 (Mar. 1950): 34-47; Wood, "Evangelical America and Early Mormonism," 370.

55. Hatch, *The Democratization of American Christianity*, 58.

56. Harrison, *The Second Coming*, 223; Lawrence Foster, *Religion and Sexuality: The Shakers, the Mormons, and the Oneida Community* (1981; reprint, Urbana: University of Illinois Press, 1984); Louis J. Kern, *An Ordered Love: Sex Roles and Sexuality in Victorian Utopias–The Shakers, the Mormons, and the Oneida Community* (Chapel Hill: University of North Carolina Press, 1981). With 50,000 members at its peak, Millerism was the early nineteenth century's largest millenarian group. Millerism's distinctness was its willingness to set an exact date for Christ's return, predicting that the advent would begin between 21 March 1843 and 22 October 1844. See Jonathan

In many ways the evangelical revivalism of the Second Great Awakening combined elements of the past and the future, tenuously walking a line between secular progress and premillennial apocalyptism which became more difficult to assimilate. Although Christ reigned supreme, common people sought personal responsibility for their salvation. Old folkways combined with enlightening science, and communal fellowship with a unique individualism, all striving for Christian unity, yet divided as never before. And people were on the move, individuals and families uprooting themselves as never before. With no solid ground, no religious center, new movements based on prophets found a home for those seeking religious authority.[57]

Prior to the nineteenth century millenarian movements were typically small unorganized groups of followers usually centered around a prophetic or charismatic leader. With American revivalism the environment changed dramatically and Millerites, Shakers, Mormons, and Jehovah's Witnesses all used millennialism to solidify beliefs, values, cohesiveness, and to mobilize adherents.[58] Endowed

---

Butler, "From Millerism to Seventh-day Adventism: 'Boundlessness to Consolidation,'" *Church History* 55 (Mar. 1986): 50-64; Barkun, *Crucible of the Millennium*, 33-39. Although modern scholarship has rejected previous notions that millenarians were "crackpots," until the 1890s U.S. millenarianism battled to be viewed as not just a group of lunatics on the fringe of society. See Moorhead, "Searching for the Millennium in America," 18-19; Sandeen, *The Roots of Fundamentalism*, 41-61.

57. Wood, "Evangelical America and Early Mormonism," 361-65; Hatch, *The Democratization of American Christianity*, 65.

58. Buss, "Meeting of Heaven and Earth," 13. A new phase of millenarianism developed in the United States in the years 1845-80. Reviving premillennial tenets, theologians like William Aberhart preached that history's downward course could only be redeemed by divine intervention. See David R. Elliott, "The Devil and William Aberhart: The Nature and Function of His Eschatology," *Studies in Religion* 9 (1980): 325-37. Dwight L. Moody expressed these same sentiments, stating, "I look on this world as a wrecked vessel. God had given me a life-boat, and said to me, 'Moody, save all you can.'" See James F. Findlay, Jr., *Dwight L. Moody: American Evangelist, 1837-1899* (Chicago: University of Chicago Press, 1969), 253. See also William G. McLoughlin, ed., *The American Evangelicals, 1800-1900: An Anthology* (New

with extraordinary powers, their charismatic prophet-leaders were understood to be divinely inspired, not bound by existing societal norms or laws and, due to their revelatory nature, not required to remain static. No rule was unbreakable, for "rule-breaking validated spiritual superiority" and prophetic declaration necessarily superseded community standards.[59]

Antebellum America provided an ideal environment for Mormonism's genesis, and within this context the movement originating with Joseph Smith came into being. Competition in the religious market place had muted the previous inherent authority of orthodox churches, giving credence to religious insurgents whose message of hope basked in the light of their new-found legitimacy. Emphasizing standard millenarian tenets, Joseph Smith's prophetic calling, supported by sacred scripture in the form of the Book of Mormon, provided revelatory answers to religious "seekers." Searching for spiritual authority, social cohesiveness, and divine direction in their

---

York: Harper Torchbooks, 1968), 171-85; Sandeen, *The Roots of Fundamentalism*, 62-63, 172. This new premillennialism, termed dispensationalism, developed a distinct interpretation of millennial theology believing that when Christ returns Christians would be removed for their safety. This event, called the Rapture, could happen at any moment. Dating back to John Nelson Darby and the Plymouth Brethren in 1830 England, the uniqueness of the Rapture doctrine was its dividing the return of Christ into two phases: first, Christ would appear at the Rapture *for* the true believing Christians; then, after seven years of tribulation, he would return *with* the Christians. Dispensationalism gained prominence at the end of the nineteenth century and was the beginning of many modern-day fundamentalist movements. See Elliott, "The Devil and William Aberhart," 326-33. On dispensationalism, see Timothy P. Weber, *Living in the Shadow of the Second Coming: American Premillennialism, 1875-1925* (New York: Oxford University Press, 1979), 13-32; Timothy P. Weber, "Premillennialism and the Branches of Evangelicalism," in *The Variety of American Evangelicalism*, eds. Donald W. Dayton and Robert K. Johnston (Knoxville: University of Tennessee Press, 1991), 5-21; George M. Marsden, *Fundamentalism and American Culture: The Shaping of Twentieth-Century Evangelicalism: 1870-1925* (New York: Oxford University Press, 1980), 11-62.

59. Barkun, *Crucible of the Millennium*, 126-27.

lives, these "seekers" hoped to join God's elect saints gathered in the New Jerusalem on American soil. Here they would establish both physical and social boundaries, and consummate their American millennial dream. As the new elect of God, they were then prepared to meet the Savior at his glorious advent.[60]

60. Ibid., 135-37.

CHAPTER THREE

MODERN REVELATION: ORIGINS OF A SEPARATIST THEOLOGY

The quest for perfectionism, to bring Jesus Christ into all aspects of one's life, became a catalyst for interest in revivalism.[1] Religious revivals would initiate a change of heart among the people inaugurating Christ's thousand-year reign prior to the end of the world.[2] In the explosive revival atmosphere described by Perry Miller as a "volcano," ministers found converts with dreams of millennial empire.[3] Preaching in 1823 western New York, Charles Finney reported how those attending revivals became "so thoroughly wrought up that they literally fell off their seats in a state of shock and ecstasy."[4] Others also preached the imminence of the Millennium, some believing it would occur within fifty to 200 years. John Noyes remembered the year 1831 was "almost as fanatical as the [future]

---

1. For the connection among revivalism, perfectionism, and millennialism during this period, see Sydney E. Ahlstrom, *A Religious History of the American People* (New Haven, CT: Yale University Press, 1972), 474-81; Marvin S. Hill, "The Rise of Mormonism in the Burned-over District: Another View," *New York History* 61 (Oct. 1980): 421.

2. Michael Barkun, *Crucible of the Millennium: The Burned-Over District of New York in the 1840s* (Syracuse: Syracuse University Press, 1986), 24-27.

3. Perry Miller, *The Life of the Mind in America: From the Revolution to the Civil War* (New York: Harcourt, Brace and World, 1965), 7-34.

4. William G. McLoughlin, *Revivals, Awakenings, and Reform* (Chicago: University of Chicago Press, 1978), 123.

Millerites." The whole decade of the 1830s saw intense millennial expectations.[5] Founded in 1830, Mormonism was one of many religious movement then occurring in New York's revival-driven, burned-over district.[6]

Revivalism gave people new-found freedom. Sin was no longer permanently ingrained in humanity but could be eliminated by action and exertion. And because the relationship with God was now an individual one, people could move from sect to sect or join new religious groups while still seeking signs, prophets, visions, or millennial hope.[7] Although the Second Great Awakening caused more Americans to be church goers, institutional churches lost appeal to individual delineation and denominational schisms. Church members argued endlessly over doctrine, and the new ability to drift caused rivaling sects to vie for converts. Religious unity unraveled as old sects broke into factions, some forming new denominations around dynamic leaders, others organizing their own congregations, while isolated evangelicals "roamed the countryside in search of lost souls."[8] This religious milieu caused many to conclude that only the

---

5. Whitney R. Cross, *The Burned-over District: The Social and Intellectual History of Enthusiastic Religion in Western New York, 1800-1850* (Ithaca, NY: Cornell University Press, 1950), 200-201.

6. Kenneth H. Winn, *Exiles in a Land of Liberty: Mormons in America, 1830-1846* (Chapel Hill: University of North Carolina Press, 1989), 40-44. Other groups which are claimed to have originated in the burned-over district were Anne Lee's Shakers, the Millerites, followers of Jemima Wilkinson, the Fox sisters, the Spiritualists, and the Oneida community. See Carl Carmer, *Listen for a Lonesome Drum* (New York: Farrar and Rinehart, 1936), 115. Marvin Hill disputes the notion that all of these groups came from the burned-over district. See Hill, "The Rise of Mormonism in the Burned-over District," 415-16. For a discussion of Mormonism in the context of Frederick Jackson Turner's frontier thesis, see Alexander Evanoff, "The Turner Thesis and Mormon Beginnings in New York and Utah," *Utah Historical Quarterly* 33 (Spring 1965): 157-73.

7. A valuable work on the effect of 1830 revivalism on one New York town is Paul E. Johnson, *A Shopkeeper's Millennium: Society and Revivals in Rochester, New York, 1815-1837* (New York: Hill and Wang, 1978).

8. Gordon S. Wood, "Evangelical America and Early Mormonism,"

coming of Christ could transform the competing sects into a united body.

The economic uncertainties of this period reinforced a sense of social displacement. Colonial patterns and customs had begun to dissolve under economic uncertainty and the expansion of republicanism. Previous stabilizing institutions fell to commerce and real estate transactions, with families moving frequently leaving roots and security behind. Millennialism became a means of explaining the upheaval and displacement society experienced following the Revolution.[9]

To the socially disoriented, the message of the revival movement was that they must belong to a church. This only further augmented the religious guilt feelings of those who had not found spiritual solace in any contemporary denomination.[10] Religious revivals instilled in those affected by the Second Great Awakening, who later became Mormon converts, an unfulfilled desire to find a place where true Christianity was left undefiled by clerical disputations.[11] As Nathan Hatch concludes, Mormonism's followers were gathered mostly from a faithful remnant whose social and religious aspirations had been destroyed by changing Jacksonian values.[12]

New York's burned-over district was settled primarily from western New Englanders who brought their towns and cultures with them, including a millennial world view.[13] Vermont immigrants in particular moved west into New York. Somewhat isolated from the rest of New England, their rural mountain roots and relative seclusion had created an ideological atmosphere which was less rigid than in more

---

New York History 61 (Oct. 1980): 375.

9. Ibid., 376; Kenelm Burridge, *New Heaven, New Earth: A Study of Millenarian Activities* (New York: Schocken Books, 1969), 9-11.

10. Hill, "The Rise of Mormonism in the Burned-over District," 422-23.

11. Winn, *Exiles in a Land of Liberty*, 47.

12. Nathan O. Hatch, "Mormon and Methodist: Popular Religion in the Crucible of the Free Market," *Journal of Mormon History* 20 (Spring 1994): 38.

13. Barkun, *Crucible of the Millennium*, 103-104; Stephen A. Marini, *Radical Sects of Revolutionary New England* (Cambridge, MA: Harvard University Press, 1982), 27-30.

traditional New England environments. But after moving to New York, many still did not find the promised economic prosperity and security they sought. Three decades of disasters and the inability of western New England farmers to withstand continuing crop failures called into question their postmillennial world view.[14]

At the same time the traditional family structure was challenged as both natural and economic disasters demonstrated that the central economic unit, the family farm, could no longer protect individuals and families from economic upheaval.[15] Back country economic realities failed to keep pace with expectations, leading some to search for the supernatural in their economic pursuits as well as in their religious ones.[16] Joseph Smith Sr.'s family is an example of New Englanders who never broke the bands of poverty despite the post-Revolutionary era of hope. Early in his life Joseph Smith, Jr., displayed a gift as a charismatic seer and developed a reputation for having mystical, revelatory powers. It was a "spiritual gift," says historian Hatch, that Joseph Jr. and his family "hoped would lead to the discovery of treasure".[17]

---

14. Barkun, *Crucible of the Millennium*, 105-17; Cross, *The Burned-over District*, 55-57, 65, 83; Michael Barkun, *Disaster and the Millennium* (New Haven, CT: Yale University Press, 1974), 1. Marvin Hill and David Rowe disagree with Cross's frontier explanation for the rise of sects. See Hill, "The Rise of Mormonism in the Burned-over District," 421; David Rowe, "A New Perspective on the Burned-over District: Millerites in Upstate New York," *Church History* 47 (Dec. 1978): 408-20.

15. Barkun, *Crucible of the Millennium*, 117-19.

16. Alan Taylor, "The Early Republic's Supernatural Economy: Treasure Seeking in the American Northeast, 1780-1830," *American Quarterly* 38 (1986): 18-19.

17. Nathan O. Hatch, *The Democratization of American Christianity* (New Haven, CT: Yale University Press, 1989), 114. Joseph Smith's pre-Book of Mormon treasure-seeking activities are detailed in Dan Vogel, "The Locations of Joseph Smith's Early Treasure Quests," *Dialogue: A Journal of Mormon Thought* 27 (Fall 1994): 197-231; D. Michael Quinn, *Early Mormonism and the Magic World View* (Salt Lake City: Signature Books, 1987), 27-52; and H. Michael Marquardt and Wesley P. Walters, *Inventing Mormonism: Tradition and the Historical Record* (San Francisco: Smith Research Associates, 1994),

Millennialism flourished more strongly in upper New York than anywhere else in the country, and those seeking the coming Millennium were inspired to participate in the revival conversion spirit.[18] In the New York town of Palmyra the local newspaper voiced the common sentiment: "The millennial state of the world is about to take place; that in seven years literally [1830], there would scarce a sinner be found on earth; that the earth itself, as well as the souls and bodies of its inhabitants, should be redeemed, as before the fall, and become as the garden of Eden."[19]

Yet the pressures of sectarian competition caused many to be guilt-ridden and frustrated in their millennial anticipations.[20] Like other Americans, the Joseph Smith, Sr., family were seekers, searching for the right place to raise a family, pursue material security, and find the right church.[21] Dan Vogel differentiates between primitivists,

---

63-87. An apologetic approach to Smith's pursuit of buried treasure is in Richard Lloyd Anderson, "The Mature Joseph Smith and Treasure Searching," *Brigham Young University Studies* 24 (Fall 1984): 489-560. Many of Anderson's arguments are examined and rejected in Rodger I. Anderson, *Joseph Smith's New York Reputation Reexamined* (Salt Lake City: Signature Books, 1990), 43-62. On placing the Smith family's treasuring seeking in the context of the late-eighteenth-early-nineteenth-century American treasuring hunting tradition, see Marvin S. Hill, "Money-Digging Folklore and the Beginnings of Mormonism: An Interpretive Suggestion," *Brigham Young University Studies* 24 (Fall 1984): 473-88; Ronald W. Walker, "The Persisting Idea of American Treasure Hunting," *Brigham Young University Studies* 24 (Fall 1984): 429-59.

18. Cross, *The Burned-over District*, 79; Barkun, *Crucible of the Millennium*, 2.

19. *Wayne Sentinel*, 23 Oct. 1823, in Marvin S. Hill, *Quest for Refuge: The Mormon Flight from American Pluralism* (Salt Lake City: Signature Books, 1989), 8.

20. Hill, *Quest for Refuge*, 4-8.

21. Many "seekers" were the socially disinherited, a label which would certainly have fit the Joseph Smith, Sr., family's seven moves in fourteen years in the early 1800s. See Wood, "Evangelical America and Early Mormonism," 361-65. Nathan Hatch identifies "seekers" as believers in a better life where God would level the playing field between them and their social betters. See

uch as Alexander Campbell, who saw a need to restore the concepts of the original apostolic church, believing the Bible contained all the necessary authority to accomplish the task, and true "seekers" who believed that a literal, direct, divine endowment of power and authority was necessary for Christ's true church to be restored, and anxiously anticipated its arrival. Mormonism came into being at the same time orthodox religious belief was giving way to individual consciousness, morals, and standards. Religious seekers in Joseph Smith Sr.'s day wanted God's rule in their lives, and many who "found" Mormonism were seeking religious authority, stability, and certainty, longing for solid ground and relatively few choices.[22] The secular influences of pluralism needed to be put aside for unity under God's one plan.[23]

The intense rivalry among sects in upper New York forced churches to compete for converts and numerical strength, and the conflicting denominations caused the young Joseph Smith, Jr., great personal anxiety.[24] Marvin Hill describes Smith's inter-

---

Nathan O. Hatch, "The Christian Movement and the Demand for a Theology of the People," *Journal of American History* 67 (Dec. 1980): 546-61; Hatch, *The Democratization of American Christianity*, 68-81. See Vogel, *Religious Seekers and the Advent of Mormonism* (Salt Lake City: Signature Books, 1988), ix-xiii.

22. Mario S. De Pillis, "The Quest for Religious Authority and the Rise of Mormonism," *Dialogue: A Journal of Mormon Thought* (Mar. 1966): 68-88; Klaus J. Hansen, *Mormonism and the American Experience* (Chicago: University of Chicago Press, 1981), 20; John Lofland, *Doomsday Cult* (Englewood Cliffs, NJ: Prentice-Hall, 1966), 7-8. Although early Mormon converts often came from economically disadvantaged circumstances, most still held a marginal degree of respectability. Most early converts were simply young people who had yet to establish themselves economically with over 80 percent of Mormon converts before 1846 under the age of thirty, the median age falling between twenty and twenty-five. See Winn, *Exiles in a Land of Liberty*, 47; Hill, "The Rise of Mormonism in the Burned-over District," 421-28; Hatch, *The Democratization of American Christianity*, 121-22.

23. Peter L. Berger, *The Sacred Canopy: Elements of a Sociological Theory of Religion* (Garden City, NY: Doubleday and Co., 1967); 106-35; Hill, *Quest for Refuge*, 14.

24. Joseph Smith, *History of the Church of Jesus Christ of Latter-day Saints*, 7 vols., 2d ed. rev., introduction and notes by B. H. Roberts (Salt Lake City:

nal conflict as follows: "It was the excitement of the revivals with
their appeal for Christian conversion which stirred him and the
war among contending sects which repelled him."[25] Joseph's alienation from society had many internal sources. These included
contending protestant sects, his own spiritual conscience, and rec-
onciling religious differences between his mother and father.[26]
Smith's personal tension also had deep roots. Poverty leading to
treasure-seeking activities, court trial embarrassment, in-law disputes, elopement, and expulsion from contact with his wife's
Methodist church in Harmony, Pennsylvania, all fed his sense of
social displacement.[27]

Deseret Book Co., 1974-76), 1:3-4; Susan Curtis, "Early Nineteenth-Century
America and the Book of Mormon," in *The Word of God: Essays on Mormon
Scripture*, ed. Dan Vogel (Salt Lake City: Signature Books, 1990), 88.

25. Hill, *Quest for Refuge*, 11.

26. Dan Vogel contends Smith's parents differed on religious matters.
Lucy Mack Smith, Joseph Smith Sr.'s wife, and some of her children
eventually joined the Palmyra Presbyterian church, while both Joseph Smith
Jr. and Sr. remained aloof. See Vogel, *Religious Seekers and the Advent of
Mormonism*, 25-31; William Smith, *William Smith on Mormonism* (Lamoni, IA,
1883), in William Mulder and A. Russell Mortensen, eds., *Among the Mormons:
Historic Accounts by Contemporary Observers* (New York: Alfred A. Knopf, 1958),
25.

27. Hill, *Quest for Refuge*, 12; Linda King Newell and Valeen Tippetts
Avery, *Mormon Enigma: Emma Hale Smith, Prophet's "Elect Lady," Polygamy's
Foe, 1804-1879* (Garden City, NY: Doubleday and Co., 1984), 25. Jan Shipps
has emphasized the need to understand Smith's total character within the
ambiguities and complexities of nineteenth-century America. See Shipps,
"The 'Prophet Puzzle': Suggestions Leading Toward a More Comprehensive
Interpretation of Joseph Smith," *Journal of Mormon History* 1 (1974): 3-20. See
also Marvin S. Hill, "The 'Prophet Puzzle' Assembled; or, How to Treat Our
Historical Diplopia Toward Joseph Smith," *Journal of Mormon History* 3
(1976): 101-105. The earliest psychological approach to Joseph Smith is Isaac
Woodbridge Riley, *The Founder of Mormonism: A Psychological Study of Joseph
Smith, Jr.* (New York: Dodd, Mead, 1902). Perhaps the most well-known work
is Fawn M. Brodie, *No Man Knows My History: The Life of Joseph Smith, the
Mormon Prophet*, 2d enl. rev. ed. (New York: Alfred A. Knopf, 1985), 405-25.
Marvin Hill's "Secular or Sectarian History? A Critique of *No Man Knows My*

Based on Joseph Smith Jr.'s confusion regarding his place in society, Mormonism from its earliest beginnings held a deep aversion to religious diversity. In the early Mormon newspaper *Messenger and Advocate*, Book of Mormon scribe Oliver Cowdery expressed the Mormon view that "Certain [it is that] the Gentile world, with all its parties, sects, denominations, reformations, revivals of religion, societies and associations, are [sic] devoted to destruction."[28] In rejecting pluralism, Joseph Smith and his early followers repudiated the basic social/political tenets of developing Jacksonian democracy.[29]

In Smith's town five denominations competed for members and this multiplicity confirmed his belief that the whole religious world abounded in turmoil.[30] Smith saw the existing religious sects as

History," Church History 33 (Mar. 1974): 78-96, criticizes a number of Brodie's assumptions. See also Bernard De Voto, "The Centennial of Mormonism," *American Mercury* 19 (Jan. 1930): 1-13; Lawrence Foster, *Religion and Sexuality: The Shakers, the Mormons, and the Oneida Community* (1981; reprint, Urbana: University of Illinois Press, 1984), 128-80; Foster, "First Visions: Personal Observations on Joseph Smith's Religious Experience," *Sunstone* 8 (Sept.-Oct. 1983): 39-43; Foster, "The Psychology of Religious Genius: Joseph Smith and the Origins of New Religious Movements," *Dialogue: A Journal of Mormon Thought* 26 (Winter 1993): 1-22; Louis J. Kern, *An Ordered Love: Sex Roles and Sexuality in Victorian Utopias–The Shakers, the Mormons, and the Oneida Community* (Chapel Hill: University of North Carolina Press, 1981), 137-43; Robert D. Anderson, "Toward an Introducion to a Psychobiography of Joseph Smith," *Dialogue: A Journal of Mormon Thought* 27 (Fall 1994): 249-72; Gary James Bergera, "Toward 'Psychologically Informed' Mormon History and Biography," *Sunstone* 15 (Dec. 1991): 27-31; T. L. Brink, "Joseph Smith: The Verdict of Depth Psychology," *Journal of Mormon History* 3 (1976): 73-83. Contrast J[ohn]. F. C. Harrison, *The Second Coming: Popular Millen- arianism, 1780-1850* (New Brunswick, NJ: Rutgers University Press, 1979), 203-205, 217.

28. "Is the End Near?" *Messenger and Advocate,* July 1835; see also *Times and Seasons* 15 (Mar. 1842).

29. Hill, *Quest for Refuge*, xii; R. Laurence Moore, *Religious Outsiders and the Making of Americans* (New York: Oxford University Press, 1986), 27-38.

30. For a discussion of the specific revivals in the immediate area surrounding the Joseph Smith, Sr., home, see Milton V. Backman, Jr., "Awakenings in the Burned-over District: New Light on the Historical Setting

corrupt, hypocritical, and full of contention, falling far short of the unity preached in the Bible. Smith expressed deep personal disturbance, saying that "great confusion and bad feeling ensued; Priest contending against priest, and convert against convert."[31] Seeking personal solace, Smith retired to a wooded area near his home to pray for answers to his religious questions.[32]

According to Smith's account, while petitioning deity, he was seized by a force of darkness, then released and overcome by a pillar of light. Two beings, pronouncing themselves to be God the Father and Jesus Christ, then appeared to Smith. They counseled him to join no contemporary church, "they were all wrong, and ... their Creeds were an abomination in his [God's] sight," with "none acknowledged of God, as his church and kingdom."[33] Warning the

of the First Vision," *Brigham Young University Studies* 9 (Spring 1969): 301-20. For a dissenting view, see Wesley P. Walters, "New Light on Mormon Origins from a Palmyra Revival," *Dialogue: A Journal of Mormon Thought* 4 (Spring 1969): 60-81; Marquardt and Walters, *Inventing Mormonism*, 15-41.

31. Dean C. Jessee, comp. and ed., *The Personal Writings of Joseph Smith* (Salt Lake City: Deseret Book Co., 1984), 198; Smith, *History of the Church*, 1:3.

32. Smith, *History of the Church*, 1:4-5; Jessee, *The Personal Writings of Joseph Smith*, 199.

33. Jessee, *The Personal Writings of Joseph Smith*, 200; Smith, *History of the Church*, 1:6; Dean C. Jessee, ed., *The Papers of Joseph Smith*, 2 vols. (Salt Lake City: Deseret Book Co., 1989-92), 1:7, 273; Lucy Smith, *Biographical Sketches of Joseph Smith the Prophet and His Progenitors for Many Generations* (1912; reprint, Independence, MO, 1969), 80; Orson Pratt, "A[n] Interesting Account, 1840," in Jessee, *The Papers of Joseph Smith*, 1:391. Although Smith did not record an account of this first religious experience for over a decade, the significance of his interpretation of the experience became part of Mormonism's theological framework from its beginnings. For discussion of the first vision narrative's development, see Milton V. Backman, Jr., *Joseph Smith's First Vision: The First Vision in Historical Context* (Salt Lake City: Bookcraft, 1971); James B. Allen, "The Significance of Joseph Smith's 'First Vision' in Mormon Thought," *Dialogue: A Journal of Mormon Thought* 1 (Autumn 1966): 30; James B. Allen, "Emergence of a Fundamental: The Expanding Role of Joseph Smith's First Vision in Mormon Religious Thought," *Journal of Mormon History* 7 (1980): 43-61; Dean C. Jessee, "Early

petitioner that his "anger is kindling against the inhabitants of the earth," Christ promised the young Joseph that he would soon return to the earth for "lo I come quickly ... in the glory of my Father."[34] Joseph Smith's vision, declaring that all religious denominations were false, is more than just a conversion story; it proclaims the "radical discontinuity of Mormonism with the Christianity of its day."[35] Smith's vision contradicted the optimism of contemporary postmillennialism, leaving little hope for the plight of humankind.

Smith's first religious experience became a metaphor for the future restored Mormon gospel. "The light of the latter day glory begins to break forth through the dark atmosphere of sectarian wickedness" that had, he said, "enveloped the Christian world since the age of the apostles."[36] The official account of this vision, Mormonism's "creation myth," employs classic millenarian allegorical

---

Accounts of Joseph Smith's First Vision," *Brigham Young University Studies*, 9 (Spring 1969): 275-94; Richard L. Anderson, "Circumstantial Confirmation of the First Vision Through Reminiscences," *Brigham Young University Studies* 9 (Spring 1969): 373-404; James B.Allen, "Eight Contemporary Accounts of Joseph Smith's First Vision: What Do We Learn from Them?" *Improvement Era* 73 (Apr. 1970): 4-13; Walters, "New Light on Mormon Origins from Palmyra Revival," 60-81; Richard L. Bushman, "The First Vision Story Revived," *Dialogue: A Journal of Mormon Thought* 4 (Spring 1969): 82-93; Hansen, *Mormonism and the American Experience*, 22-24, 221n30; and Brodie, *No Man Knows My History*, 23-25.

34. Scott H. Faulring, ed., *An American Prophet's Record: The Diaries and Journals of Joseph Smith* (1987; reprint, Salt Lake City: Signature Books in association with Smith Research Associates, 1989), 6; Jessee, *The Papers of Joseph Smith*, 1:7; Jessee, *The Personal Writings of Joseph Smith*, 6.

35. John G. Gager, "Early Mormonism and Early Christianity: Some Parallels and Their Consequences for the Study of New Religions," *Journal of Mormon History* 9 (1982): 59. Smith's nineteenth-century social disorientation was not unique. David Rowe contends that the formation of radical Millerites was a protest against both existing churches and society; see his "A New Perspective on the Burned-over District."

36. Joseph Smith, Jr., to N. C. Saxton, 4 Jan. 1833, in Jessee, *The Personal Writings of Joseph Smith*, 272; Hatch, "Mormon and Methodist," 36.

symbols by contrasting two opposing forces, sacred and secular, representing heaven and earth. As the narrative develops, the sacred or heavenly kingdom of God is magnified, and the worldly earth diminished, until God's kingdom overcomes the world transforming it into a new heaven. Once reduced to writing, the first vision story itself is an example of Smith's conceptual hope for the Mormon kingdom.[37] In spite of not knowing the first vision's specifics, early converts commonly believed that Smith had received personal and direct communication from God.[38] The guiding notion of that revelation was divine condemnation of all existing religious denominations.[39]

According to Smith, some three years later he experienced a second religious manifestation, a visit from a heavenly messenger, which inaugurated his soon prophet-to-be role. Smith's account reports the "angel" identified himself as Moroni, an ancient prophet who had lived on the American continent among a people known as Nephites. Moroni cited eschatological prophecies familiar to Smith from both the Old and New Testaments, including passages associated with the Millennium, the last days, and the coming of Christ.[40] Moroni warned Smith, "For behold the day cometh that shall burn as an oven, and all the proud, yea, and all that do wickedly shall burn as stubble; for they that come shall burn them, saith the Lord of hosts, that it shall leave them neither root nor branch."[41] Moroni's admonition validated much of what the local clergy's numerous revival teachings had passionately proclaimed: Christ's return was near. The texts quoted by Moroni were those used by preachers to point to the

---

37. Steven L. Olsen, "Joseph Smith and the Structure of Mormon Identity," *Dialogue: A Journal of Mormon Thought* 14 (Autumn 1981): 89-99.

38. Allen, "Emergence of a Fundamental," 44-45. Donna Hill, *Joseph Smith: The First Mormon* (Midvale, UT: Signature Books, 1977), 53. Early Mormons Martin Harris, Oliver Cowdery, Parley Pratt, and Peter Whitmer spoke of heavenly beings appearing to Smith in dreams. See Quinn, *Early Mormonism and the Magic World View*, 114-15.

39. Olsen, "Joseph Smith and the Structure of Mormon Identity," 92.

40. Jessee, *The Personal Writings of Joseph Smith*, 203-204, 214.

41. Smith, *History of the Church*, 1:12.

imminence of the Millennium. Either the verses were well known to Smith or Moroni's repetition of the theme four times planted the text distinctly in Smith's mind.[42]

Most important, Smith learned *he* was to be an instrument to prepare humankind for Christ's return. This was to be accomplished by bringing forth the record of an ancient American people whose prophets had recorded God's teachings and prophecies.[43] This record, and the gospel it contained, was to be restored in the *last days* to bring both Jew and gentile to a knowledge of Christ, who was to return to the earth in short order.[44] The records would be found on metal plates buried in a hill near the Smith farm. With this ancient source of scripture Joseph would be an instrument in God's hand. Moroni's millennial announcement was clear, although "the day had not yet come 'when they who would not hear his voice should be cut off from among the people,' but soon would come."[45] Prophecy was soon to be fulfilled.

Moroni's message held three primary themes. First, Christ's return was imminent. Moroni's appearance to Smith was merely the beginning of "The ushering in of the fullness of the gospel, to prepare the way for the second advent of the Messiah."[46] Second, those who were not prepared for his coming would be cut off and destroyed. Third, Smith would be God's agent in fortifying a righteous community worthy to possess Christ's kingdom at his return. A great work "was speedily to commence ... that a people might be prepared with faith and righteousness, for the Millennial reign of universal peace

---

42. Jessee, *The Personal Writings of Joseph Smith*, 7; Faulring, *An American Prophet's Record*, 6; Philip L. Barlow, *Mormons and the Bible: The Place of the Latter-day Saints in American Religion* (New York: Oxford University Press, 1991), 18.

43. Smith, *History of the Church*, 1:12-13; Richard L. Bushman, *Joseph Smith and the Beginnings of Mormonism* (Urbana: University of Illinois Press, 1984), 62.

44. Smith, *History of the Church*, 1:12-13; Book of Mormon, title page.

45. Smith, *Biographical Sketches of Joseph Smith the Prophet and His Progenitors*, 85.

46. Jessee, *The Papers of Joseph Smith*, 1:73, 279.

and joy."[47] The records would be God's means for restoring the gospel prior to the Millennium. Mormon eschatology, alluded to in Smith's first vision experience, now took on a new urgency with Smith occupying a central role.

In 1827 Smith finally obtained the plates and over the next three years the translation and publication of the record was completed. Thematically the Book of Mormon fit the concerns of the day. Criticizing the new "Mormon Bible," Disciples of Christ founder Alexander Campbell claimed Smith's Book of Mormon brought together "every error and almost every truth discussed in New York for the last ten years."[48] But to Smith and his followers, the purpose of the Book of Mormon was clear: to "be united with the Bible for the accomplishment of the purposes of God in the *last days*."[49]

Three Book of Mormon themes characterized the relationship between God's Saints and the rest of humanity, both in ancient times and in the latter days, predicting the shape of the new millenarian movement. First, all contemporary churches were wrong and a new restored gospel was necessary to return ancient/pure Christianity to the world. The Book of Mormon prophesied that all churches of the last days had fallen into apostasy. "They have all gone astray save it be a few, who are the humble followers of Christ; nevertheless, they are led, that in many instances they do err because they are taught by the precepts of men" (2 Ne. 28:14). Joseph's mother, Lucy Mack Smith, declared the Book of Mormon's message was: "the eyes of the whole world are blinded; that the churches have all become corrupt, yea every church upon the face of the earth; that the Gospel of Christ is nowhere preached."[50]

Second, the book internally described two great civilizations. Much of its nearly 600-page narrative contrasts these two warring

---

47. Ibid., 1:393.

48. "The Mormonites," *Millennial Harbinger* 2 (Feb. 1830): 93.

49. Joseph Smith to John Wentworth, in *Times and Seasons* (1 Mar. 1842), emphasis mine.

50. Lucy Mack Smith to Solomon Mack, 6 Jan. 1831, in Bushman, *Joseph Smith and the Beginnings of Mormonism*, 140.

peoples—the Nephites, righteous, fair, and delightsome; and the Lamanites, wicked, wild, ferocious, bloodthirsty.[51] Both groups descended from one family that had left Jerusalem in 600 B.C., led by
divine guidance to a new "promised land"—the American continent.
Both Nephites and Lamanites were literal branches of the tribe of
Israel, although through wickedness the Lamanites had lost claim to
the blessings of Abraham's lineage. Emphasizing scriptural literalism,
and placed inside a sacred historical narrative, dualist early Mormons
envisioned themselves as God's new covenant people. As the new
Israel in America, they were analogous to the Book of Mormon
Nephites, and the parallel between the ancient unrighteous Laman-
ites and the gentiles of Smith's day soon became a part of early
Mormon cosmology.

Third, the book signaled the beginning of the promised winding-
up scene prior to the glorious day of Christ's return. Smith's Palmyra
neighbors understood the book predicted "the Millennium day [and]
... when it is going to take place." Early converts found in Mormon
eschatology the answers they were seeking regarding the Second
Coming.[52] Emphasizing the great reversal, the Book of Mormon
confirmed biblical prophecy which promised reward for the righteous and destruction of the wicked at Christ's return.[53] Smith warned

---

51. Brodie, *No Man Knows My History*, 43-44.

52. Lucius Fenn to Birdseye Bronson, 12 Feb. 1830, in Mulder and
Mortensen, *Among the Mormons*, 28. See also Timothy L. Smith, "The Book
of Mormon in a Biblical Culture," *Journal of Mormon History* 7 (1980): 6; Ernest
R. Sandeen, *The Roots of Fundamentalism: British and American Millenarianism
1800-1930* (Chicago: University of Chicago Press, 1970), 13-27; David Arthur,
"Millerism," in *The Rise of Adventism: Religion and Society in Mid-
Nineteenth-Century America*, ed. Edwin S. Gaustad (New York: Harper and
Row, 1974), 154-61. In his first encounter with Mormon missionaries in July
1831, early Mormon convert William E. McLellin learned the Book of
Mormon would show "when the Savior shall come to destroy iniquity off the
face of the earth, and *reign* with his saints in the Millennial *Rest*." See Jan
Shipps and John W. Welch, eds., *The Journals of William E. McLellin,
1831-1836* (Provo, UT: BYU Studies, 1994), 80.

53. The parts of Isaiah in the Book of Mormon are some of the Bible's
most dramatic prophecies regarding the destruction to occur in the last days

a cousin in St. Lawrence County that "the sword of vengeance of the Almighty hung over this generation and except they repent and obeyed the Gospel, and turned from their wicked ways, humbling themselves before the Lord, it would fall upon the wicked, and sweep them from the earth."[54] Believing impending doom was near, Martin Harris, financial supporter of the first edition of the Book of Mormon and one of the book's three witnesses, told Columbia College Professor Charles Anthon that the book would "produce an entire change in the world and save it from ruin."[55] To early Mormon apostle Parley Pratt, the Book of Mormon confirmed the arrival of a new dispensation, "in fulfillment of prophecy, and for the restoration of Israel, and to prepare the way before the second coming of the Lord."[56] Rather than following postmillennialism's model of America's profound destiny, the Book of Mormon stressed the premillennial tenet that society had fallen into disrepair and that religious and cultural decay was beyond repair (2 Ne. 28:11-14; Morm. 8:31).[57]

Emphasizing America's role in God's plan, the Book of Mormon recognized two "Jerusalems" where Jews and believing gentiles would congregate. The Jews would gather in the ancient holy land of Israel and converted gentiles in the "New Jerusalem" on the American continent. The Book of Mormon also identified Native American Indians as Lamanites, a remnant of "lost Israel." Zion, the new Jerusalem in America, was designated to be the gathering site for

---

and the peace of the Millennium. See Hatch, *The Democratization of American Christianity*, 117-19.

54. Joseph Smith to George A. Smith, 1828, in Hill, *Joseph Smith: The First Mormon*, 83-84.

55. Charles Anthon to Eber D. Howe, 17 Feb. 1834, in Francis W. Kirkham, *A New Witness for Christ in America*, 2 vols. (1942; reprint, Salt Lake City: Utah Printing Co., 1967), 1:415.

56. Parley P. Pratt, *Autobiography of Parley Parker Pratt* (1938; reprint, Salt Lake City: Deseret Book Co., 1979), 38.

57. See also Thomas F. O'Dea, *The Mormons* (Chicago: University of Chicago Press, 1957), 26; Sandeen, *The Roots of Fundamentalism*, 13, 22; Marvin S. Hill, "The Shaping of the Mormon Mind in New England and New York," *Brigham Young University Studies* 9 (Spring 1969): 354.

converted gentiles and Indians. The unique Mormon theology of two gatherings, Jews to Jerusalem and others to Zion in America, gave American Indians an unprecedented role in the last days.[58] In Andrew Jackson's Indian removal policy, Mormons saw God's hand in gathering the Indians (Lamanites) by the borders of Zion (Missouri) where they would assist in building the New Jerusalem and become a tool in God's hand to destroy the gentiles (3 Ne. 20:10-22, 21:14, 22-25).[59]

America was a promised land to both the ancient Nephites and believers in the restored gospel living in the latter days. The Book of Mormon doctrine associating American Indians with the lost tribes of Israel supported theories dating back to before the Puritan era.[60] Early Mormon converts William W. Phelps and Parley Pratt acknowledged that Indian origin questions were "done away [with] by the Book of Mormon," declaring it "reveals the origin of American Indians, which was before a mystery."[61] The new Mormon "Zion was to be built in the American West, and that in the near future," giving Mormon kingdom building an urgency.[62] Mormon millennialism was

---

58. Ronald W. Walker, "Seeking the 'Remnant': The Native American During the Joseph Smith Period," *Journal of Mormon History* 19 (Spring 1993): 1-33.

59. Independence, Missouri, would later be designated as the site of the New Jerusalem. In Missouri this pro-Indian rhetoric would feed Mormon-gentile antagonism as non-Mormons envisioned a Mormon-Indian conspiracy against established settlers, a view unwelcome on the western frontier. See E[ber]. D. Howe, *Mormonism Unvailed: or A Faithful Account of that Singular Imposition and Delusion, from Its Rise to the Present Time* (Painesville, OH: E. D. Howe, 1834), 145-46, 197; Grant Underwood, *The Millenarian World of Early Mormonism* (Urbana: University of Illinois Press, 1993), 81.

60. Dan Vogel, *Indian Origins and the Book of Mormon* (Salt Lake City: Signature Books, 1986); B[righam]. H. Roberts, *A Comprehensive History of the Church of Jesus Christ of Latter-day Saints*, 6 vols. (1930; reprint, Provo, UT: Brigham Young University Press, 1965), 1:219-20.

61. *Evening and Morning Star,* Jan. 1833; Parley P. Pratt, *A Voice of Warning* ... (New York: W. Sanford, 1837), 135.

62. Harrison, *The Second Coming*, 181-82.

not just for the future but for the here and now, and Mormons were directed to begin building an empire worthy of Christ at his return.[63] The Book of Mormon would precede the last act of history and Israel's triumph would be the hour of judgement for the world. The Jews in the East and the New Israel in the Western Hemisphere would each prepare and enthrone the returning Messiah who would then inaugurate his millennial reign (2 Ne. 6:8-18; 30:3-18; 3 Ne. 16:1-20; 21:1-29, 25:1-6; Morm. 8:27-41).[64] Believers would become part of Israel and "be a blessed people upon the promised land forever" (1 Ne. 14:2). Those who rejected the restored gospel would be cast off. In either case the last days had arrived. Israel would soon be restored to righteousness, not by any existing Christian denomination, but by the Book of Mormon (1 Ne. 13:4-41; 14:2-7; 2 Ne. 10:18-19; 28:1-32, 29:1-14, 30:1-18; 3 Ne. 16:1-20, 21:1-29).[65]

But the Book of Mormon did more than address the mystery of Indian origins, it also answered basic theological questions regarding God's relationship to humankind, good versus evil, and personal salvation. By offering security to the soul, religious seekers could find in the Book of Mormon certainty and the spiritual and moral solutions to life's problems. Once chosen, the road to redemption was clearly marked, its travelers easily identified.[66] Gordon Wood recognized the Book of Mormon as "undoubtedly the most distinctive and important force in establishing the new faith."[67] Mormon apostle Parley Pratt's sentiments typify the book's significance to early converts, declaring it "was the principal means . . . of directing the entire course of my future life."[68] Characterized by Smith as "the most correct of any book on earth," the new scripture symbolized Mormon-

---

63. Klaus J. Hansen, *Quest for Empire: The Political Kingdom of God and the Council of Fifty in Mormon History* (Lansing: Michigan State University Press, 1970), 28-31.

64. See also Smith, "The Book of Mormon in a Biblical Culture," 8.

65. See also Bushman, *Joseph Smith and the Beginnings of Mormonism*, 139.

66. Underwood, *The Millenarian World of Early Mormonism*, 45.

67. Wood, "Evangelical America and Early Mormonism," 380.

68. Pratt, *Autobiography of Parley Parker Pratt*, 37.

ism's break with conventional Protestantism.[69] The book itself was of revolutionary intent for it circumvented all human reforms. The Book of Mormon, it was believed, came to Smith without the corruption of time, bypassing imperfect Christian practices and the problems of translation inherent in the Bible. True Christianity was brought to America, not through human agents, but by heavenly messengers directly to Joseph Smith.[70]

Within the Book of Mormon narrative, the destruction in the New World at Christ's death and his arrival in America as a resurrected being portrayed earth's imminent destruction prior to the Second Coming, something not missed by the book's readers (see Matt. 24; 3 Ne. 8).[71] Drawing from the religious culture of his time, Smith and his contemporaries took biblical accounts, the Millennium, and the primitive church seriously. Bible events were actual, and prophecies would be literally fulfilled.[72] Even before the church's official organization, Smith saw events in his own life as a fulfillment and continuation of scriptural history contained in the Bible.[73] Not

---

69. Smith, *History of the Church*, 4:461; James B. Allen, *Trials of Discipleship: The Story of William Clayton, a Mormon* (Urbana: University of Illinois Press, 1987), 3.

70. Gager, "Early Mormonism and Early Christianity," 59-60; Jon Butler, *Awash in a Sea of Faith: Christianizing the American People* (Cambridge, MA: Harvard University Press, 1990), 242.

71. See also *Journal of Discourses*, 26 vols. (Liverpool, Eng.: F.D. Richards, 1855-86), 8:123.

72. Perry Miller, "The Old Testament in Colonial America," in *Historical Viewpoints*, ed. John A. Garraty (New York: Harper and Row, 1970), 1-95; George M. Marsden, "Everyone One's Own Interpreter? The Bible, Science, and Authority in Mid-Nineteenth-Century America," in *The Bible in America: Essays in Cultural History*, eds. Nathan O. Hatch and Mark A. Noll (New York: Oxford University Press, 1982), 79-100.

73. An example is the church's understanding of Charles Anthon's rejection of Book of Mormon origins as fulfillment of "the prophecy of Isaia [sic] ... writ[t]en in the 29 Chapter concerning the book [of Mormon]." See Joseph Smith Letter Books, 5, quoted in Hill, *Joseph Smith: The First Mormon*, 78. See also Oliver Cowdery in *Messenger and Advocate* 1 (Feb 1835): 80; Orson Pratt, *Journal of Discourses*, 2:287-88, 7 Jan. 1855.

only did Smith place himself inside the biblical narrative, so did his followers. On the church's move to Kirtland, the prophet's mother reflected, "I then called the brethren and sisters together and reminded them that we were traveling by the commandment of the Lord, as much as [Book of Mormon] father Lehi was, when he left Jerusalem; and if faithful, we had the same reason to expect the blessings of God."[74]

The new church combined New Testament Christian primitiveness with Old Testament Hebrew-covenant consciousness, Mormons perceiving themselves as the new Israel, the chosen people of the last days.[75] Mormons were not merely re-creating past biblical narrations, they were living as God's new Israel in the latter days, "reestablishing the covenant, gathering the Lord's elect, separating Israel from the Gentiles, organizing the church, preaching the gospel, building up the kingdom, living in sacred space and time."[76] Smith's continuing revelations fed the theological assumption that as recipients of new scripture, paralleling ancient Israel, Mormons were living biblical-like events reserved by God for his people in the last days.[77]

Although in the "enthusiasm" of the Second Great Awakening visions in general were not unheard of, Smith's heavenly messengers were supplemented by literal/physical things. Items such as gold

---

74. Smith, *Biographical Sketches of Joseph Smith the Prophet and His Progenitors*, 210.

75. Barlow, *Mormons and the Bible*, 21, 68-71. See also Jan Shipps, *Mormonism: The Story of a New Religious Tradition* (Urbana: University of Illinois Press, 1985), 119; Nathan O. Hatch and Mark A. Noll, eds., *The Bible in America: Essays in Cultural History* (New York: Oxford University Press, 1982), 44-51; Underwood, *The Millenarian World of Early Mormonism*, 58; John F. Wilson, "Some Comparative Perspectives on the Early Mormon Movement and the Church-State Question, 1830-1845," *Journal of Mormon History* 8 (1981): 67-68.

76. Barlow, *Mormons and the Bible*, 69; Shipps, *Mormonism*, 34-39, 51-65, 81-83.

77. Barlow, *Mormons and the Bible*, 95; Gordon Irving, "The Mormons and the Bible in the 1830's," *Brigham Young University Studies* 13 (Summer 1973): 476-78.

plates, a Urim and Thummim, and eventually new holy scripture all provided additional legitimacy to Smith's message.[78] Enough of the old folk traditions and belief in godly intervention, angels, divine interpreters, and ancient prophets remained for Book of Mormon origins to be accepted by common people. Yet sufficient societal turmoil existed for people to cast off previous religious loyalties to find a religion which answered their quest for revelation, visions, and authority. To religious seekers, Smith's Book of Mormon convinced them that a new dispensation had arrived, the silence between humanity and God had ceased, and a new apostolic order was to be established.[79] In many ways Mormonism offered the best of all worlds, evangelical millennialism under the guidance of a restored church structure, backed by mysterious truths, rituals, and a priesthood which traced its authoritative lines back to apostolic times.[80] Mormonism combined religion with the emerging secular need for verification producing a literal book of scripture sustained by living witnesses.

But Mormonism took literalness to new heights, further separating the new church from other religious traditions. Mormon conviction revolved around actual events, not mere theology or doctrine. The historical certainty of what had happened to Smith, to ancient Nephite prophets, and what would happen to the restored church was as important as religious tenets. Mormonism was rooted in history not theology. Richard Bushman affirms, "The test of faith was

---

78. Barlow, *Mormons and the Bible*, 16. Smith obtained the Urim and Thummim with the plates, describing it as "two transparent stones set in the rim of a bow fastened to a breast plate." See Jessee, *The Personal Writings of Joseph Smith*, 215. The term "Urim and Thummim" sometimes referred to seer stones used by Joseph Smith. See Richard Van Wagoner and Steve Walker, "Joseph Smith: 'The Gift of Seeing,'" *Dialogue: A Journal of Mormon Thought* 15 (Summer 1982): 49-68.

79. Hatch, *The Democratization of American Christianity*, 168-69.

80. Wood, "Evangelical America and Early Mormonism," 381-84. For notions of authority based on a link to the apostleship, see Pratt, *Autobiography of Parley Parker Pratt*, 32, 39, 43; Vogel, *Religious Seekers and the Advent of Mormonism*, 1-66.

not adherence to a certain confession of faith but belief that Christ was resurrected, that Joseph Smith saw God, that the Book of Mormon was true history."[81] Early Mormons interpreted the Bible to say that Christ's second coming would coincide with renewed revelation from God. Thus the Book of Mormon became a tangible fulfillment of prophecy.[82]

Smith's early religious experiences and the Book of Mormon clearly initiated Mormonism's premillennial eschatology. By collectively gathering the elect at the Mormon "Zion" in America, Smith's new movement hoped to effect a dualist separation from the rest of society.[83] Specifically, Smith and his early followers believed the Book of Mormon's description of two main factions—true Christians under a theocratic government, and atheists who waged war against the righteous—prophesied the reality of their day. Never the aggressors in the Book of Mormon, the Nephites defended liberties, families, wives, and children, sending out missionaries to convert the wicked, while the Lamanites continually battled the people of God.[84] Written from a Christian prophet's perspective, dissent and pluralism were always destructive and evil. The ideal Book of Mormon government was led by a prophet-king, and only when separated from the wicked was ancient Nephite society able to remain pure to God's teachings and laws (Mosiah 29:13; 4 Ne. 1-18). By gathering the righteous, Smith hoped to achieve a society led by a modern prophet, prepared for the total, imminent, miraculous transformation of the earth into a millennial kingdom at Christ's coming.

The Book of Mormon also predicted that an ominous cloud of apocalyptic judgement hung over businessmen of Jacksonian America. The book testified against contentions and class differences where people are "distinguished by ranks, according to

---

81. Bushman, *Joseph Smith and the Beginnings of Mormonism*, 188.

82. *Times and Seasons* 2 (Mar. 1841): 351. For an example, see Orson Pratt, *Journal of Discourses*, 15:178-79, 22 Sept. 1872.

83. Mark D. Thomas, "Scholarship and the Book of Mormon," in *The Word of God*, 63-64.

84. O'Dea, *The Mormons*, 32-33.

their riches and their chances for learning" (3 Ne. 6:12).[85] As such, Nathan Hatch calls the Book of Mormon "a document of profound social protest," which guaranteed the rich, the proud, and the learned would be judged of God.[86] Smith declared, "We rejoice that the time is at hand, when the wicked who will not repent will be swept from the earth as with a besom of destruction, and the earth become an inheritance of the poor and the meek."[87] Mormonism, at its heart, rejected entrepreneurial ventures, religious competition, and freedom of thought which led to secularization.[88] The Nephites, like the Puritans, wanted religious freedom to preserve their own "true religion" but were unable to concede the same rights to others.[89] In speculating about a kingdom of peace, the Mormon newspaper *Evening and Morning Star* expressed nostalgic desire for a theocratic kingdom where prophets "put an end to all strife" and were "of one heart and one mind."[90] One of the Book of Mormon's dominant themes is that only under a theocratic government, ruled by men of God, can a society survive and prosper (Mosiah 29:13; Alma 30).[91]

---

85. See also Hill, *Quest for Refuge*, 21.

86. Hatch, *The Democratization of American Christianity*, 116-17. For association of wickedness with wealth and pride, see 4 Ne. 1:24-27.

87. Smith, *History of the Church*, 2:323-24.

88. Hatch, "Mormon and Methodist," 26-27. Marvin Hill contends the anti-capitalistic quality of the early Mormon movement "had more to do with the divisive, pluralistic character of capitalism than to permanent ideological objections to it." See Hill, *Quest for Refuge*, 17.

89. Hill, *Quest for Refuge*, xii.

90. *Evening and Morning Star* 2 (Aug. 1834): 177. See also *Messenger and Advocate* 3 (Dec. 184): 40.

91. For a rejection of Jacksonian principles in the Book of Mormon and in Mormonism in general, see Grant Underwood, "Early Mormon Perceptions of Contemporary America: 1830-1846," *Brigham Young University Studies* 26 (Summer 1986): 49-61; Hill, "Quest for Refuge," 3-20; Leonard J. Arrington, Feramorz Y. Fox, and Deal L. May, *Building the City of God: Community & Cooperation Among the Mormons* (Salt Lake City: Deseret Book Co., 1976), 3, 5, 15.

The Book of Mormon revered America, the continent, as sacred; American civilization held no such honor.[92] The volume not only described the destruction of two great ancient American civilizations, but uttered looming predictions which would befall its latter-day American readers' own society. The Book of Mormon declared a dualistic world view, proclaiming two realms of society only—the church of the Lamb of God and the church of the devil (1 Ne. 14:10; Moro. 7:12-19).[93] In an 1832 revelation Smith defined the "wicked" as those who rejected Mormon professions, for, "whoso cometh not unto me is under the bondage of sin ... and by this you may know the righteous from the wicked."[94] Believers were described as Saints, Israel, the elect; non-believers as sinners, gentiles, and the wicked. For early Latter-day Saints, good-evil, saint-gentile, friend-foe, were easily defined. James Davidson describes this phenomenon as the "rhetoric of polarization" and Mormonism is a classic example of millenarian dualism.[95]

---

92. Bushman, *Joseph Smith and the Beginnings of Mormonism*, 139.

93. Underwood, *The Millenarian World of Early Mormonism*, 43.

94. *Doctrine and Covenants of the Church of the Latter Day Saints: Carefully Selected from the Revelations of God*, comps., Joseph Smith, Junior, Oliver Cowdery, Sidney Rigdon, and Frederick G. Williams (Kirtland, OH: F.G. Williams and Co., 1835), 91.

95. James West Davidson, *The Logic of Millennial Thought: Eighteenth-Century New England* (New Haven, CT: Yale University Press, 1977), 163-65, 281-87; Grant Underwood, "Millenarianism and the Early Mormon Mind," *Journal of Mormon History* 9 (1982): 43. For similar notions of dualism, see James H. Moorhead, *American Apocalypse: Yankee Protestants and the Civil War, 1860-1869* (New Haven, CT: Yale University Press, 1978), 7; John M. Werly, "Premillennialism and the Paranoid Style," *American Studies* 18 (Spring 1977): 39-55. This dualism is similar to early Christianity, as noted in John G. Gager, *Kingdom and Community: The Social World of Early Christianity* (Englewood Cliffs, NJ: Prentice-Hall, 1975), 25. Kenelm Burridge shows how millenarian movements take society's complexities and re-order them as "sharply contrasted contraries." See Burridge, *New Heaven, New Earth: A Study of Millenarian Activities* (New York: Schocken Books, 1969), 147. See Mary Douglas, *Natural Symbols: Explorations in Cosmology* (London: Cresset Press, 1970), 118-19, where she states the ideas of "inside and outside, purity within,

The new religion declared that all existing denominations lacked authority or legitimacy, including Protestants, Catholics, Masons, all who were not Mormons.[96] Condemning the proliferation of sects, the Book of Mormon predicted there would be in the last days many "churches which are built up ... not unto the Lord," and promised to end religious conflict and confusion by resolving doctrinal differences dividing 1830 Protestantism (2 Ne. 28:3-4; 26:20-21).[97] The Book of Mormon paralleled contemporary anti-Catholic rhetoric condemning the sale of indulgences and labeling the Catholic church as the "whore of all the earth," a "church which is most abominable above all other churches" (1 Ne. 14:9-10; 13:26-29).[98] Mormon apostle John Taylor associated Babylon with the Catholic church, declaring that the identity of the mother of harlots in John's Apocalypse was not in dispute, "it needs no prophetic vision to unravel such mysteries. The old church is the mother, and the protestants are the lewd daughters."[99] Martin Harris identified the Book of Mormon as "the Anti-masonick Bible, and that all who do not believe it will be damned."[100] Both Mor-

---

corruption without" are "common to small bounded communities ... a form of metaphysical dualism."

96. Hill, *Quest for Refuge*, 28.

97. See also Susan Curtis, "Early Nineteenth Century America and the Book of Mormon," in *The Word of God*, 89.

98. Thomas O'Dea associates the Book of Mormon's great and abominable church with the general Protestant, anti-Catholic rhetoric, and cites other Book of Mormon references which include 1 Ne. 13:4-9, 26-29, 14:3, 9-17, 22:13-14; 2 Ne. 6:12, 28:18; Morm. 8:32. See O'Dea, *The Mormons*, 34, 268n24. See also *Evening and Morning Star,* June 1832. For the contemporary anti-Catholic mood, see Cross, *The Burned-over District*, 83-84, 231-33.

99. *Times and Seasons* 3 (15 Feb. 1845): 811. See also Taylor's comments in Faulring, *An American Prophet's Record*, 358; 1 Ne. 14:17, *Times and Seasons* 6 (15 June 1845): 939; Underwood, "Millenarianism and the Early Mormon Mind," 44.

100. Ohio's *Geauga Gazette,* 15 Mar. 1831, in Dan Vogel, "Mormonism's 'Anti-Masonick Bible,'" *John Whitmer Historical Association Journal* 9 (1989): 17. Vogel also cites the *Ohio Star,* 24 Mar. 1831, whose editor

mons and non-Mormons would have agreed on the Book of Mormon's anti-Masonic sentiments, which warned that democracy would be destroyed by "secret combinations."[101] On the other hand, Jacksonian values would not have comported with the book's anti-factional stance and its notion of combining church and state under a prophetic theocracy.[102]

For Mormons, who saw non-Mormons as part of Satan's forces who would block the kingdom's progress, persecution soon validated their millenarian, dualistic world view and intensified apocalyptic expectations. Opposition only proved to the believer that "the millennium was indeed approaching, and that his zeal should be redoubled," for the Lord has "in reserve a swift judgement ... for them all."[103] Religious dualism quickly led to social dualism as only the

---

declared, "The Mormon Bible is anti-masonic." See also Howe, *Mormonism Unvailed*, 81; Alexander Campbell, "The Mormonites," *Millennial Harbinger* 2 (Feb. 1831): 93. References seen as anti-Masonic in the Book of Mormon include 2 Ne. 10:15, 26:22; Alma 37:29,; Hel. 2:8, 3:23, 6:18-39, 7:4, 25, 8:1, 28, 10:3, 11:2, 10, 26-27; 3 Ne. 2:11, 3:9, 5:6, 7:9, 9:9; Morm. 1:18, 8:27; Ether 8:15-26, 9:5-7, 10:33, 11:15, 22. See O'Dea, *The Mormons*, 35, 269n28. Works which dispute the implication of an anti-Masonic influence in the Book of Mormon include those of Bushman, *Joseph Smith and the Beginnings of Mormonism*, 128-31; Blake T. Ostler, "The Book of Mormon as a Modern Expansion of an Ancient Source," *Dialogue: A Journal of Mormon Thought* 20 (Spring 1987): 73-76; Quinn, *Early Mormonism and the Magic World View*, 160-65. Whitney Cross contended anti-Masonry became another means of cleansing the political environment and ushering in the Millennium. See Cross, *The Burned-over District*, 123. Enough contemporary anti-Masonic sentiment existed to ignite an anti-Masonic party. See William Preston Vaughn, *The Antimasonic Party in the United States, 1826-1843* (Lexington: University of Kentucky Press, 1983).

101. The term "secret combinations" was used almost exclusively to refer to Freemasonry, and the 1826 William Morgan kidnapping fit this environment. See Curtis, "Early Nineteenth Century America and the Book of Mormon," 91; Vogel, "Mormonism's 'Anti-Masonick Bible,'" 24.

102. Vogel, "Mormonism's 'Anti-Masonick Bible,'" 24; Hill, *Joseph Smith: The First Mormon*, 110-11.

103. James H. Moorhead, "Social Reform and the Divided Conscience of Antebellum Protestantism," *Church History* 48 (Dec. 1979): 421; Smith,

elect accept God's call. Wicked, non-Mormon unbelievers, on the other hand, rejected the latter-day message. Steeped in dualism Mormons expected opposition. Viewed as the refiner's fire, persecution both fulfilled prophecy and was necessary prior to Christ's return. This in turn led to a siege mentality.[104] When the Saints' early mistreatment validated their dualist philosophy, a cycle of apocalyptic belief and rhetoric led to additional persecution which further fed millennial anticipation.[105] As Grant Underwood described it, "Dualist distinctions coupled with vivid apocalyptic imagery did not augur well for peaceful interaction between Mormons and Gentiles. ... Mormon millenarianism must be identified as a major source of the animosity felt towards the Saints."[106]

During and immediately following the Book of Mormon's translation/publication phase, Smith also began producing revelations. Although many of these pronouncements addressed specific individuals or temporal problems associated with the new movement, a number centered on the Second Advent, the coming Millennium, and the building up of the New Jerusalem.[107] In September 1830 Smith pronounced a revelation declaring,

---

History of the Church, 3:294. See similar expectation that Christ would soon destroy their enemies in *Times and Seasons* 6 (July 1845): 951-52.

104. Underwood, "Millenarianism and the Early Mormon Mind," 44; Davidson, *The Logic of Millennial Thought,* 83; Underwood, *The Millenarian World of Early Mormonism,* 43; *Times and Seasons* 4 (Mar. 1843): 141.

105. Therald N. Jensen, "Mormon Theory of Church and State," Ph.D. diss., University of Chicago, 1938, 67-68; Hansen, *Quest for Empire,* 22; Louis G. Reinwand, "An Interpretive Study of Mormon Millennialism During the Nineteenth Century with Emphasis on Millennial Developments in Utah," M.A. thesis, Brigham Young University, 1971, 11; Underwood, *The Millenarian World of Early Mormonism,* 45-47. See also *Times and Seasons* 2 (15 Feb.1841): 332.

106. Underwood, *The Millenarian World of Early Mormonism,* 46.

107. Examples include *A Book of Commandments for the Government of the Church of Christ, Organized According to Law, on the 6th of April, 1830* (Zion [Independence], MO: W.W. Phelps and Co., 1833), 61 (Sept. 1830), 73-74 (Oct. 1830), 74-75 (Nov. 1830), 79 (Dec. 1830), 81 (Jan. 1831), 82 (Jan. 1831), 99-100 (Feb. 1831), 105 (Mar. 1831), 116 (Mar. 1831). See also Effie Marion

For the hour is nigh, and the day soon at hand, when the earth is ripe: And all the proud, and they that do wickedly, shall be as stubble, and I will burn them up, saith the Lord of Hosts, that wickedness shall not be upon the earth: For the hour is nigh, and that which was spoken by mine apostles must be fulfilled; for as they spoke so shall it come to pass; For I will reveal myself from heaven with power and great glory, with all the hosts thereof, and dwell in righteousness with men on earth a thousand years, and the wicked shall not stand.[108]

Smith's revelations advised the Saints to prepare "the way of the Lord for his second coming: for behold, verily I say unto you, the time is soon at hand, that I shall come in a cloud with power and great glory, and it shall be a great day at the time of my coming, for all nations shall tremble."[109]

Since the world's destruction was assured, the only safety was in accepting the restored gospel.[110] But early church members did not fare well with their non-believing neighbors and began to suffer both social ostracism and physical persecution. Propelled by dualist literalism, the new religious movement soon began to fall into sect development patterns where the difference between its values and those of secular society necessitated separation from the world.[111] In January 1831 Joseph Smith resolved early Mormonism's separatism dilemma by relocating the church to the nation's frontier.

Chadwick, "Extent to Which Early Mormon Beliefs and Practices Reflected the Environment of That People," M.A. thesis, Brigham Young University, 1940, 8-9.

108. *Book of Commandments*, 62.

109. Ibid., 75.

110. *Evening and Morning Star* 2 (Jan. 1834): 126.

111. Bryan R. Wilson, "An Analysis of Sect Development," *American Sociological Review* 24 (Feb. 1959): 12-13. An example is Joseph Smith's two arrests in less than a day for public nuisance by "preaching" the Book of Mormon, and to "check the progress of the delusion, and open the eyes and understanding of those who blindly followed him." See A. W. Benton to *Evangelical Magazine and Gospel Advocate*, 9 Apr. 1831, in Hill, *Joseph Smith: The First Mormon*, 111, 113.

Months after the Book of Mormon's publication, Smith received a revelation commanding the Saints in western New York to gather in Ohio.[112] The move was motivated by fear of their enemies, and by missionary success among Campbellites near Kirtland.[113] The Saints interpreted the migration as initiating the long-awaited gathering of Israel prior to Christ's return.[114] Dictating a revelation, Smith told the church, "Ye are called to bring to pass the gathering of mine elect, ... Wherefore the decree hath gone forth from the Father, that they shall be gathered in unto one place, upon the face of this land, to prepare their hearts, and be prepared in all things against the day when tribulation and desolation are sent forth upon the wicked."[115] He declared in the west they would find their anticipated inheritance, a "land of promise ... upon which there shall be no curse when the Lord comes," and which would endure as the "inheritance of your children forever."[116] The prophet's mother confided to her brother that God "has now made a new and everlasting covenant, ... He says they shall be gathered together into a land of promise and He himself will come and reign on earth with them a thousand years."[117]

Millennial prophecies began to arrive in a flurry setting the tone for the new millenarian movement. When Smith, now relocated in Ohio, produced revelations promising soon to identify the location "where the New Jerusalem shall be built ... that ye may be gathered,"

---

112. *Book of Commandments*, 80-84.

113. Campbellite preacher Sidney Rigdon's conversion was based on the Book of Mormon's teachings concerning an imminent millennium. See Richard S. Van Wagoner, *Sidney Rigdon: A Portrait of Religious Excess* (Salt Lake City: Signature Books, 1994), 60; Hill, *Joseph Smith: The First Mormon*, 122.

114. *Book of Commandments*, 81, 83. See also Joseph Smith to Hyrum Smith, 3 Mar. 1831, in Jessee, *The Personal Writings of Joseph Smith*, 231; Bushman, *Joseph Smith and the Beginnings of Mormonism*, 175.

115. *Book of Commandments*, 61.

116. Ibid., 82.

117. Lucy Mack Smith to Solomon Mack, 6 Jan. 1831, in Bushman, *Joseph Smith and the Beginnings of Mormonism*, 243n90.

hope began to mount that the much anticipated Millennium was upon them.[118] Smith's declarations warned, "Prepare ye, prepare ye for that which is to come, for the Lord is nigh; And the anger of the Lord is kindled, and his sword is bathed in heaven, and it shall fall upon the inhabitants of the earth."[119] Gathered in the west, and awaiting command to initiate building the City of Zion, the New Jerusalem, the Saints were posed to abandon the gentiles to their doom, to inaugurate the Millennium, and to receive their own paradisiacal reward with the Savior at his return.

Mormon eschatology was explicitly American, incorporating the nation's landscape into God's teleological plan. Reserved by God for the last days, America, the land and the people, had special characteristics allowing the restored gospel to be born and to flourish.[120] Patterned on the New England heritage of their Puritan grandfathers, Mormonism sought to establish a society which rejected Jacksonian progressive ideals and individualism. As a quest for order, Mormonism's total theology provided a "counter ideology" acting against the basic assumptions built into the new civil religion.[121]

Smith's movement differed from other primitivist-seeking churches for he offered not only a literal interpretation of the Bible, but direct revelation from God—a link of authority Mormons felt none could challenge. To Smith the unaided Bible was inadequate for guidance in one's life. But where contemporaries sought scholarly insight to overcome perceived biblical inadequacies, Smith produced more scripture, both in the form of restored historical records and in personal and visionary revelation. The return to primitivism that Alexander Campbell and others taught was merely a way-station to Christ's true church.[122]

Mormons remedied the problem of religious authority through

---

118. *Book of Commandments*, 90-95.

119. Ibid., 3.

120. Hatch, *The Democratization of American Christianity*, 187-89; Jon Butler, *Awash in a Sea of Faith*, 242.

121. Hill, *Quest for Refuge*, 28, 203-204.

122. Barlow, *Mormons and the Bible*, 11.

divine communication to prophets, their modern scripture transcending denominational rivalry and conflict, uniting under one head the true apostolic church. Established in an era of tension, Mormonism defied both old established religions and new revivalist movements. When Alexander Campbell said Mormonism's Book of Mormon answered "every error and almost every truth discussed in New York for the last ten years," he was not exaggerating but commenting on the many divisions Mormonism was attempting to breach: mystical-empirical, spiritual-secular, pessimistic-progressive, collective-individualist, authoritative-democratic, sacred-profane.[123]

Modern revelation gave Mormonism an authoritative position unmatched by other religions. The Book of Mormon broke through denominational disputes over scriptural interpretation, updating the Bible, giving common people plain doctrine, carrying biblical history from the Old World to the New, testifying of God's presence in their everyday lives.[124] Although new, Mormonism did not see itself as another denomination; it was to be unique, the only true church on the face of the earth, in a sense hoping "to establish a sect to end all sects."[125]

---

123. Wood, "Evangelical America and Early Mormonism," 379-80.

124. Hatch, *The Democratization of American Christianity*, 121; De Pillis, "The Quest for Religious Authority and the Rise of Mormonism." Some scholarship has indicated the Book of Mormon's influence on early events in Mormon history was limited. See Richard L. Bushman, "The Book of Mormon in Early Mormon History," in *New Views of Mormon History*, eds. Davis Bitton and Maureen Ursenbach Beecher (Salt Lake City: University of Utah Press, 1987), 3-18; Bushman, *Joseph Smith and the Beginnings of Mormonism*, 142; Grant Underwood, "Book of Mormon Usage in Early LDS Theology," *Dialogue: A Journal of Mormon Thought* 17 (Autumn 1984): 35-74. Yet Underwood concludes the Book of Mormon's "earliest uses were primarily eschatological ... [and] the theological millenarianism derived from the Book of Mormon was both complex and pervasive" (60). See also Underwood, *The Millenarian World of Early Mormonism*, 96.

125. De Pillis, "The Quest for Religious Authority and the Rise of Mormonism," 88. John Gager argues Mormonism wished to "short-circuit all historical continuity with Christianity and Judaism and thereby to eliminate both as competitors for the claim to represent the true people of God." See

Meeting a variety of needs, Mormonism offered hope and promise to the troubled who had sought in vain the primal manifestations of divine power.[126] Those who accepted the restored gospel would be saved from divine wrath and prepared for Christ's millennial reign. As summarized by Nathan Hatch: "[P]rimitive Mormonism was a radical, apocalyptic sect that invoked and anticipated divine wrath upon the core institutions and values of Jacksonian America—its pluralism, enlightened rationality, religious optimism, and reform, and its successful entrepreneurs and managers."[127]

When in April 1830 believers in the Book of Mormon became a church, sect-like development patterns began to emerge. Mormons were joined together by a sense of central religious values, beliefs, regulations, and loyalty to a modern prophet. A community of believers now derived their identity from a common conviction that they were endowed with supernatural power, coupled with a sense of distinctiveness which established the boundary between themselves and outsiders. As a peculiar people, they were distinguished by their opposition to and separation from the larger society.[128]

---

his "Early Mormonism and Early Christianity," 59-60. Paul Edwards contends Smith "wished to end it [contention] not replace it." See Paul M. Edwards, "The Secular Smiths," *Journal of Mormon History* 4 (1977): 5n4. For works which contend Mormonism wished "to be to Christianity what Christianity was to Judaism: that is, a reform and a consummation," see Brodie, *No Man Knows My History*, viii; Hansen, *Mormonism and the American Experience*, 18; Shipps, *Mormonism*, 85.

126. Harrison, *The Second Coming*, 184, 191; Wood, "Evangelical America and Early Mormonism," 380.

127. Hatch, "Mormon and Methodist," 38. See also Sandeen, *The Roots of Fundamentalism*, 47.

128. Wilson, "An Analysis of Sect Development," 4; Max Weber, *Economy and Society*, 3 vols. (New York: Bedminister Press, 1968), 3:1204; Rex Eugene Cooper, *Promises Made to the Fathers: Mormon Covenant Organizations* (Salt Lake City: University of Utah Press, 1990), 9; Larry M. Logue, *A Sermon in the Desert: Belief and Behavior in Early St. George, Utah* (Urbana: University of Illinois Press, 1988), 33. Leonard Arrington identifies five Mormon themes initiated in New York which have endured: (1) heavenly visitations, visions, and revelations, (2) translation and publication of the Book of Mormon, (3)

Modern revelation, both in the form of direct communication with the divine and in new scripture, proclaimed great messages to the Saints of the latter days. Convinced that all existing sects and denominations were wrong, a new restored religion was believed necessary to redeem humankind. As such, the Book of Mormon had been brought forth both to profess Christ to the world and to testify of the mission of the young prophet Joseph Smith. With society on the brink of destruction, restoration of apostolic power would prepare a people for Christ's return.[129] Based on apocalyptic literalism, the Saints would attempt to initiate immediately the building of God's kingdom on earth. Soon the elect would be gathered from the gentiles and the lost house of Israel (Indians) to build the New Jerusalem, the holy City of Zion in America, where the righteous would flee for safety and security while Christ's cataclysmic return destroyed the wicked and purified the earth.

---

organization of the Church of Christ, (4) inauguration of missionary work, and (5) commencement of mutual aid, a forerunner to communitarianism. See Arrington, "Mormonism: From Its New York Beginnings," *New York History* 61 (Oct. 1980): 387.

129. Hatch, *The Democratization of American Christianity*, 167-68.

CHAPTER FOUR

EARLY MORMON MILLENNIALISM

America's religious history has demonstrated an evolution and sometimes a merging of the different aspects of millennialism. In this study I employ a fairly narrow definition. Premillennialists (millenarians) are defined as literalists who emphasized the difference between the profane world and the future kingdom of Christ, awaiting two parousias, two physical resurrections, and two judgements. The first resurrection would be of the faithful where Christ would reign personally on the earth, with the rest of humanity resurrected at the end of a thousand years. Postmillennialists believed the Savior's return, the resurrection, and the day of judgement would all close the Millennium. Here on earth God's kingdom would be manifested through the Holy Spirit's influence over human hearts rather than in a literal return of Christ.[1]

Joseph Smith's revelations regarding the imminence of the Second Coming fell carefully into place with the millennial wave of the day.[2] Consequently early Mormon eschatology displayed many sides, including the notion that the Saints must build up and establish the kingdom of God on earth. At the same time Mormons admitted the

1. Robert G. Clouse, ed., *The Meaning of the Millennium: Four Views* (Downers Grove, IL: InterVarsity Press, 1977), 7.

2. Richard L. Bushman, *Joseph Smith and the Beginnings of Mormonism* (Urbana: University of Illinois Press, 1984), 170.

Millennium would come without their assistance in the "twinkling of an eye."[3]

Due to the restoration emphasis in their religious thought, Mormons could incorporate diverse facets of previous millennial movements, giving their theology the flexibility to avoid fixed events and dates.[4] As such, some historians have claimed Mormonism's beginnings displayed aspects of both pre- and postmillennialism. But the most recent scholarship has demonstrated that apocalyptism was the predominant early Mormon cosmology. Early Mormonism fits closely into Norman Cohn's model as collective, terrestrial, total, imminent, miraculous, and can be placed clearly in the millenarian camp.[5]

---

3. *A Book of Commandments for the Government of the Church of Christ, Organized According to Law, on the 6th of April, 1830* (Zion [Independence], MO: W.W. Phelps and Co., 1833), 3-6; Marvin S. Hill, *Quest for Refuge: The Mormon Flight from American Pluralism* (Salt Lake City: Signature Books, 1989), xx.

4. Louis G. Reinwand, "An Interpretive Study of Mormon Millennialism During the Nineteenth Century with Emphasis on Millennial Developments in Utah," M.A. thesis, Brigham Young University, 1971, 33, 67. At least twice, in 1835 and 1843, Smith indicated the Millennium would arrive in 1890-91. Apparently failing to dampen Mormon apocalyptism in the 1830s-40s, these prophesies would later take on increased importance during the anti-polygamy campaign of the 1870s and 1880s.

5. Although labeling the movement a "uniquely American form of millenarianism," Ernest Lee Tuveson also sees Joseph Smith's idea of eternal progress as the epitome of the idea of natural progress. See Tuveson, *Redeemer Nation: The Idea of America's Millennial Role* (Chicago: University of Chicago Press, 1968), 34n11, 175-76, 186. Ernest R. Sandeen contends Mormon millennialism was mixed. Even though Mormons believed the destruction of the world was near, they still labored to gather in the elect and build a New Jerusalem in America. See Sandeen, *The Roots of Fundamentalism: British and American Millenarianism, 1800-1930* (Chicago: University of Chicago Press, 1970), 12-14, 23, 48. Works which hold Mormonism vacillated between pre- and postmillennialism include Klaus J. Hansen, *Quest for Empire: The Political Kingdom of God and the Council of Fifty in Mormon History* (Lansing: Michigan State University Press, 1970), 20-21; Klaus J. Hansen, *Mormonism and the American Experience* (Chicago: University of Chicago Press, 1981), 118;

Mormonism publicly announced its preoccupation with Christ's return in the inclusion of the term "Latter-day Saints" as part of the church's official name.[6] This theme was also symbolized by the titles of its early publications, *Evening and Morning Star*, *Times and Seasons*, and *Millennial Star*, which extensively expounded millennialism.[7] Editor William W. Phelps defined the mission of the church's Independence, Missouri, newspaper *(Evening and Morning Star)* as warning humankind "that a wicked world may know that Jesus Christ, the Redeemer, who shall come to Zion will

---

Reinwand, "An Interpretive Study of Mormon Millennialism," 11-12, 47-48; Keith E. Norman "How Long, O Lord? The Delay of the Parousia in Mormonism," *Sunstone* 8 (Jan.-Apr. 1983): 49-58; David E. Smith, "Millenarian Scholarship in America," *American Quarterly* 17 (Fall 1965): 542; Bushman, *Joseph Smith and the Beginnings of Mormonism*, 170; J[ohn]. F. C. Harrison, *The Second Coming: Popular Millenarianism, 1780-1850* (New Brunswick, NJ: Rutgers University Press, 1979), 176-92. Grant Underwood contends that "even though the Saints urged human efforts to build the kingdom, or were mission minded, or occasionally waned in the enthusiasm for the imminence of paradisiacal glory, these attitudes do not warrant changing the classification of Mormons as premillennialists." See Underwood, *The Millenarian World of Early Mormonism* (Urbana: University of Illinois Press, 1993), 6-8, 24-41. See also Malcolm R. Thorp, review of *The Second Coming: Popular Millenarianism, 1780-1850*, by J. F. C. Harrison, *Brigham Young University Studies* 21 (Fall 1981): 534-36; Dan Vogel, *Religious Seekers and the Advent of Mormonism* (Salt Lake City: Signature Books, 1988), 181-205.

6. The church's official name evolved from The Church of Christ (April 1830) to The Church of the Latter Day Saints (May 1834) to The Church of Jesus Christ of Latter-day Saints (April 1838). See James B. Allen and Glen M. Leonard, *The Story of the Latter-day Saints* (Salt Lake City: Deseret Book Co., 1976), 47.

7. These newspapers were the equivalents of the *Harbingers* and *Watchmen* prevalent among other contemporary sects. See William Mulder, "Mormonism's 'Gathering': An American Doctrine with a Difference," *Church History* 23 (Sept. 1954): 256; Stephen J. Stein, "Signs of the Times: The Theological Foundations of Early Mormon Apocalyptic," *Sunstone* 8 (Jan.-Apr. 1983): 59-65; Reinwand, "An Interpretive Study of Mormon Millennialism," 13.

soon appear."[8] Published in England and edited by Apostle Parley
P. Pratt, the *Millennial Star* reiterated its American counterpart's
role as a "special messa[n]ge[r] to all the nations of earth, in order
to prepare all who will harken for the Second Advent of Messiah,
which is now near at hand."[9]

Early Mormons constantly spoke of the imminence of Christ's
return and scouted for signs of providential anger, judgement, pesti-
lences, tumult, earthquakes, and storms. These were faithfully chron-
icled as evidences of the coming apocalypse, a "sure sign that the
coming of Christ is close at hand."[10] In a recurring column titled
"Signs of the Times," the *Evening and Morning Star* declared,

> We live in a great time; one of the most eventful periods that has
> ever been; ... it is the time when the wicked shall be destroyed; when
> the earth shall be restored to its former beauty and goodness, and
> shall yield its increase, when plagues shall be sent to humble the
> haughty, and bring them, if they will, to a knowledge of God; Yea,
> it is a time when the wicked can not expect to see the next genera-
> tion; yea it is that great time, when none shall live in the next
> generation unless they are pure in heart.[11]

---

8. Joseph Smith, *History of the Church of Jesus Christ of Latter-day Saints*,
7 vols., 2d ed. rev., introduction and notes by B. H. Roberts (Salt Lake City:
Deseret Book Co., 1974-76), 1: 259; *Evening and Morning Star* 1 (June 1832).
See also *Times and Seasons* 5 (15 Aug. 1844): 610; 1 (Nov. 1839): 1; *Journal of
Discourses*, 26 vols. (Liverpool, Eng.: F. D. Richards, 1855-86), 9:346; Loy Otis
Banks, "The Evening and Morning Star," *Missouri Historical Review* 43 (July
1949): 319-33.

9. *Millennial Star* 1 (May 1840): 1; Alan K. Parrish, "Beginnings of the
Millennial Star: Journal of the Mission to Great Britain," in *Regional Studies
in Latter-day Saint Church History: British Isles*, ed. Donald Q. Cannon (Provo,
UT: Brigham Young University, 1990), 133-49.

10. Scott. H. Faulring, ed., *An American Prophet's Record: The Diaries
and Journals of Joseph Smith* (1987; reprint, Salt Lake City: Signature Books in
association with Smith Research Associates, 1989), 14; Smith, *History of the
Church*, 1:439; 2:464; 4:201-203, 381; Harrison, *The Second Coming*, 181.

11. *Evening and Morning Star*, Feb. 1833. Other examples include
"Foreign News," *Evening and Morning Star* 1 (July 1832): 14; "The Judgments
of God," 1 (Oct. 1832): 37; "The Gathering," 1 (Nov. 1832): 45-46; "Another

Early Mormon hymn books devoted whole sections to the "Gathering of Israel" and "The Second Coming of Christ," the Saints looking forward to the time when the wicked "will be swept from the earth."[12]

Departing from their postmillennial neighbors who saw God working through humanity to regenerate the world, Latter-day Saints understood only the sinful majority's future destruction. To Mormons the aspirations of reform movements merely squandered precious time on counterfeit solutions.[13] Prominent Mormon Sidney Rigdon declared that "the ignorance of the religious teachers of the day never appeared more glaring in anything than in an attempt to create a Millennium by converting this generation."[14] Part of Rigdon's disagreement with his former associate, Alexander Campbell, was over a different millennial vision, and many of the Campbellites who joined the Mormon church were those who expected Christ's speedy literal return.[15]

'Shower of Flesh And Blood' In Our Own Neighborhood," *Times and Seasons* 2 (15 Nov. 1841): 587; "Full Particulars of the Wonderful Sights Seen By the Pilot Of The William Penn In The Sky On Tuesday Night, March 21," 4 (Apr. 1843): 149-50; "History of Joseph Smith," 6 (15 Dec. 1845): 1060.

12. Smith, *History of the Church*, 2:324; Mulder, "Mormonism's 'Gathering,'" 260-61n8. See also *Evening and Morning Star* 1 (May 1833): 96.

13. Michael Barkun, *Crucible of the Millennium: The Burned-Over District of New York in the 1840s* (Syracuse: Syracuse University Press, 1986), 17.

14. *Evening and Morning Star* 2 (June 1834): 163. See also *Messenger and Advocate* 3 (Nov. 1836): 401-404. For examples of Oliver Cowdery's criticism of postmillennialism, see *Evening and Morning Star* 2 (Apr. 1834): 145; 2 (May 1834): 153; 2 (June 1834): 163. For other nineteenth-century pre-millennialists, such as William Miller's followers, who showed little interest in the reform measures of the 1830s, see Whitney R. Cross, *The Burned-over District: The Social and Intellectual History of Enthusiastic Religion in Western New York, 1800-1850* (Ithaca: Cornell University, 1950), 235.

15. Richard S. Van Wagoner, *Sidney Rigdon: A Portrait of Religious Excess* (Salt Lake City: Signature Books, 1994), 50-55; Milton V. Backman, Jr., *The Heavens Resound: A History of the Latter-day Saints in Ohio, 1830-1838* (Salt Lake City: Deseret Book Co., 1983), 15; Underwood, *The Millenarian World of Early Mormonism*, 26-28. Just months before Mormon missionaries arrived in Ohio, Rigdon preached that something important was to occur "in the near future,"

Joseph Smith's revelations described the awful calamities which would befall the earth prior to Christ's return. Plagues of flies, maggots, hailstorms, fires, flesh falling from bones and eyes from sockets were all destined to take place in the last days.[16] Rhetorically Latterday Saints held change could still happen. Modern revelation promised that if "this generation harden not their hearts, I [God] will work a reformation among them," and Mormons believed it was their duty to preach repentance in the last days. But in reality few believed the world would heed the call.[17] As millenarians, Mormons recognized humanity's perfection would only come with the destruction of the wicked, for "as it was in the days of Noah, so shall it be at the coming of the Son of man."[18] Smith, blessed by his father that he would continue in office until Christ came, described the mood of his age when he wrote in 1832, "It is a day of strange appearances. Everything indicates something more than meets the eye. ... The end is nigh."[19]

---

and Rigdon interpreted Mormonism to be the extraordinary thing he expected, believing the restoration of the gospel was a sign the Millennium was near. See Van Wagoner, *Sidney Rigdon*, 50-55. Non-Mormons in Ohio were aware of the early Latter-day Saints' belief in the imminence of the Millennium. See Robert Richardson, ed., *Memoirs of Alexander Campbell*, 2 vols. (1868-70; reprint, Cincinnati: Standard Publishing Co., 1913), 2:345-47; Alanson Wilcox, *A History of the Disciples of Christ in Ohio* (Cincinnati: Standard Publishing, 1918), 125. From December 1835 to May 1836 Rigdon produced a fourteen-article series on the Millennium which criticized postmillennialism. See *Evening and Morning Star* 2 (Dec. 1833): 117; 2 (Jan 1834): 126; 2 (June 1834): 163. For Alexander Campbell's postmillennial eschatology, see Hiram J. Lester, "Alexander Campbell's Millennial Program," *Discipliana* 48 (Fall 1988): 35-39; Richard T. Hughes, "The Apocalyptic Origins of the Churches of Christ and the Triumph of Modernism," *Religion and American Culture: A Journal of Interpretation* 2 (Summer 1992): 181-214.

16. *Book of Commandments*, 63. See also Bushman, *Joseph Smith and the Beginnings of Mormonism*, 170.

17. *Book of Commandments*, 11.

18. *Evening and Morning Star* 2 (July 1834): 169. See also 2 (June 1834): 163.

19. Smith, *History of the Church*, 1:281, 323; 2:32. Examples of the

Mormons were consistent in their belief that Christ's return was imminent. In the early 1830s Book of Mormon scribe Oliver Cowdery concluded the end of the world would arrive in fifteen years. Predicting "there would never be another President of the United States elected," Martin Harris declared: "[S]oon all temporal and spiritual power would be given over to the prophet Joseph Smith and the Latter Day Saints," and only those who believed in the Book of Mormon would remain to "see Christ."[20]

Apostle George A. Smith recalled that members in the early 1830s believed that not more than "nine or ten years would be sufficient to wind up the whole matter of warning the wicked nations and the gathering of the Saints preparatory to the coming of the

---

concern Mormonism had with these things include: ibid., 1:176n, 316; 2:447-48, 464; 3:67, 286, 390; 4:201-203, 381, 401, 414; 5:301, 336; 6:516, 560; Scott G. Kenney, ed., *Wilford Woodruff's Journal, 1833-1898*, 9 vols. (Midvale, UT: Signature Books, 1983-85), 1:123, 25 Jan. 1837; 1:491-92, 12 Aug. 1840; Parley P. Pratt, *Autobiography of Parley Parker Pratt* (1938; reprint, Salt Lake City: Deseret Book Co., 1979), 44; Brigham Young, *Journal of Discourses*, 9:231, 13 July 1855; Orson Pratt, ibid., 3:17, 20 May 1855; Charles C. Rich, ibid., 19:161, 11 Nov. 1877.

20. *Painesville Telegraph* 2 (16 Nov. 1830): 3; 2 (15 Mar. 1831); *Ohio Star* 1 (9 Dec. 1830): 2; Albert Chandler to William A. Linn, 22. Dec. 1898, in William Alexander Linn, *The Story of the Mormons* (1902; reprint, New York: Russell and Russell, 1963), 48-49. Chandler was an apprentice in the book-binding operation of Egbert B. Grandin and in 1830 helped to collate and stitch the first edition of the Book of Mormon. Martin Harris is also quoted as predicting that "Within four years from September 1832, there will not be one wicked person left in the United States; that the righteous will be gathered to Zion, [Missouri,] and that there will be no President over these United States after that time. ... I do hereby assert and declare that in four years from the date hereof, every sectarian and religious denomination in the United States, shall be broken down, and every Christian shall be gathered unto the Mormonites, and the rest of the human race shall perish." See E[ber]. D. Howe, *Mormonism Unvailed: or A Faithful Account of that Singular Imposition and Delusion, from Its Rise to the Present Time* (Painesville, OH: E. D. Howe, 1834), 14. See also Max H. Parkin, "The Nature and Cause of Internal and External Conflict of the Mormons in Ohio Between 1830 and 1838," M.A. thesis, Brigham Young University, 1966, 53-54.

Messiah."[21] Early Mormon historian John Whitmer acknowledged "there was a tradition among some of the early disciples, that those who obeyed the covenant in the last days, would never die."[22] Mormon apostle Parley Pratt prophesied that the governments on the American continent would soon be overthrown and that within fifty years no unbelieving gentile would be left.[23] On more than one occasion Joseph Smith himself asserted that members of his own generation would yet witness the Second Coming, predicting that the great temple spoken of by the biblical prophet Malachi would be built in America before those now alive would "pass away."[24] No exact date was given but all believed they were "on the eve of the second coming," living in the generation that would see Christ usher in the Millennium.[25]

Not only Joseph Smith but devout followers Brigham Young, John Taylor, and Wilford Woodruff were also ardent millennialists who proclaimed and taught it during their successive terms as president of the LDS church.[26] Smith, Young, Taylor, and Woodruff were

21. George A. Smith, *Journal of Discourses*, 9:346, 11 May 1862. See also Charles C. Rich, ibid., 19:161, 11 Nov. 1877; Joseph Young, ibid., 9:231, 13 July 1855.

22. F. Mark McKiernan and Roger D. Launius, eds., *An Early Latter Day Saint History: The Book of John Whitmer, Kept by Commandment* (Independence, MO: Herald Publishing House, 1980), 45; Backman, *The Heavens Resound*, 59. Some members went so far in the belief that they would "never die" that they refused to call a physician. See *Wayne Sentinel*, 18 Apr. 1832; *Painesville Telegraph*, 5 Apr. 1831.

23. Parley P. Pratt, *Mormonism Unveiled*... (New York: Orson Pratt and Elijah Fordham, 1838), 15.

24. Smith, *History of the Church*, 1:316, 5:336; *Messenger and Advocate* 2 (Oct. 1835): 206; John Henry Evans, *Joseph Smith: An American Prophet* (1933; reprint, Salt Lake City: Deseret Book Co., 1989), 81; "Levi Hancock Journal," June 1831, in Vogel, *Religious Seekers and the Advent of Mormonism*, 188.

25. *Messenger and Advocate* 1 (Jan. 1835): 58; *Evening and Morning Star* 2 (June 1834): 162.

26. Examples include John Taylor, *Journal of Discourses*, 10:146-48, 6 Apr. 1863; Wilford Woodruff, ibid., 18:113-14, 12 Sept. 1875; Brigham Young, ibid., 19:4-5, 29 Apr. 1877; Wilford Woodruff, ibid., 25:11, 6 Jan.

the first four presidents of the Mormon church with Woodruff's administration ending near the close of the nineteenth century. Woodruff was particularly apocalyptic.[27] Concurring with Joseph Smith who prayed God would hasten the Millennium that "thy church may come forth out of the wilderness," Woodruff had looked for a church that would "call us out of Babylon ... [where the] Sword of God is ... soon to fall upon the inhabitants of the earth."[28] Once joined with the Mormons, Woodruff found his millennial anticipations confirmed in a patriarchal blessing under the hands of Patriarch Joseph Smith, Sr.[29] Woodruff's blessing promised that he would witness the winding-up scene in the flesh and would "remain on the earth to behold thy Savior Come in the Clouds of heaven."[30] Just as

---

1884; B[righam]. H. Roberts, *A Comprehensive History of the Church of Jesus Christ of Latter-day Saints*, 6 vols. (1930; reprint, Provo, UT: Brigham Young University Press, 1965), 5:136. See also Thomas G. Alexander, *Things in Heaven and Earth: The Life and Times of Wilford Woodruff, a Mormon Prophet* (Salt Lake City: Signature Books, 1991), 16; Reinwand, "An Interpretive Study of Mormon Millennialism," 58.

27. Woodruff's millennialism is so pervasive that a recent abridged version of his journal was titled *Waiting for World's End*. See Susan Staker, ed., *Waiting for World's End: The Diaries of Wilford Woodruff* (Salt Lake City: Signature Books, 1993).

28. Wilford Woodruff to Aphek Woodruff, 15 Mar. 1834, in Alexander, *Things in Heaven and Earth*, 22.

29. As part of Mormonism's restoration of Old Testament theology, tying modern Israel to ancient rites, the church introduced blessings mirroring Old Testament patriarchs who blessed their children. See Gen. 28:4, 49:1-28. Joseph Smith's father was ordained to the office of patriarch in December 1834. See Roberts, *A Comprehensive History of the Church*, 1:387; William James Mortimer, "Patriarchal Blessings," in *Encyclopedia of Mormonism*, 5 vols., ed. Daniel H. Ludlow (New York: Macmillan Publishing Company, 1992), 3:1066-1067. See also John Taylor, "Patriarchal," *Times and Seasons* 6 (1 June 1845): 920-22.

30. Kenney, *Wilford Woodruff's Journal*, 1:142-43, 15 Apr. 1837. Woodruff's belief in this promise apparently did not wane. Thirteen years later he recopied this blessing into his journal on the day his father Aphek Woodruff received his patriarchal blessing. See ibid., 3: 583-88, 20 Dec. 1850. At least sixty-one other early Saints including Hyrum Smith, Orson Pratt,

John the Baptist had prepared the way for Jesus' coming, so now was Joseph Smith looked upon as a latter-day voice, crying in the wilderness, preparing the way for the Lord.[31]

Conforming to the role of millenarian prophet, Joseph Smith condemned the society around him. His view of the world and of established religion's state of apostasy fed the new movement's millennialism. "The world," Smith said, "has had a fair trial for six thousand years; the Lord will try the seventh thousand Himself."[32] As the seer of the coming millennium, he believed that contemporary mainstream America was ripe with iniquity, on the verge of destruction.[33] Although America was still a promised land, choice above all others, editor William Phelps saw the country fulfilling its destiny just as the Nephites of old had done. Soon wars would be at the nation's door, with pestilence, famine, earthquakes, and other disasters acting as signs that the Lord was warning the wicked of his imminent return.[34]

Lyman Johnson, Heber C. Kimball, William Smith, and Orson Hyde were told in patriarchal blessings they would "stand upon the Earth when the Savior makes his appearance" and live during "the Millennial Reign." See Irene M. Bates, "Patriarchal Blessings and the Routinization of Charisma," *Dialogue: A Journal of Mormon Thought* 26 (Fall 1993): 9-10, 21; Van Wagoner, *Sidney Rigdon*, 154; "Caroline Barnes Crosby Journal," 21 Feb. 1836, in Vogel, *Religious Seekers and the Advent of Mormonism*, 197-98.

31. Timothy L. Smith, "The Book of Mormon in a Biblical Culture," *Journal of Mormon History* 7 (1980): 19; Parley P. Pratt, *A Voice of Warning ...* (New York: W. Sanford, 1837), 96-99.

32. Smith, *History of the Church*, 5:64.

33. Dean C. Jessee, comp. and ed., *The Personal Writings of Joseph Smith* (Salt Lake City: Deseret Book Co., 1984), 270-72; Harrison, *The Second Coming*, 183; Thomas F. O'Dea, *The Mormons* (Chicago: University of Chicago Press, 1957), 27; Kenneth H. Winn, *Exiles in a Land of Liberty: Mormons in America, 1830-1846* (Chapel Hill: University of North Carolina Press, 1989), 39.

34. *Evening and Morning Star* 1 (Mar. 1833). See also *Messenger and Advocate*, Feb. 1837; Wilford Woodruff to Axmon and Thompson Woodruff, 29 Nov. 1834, in Alexander, *Things in Heaven and Earth*, 33; *Book of Commandments*, 48:57; Winn, *Exiles in a Land of Liberty*, 49, 78-79.

Apostle Parley Pratt foresaw the destiny of American society if it rejected the restored gospel: "[they] shall be cut off from among the people ... This destruction includes an utter overthrow, and desolation of all our cities, Forest, Strong Holds—and entire annihilation of our race, except such as embrace the covenant, and are numbered with Israel."[35] In 1832 Smith received a revelation specifically warning New York, Albany, and Boston of the "desolation and utter abolishment" awaiting them if they rejected the gospel.[36] Ten years later Mormon elder Freeman Nickerson published a renewed admonition to Boston inhabitants warning them of "the destruction which will take place in this generation that is now on earth," advising them what to do to survive "the day of the second coming of Christ."[37]

Believing that only the restored church represented true freedom as envisioned by the Founding Fathers, Mormons saw their relationship with the gentiles as a struggle between good and evil, light and darkness. The flaws of the U.S. Constitution emphasized that only during a millennial kingdom could liberty remain. When America, the world's last great hope, began to flounder in disbelief and corruption, the Saints would know the Millennium was nigh.[38]

Early Mormon millennialism is exemplified by Joseph Smith's so-called "Revelation and Prophecy on War" dictated on 25 December 1832 in Kirtland, Ohio. Describing the devastating forces that would strike the wicked—famine, plague, earthquakes, thunder, and lightening—Smith then prophesied that a "rebellion" beginning in

---

35. Pratt, *Mormonism Unveiled*, 15.

36. *Doctrine and Covenants of the Latter Day Saints: Carefully Selected from the Revelations of God*, comps., Joseph Smith, Junior, Oliver Cowdery, Sidney Rigdon, and Frederick G. Williams (Kirtland, OH: F.G. Williams and Co., 1835), 95; Smith, *History of the Church*, 1:294-95.

37. *Dollar Weekly Bostonian* as reprinted in *Times and Seasons* 3 (16 May 1842): 798; Vogel, *Religious Seekers and the Advent of Mormonism*, 188-89. Alongside the report of a destructive fire in Albany in 1848, the *Millennial Star* reprinted Smith's 1832 prophecy. See *Millennial Star* 10 (15 Sept. 1848): 286-87. In Utah Wilford Woodruff continued to prophecy of the destruction of these cities. See Kenney, *Wilford Woodruff's Journal*, 6:421-23, 22 Aug. 1868.

38. Winn, *Exiles in a Land of Liberty*, 37, 185-86.

South Carolina would occur.[39] This revelation, received at the height of the 1832 nullification crisis, proclaimed an intensified "voice of warning" to the world.

Against the backdrop of the tariffs of 1828 and 1832, on 24 November 1832 South Carolina passed legislation aimed specifically at nullifying federal tariff laws beginning 1 February 1833. When President Andrew Jackson gained congressional authority to crush the rebellion and hold South Carolina in line, by force if necessary, anxieties grew that a national crisis was at hand.[40] Twelve miles from the Mormon stronghold of Kirtland, Eber D. Howe's *Painesville Telegraph* predicted "civil war" was near and perhaps "our national existence is at an end."[41] Four days later Joseph Smith prophesied

> Verily thus saith the Lord, concerning the wars that will shortly come to pass, beginning at the rebellion of South Carolina, which will eventually terminate in the death and misery of many souls. The days will come that war will be poured out upon all nations, beginning at that place; for behold, the Southern States shall be divided against the Northern States, ... and thus war shall be poured out upon all nations. ... after many days, slaves shall rise up against their Masters, who shall be marshalled and disciplined for war; And it shall come to pass also, that the remnants who are left on the land will marshall themselves, and shall become exceeding angry, and shall vex the Gentiles with a sore vexation; and thus, with the sword,

39. *The Pearl of Great Price: Being a Choice Selection from the Revelations, Translations, and Narrations of Joseph Smith* (Liverpool, Eng.: F.D. Richards, 1851), 35; Richard P. Howard, "Christmas Day, 1832: Joseph Smith Responds to the Nullification Crisis," *Saints Herald* 116 (May 1969): 54; Lyndon W. Cook, *The Revelations of the Prophet Joseph Smith: A Historical and Biographical Commentary of the Doctrine and Covenants* (1981; reprint, Salt Lake City: Deseret Book Co., 1985), 180; Backman, *The Heavens Resound*, 226-28.

40. Richard E. Ellis, *The Union at Risk: Jacksonian Democracy, States' Rights and the Nullification Crisis* (New York: Oxford University Press, 1987); William W. Freehling, *Prelude to Civil War: The Nullification Controversy in South Carolina, 1816-1836* (New York: Harper and Row, 1965); Robert V. Remini, *The Life of Andrew Jackson* (1988; reprint, New York: Penguin Books, 1990), 233-51.

41. *Painesville Telegraph,* 21 Dec. 1832.

and by bloodshed, the inhabitants of the earth shall ... feel the wrath, and indignation and chastening hand of an Almighty God, until the consumption decreed, hath made a full end of all nations; that the cry of the Saints, and of the blood of the Saints, shall cease to come up into the ears of the Lord of Sabbaoth, from the earth, to be avenged of their enemies. Wherefore, stand ye in holy place, and be not moved, until the day of the Lord come; for behold it cometh quickly, saith the Lord.[42]

Less than two weeks following the "civil war prophecy," Smith penned a letter to Rochester, New York, newspaper editor N. C. Saxton, announcing, "I am prepared to say by the authority of Jesus Christ, that not many years shall pass away before the United States shall present such a scene of bloodshed as has not a parallel in the hystory [sic] of our nation."[43] Employing standard millenarian imagery, Smith continued,

pestalance hail famine and earthquake will sweep the wicked of this generation from the face of this Land ... I declare unto you the warning which the Lord has commanded me to declare unto this generation ... the hour of his Judgement is come. ... For there are those now living upon the earth whose eyes shall not be closed in death until they see all these things which I have spoken fulfilled.[44]

Following Smith's lead, William W. Phelps understood the "dissolution of South Carolina from the Union" to be a sign that the Millennium would soon arrive.[45]

---

42. *The Pearl of Great Price*, 35; Smith, *History of the Church*, 1:301-302.

43. Joseph Smith to N. C. Saxton, 4 Jan. 1833, in Jessee, *The Personal Writings of Joseph Smith*, 273.

44. Ibid., 273-74. When Smith observed his letter had appeared in the newspaper in an abbreviated form, he wrote to Saxton a second time urging publication of his letter in its entirety. See Joseph Smith to N. C. Saxton, 12 Feb. 1833, in ibid., 275-76. The published portion of Smith's letter appeared in the *American Revivalist, and Rochester Observer*, 2 Feb. 1833. See Vogel, *Religious Seekers and the Advent of Mormonism*, 188, 207n42. See also Smith, *History of the Church*, 1:312-16.

45. *Evening and Morning Star* 1 (Jan. 1833). See also Max H. Parkin, "Mormon Political Involvement in Ohio," *Brigham Young University Studies* 9

The national crisis was avoided when Congress met in January 1833 to discuss lowering the tariff and South Carolina suspended its nullification ordinance. In the early 1830s both Phelps and Frederick G. Williams included Smith's prophecy in their own compilations of revelations.[46] Yet in 1835 when Smith began to assemble the church's revelations for publication, the nullification crisis had subsided and he chose not to include the prophecy in the *Doctrine and Covenants*. The "civil war prophecy" was not published for church members generally until 1851, seven years after Smith's death, following renewed national anxiety over the 1850 compromise.[47] While Mormon tradition holds that this prophecy was fulfilled in the American Civil War, in the church's history Joseph Smith identified the nullification crisis as the background for the revelation.[48] As Richard Howard and

---

(Summer 1969): 485-86.

46. Williams recorded the prophecy in a bound volume titled "Kirtland Revelations," and Phelps's copy is in Book "B" of the "Book of Commandments, Laws, and Covenants," both of which are held in the archives of the historical department of the LDS church. See Earl E. Olson, "The Chronology of the Ohio Revelations," *Brigham Young University Studies* 11 (Summer 1971): 333-35, 347.

47. The "prophecy on war" was first published unofficially in 1851 in England by the president of the Mormon English mission, Franklin D. Richards, as part of *The Pearl of Great Price*, but was not included in the *Doctrine and Covenants* until the 1876 edition. See Rodney Turner, "Franklin D. Richards and the Pearl of Great Price," in *Regional Studies in Latter-day Saint Church History: British Isles*, ed., Donald Q. Cannon (Provo, UT: Brigham Young University, 1990), 177-91. In 1860 Brigham Young explained that the deletion of this prophesy from the *Doctrine and Covenants* published in 1835 was intentional because, although true, it was "not wisdom to publish it to the world." See Young, *Journal of Discourses*, 8:58, 29 May 1860. In the 1860s and 1870s apostles Orson Pratt and Wilford Woodruff claimed they promulgated this prophecy in the 1830s. See Prat, ibid., 17:319, 28 Feb. 1875; Pratt, ibid., 13:135, 10 Apr. 1870; Pratt, ibid., 18: 224-25, 26 Aug. 1876; Pratt, ibid., 18:340, 25 Feb. 1877; Woodruff, ibid., 14:2, 1 Jan. 1871; Cook, *The Revelations of the Prophet Joseph Smith*, 318, sec. 87 n3; Vogel, *Religious Seekers and the Advent of Mormonism*, 189-90; Newell G. Bringhurst, *Saints, Slaves, and Blacks* (Westport, CT: Greenwood Press, 1981), 17, 28nn15-17.

48. Smith, *History of the Church*, 1:301.

Anthony Hutchinson have pointed out, contemporary Saints down-played the possible Civil War rhetoric only after the crisis had sub-sided, believing the Union's division was a prelude to the apocalypse soon to sweep the earth.[49]

A decade later, as part of a myriad of instruction and scripture clarification to a handful of close associates, Smith reported that the catalyst for the great tribulation prior to the Second Coming would be American slavery. "I prophecy in the Name of the Lord God," he declared, "that the commencement of bloodshed as preparatory to the coming of the Son of Man will commence in South Carolina. (It probably may come through the slave trade[.]) This the voice declared to me while I was praying earnestly on the subject 25 December 1832."[50] The revised prophecy followed Smith's recounting of a 9 March 1843 dream, interpreted by Orson Hyde without comment, that the "Government of these United States, ... will be invaded by a foreign foe, probably England. [The] U.S. government will call on Gen[eral] Smith to defend probably all this western territory and offer him any amount of men he shall desire and put them under his command."[51]

---

49. Howard, "Christmas Day 1832: Joseph Smith Responds to the Nullification Crisis," 54; Anthony A. Hutchinson, "Prophetic Fore-knowledge: Hope and Fulfillment in an Inspired Community," *Sunstone* 11 (July 1987): 16-17. See also Vogel, *Religious Seekers and the Advent of Mormonism*, 208n48.

50. Faulring, *An American Prophet's Record*, 340, 2 Apr. 1843; Joseph Smith Diary, by Willard Richards, in Andrew F. Ehat and Lyndon W. Cook, comps. and eds., *The Words of Joseph Smith: The Contemporary Accounts of the Nauvoo Discourses of the Prophet Joseph* (1980 reprint; Orem, UT: Grandin Book Co., 1991), 172, 2 Apr. 1843, emphasis mine; George D. Smith, ed., *An Intimate Chronicle: The Journals of William Clayton* (Salt Lake City: Signature Books in association with Smith Research Associates, 1991), 97, 2 Apr. 1843. This prophecy is found in the *Doctrine and Covenants* (Salt Lake City: The Church of Jesus Christ of Latter-day Saints, 1981), 130:12-13. Section 130 was first published in the *Deseret News*, 9 July 1856. See Cook, *The Revelations of the Prophet Joseph Smith*, 291.

51. Faulring, *An American Prophet's Record*, 340, 2 Apr. 1843; Smith, *An Intimate Chronicle*, 97, 2 Apr. 1843. See also Hutchinson, "Prophetic Fore-

Although Smith's prediction was not immediately fulfilled, sub-sequent Mormon persecution in Missouri further fed the Saints' yearnings for justice and vindication, anticipating divine retribution upon the United States. Apostle Wilford Woodruff chided the nation for driving the Saints "from place to place," and lamented its destiny:

> O America ... From this time forth perplexity shall rest upon the nation, confusion reign in thy government wisdom righteousness & truth will depart from thy senator & rulers, Discord & folly shall sit in thy congress & senate. Thy shame shall be known among the nations of the Earth. They pride shall be humbled in the dust & thy haughtiness laid low. The heads of they rulers shall be cut off & lade in the Dust.
>
> It shall be a vexation to understand the report of the Sorrow pain & wo that Shall come upon thee by Sword, fire, tempest, Earthquakes, & pestilence from the hand of God. Even these things shall come upon thee untill thy government is broken up & thou art destroyed as a nation from under Heaven.[52]

The apocalyptic spirit penetrated all aspects of early Mormon life, including missionary work. According to future church president John Taylor, modern revelation commanded the church to clearly set forth the desolation of abomination to fall upon the world in the last days.[53] Apostle Orson Hyde wrote in his missionary tract, *A Timely Warning to the People of England,*

---

knowledge: Hope and Fulfillment in an Inspired Community," 17. Smith's revised prophecy was first canonized in section 130 of the 1876 edition of the *Doctrine and Covenants*. The 1876 editor, Orson Pratt, included section 130 under the direction of Brigham Young. See Robert J. Woodford, "The Historical Development of the Doctrine and Covenants," Ph.D. diss., Brigham Young University, 1974, 70, 75-76, 1710.

52. Kenney, *Wilford Woodruff's Journal*, 2:43-44, 12 Feb. 1841. See also Jessee, *The Personal Writings of Joseph Smith*, 389-407; Smith, *History of the Church*, 6:116.

53. John Taylor, *The Government of God* (Liverpool, Eng.: S.W. Richards, n.d.). Examples include Elden J. Watson, ed., *The Orson Pratt Journals* (Salt Lake City: Elden Jay Watson, 1975), 22-24, 31, 40, 78; Jan Shipps

The time has come for him [the Lord] to set his hand the second and last time to gather the remnants of Israel; and with them the fulness of the Gentiles— to establish permanant peace on Earth for one thousand years. ... As John was sent before the face of the Lord to prepare the way for his coming, even so has the Lord now sent forth his servants for the last time, to labour in his vineyard at the eleventh hour, to prepare the way for his second coming.[54]

Raising the apocalyptic alarm defined the Latter-day Saints' charge to "warn the wicked and to gather the elect."[55] Living on the eve of the Millennium, the "great and dreadful day of the Lord" would not dawn until the elect "shall all have come from one end of heaven to the other, and not one [is] left in all nations ... under heaven, and then and not until then will Christ come."[56] As such, missionary work was the worldwide recruitment of obedient gentiles who would heed the call. Those who came to the gospel by faith and baptism would become God's chosen people, accomplishing the gathering necessary to precede the Lord's day of judgement.[57] Those who rejected the message must yield to "the judgements of God [which will] sweep you from the face of the earth."[58]

Although missionaries were sent to the eastern states and Canada, the greatest success came from the British Isles, achieving what one author called "the most spectacular harvest of souls since Wesley's time."[59] In less than a decade over 54,000 British converts

---

and John W. Welch, eds., *The Journals of William E. McLellin, 1831-1836* (Provo, UT: BYU Studies, 1994), 62, 65, 80, 85, 143.

54. Orson Hyde, in James B. Allen, *Trials of Discipleship: The Story of William Clayton, A Mormon* (Urbana: University of Illinois Press, 1987), 6-7.

55. "Kirtland Council Minute Book," 174, in Grant Underwood, "Millenarianism and the Early Mormon Mind," *Journal of Mormon History* 9 (1982): 48. See also *Times and Seasons* 2 (July 1841): 461.

56. *Messenger and Advocate* 3 (Nov. 1836): 404.

57. Smith, "The Book of Mormon in a Biblical Culture," 12; Barbara McFarlane Higdon, "The Role of Preaching in the Early Latter Day Saint Church, 1830-1846," Ph.D. diss., University of Missouri, 1961.

58. *Messenger and Advocate* 1 (Jan 1835): 61.

59. W[alter]. H. G. Armytage, *Heavens Below: Utopian Experiments in*

joined the Mormon church; by 1870 Mormons had baptized 100,000 people in England.[60] Most English-Mormon converts came from cities and the urban working class, mainly manufacturers and mechanics, those disturbed by secularization and sectarian conflict, much like Joseph Smith's American followers in the 1820s-30s.[61] Whether in America or England, a certain type of "seeker" found Mormonism's themes—emphasis on the last days, the restoration of Israel (including ideas about American Indians), the need for prophets, and separating the righteous from the wicked—a persuasive theology.[62] Professing the restored gospel with a doomsday trumpet, missionaries patterned their voice of warning after biblical prophets, centering on the imminence of Christ's reign and the destruction of the wicked.[63]

By exhorting millennialism, Mormon missionaries in England had great success among those who awaited Christ's return, converts hoping for and experiencing the charismatic gifts of the Spirit that British millenarians believed would accompany the last days.[64] Eng-

---

England, 1560-1960 (Toronto: Toronto University Press, 1961), 260.

60. M. Hanlin Cannon, "Migration of English Mormons to America," *American Historical Review* 52 (Apr. 1947): 441; Armytage, *Heavens Below*, 268.

61. James B. Allen and Malcolm. R. Thorp, "The Mission of the Twelve to England, 1840-41: Mormon Apostles and the Working Classes," *Brigham Young University Studies*, 15 (Summer 1975): 499-526; James B. Allen and Thomas G. Alexander, eds., *Manchester Mormons: The Journal of William Clayton, 1840-1842* (Santa Barbara, CA: Peregrine Smith, 1974), 20-31; Marvin S. Hill, "The Rise of Mormonism in the Burned-over District: Another View," *New York History*, Oct. 1980, 416-19.

62. Harrison, *The Second Coming*, 190-205, 217; Allen, *Trials of Discipleship*, 23-24.

63. *Book of Commandments*, 15; Underwood, "Millenarianism and the Early Mormon Mind," 49-50; Letter from Warren Parrish in Smith, *History of the Church*, 2:447-48.

64. Smith, "The Book of Mormon in a Biblical Culture," 7; Alexander, *Things in Heaven and Earth*, 90; Armytage, *Heavens Below*, 268; James B. Allen, Ronald K. Esplin, and David J. Whittaker, *Men with a Mission: 1837-1841, The Quorum of the Twelve Apostles in the British Isles* (Salt Lake City: Deseret Book Co., 1992), 86-88, 259; Malcolm R. Thorp, "The Religious Backgrounds of

lish audiences heard Mormon apostle Heber C. Kimball declare that he "would not suffer death before Christ's second coming, and prophesy that within ten or fifteen years the sea between Liverpool and America would dry up."[65] "Under the spirit of prophecy," Apostle Wilford Woodruff told British converts they would remain on earth "until the coming of Christ."[66] Parley Pratt even wrote to Queen Victoria that the Lord was soon to establish "a new and universal Kingdom, under the immediate administration of the Messiah and his [Latter-day] Saints."[67] Soon the elevation of the righteous and the "destruction of the gentiles" would unite the Saints with their returning Savior.[68]

Much early Mormon energy and momentum derived from the Saints' sense of being God's chosen people, living in the final era of history. Yet preparing for the "last days," and transforming a society,

---

Mormon Converts in Britain, 1837-52," *Journal of Mormon History* 4 (1977): 53. Although Thorp contends millennialism was not as important as "primitive simplicity," he notes Parley Pratt's highly millennial tract *A Voice of Warning* was "mentioned almost as often as the Book of Mormon in influencing conversion." Ibid., 63. Kenneth Winn calls Pratt's *A Voice of Warning* "the greatest proselyting tract in Mormon history." See Winn, *Exiles in a Land of Liberty*, 49. Grant Underwood sees *A Voice of Warning*, the most reprinted work aside from the Book of Mormon, as the premiere eschatological work of early Mormon thought. See Underwood, "Early Mormon Perceptions of Contemporary America: 1830-1846," *Brigham Young University Studies* 26 (Summer 1986): 28. See also Peter Crawley, "Parley P. Pratt: Father of Mormon Pamphleteering," *Dialogue: A Journal of Mormon Thought* 15 (Autumn 1982): 13-26; David J. Whittaker, "Early Mormon Pamphleteering," Ph.D. diss., Brigham Young University, 1982.

65. Armytage, *Heavens Below*, 260.

66. Kenney, *Wilford Woodruff's Journal*, 1:411, 26 Jan. 1840.

67. Parley P. Pratt to *Her Gracious Majesty, Queen Victoria* (Manchester, Eng., 1841), 5, in Hansen, *Quest for Empire*, 4. Other examples are found in Stanley B. Kimball, ed., *On the Potter's Wheel: The Diaries of Heber C. Kimball* (Salt Lake City: Signature Books in association with Smith Research Associates, 1987), 8, 22 July 1837; Kenney, *Wilford Woodruff's Journal*, 1:411, 26 Jan. 1840; 1:502-504, 30 Aug. 1840; 1:540, 24 Oct. 1840.

68. Smith, *An Intimate Chronicle*, 43, 6 Apr. 1840.

was not easy or conventional. As such, proselyting and withdrawal were used as alternate strategies for survival and sustaining members' commitment, some adherents gaining strength by converting non-believers, others by separating themselves from the "wicked." Consequently Mormons attempted to maintain a balance between separation from and engagement with secular society.[69] Merging secular with religious themes, aspirations of an earthly utopia fostered Mormon millennialism's separatist tendencies.

With early converts coming from dislocated backgrounds, a search for economic stability was natural. No doubt Sidney Rigdon's previous communitarian experience influenced early Mormon thought. Months before Rigdon's conversion to Mormonism, he had established a small "family commonwealth" near Kirtland, and it was his desire to implement a communal order that led to his conflict and eventual break with Alexander Campbell.[70] As an example of righteousness, the Saints looked to communitarian sentiments in both the book of Acts (4:32) and the Book of Mormon (4 Ne. 3) where disciples held "all things common among them; therefore there were not rich and poor, bond and free, but they were all made free, and partakers of the heavenly gift."[71] In February 1831 Joseph Smith dictated a revelation known as the "Law of Consecration," or "United Order," commanding Ohio converts to live "the more perfect law of the Lord."[72] Not just avoiding sin but actively participating in the pursuit of perfection is what would prepare men and women for the soon-to-be Millennium.[73] This new economic system, what one author

---

69. John G. Gager, "Early Mormonism and Early Christianity: Some Parallels and Their Consequences for the Study of New Religions," *Journal of Mormon History* 9 (1982): 56; Barkun, *Crucible of the Millennium*, 48, 89; Reinwand, "An Interpretive Study of Mormon Millennialism," 32.

70. Van Wagoner, *Sidney Rigdon*, 49-51; Donna Hill, *Joseph Smith: The First Mormon* (Midvale, UT: Signature Books, 1977), 121.

71. See also *Evening and Morning Star,* Aug. 1831.

72. Smith, *History of the Church,* 1:146-47; *Book of Commandments,* 89-96; Backman, *The Heavens Resound,* 15; Van Wagoner, *Sidney Rigdon,* 79-89.

73. Leonard J. Arrington, Feramorz Y. Fox, and Dean L. May, *Building the City of God: Community and Cooperation Among the Mormons* (Salt Lake City:

termed a combination of "Yorker independence with Rigdonite communism," would bring order from the chaos of America's individualistic-capitalist economic structure.[74]

Based on the principle that the earth belongs to the Lord, with men serving as stewards, members were to "consecrate" their property to the church which would then in turn allocate the land and goods to families based on need. As Leonard Arrington observed, eighty-eight of Smith's 112 published revelations dealt with economic matters.[75] Placing economics on par with religion, the Law of Consecration was not mere piety but involved specific programs leading to society's perfection, raising members' commitment to their new religion.[76] The Law of Consecration served many functions, but specifically it provided, through religious dictum, motivation for the Ohio Saints to accommodate poor Mormons who had abandoned their New York homes and followed the young prophet to Ohio. The principle also allowed the church to accumulate the necessary funds to build meetinghouses, purchase printing presses, and in general support the movement's religious purposes.[77]

Deseret Book Co., 1976), 2-3.

74. O'Dea, *The Mormons*, 41-42.

75. Leonard J. Arrington, *Great Basin Kingdom: An Economic History of the Latter-Day Saints, 1830-1900* (1958; reprint, University of Nebraska Press, 1966), 6.

76. Arrington, Fox, and May, *Building the City of God*, 2-3; Arrington, *Great Basin Kingdom*, 5. Later, in Utah, Brigham Young candidly declared, "We cannot talk about spiritual things without connecting with them temporal things, neither can we talk about temporal things without connecting spiritual things with them. They are inseparably connected. ... We, as Latter-day Saints, really expect, look for and we will not be satisfied with anything short of being governed and controlled by the word of the Lord in all our acts, both spiritual and temporal. If we do not live for this, we do not live to be one with Christ." See Young, *Journal of Discourses*, 10:329, 22-29 June 1864.

77. Arrington, Fox, and May, *Building the City of God*, 15-20; Leonard J. Arrington, "Early Mormon Communitarianism: The Law of Consecration and Stewardship," *Western Humanities Review* 7 (Autumn 1953): 341-369;

The new economic theology fell into place with revelations received as early as September 1830 in which Smith pronounced, in the name of the Lord, that "all things unto me are spiritual, and not at any time have I given unto you a law which is temporal."[78] Here Momon communalism merged with folk religious tradition to draw no clear distinction between matter and spirit, all aspects of the physical world corresponding to the spiritual realm.[79] Philosophically Mormons were following in the footsteps of other utopian communities which attempted to separate themselves from society and radically alter traditional norms regarding property.[80]

Smith's first attempt to implement the United Order came in Ohio in an effort to facilitate assimilation of destitute converts who had migrated as a group from Colesville, New York. But when Ohio land-owners backed out of the plan, the Colesville Saints were called to settle Jackson County, Missouri, where Smith declared the "New Jerusalem" would be built. In July 1831 Smith personally led the Colesville Saints to Missouri. Subsequent to the Mormon arrival,

---

Lyndon W. Cook, *Joseph Smith and the Law of Consecration* (Provo, UT: Grandin Book Co., 1985).

78. *Evening and Morning Star* 1 (Sept. 1832): 2; *Book of Commandments*, 65.

79. Harrison, *The Second Coming*, 40, 183; O'Dea, *The Mormons*, 27; Harold Bloom, *The American Religion: The Emergence of the Post-Christian Nation* (New York: Simon and Schuster, 1992), 110.

80. Barkun, *Crucible of the Millennium*, 63-64. In order to clarify to non-Mormons who associated Smith's new economic order with groups who abided by common stock tenets, W. W. Phelps and Joseph Smith both published articles attempting to differentiate Mormon communal principles from those of contemporary communitarian societies such as the Shakers, Harmonists, and Ephratists. See Howe, *Mormonism Unvailed*, 129; *Messenger and Advocate* 2 (Dec. 1835): 230; *Elders' Journal* 1 (July 1838): 43; Arrington, Fox, and May, *Building the City of God*, 25, 433n36. For a discussion of other contemporary utopian groups established in Missouri, see H. Roger Grant, "Missouri's Utopian Communities," *Missouri Historical Review* 56 (Oct. 1971): 20-48.

within two years the United Order assisted almost 1,200 settlers to assemble around Independence.[81]

The merging of temporal and spiritual realms would eventually lead to internal dissent, but at its inception Smith's economic system was based on belief in an imminent millennium. While the Saints were still forced to struggle economically, as a community their sacrifice and hardships were now for the kingdom of God. The Law of Consecration would be the instrument to restructure the economic institution of Smith's followers, as well as a model for the rest of society when the Savior returned. Divested of greed and selfishness, an ideal community of cooperation and unity would be organized to prepare for the Parousia, and the Saints would be ready to administer Christ's Kingdom at the commencement of his millennial reign.

Although willing to take advantage of Mormon numbers to obtain political power and influence, in the 1830s the church still hoped for deliverance through God's destruction of the wicked rather than through earthly political victory.[82] Yet the idea that a political kingdom may be necessary to usher in Christ's reign soon developed, based on Mormon confidence that they would one day rule the entire world. Instilled with great hope for the future, Latter-day Saint grandeur was envisioned within the new church's first year. "We were maturing plans fourteen years ago," acknowledged Sidney Rigdon, to prepare the church for

> people coming as doves to the window; and that nations would flock unto it. ... in the year 1830 I met the whole Church of Christ in a little old log-house about 20 feet square, near Waterloo, N.Y., and we began to talk about the kingdom of God as if we had the world at our command. We talked with great confidence, and talked big things. ... We began to talk like men in authority and power.[83]

As literalists, Mormons expected unequivocal fulfillment of

---

81. Arrington, Fox, and May, *Building the City of God*, 22.

82. Winn, *Exiles in a Land of Liberty*, 79-80.

83. Sidney Rigdon, in Smith, *History of the Church*, 6:288-90. See also Nathan O. Hatch, *The Democratization of American Christianity* (New Haven, CT: Yale University Press, 1977), 187-89.

apocalyptic prophecy and the establishment of Christ's kingdom on earth. The desire for political power came from a hope that human efforts might hasten the Millennium by preparing the way for the Lord.[84] Believing they were "laying the foundation of a kingdom that shall last forever," the Saints looked forward to the Millennium where they would finally govern.[85] Rigdon declared "when God sets up a system of salvation, He sets up a system of government ... that shall rule over temporal and spiritual affairs."[86] But by intertwining the future millennial kingdom with the temporal kingdom of the here and now, Mormons blurred the distinction between what should happen prior to and during the millennial reign.[87]

As a "peculiar people," isolated from gentile society, converts left the uncertainty of religious confusion and were put to work building the kingdom.[88] Bustling with energy and enthusiasm, Mormons saw not their own struggles but the vision of the coming kingdom of God, developing a sense of community where burdens are shared. With the Millennium just around the corner, Mormon life was a daily routine of sermons, church meetings, ordinance ceremonies, and mission calls.[89] As religious and secular pursuits combined, building

---

84. Smith, "The Book of Mormon in a Biblical Culture," 17-19. See also Pratt, *A Voice of Warning*, 9-49, 106-108; Brigham Young, *Journal of Discourses*, 1:203, 6 Apr. 1852; Marvin S. Hill contends the Saints understood they were to rule politically *prior* to the advent of the Millennium. See Hill, "The Shaping of the Mormon Mind in New England and New York," *Brigham Young University Studies* 9 (Spring 1969): 369.

85. John Taylor, in Smith, *History of the Church*, 6:293.

86. Smith, *History of the Church*, 6:292.

87. Hill, *Quest for Refuge*, xvi-xviii; Hansen, *Quest for Empire*, 20-21; *Quincy Whig*, 17 Oct. 1840, in William Mulder and A. Russell Mortensen, eds., *Among the Mormons: Historic Accounts by Contemporary Observers* (New York: Alfred A. Knopf, 1967), 115.

88. Harrison, *The Second Coming*, 176-80.

89. Robert Kent Fielding, "The Growth of the Mormon Church in Kirtland, Ohio," Ph.D., diss., Indiana University, 1957, 153-56; Winn, *Exiles in a Land of Liberty*, 54-55.

a kingdom based on righteous principles required further separation from the world.[90]

By reversing the American notion of the separation of church and state, Mormonism established a community that completely oversaw all aspects of private life. But the cost of this economic/societal security was high, a complete abdication of individual decision-making and total absorption into Mormon society.[91] When asked, "Will everybody be damned but Mormons?" Joseph Smith answered, "Yes, and a great portion of them, unless they repent and work righteousness."[92] Not only did this belief system set boundaries, it invited conflict and hostility, particularly as the group was seen as aggressive and expanding.[93] By isolating themselves from the outside world, Mormons ironically provoked confrontation.

While Mormons believed their "gathering" was to separate themselves from corruption, non-Mormons held the Saints' exclusivity placed them on the periphery of society. Most non-Mormons could and would take offense from the Mormons' view of outsiders as the prophesied "Babylon," to be destroyed at Christ's return, and understood the term "gentile" was pejorative.[94] Ohio newspaper editor

---

90. Winn, *Exiles in a Land of Liberty*, 56.

91. Leonard J. Arrington and Davis Bitton, *The Mormon Experience: A History of the Latter-day Saints*, 2d ed. (Urbana: University of Illinois Press, 1992), 41-43.

92. *Elders' Journal* 1 (July 1838): 42. See also *Times and Seasons* 1 (Nov. 1839): 10; 4 (Feb. 1843): 106; Grant Underwood "'Saved or Damned': Tracing a Persistent Protestantism in Early Mormon Thought," *Brigham Young University Studies* 25 (Summer 1985): 85-103; Underwood, *The Millenarian World of Early Mormonism*, 42.

93. Lawrence Foster, "Cults in Conflict: New Religious Movements and the Mainstream Religious Tradition in America," in *Uncivil Religions: Interreligious Hostility in America*, eds. Robert N. Bellah and Frederick E. Greenspahn (New York: Crossroad Publishing Co., 1987), 190. For boundary maintenance, see Kai Erickson, *Wayward Puritans: A Study in Sociological Deviance* (New York: John Wiley, 1966), 3-29.

94. Winn, *Exiles in a Land of Liberty*, 64. For reaction to Mormon self-righteousness, see Hill, "The Shaping of the Mormon Mind in New England and New York," 358, and Underwood, "'Saved or Damned,'" 85-103.

E. D. Howe viewed Mormon seclusion as a controlled environment which Smith maintained to prohibit debate. Howe believed that Smith sent members to Missouri to continue their lives as a "distinct" people when their contact with the outside community began to shake their faith.[95]

As millennial rhetoric and hope increased, so did non-Mormon hostility.[96] But anti-Mormonism only confirmed Mormon belief in the truthfulness of their message. Their theology prepared them, as God's children, for persecution. They viewed their trials no differently than those endured by righteous martyrs of all ages.[97] Living in the last days, Mormons knew their suffering would end and be replaced by the millennial bliss shortly to come. The Lord's judgement would be swift, delivering his saints from the hands of their enemies.[98]

Mormonism's vision of America's destiny created a unique form of millennial hope where the building of a physical City of Zion within the borders of the United States and the gathering of the elect merged into a wondrous design to prepare the world for Christ.[99] Zion was a specific place the Lord had designated as "a defense and for a refuge from the storm, and from wrath, when it shall be poured out without mixture upon the whole Earth."[100]

Whether preaching the gospel, condemning contemporary society, building a righteous earthly kingdom, or implementing economic communal principles, millennialism dominated all aspects of early

---

95. Howe, *Mormonism Unvailed*, 126; Winn, *Exiles in a Land of Liberty*, 72.

96. Winn, *Exiles in a Land of Liberty*, 75.

97. See *Messenger and Advocate*, Mar. 1837; Winn, *Exiles in a Land of Liberty*, 74-75.

98. *Book of Commandments*, 19.

99. Robert Flanders, "To Transform History: Early Mormon Culture and the Concept of Time and Space," *Church History* 40 (Mar. 1971): 108-117; Gordon S. Wood, "Evangelical America and Early Mormonism," *New York History* 61 (Oct. 1980): 386; Bushman, *Joseph Smith and the Beginnings of Mormonism*, 170.

100. *Elders' Journal* 4 (Aug. 1838): 52.

Mormon theology. In their millennial world view, Mormons many times shifted their strategy. Sometimes they acted, as one writer has termed, like "arrogant empire builders, dreaming of theocratic rule over a vice-ridden world." While at other times they wanted to be left alone to live quiet lives, separated from non-Mormon society, seeking solace in the hope of Christ's imminent return and in the fellowship of the gathering.[101]

Like Puritans before them, Mormons believed the execution of God's plan required work, and Mormon kingdom building was ultimately tied to millennial aspirations, attempting to create a theocracy based on what Klaus Hansen calls dreams of "not only a religious but a social, economic, and political millennium."[102] The church could not be passive and just sit and wait; it had a work to do. The New Jerusalem was to be built where the righteous would gather, and the Saints were to actively seek out God's "elect" from among the world's meek and poor.

As a "new Israel," the Mormon sense of tribal loyalty and self-identity differed from mainstream America's religious pluralism.[103] Physical exclusivity further alienated non-Mormon society. Urging all to "embrace the everlasting covenant," Joseph Smith warned humankind to "flee to Zion before the overflowing scourge overtakes you."[104] The world would have two choices: join the restored gospel and be adopted into Israel or be destroyed. Mormon missionaries would call in the elect, and converted gentiles would be gathered to the City of Zion for refuge pending the imminent and cataclysmic return of the Savior. Here the Saints would be safe until Christ's millennial reign would allow the gospel to flow to the rest of humanity.[105]

---

101. Winn, *Exiles in a Land of Liberty*, 182.

102. Hansen, *Mormonism and the American Experience*, 121-22; Gustav H. Blanke and Karen Lynn, "'God's Base of Operations': Mormon Variations on the American Sense of Mission," *Brigham Young University Studies* 20 (Fall 1979): 83-92.

103. Foster, "Cults in Conflict," 193.

104. Smith, *History of the Church*, 1:315-16.

105. Ibid., 1:127, 315-16; 2:52.

CHAPTER FIVE

THE GATHERING:
SEPARATISM SHAPES A SOCIETY

Armed with Christ's restored gospel, as evidenced by modern scripture and a latter-day prophet, Joseph Smith's followers began to prepare for the Millennium. Less than six months after the church was organized, Smith dictated a revelation to "bring to pass the gathering of mine elect," providing both a means and a place of escape from the tribulation of the last days.[1] To early Mormons this "gathering" was a prelude to the imminent end of the world when "the heaven and earth shall be consumed, and pass away, and there shall be a new heaven and a new earth."[2]

The importance of early Mormon gathering as a millennial event cannot be over-emphasized. Joseph Smith declared,

> Take away the Book of Mormon and the revelations, and where is our religion? We have none; for without Zion, and a place of deliverance, we must fall; because the time is near when the sun will be darkened, and the moon turn to blood, and the stars fall from

---

1. *A Book of Commandments for the Government of the Church of Christ, Organized According to Law, on the 6th of April, 1830* (Zion [Independence], MO: W.W. Phelps and Co., 1833), 61; *Evening and Morning Star* 1 (Sept. 1832); F. Mark McKiernan and Roger D. Launius, *An Early Latter Day Saint History: The Book of John Whitmer, Kept by Commandment* (Independence, MO: Herald Publishing House, 1980), 81-83.

2. *Book of Commandments*, 63.

heaven, and the earth reel to and fro. Then, if this is the case, and
if we are not sanctified and gathered to the places God has appointed ... we must fall; we cannot stand; we cannot be saved; for
God will gather out His Saints from the Gentiles; and then comes
desolation and destruction, and none can escape except the pure in
heart who are gathered.[3]

Grant Underwood contends that by concentrating the Saints together for mutual support in preparation for Christ's return, the
gathering became "the pivotal premillennial event in Mormon eschatology."[4]

Within Mormon theology of the 1830s-40s, millennialism, separatism, the "New Jerusalem," and the "gathering" were intertwined.[5]
The most important sign that the gathering of God's elect had begun
was the coming forth of the Book of Mormon (3 Ne. 21:1-7).[6] Although Mormons viewed the new book of scripture as the authoritative voice among conflicting sects of the day, its main mission was to
recover the lost remnant of the house of Israel. "The Book of Mormon," it was told, "has made known who Israel is, upon this continent," and even before the church's move to Ohio missionaries were
sent to Missouri to preach to the Indians, the presumed descendants
of Book of Mormon authors.[7]

---

3. Joseph Smith, *History of the Church of Jesus Christ of Latter-day Saints*,
7 vols., 2nd ed. rev., introduction and notes by B. H. Roberts (Salt Lake City:
Deseret Book Co., 1974-76), 2:52.

4. Grant Underwood, *The Millenarian World of Early Mormonism*
(Urbana: University of Illinois Press, 1993), 29. Underwood argues that just
as the Rapture provided late-nineteenth-century dispensationalists with an
escape for the righteous, so "the Mormon doctrine of the 'gathering' served
to provide a means of escape from much of the anticipated tribulation of the
last days."

5. *Book of Commandments*, 76-78, 80-82, 85-87, 90-92, 98-100, 104-11,
152-54.

6. *Millennial Star* 1 (Aug. 1840): 75; *Times and Seasons* 2 (Mar. 1841):
351.

7. Smith, *History of the Church*, 2:358; Ronald W. Walker, "Seeking the
'Remnant': The Native American During the Joseph Smith Period," *Journal*

But in the fall of 1830 this mission to the "Lamanites" took on a greater role. It became part of the larger plan to prepare a place for the temple of God. The Book of Mormon prophet, Ether, had foretold a New Jerusalem to be "built up upon this land," implying a physical city to be constructed by the new Israel. The mission to the Indians was full of excitement, for the Saints were told the City of Zion "shall be on the borders of the Lamanites."[8] Oliver Cowdery was to locate the place where the holy city would be built, not just for the Indians, but for the whole world.[9]

Through the Book of Mormon the New World's importance was brought forth. Modern revelation identified the location of Zion, and Mormons could now focus on gathering in America. They no longer had to wait for the Jews to repossess ancient Palestine.[10] "The city of Zion spoken of by David, in the one hundred and second Psalm," Smith declared, "will be built upon the land of America."[11] "Righteousness and truth will I cause to sweep the earth as with flood," God revealed through Smith.[12] He further promised "to gather out mine [God's] elect from the four quarters of the earth, unto a place which I shall prepare, an Holy City, that my people may gird up their loins, and be looking forth for the

of Mormon History 19 (Spring 1993): 1-9; Ronald E. Romig, "The Lamanite Mission," John Whitmer Historical Association Journal 14 (1994): 25-33; Parley P. Pratt, The Autobiography of Parley Parker Pratt (1938; reprint, Salt Lake City: Deseret Book Co., 1979), 54-56; B[righam]. H. Roberts, A Comprehensive History of the Church of Jesus Christ of Latter-day Saints, 6 vols. (1930; reprint, Provo, UT: Brigham Young University Press, 1965), 1:173-74.

8. See Ether 13:4-6, 13:8-10; Rev. 2:21; Book of Commandments, 67-68. See also Richard L. Bushman, Joseph Smith and the Beginnings of Mormonism (Urbana: University of Illinois Press, 1984), 169.

9. Book of Commandments, 8-9.

10. Times and Seasons 3 (1 Mar. 1842): 710. See also Underwood, The Millenarian World of Early Mormonism, 29-31.

11. Smith, History of the Church, 1:315; Dean C. Jessee, comp. and ed., The Personal Writings of Joseph Smith (Salt Lake City: Deseret Book Co., 1984), 273.

12. Smith, History of the Church, 1:138.

time of my coming; for there shall be my tabernacle, and it shall be called Zion, a New Jerusalem."[13]

At the coming of Christ a remnant of the tribe of Joseph, the Indians, would be identified through revelation, learn of their covenanted history from the Book of Mormon, and convert to the restored gospel. And by joining the church, righteous gentiles would be adopted into the House of Israel and receive the blessings of the Abrahamic covenant.[14] Mormons saw in Andrew Jackson's Indian relocation policies God's hand in gathering the Indians on the nation's western border.[15] The uniqueness of Mormonism's two gatherings gave the American Indians a previously unprecedented role in the last days, for now part of the gathering of Israel would be that of Indians locating at the site of the New Jerusalem. If gentiles continued in unrighteousness, these latter-day Lamanites would rise from the dust and begin to destroy them "as a young lion among the flocks of sheep" (3 Ne. 20:16).[16]

Smith's early revelations regarding the building of a city as a

---

13. Ibid.

14. 3 Ne. 21:21-24; *Doctrine and Covenants of the Church of the Latter Day Saints: Carefully Selected from the Revelations of God*, comps., Joseph Smith, Junior, Oliver Cowdery, Sidney Rigdon, and Frederick G. Williams (Kirtland, OH: F.G. Williams and Co., 1835), 247-50; Edward Partridge to Dear Friends and Neighbors, 31 Aug. 1833, in *Messenger and Advocate* 1 (Jan. 1835): 56-61. See also Rex Eugene Cooper, *Promises Made to the Fathers: Mormon Covenant Organizations* (Salt Lake City: University of Utah Press, 1990), 81.

15. 3 Ne. 21:22-24; *Evening and Morning Star* 1 (Jan. 1833); ibid. 1 (Sept. 1832); ibid. 1 (Dec. 1832); 54; Smith, *History of the Church*, 1:358-62; Parley P. Pratt, *A Voice of Warning* ... (New York: W. Sanford, 1837), 185-91. Later disappointment with the Indian removal policy is found in *Times and Seasons* 6 (Mar. 1845): 829-30, which emphasized "God, not man" will bring to pass the restoration of the Lamanites' inheritance. See also Underwood, *The Millenarian World of Early Mormonism*, 66, 80-83; Grant Underwood, "Seminal Versus Sesquicentennial Saints: A Look at Mormon Millennialism," *Dialogue: A Journal of Mormon Thought* 14 (Spring 1981): 39.

16. See also Kenneth H. Winn, *Exiles in a Land of Liberty: Mormons in America, 1830-1846* (Chapel Hill: University of North Carolina Press, 1989), 37-38.

prelude to Christ's advent caused great anticipation and provided much of the incentive for his early followers to uproot their families in pursuit of the millennial dream.[17] In the West God assured them a significant legacy awaited, "a land of promise; a land flowing with milk and honey, upon which there shall be no curse when the Lord cometh, and I will give it unto you for the land of your inheritance ... And this shall be my covenant with you, ye shall have it for the land of your inheritance, and for the inheritance of your children forever."[18] As Smith later recorded, "the mission to Western Missouri and the gathering of the Saints to that place was the most important subject which then engrossed the attention of the church."[19]

To Mormons the City of Zion held two purposes. First, it would be the converging point for the house of Israel in the last days. Second, it would be a refuge from the wicked and from the calamities associated with the coming destruction.

> When the God of heaven sent a messenger to proclaim judgement on the old world, he provided an ark for the safety of the righteous: when Sodom was burned, there was Zoar provided for Lot and his family ... in the last days, when the Lord brings judgement on the world, there will be a Mount Zion, and a Jerusalem, where there will be deliverance.[20]

But the revelations also left many unanswered questions. For example, where exactly were they to gather, and what requirements

---

17. Louis G. Reinwand, "An Interpretive Study of Mormon Millennialism During the Nineteenth Century with Emphasis on Millennial Developments in Utah," M.A. thesis, Brigham Young University, 1971, 62; Steven L. Olsen, "Zion: The Structure of a Theological Revolution," *Sunstone* 6 (Nov.-Dec. 1981): 22.

18. *Book of Commandments*, 82. No doubt Mormons understood the parallel between the new church and the pledge given to the Nephites in the Book of Mormon who also obtained in America "a land of promise, a land which is choice above all other lands ... Yea, the Lord hath covenanted this land unto me, and to my children forever" (2 Ne. 1:5).

19. Smith, *History of the Church*, 1:182.

20. *Evening and Morning Star* 2 (Jan. 1834): 126.

would the Lord make prior to the Second Coming?[21] For now God decreed through Joseph, "I have a great work laid up in store: For Israel shall be saved," and the Saints were promised the day would come when the "veil of darkness shall soon be rent" and they would see the Lord's face.[22] In the meantime, through Smith as oracle, the church was commanded to establish a temporary location in Ohio for the righteous in preparation for the true gathering to take place in Zion. The new religion then initiated its first exodus to the Mormon promised land.

The church's term in Ohio would last seven years. But with the New Jerusalem soon to be built on the borders of Indian country, Kirtland was always viewed as a temporary stop, the first step toward Zion. Though headquartered in the Western Reserve, the Saints' thoughts continued to center on the New Jerusalem and the Millennium. Here God's elect primed themselves to become a covenant people, looking for the day when the great temple would receive Christ.[23]

Four months after Smith relocated the church to Kirtland in May, 1831, missionary Parley Pratt returned from Jackson County, Missouri, with vivid accounts of the land near Indian territory. The following month a revelation commanded Smith and many of the church's leading elders to journey to Missouri. Here they would unite with Oliver Cowdery who had remained in Independence anxiously awaiting their arrival, believing he had found many "earnestly searching for the truth."[24] That same month the Colesville Saints, having

---

21. Smith, *History of the Church*, 2:52-53. See also Bushman, *Joseph Smith and the Beginnings of Mormonism*, 170-71.

22. *Book of Commandments*, 83, 81.

23. Milton V. Backman, Jr., *The Heavens Resound: A History of the Latter-day Saints in Ohio, 1830-1838* (Salt Lake City: Deseret Book Co., 1983), 43; William Mulder, "Mormonism's 'Gathering': An American Doctrine with a Difference," *Church History* 23 (Sept. 1954): 254; James B. Allen and Glen M. Leonard, *The Story of the Latter-day Saints* (Salt Lake City: Deseret Book Co., 1976), 93.

24. Oliver Cowdery to Our Dear Beloved Brethren, 7 May 1831, in Romig, "The Lamanite Mission," 31; McKiernan and Launius, *The Book of*

relocated in Ohio from New York and living under the communal
Law of Consecration, were ejected from their land by a disgruntled
participant. Smith now announced they were also to make the 800-
mile journey to Missouri.

In mid-July 1831 Smith and his party arrived at Independence
where they were to be shown "the land of [their] inheritance.[25]
Smith proclaimed Missouri set apart by God for the gathering of
his people, identified Independence as the center place, and urged
them to buy all available property. He announced, "[T]his is the
land of promise, and the place for the city of Zion."[26] The Colesville group also arrived in July and the Saints proceeded at break-
neck pace to build a community. The first cabin was begun in August, a temple site selected, the land dedicated for the gathering,
a mercantile house, a printing office and the newspaper the *Evening and Morning Star* initiated, and a conference held.[27] "The City
of New Jerusalem," pronounced Smith, "shall be built, beginning
at the temple lot ... [and] shall be built by the gathering of the
saints, beginning at this place, even the place of the temple, which
temple shall be reared in this generation."[28] Thus the physical location for the Mormon kingdom was designated, providing a link
between heaven and earth, and Mormons claimed territorial rights

---

John Whitmer, 77-78; Phillip R. Legg, *Oliver Cowdery: The Elusive Second Elder
of the Restoration* (Independence, MO: Herald Publishing House, 1989),
59-60; Donna Hill, *Joseph Smith: The First Mormon* (Midvale, UT: Signature
Books, 1977), 134.

25. *Book of Commandments*, 127.

26. *Doctrine and Covenants*, 1835 ed., 154; Smith, *History of the Church*,
1:189-90.

27. McKiernan and Launius, *The Book of John Whitmer*, 79-80; Mulder,
"Mormonism's 'Gathering,'" 255.

28. Smith, *History of the Church*, 1:288; *Doctrine and Covenants*, 1835 ed.,
89. In June 1833 Smith would outline and forward to Missouri specific plans
for the building of the city and temple. See Smith, *History of the Church*,
1:357-62; Richard H. Jackson, "The Mormon Village: Genesis and
Antecedents of the City of Zion Plan," *Brigham Young University Studies* 17
(Winter 1977): 223-40.

for their promised "inheritance." Soon a cultural consciousness emerged.[29] With the church scarcely one year old, Mormons began to flock to Jackson County, their "New Jerusalem," where they would escape the destruction of the last days.

Although initially disappointed with Independence's frontier crudeness, and put off by the Missourians whom Smith called degraded and lean in intellect, Mormons envisioned 1831 western Missouri as their "promised land."[30] "It was to them like some limitless paradise, these immense alternating stretches of open, rolling prairie and densely wooded water courses, as compared with the closed-in heavily wooded hill country from which they had come."[31] While Smith had little knowledge of the western frontier, Missouri conformed with the belief that Indians would assist in building the "New Jerusalem." Understanding "the Lord is making short [His] work," Mormons believed mass Indian conversions would follow the church's move, thereby aiding their growth.[32] With the Book of Mormon prophesying of Indians returning to the true faith, events began leading to their logical millennial climax.[33]

After less than a month, on 8 August 1831 Smith announced a revelation commanding him to return to Ohio.[34] By the time of his departure from Independence, a Mormon settlement was flourish-

---

29. Olsen, "Zion: The Structure of a Theological Revolution," 23; Richard T. Hughes and C. Leonard Allen, *Illusions of Innocence: Protestant Primitivism in America, 1630-1875* (Chicago: University of Chicago Press, 1988), 147.

30. Smith, *History of the Church*, 1:189.

31. Roberts, *A Comprehensive History of the Church*, 1:260; Smith, *History of the Church*, 1:197-98.

32. "The Gathering," *The Evening and Morning Star* 1 (Nov. 1832): 45-46; Robert Kent Fielding, "The Growth of the Mormon Church in Kirtland, Ohio," Ph.D. diss., Indiana University, 1957, 48-55.

33. Fawn M. Brodie, *No Man Knows My History: The Life of Joseph Smith The Mormon Prophet*, 2d enl. rev. ed. (New York: Alfred A. Knopf, 1985), 121; Winn, *Exiles in a Land of Liberty*, 86-87.

34. *Book of Commandments*, 142; Hill, *Joseph Smith: The First Mormon*, 137.

ing, with more arriving daily. Once reunited with the Kirtland Saints, Smith had to subdue the enthusiastic desire to gather in Missouri and command, by revelation, key individuals to remain in Ohio.[35] As Apostle Orson Pratt later commented, many Kirtland Saints believed "Christ would come immediately ... [they] felt exceedingly anxious to have him come ... and this anxiety overcame them."[36] The church was now gathering in two main settlements, Kirtland and Independence, separated by 800 miles of wilderness.[37]

In general the first Mormon settlers were ill prepared for life on the Missouri frontier, and soon Mormons and Missourians were on a collision course. When many dislocated Saints were sent to Independence, "Zion" became a sanctuary for the Mormon downtrodden and poor.[38] Mormonism's communal economic society, the Law of Consecration, was instituted to a greater extent in Jackson County than in Kirtland, further heightening Mormon/non-Mormon differences. A collective identity emerged among members, and Mormon separateness created antagonism and an opposing group mentality on the part of the old settlers as well. This sentiment was expressed by a local citizen who noted, "[T]he very materials of which the [Mormon] society is composed must at length produce an explosion."[39]

---

35. *Book of Commandments*, 159; Underwood, *The Millenarian World of Early Mormonism*, 31-32.

36. Orson Pratt, *Journal of Discourses*, 26 vols. (Liverpool, Eng.: F.D. Richards, 1855-86), 3:17, 20 May 1855. See also Charles C. Rich, ibid., 19:161, 11 Nov. 1877; George A. Smith, ibid., 9:346, 11 May 1862.

37. Hill, *Joseph Smith: The First Mormon*, 137.

38. Winn, *Exiles in a Land of Liberty*, 89. See Smith, *History of the Church*, 1:381-82.

39. B. Pixley to the *Christian Watchman*, 12 Oct. 1832, in William Mulder and A. Russell Mortensen, eds., *Among the Mormons: Historic Accounts by Contemporary Observers* (New York: Alfred A. Knopf, 1967), 75; Val Dan MacMurray and Perry H. Cunningham, "Mormons and Gentiles: A Study in Conflict and Persistence," in *Ethnic Conflicts and Power: A Cross National Perspective*, eds. Donald E. Gelfand and Russell D. Lee (New York: John Wiley and Sons, 1973), 208-209; J. F. C. Harrison, *The Second Coming: Popular*

But it was the Saints' self-righteousness and implied superiority that raised hatred among non-Mormons. Anti-Mormons understood Mormon either/or rhetoric and exclusiveness. Even before Joseph Smith's first arrival, Jackson County had been identified as "the land of your [the Mormons'] enemies."[40] Mormon belief consigned all Missouri citizens, except the Saints, as unworthy to live in Jackson County. They defiantly believed the Lord would deliver the land of Zion into their hands and "consecrate the riches of the gentiles, unto my people."[41] Pre-Mormon Missouri settlements were merely in the way. It was but a matter of time until all Jackson County would belong to the Saints.[42]

The Book of Mormon had also foretold how the Indians would be a tool in God's hand to destroy the gentiles who reject the restored gospel of the latter days (3 Ne. 21:12-13, 16:15, 20:16-17; see also Micah 5:8). Annihilation would be literal and total with all people and cities destroyed except those of the covenant. This pro-Indian rhetoric, the immediacy of the Mormon mission to the Indians, a perceived allegiance between the two, and the threat of a Mormon-led Indian uprising antagonized and frightened whites on the fringe of civilization's western border.[43]

Millenarianism, 1780-1850 (New Brunswick, NJ: Rutgers University Press, 1979), 180; Klaus J. Hansen, *Quest for Empire: The Political Kingdom of God and the Council of Fifty in Mormon History* (Lansing: Michigan State University Press, 1970), 16-17; Romig, "The Lamanite Mission," 30; Thomas F. O'Dea, *The Mormons* (Chicago: University of Chicago Press, 1957), 43.

40. *Book of Commandments*, 127; Underwood, *The Millenarian World of Early Mormonism*, 43.

41. *Book of Commandments*, 93. See also *Messenger and Advocate* 1 (Jan. 1835): 58; Underwood, *The Millenarian World of Early Mormonism*, 46.

42. Robert Flanders, "To Transform History: Early Mormon Culture and the Concept of Time and Space," *Church History* 40 (Mar. 1971): 114; Winn, *Exiles in a Land of Liberty*, 88-90.

43. Frederick G. Williams to the Missouri Saints, 10 Oct. 1833, in Smith, *History of the Church*, 1:419; Joseph Smith to William W. Phelps, 31 July 1832, in Jessee, *The Personal Writings of Joseph Smith*, 247; Walker, "Seeking the 'Remnant': The Native American During the Joseph Smith Period," 14; Underwood, *The Millenarian World of Early Mormonism*, 80-81;

Missouri citizens believed Mormons would provoke Indians to violence against the old settlers and use force if necessary to take their lands. They also feared incitement of a slave revolt. The Mormon migration to Missouri fell into the context of pre-existing suspicions between people from slave and free states which fed Mormon-gentile conflict.[44] Missourians distrusted Mormons who, as Northerners, drew immediate suspicions from slave-holders regarding their attitude towards "free Negroes."[45] When in July 1833 *Evening and Morning Star* editor W. W. Phelps deliberated the merits of bringing to Missouri converts from "Free people of color," he furnished Missourians with added grounds for denouncing the new religion.[46] "As to slaves," he wrote, "In connection with the wonderful events of this age, much is doing towards abolishing slavery."[47] Accompanied by

Winn, *Exiles in a Land of Liberty*, 37-38; O'Dea, *The Mormons*, 22. See E[ber]. D. Howe, *Mormonism Unvailed: or A Faithful Account of that Singular Imposition and Delusion, from Its Rise to the Present Time* (Painesville, OH: E.D. Howe, 1834), 145-46, 197, where he talks of Mormon-Indian conspiracy against the U.S. This conspiracy logic was also expressed by American Indian agents. See John King to John Chambers, 14 July 1843, in Ronald W. Walker, "Seeking the 'Remnant': The Native American During the Joseph Smith Period," 27. See *Millennial Star* 2 (July 1841): 43 and *Messenger and Advocate* 2 (Aug. 1836): 357, where the Saints try to deflect any thought of a Mormon-Indian joint venture in Missouri.

44. Editor W. W. Phelps commented that the Missourians "hate Yankees worse than snakes." Phelps to Canadaigua (New York) *Ontario Phoenix*, 23 July 1831, in Richard Lloyd Anderson, "Jackson County in Early Mormon Descriptions," *Missouri Historical Review* 65 (Apr. 1971): 276. Richard S. Van Wagoner contends the slave issue has been overplayed. See Van Wagoner, *Sidney Rigdon: A Portrait of Religious Excess* (Salt Lake City: Signature Books, 1994), 145.

45. Winn, *Exiles in a Land of Liberty*, 88-91.

46. "Free People of Color," *Evening and Morning Star* 2 (July 1833): 109. See also Loy Otis Banks, "The Evening and Morning Star," *Missouri Historical Review* 43 (July 1949): 326.

47. *Evening and Morning Star* 2 (July 1833): 111. Joseph Smith's 1832 prophecy on war had suggested a slave uprising would accompany the apocalyptic events of the Second Coming by prophesying, "And it shall come to pass, after many days, slaves shall rise up against their masters, who shall

continual migration, Mormon openness towards possible recruitment of Negroes solidified non-Mormon opposition.

Despite an attempt to clear up any misunderstanding, the dam-
age had been done.[48] Missouri citizens saw a Mormon alliance with
either Indians or Negroes as a threat to their safety.[49] And if these
two did not happen, through immigration Mormons would shortly
outnumber old settlers and exercise political control over Missouri
lands.[50] The 1830 census showed 2,823 citizens in Jackson County
with surrounding counties populated less sparsely.[51] With Mormon

---

be marshalled for war." See previous chapter; also Newell G. Bringhurst,
Saints, Slaves, and Blacks (Westport, CT: Greenwood Press, 1981), 17.

48. On 16 July 1833 a follow-up *Star Extra* handbill was issued,
adamantly stating "that our intention was not only to stop free people of
color from emigrating to this state, but to prevent them from being admitted
as members. See *Star Extra*, reprinted in *Times and Seasons* 6 (Mar. 1845): 818,
and Smith, *History of the Church*, 1:378-79. In a specific reference to the
Evening and Morning Star, both John Whitmer and Parley Pratt quoted a
declaration written by Jackson County citizens that condemned the Mormons
for publishing "an article inviting free negroes and mulattoes from other
States, to become Mormons, and remove and settle among us." See
McKiernan and Launius, *The Book of John Whitmer*, 90; Parley P. Pratt, *History
of the Late Persecution Inflicted By the State of Missouri Upon the Mormons*
(Detroit: Dawson and Bates, Printers, 1839), reprinted in Clark V. Johnson,
ed., *Mormon Redress Petitions: Documents of the 1833-1838 Missouri Conflict* (Salt
Lake City: Bookcraft, 1992), 62. A copy of the declaration is given in the
Evening and Morning Star 2 (Dec. 1833): 114. See also Banks, "The Evening
and Morning Star," 327; Bringhurst, *Saints, Slaves, and Blacks*, 17-18; Lester
E. Bush, Jr., "Mormonism's Negro Doctrine: An Overview," in *Neither White
nor Black*, eds. Lester E. Bush, Jr., and Armand L. Mauss (Midvale, UT:
Signature Books, 1984), 54-55.

49. Smith, *History of the Church*, 1:431.

50. *Evening and Morning Star* 2 (Dec. 1833): 114; Richard L. Bushman,
"Mormon Persecutions in Missouri, 1833," *Brigham Young University Studies*
3 (Autumn 1960): 11-20; Warren A. Jennings, "Factors in the Destruction of
the Mormon Press in Missouri, 1833," *Utah Historical Quarterly* 35 (Winter
1967): 57-76; Warren A. Jennings, "Isaac McCoy and the Mormons," *Missouri
Historical Review* 61 (Oct. 1966): 64-66.

51. Hill, *Joseph Smith: The First Mormon*, 135.

population in Jackson County increasing from 300 in May 1832 to 1,200 in July 1833, the rapid growth of a solidified Mormon community reinforced Mormon confidence and exacerbated non-Mormon fears.[52]

"Zion" never became a land of peace. Established Missouri citizens opposed Mormon domination and began devising ways to rid themselves of the Mormon problem.[53] It was a combination of these primary causes—religious differences, claim to the land of Zion, and Mormon sentiments towards Indians and Negroes—which led to non-Mormon animosity, enmity, and group consciousness.[54]

In July 1833 Jackson County citizens convened to address the "fanatics" of the "sect of pretended Christians," resolving that Mormon immigration must cease and that all Mormon residents must pledge to leave the county with due haste. Demanding that the church's newspaper and all Mormon-owned enterprises close down immediately, the old settlers committed themselves to shut down by force those who failed to comply.[55] Soon the conflict erupted into armed violence.[56] When Independence Mormons were overtaken by a mob, their press destroyed and type scattered, their leaders tarred

52. D. Brent Collette, "In Search of Zion: A Description of Early Mormon Millennial Utopianism as Revealed Through the Life of Edward Partridge," M.A. thesis, Brigham Young University, 1977, 3, 64; Bringhurst, *Saints, Slaves, and Blacks*, 28n18. Total Jackson County population in 1832 was only 5,071. See also "The Gathering," *Evening and Morning Star* 1 (Nov. 1832).

53. John Whitmer reports Missouri citizens met as early as March 1832, less than a year after the Saints' arrival, to discuss ways to rid Jackson County of Mormons. See McKiernan and Launius, *The Book of John Whitmer*, 86.

54. Ephraim Edward Ericksen, *The Psychological and Ethical Aspects of Mormon Group Life* (1922; reprint, Salt Lake City: University of Utah Press, 1975), 19; Warren A. Jennings, "The City in the Garden: Social Conflict in Jackson County, Missouri," in *The Restoration Movement: Essays in Mormon History*, rev. ed., eds. F. Mark McKiernan, Alma R. Blair, and Paul M. Edwards (Independence, MO: Herald Publishing House, 1992), 103-104.

55. *Western Monitor*, 2 Aug. 1833, in Smith, *History of the Church*, 1:395-99; McKiernan and Launius, *The Book of John Whitmer*, 89-90.

56. Winn, *Exiles in a Land of Liberty*, 85-93.

and feathered and threatened with death, the Saints fled Jackson County.[57] Despite their hopes, the Saints were driven from their promised land and forced to gather in northwestern Missouri in Clay County.[58]

Now expelled from "Zion," the Saints' eschatology continued nonetheless to exhibit the importance of gathering to Missouri. They maintained that religious persecution was the cause of their problems and that soon Christ would aid in redeeming their "inheritance."[59] From Kirtland on 10 December 1833 Joseph Smith wrote to Missouri advising members they must suffer affliction to be worthy of the blessings to follow, that "it is better that you should die ... than that you give up the Land of Zion."[60] Seeing their expulsion from Jackson County as the first step in the breakdown of American democracy, Smith a week later received a revelation that the church should remain steadfast and continue to reclaim their homes and property. First, the Saints should appeal to judges, then the governor, and, if necessary, the president of the United States. If no redress was obtained, God promised his "fury would vex the nation."[61]

---

57. Jennings, "Factors in the Destruction of the Mormon Press in Missouri, 1833," 69-73.

58. McKiernan and Launius, *The Book of John Whitmer*, 91-96; Underwood, *The Millenarian World of Early Mormonism*, 33; Allen and Leonard, *The Story of the Latter-day Saints*, 81-90. Unaware of the extent of the violence, Smith was planning for the New Jerusalem and on 25 June 1833 sent to the Saints in Missouri a proposed City of Zion plot map. See Jackson, "The Mormon Village," 223-40.

59. See Brigham Young's interview with Horace Greely in 1859 where Young could only explain hatred of the Mormons as that "afforded by the crucifiction of Christ and the kindred treatment of God's ministers, prophets and saints of all ages." *New York Daily Tribune,* 20 Aug. 1859, in R. Laurence Moore, *Religious Outsiders and the Making of Americans* (New York: Oxford University Press, 1986), 214n18.

60. Joseph Smith to E. Partridge et al., 10 Dec. 1833, in Jessee, *The Personal Writings of Joseph Smith,* 310.

61. Smith, *History of the Church,* 1:463; *Doctrine and Covenants,* 1835 ed., 239. A copy of this revelation was sent to the governor of Missouri and President Andrew Jackson. See *Millennial Star* 3 (July 1840): 65.

In a final attempt to "redeem" Zion, on 24 February 1834 God commanded the Saints to raise 500 volunteers and restore their Jackson County inheritance "by power ... and my presence shall be with you even in avenging me of mine enemies."[62] Three months later in May 1834 Smith initiated a quasi-military rescue attempt labeled "Zion's Camp." Summoning as many male members as possible, Parley Pratt described their purpose as "carrying some supplies to the afflicted and persecuted Saints in Missouri, and to reinforce and strengthen them; and, if possible, to influence the Governor of the State to call out sufficient additional force to cooperate in restoring to them their rights."[63] Zion's Camp only reinforced the important role Jackson County played in Mormonism's millennial hope.

From its inception this loosely disguised band provoked fear and outrage among non-Mormons who saw in its army-like character Mormon designs to return to Missouri "by force of arms."[64] From Liberty, Missouri, William W. Phelps reported gentile sentiments: "The crisis has come," he wrote, and "all that will not take up arms with the mob and prepare to fight the 'Mormons,' have to leave Jackson county."[65] Convinced that a militia escort from Missouri governor Daniel Dunklin was forthcoming, the Saints were unaware of the intense violence which continued to erupt in Missouri. By the end of April Missourians had burned to the ground nearly all 170 buildings owned by Mormons.[66] Dunklin sought to mediate a nego-

---

62. Smith, *History of the Church*, 2:37-38. See also Ronald W. Walker, "Sheaves Bucklers and the State: Mormon Leaders Respond to the Dilemmas of War," *Sunstone* 7 (July-Aug. 1982): 44.

63. Pratt, *Autobiography of Parley P. Pratt*, 114.

64. Columbia *Missouri Intelligencer*, 7 June 1834, in Peter Crawley and Richard L. Anderson, "The Political and Social Realities of Zion's Camp," *Brigham Young University Studies* 14 (Summer 1974): 413; *Painesville Telegraph*, 9 May 1834; Roger D. Launius, *Zion's Camp: Expedition to Missouri, 1834* (Independence, MO: Herald Publishing House, 1984), 49-50, 62-65; Ronald W. Walker, "Sheaves Bucklers and the State," 44.

65. W. W. Phelps to editors, 1 May 1834, *Evening and Morning Star* 2 (May 1834): 160; Smith, *History of the Church*, 2:61-62.

66. McKiernan and Launius, *The Book of John Whitmer*, 106-11; Smith,

tiated settlement and avoid at all costs involving state troops in open warfare. No doubt Missouri officials understood that without a standing army Mormon repossession of Jackson County lands represented a temporary solution, and once the militia was withdrawn the area would again break into civil war. When the governor's hoped-for militia reinforcements never materialized, any realistic LDS prospect of marching into Independence disappeared.[67]

Traveling over 600 miles in thirty days, the "army of Israel"'s close quarters naturally led to interpersonal conflict and dissension that later reared its head in Kirtland.[68] Yet the detachment continued marching through Missouri and on 19 June camped on a plain above the Little and Big Fishing rivers, ten miles northeast of Liberty, the Clay County seat. Missourians prepared to attack on the night of 19 June when a massive rainstorm thwarted their planned offensive. With the Missourians' numerical superiority, the storm saved the Mormon expedition from destruction. When the rivers rose 30-40 feet, preventing either side from crossing, the Saints saw God's hand shielding them, just as he had protected the Hebrews from Pharaoh's armies.[69] Smith began to see the futility of his designs and on 22 June read a revelation chastising expedition members for their lack of charity. Shifting the blame to the Saints themselves, Smith declared that Zion's redemption must be delayed "for a little season."[70]

While they camped on the banks of Fishing River in eastern

History of the Church, 2:88-89; Crawley and Anderson, "The Political and Social Realities of Zion's Camp," 413: Hill, *Joseph Smith: The First Mormon*, 177-78.

67. Launius, *Zion's Camp*, 108-15; Crawley and Anderson, "The Political and Social Realities of Zion's Camp," 416-18.

68. *Times and Seasons* 6 (4 Feb. 1845): 788-89; 6 (1 Jan. 1846): 1076; John Henry Evans, *Joseph Smith: An American Prophet* (1933; reprint, Salt Lake City: Deseret Book Co., 1989), 117-18; Hill, *Joseph Smith: The First Mormon*, 173-74, 180-84; Backman, *The Heavens Resound*, 187-89.

69. *Times and Seasons* 6 (15 Feb. 1845): 803; McKiernan and Launius, *The Book of John Whitmer*, 114-15; Pratt, *Autobiography of Parley Parker Pratt*, 116; Smith, *History of the Church*, 2:105.

70. Smith, *History of the Church*, 2:108-109; *The Reed Peck Manuscript* (Salt Lake City: Utah Lighthouse Ministry, n.d.), 3.

Missouri, cholera struck on 22 June and swept through the company with a fury.[71] The disease became God's instrument of judgement. When the cholera attacks ceased, some sixty-eight participants had been stricken, of whom thirteen had died, including the prophet's cousin, Jessie J. Smith.[72] The combination of the refusal of Governor Dunklin to send a militia contingency, the near-battle of 19 June, the Fishing River revelation, and the cholera epidemic all convinced Smith that the expedition's aims were unattainable, and on 30 June he dismissed members to return home. Before returning to Ohio, Smith summoned the Clay County Saints and organized a high council, as he had in Kirtland, to administer church affairs in Missouri.[73]

In one sense the expedition has been viewed as successful since from the camp's stalwarts Smith chose his "First Seventy Elders of Israel" and Quorum of Twelve Apostles. Members of the campaign who remained faithful were also among those who would lead the church to the Great Basin.[74] But in reality the expedition's futility

71. Robert T. Divett, "His Chastening Rod: Cholera Epidemics and the Mormons," *Dialogue: A Journal of Mormon Thought* 12 (Fall 1979): 10-11; Warren A. Jennings, "The Army of Israel Marches into Missouri," *Missouri Historical Review* 62 (Jan. 1968): 133.

72. Divett, "His Chastening Rod," 12.

73. Donald Q. Cannon and Lyndon W. Cook, eds., *Far West Record: Minutes of the Church of Jesus Christ of Latter-day Saints, 1830-1844* (Salt Lake City: Deseret Book Co., 1983), 70, 3 July 1834; McKiernan and Launius, *The Book of John Whitmer*, 118; Scott G. Kenney, *Wilford Woodruff's Journal, 1833-1898*, 9 vols. (Midvale, UT: Signature Books, 1983-85), 1:13, 3 July 1834; Launius, *Zion's Camp*, 144-45.

74. Kenney, *Wilford Woodruff's Journal*, 1:118, 3 Jan. 1837; Wilford Woodruff, *Journal of Discourses*, 13:158, 12 Dec. 1869; Brigham Young, ibid., 10:20, 6 Oct. 1862; Smith, *History of the Church*, 2:xxii-xxiv, 2:182, 201-202; Launius, *Zion's Camp*, 166-67; Gregory A. Prince, *Power From On High: The Development of Mormon Priesthood* (Salt Lake City: Signature Books, 1995), 25, 75-76; Dan Vogel, *Religious Seekers and the Advent of Mormonism* (Salt Lake City: Signature Books, 1988), 202; D. Michael Quinn, "The Mormon Succession Crisis of 1844," *Brigham Young University Studies* 16 (Winter 1976): 187-223; Backman, *The Heavens Resound*, 199-200.

dampened Mormon hope in a millennial deliverance. Although Smith explained the cholera epidemic and Zion's Camp's debacle as God's "scourge ... in consequence of the[ir] fractious and unruly spirits," from a practical viewpoint the disaster of Zion's Camp, seen as failed prophesy, eroded Smith's institutional strength. It led to internal discord and weakened an already diminished level of public sympathy for the Saints.[75] Understood as a military invasion by an army of retribution, Zion's Camp gave further support to Missourians' claims that the Saints would use violence to overpower the gentiles.[76]

For some six years there remained two gathering places, Ohio and Missouri–albeit in Missouri the Saints were forced to gather outside Jackson County. Yet Mormon preoccupation with the location of the New Jerusalem refused to cease. Given its eschatological significance, the Zion Joseph Smith had prophesied maintained a special place in the Saints' hearts. In August 1834 Smith instructed the church's governing body in Missouri, Zion's high council, to purchase land around Jackson County in anticipation of reoccupying the region. Smith even identified the date of repossession–11 September 1836.[77]

---

75. Smith, *History of the Church*, 2:80; *Times and Seasons* 6 (1 Feb. 1845): 788; *Painesville Telegraph*, 15 Feb. 1838; Kenney, *Wilford Woodruff's Journal*, 1:12, 26 Apr.-3 July 1834; Pratt, *Autobiography of Parley Parker Pratt*, 116. E. D. Howe compared Zion's Camp to Cervantes' Knight of La Mancha. See Howe, *Mormonism Unvailed*, 163. See also Marvin S. Hill, "Cultural Crisis in the Mormon Kingdom: A Reconsideration of the Causes of Kirtland Dissent," *Church History* 49 (Sept. 1980): 287-89.

76. *Evening and Morning Star* 2 (July 1834): 176. After destruction of the printing press in Independence, a new press was purchased and the *Evening and Morning Star* was published in Kirtland, Ohio.

77. Joseph Smith to Edward Partridge et. al., 16 Aug. 1834, in Jessee, *The Personal Writings of Joseph Smith*, 330; Smith, *History of the Church*, 2:145; Winn, *Exiles in a Land of Liberty*, 102; Vogel, *Religious Seekers and the Advent of Mormonism*, 200. Continued reliance on the designated date of Zion's repossession is seen in Scott H. Faulring, *An American Prophet's Record: The Diaries and Journals of Joseph Smith* (1987; reprint, Salt Lake City: Signature Books in association with Smith Research Associates, 1989), 42-43, 29 Oct.

But viewing Mormon gathering and kingdom building as a kind of imperialism, Clay County citizens by 1836 were demanding that Mormons leave their county as well.[78] In mid-summer mass meetings were held in Liberty where old settlers protested Mormon immigration, pro-Indian and abolitionist sentiments, and cultural incompatibility. Admitting that their initial hospitality was based on the assumption that Clay County was to be a temporary asylum, and that a Mormon majority in their midst would not be tolerated, the permanent citizens now demanded an immediate Mormon exodus.[79] With the Saints forced to flee Clay County, the Missouri legislature created a new county, Caldwell County, in Northwestern Missouri as a Mormon refuge. Here the Saints started over once more, in Far West, to build the city based on Smith's map of Zion.[80]

With the failure of Zion's Camp Smith returned to a hostile Kirtland, where his leadership was openly challenged.[81] He placed himself on trial before the church's Kirtland high council for alleged misconduct during the Zion's Camp campaign.[82] When the high council sustained him, Smith then moved to consolidate church leadership and, for stability purposes, change its nature from charis-

---

1835. Wilford Woodruff was promised in his ordination as a "Seventy" that he would "stand upon Mount Zion in the flesh in Jackson County Missouri at the Cumming of Christ." See Kenney, *Wilford Woodruff's Journal*, 1:119, 3 Jan. 1837.

78. *Messenger and Advocate* 2 (Aug. 1836): 353-64; Smith, *History of the Church*, 2:448-62. See also Flanders, "To Transform History," 115; Bringhurst, *Saints, Slaves, and Blacks*, 22.

79. Richard Lloyd Anderson, "Atchison's Letters and the Causes of Mormon Expulsion from Missouri," *Brigham Young University Studies* 26 (Summer 1986): 11; Hill, *Joseph Smith: The First Mormon*, 206.

80. Allen and Leonard, *The Story of the Latter-day Saints*, 104-107; O'Dea, *The Mormons*, 45.

81. Backman, *The Heavens Resound*, 197; Hill, "Cultural Crisis in the Mormon Kingdom," 288-89.

82. Howe, *Mormonism Unvailed*, 163; Smith, *History of the Church*, 2:142-44. An account of the trial is given in ibid., 250-60.

matic to structural.[83] Although he had received a revelation in 1829 instructing him to choose twelve disciples (apostles), with dissension widespread now was the time to consolidate and streamline ecclesiastic power.[84] Accordingly, to augment the existing Ohio and Missouri high councils, Smith ordained apostles and seventies to provide authoritative institutionalism with himself at the head.[85] The apostles were then blessed in preparation for their millennial mission to gather in the elect of God, with many of the newly-ordained oracles promised that they would remain "in the flesh" to witness Christ usher in his millennial kingdom.[86]

One mission of the gathering was to have the faithful stand in holy places while awaiting the coming of the "Holy One of Israel." That meant leaving Babylon and uniting with God's people, building his kingdom.[87] Considering the ongoing trouble from outsiders in Missouri and insiders in Kirtland, the Saints required a unifying purpose. At this point erecting a temple took on additional importance.[88] Although moderate in proportion, the structure's comple-

---

83. John G. Gager, *Kingdom and Community: The Social World of Early Christianity* (Englewood Cliffs, NJ: Prentice-Hall, 1975), 67; Vogel, *Religious Seekers and the Advent of Mormonism*, 202.

84. *Book of Commandments*, 37-38; McKiernan and Launius, *The Book of John Whitmer*, 140.

85. Smith, *History of the Church*, 2:180-204. Individuals called as "seventies" were to become traveling missionaries under the direction of the twelve apostles. See ibid., 2:201-202; D. Michael Quinn, "The Evolution of the Presiding Quorums of the LDS Church," *Journal of Mormon History* 1 (1974): 31-32; Prince, *Power From On High*, 22-27, 75-78.

86. The selection and blessing of the twelve apostles is found in Smith, *History of the Church*, 2:180-200. The official account omits the millennial promises which can be found in "History of Joseph Smith," *Millennial Star* 15 (26 Mar. 1853): 206-208, and ibid., 15 (2 Apr. 1853): 209-13. See also Marvin S. Hill, *Quest for Refuge: The Mormon Flight from American Pluralism* (Salt Lake City: Signature Books, 1989), 47; Vogel, *Religious Seekers and the Advent of Mormonism*, 203, 212n119.

87. Mulder, "Mormonism's 'Gathering,'" 250.

88. Danny L. Jorgensen, "Dissent and Schism in the Early Church: Explaining Mormon Fissiparousness," *Dialogue: A Journal of Mormon Thought*

tion was the result of dedication, cooperation, and sacrifice in the face of the new movement's already strained resources. But it helped resolve the church's internal discord.[89]

At the temple's March 1836 dedication, millennial anticipation and Zion's "redemption" remained themes, and many members interpreted divine manifestations and rejuvenation as a sign that the spiritual endowment necessary to restore their Missouri inheritance had arrived.[90] In dualist language Smith's dedicatory prayer proclaimed if any people "shall smite this people, thou wilt smite them—thou wilt fight for thy people as thou didst in the day of battle, that they may be delivered from the hands of their enemies."[91] The following month a special committee was initiated to raise funds to purchase Missouri land.[92]

Subsequently, Joseph Smith and Oliver Cowdery received visions from Christ and many biblical prophets in their new temple. Israel by blood and by adoption began to be called home. Moses's appearance confirmed that the gathering of Israel had commenced. "The keys of this dispensation," Smith was promised, "are committed into your hands; and by this ye may know that the great and dreadful day of the Lord is near, even at the doors."[93] Passing the torch from the ancient patriarchs to Joseph Smith was no longer figurative. As a modern Moses, Smith was to lead the people as a chosen nation, his kingdom-building endeavors to include

28 (Fall 1995): 28.

89. Smith, *History of the Church*, 2:167; George A. Smith, *Journal of Discourses*, 11:11, 15 Nov. 1864; Allen and Leonard, *The Story of the Latter-day Saints*, 98-99; Hill, *Quest for Refuge*, 51.

90. *Messenger and Advocate* 2 (Mar. 1836): 273-88; Smith, *History of the Church*, 2:112-13, 2:431-34; McKiernan and Launius, *The Book of John Whitmer*, 128-29; *Doctrine and Covenants of the Church of Jesus Christ of Latter-day Saints* (Salt Lake City: Church of Jesus Christ of Latter-day Saints, 1981), 109:47, 51-52, 58; 105:9-13; Vogel, *Religious Seekers and the Advent of Mormonism*, 200.

91. *Messenger and Advocate* 2 (Mar. 1836): 278.

92. Smith, *History of the Church*, 2:434; Vogel, *Religious Seekers and the Advent of Mormonism*, 201.

93. Smith, *History of the Church*, 2:435-36.

planning, colonizing, promoting, and financing, living in but not of the world, gathering the repentant to Zion's bosom.[94] The temple ceremony initiated in Kirtland further linked the Saints to the spirit world, supporting a continued millennial world view.[95]

The move to Ohio had been the first attempt to live as a distinct community separate from the world, and as missionaries were sent forth their message was to gather to Kirtland.[96] Mormons saw material prosperity as a sign of God's pleasure as the Book of Mormon had promised, and church members' apparent economic success verified their hope of a "promised land" in the West.[97] But with the influx of Mormons to a central location, Ohioans also began to fear Mormon numbers who, by 1835, controlled the Kirtland township, and again anti-Mormon activity began to threaten the Saints.

But the church in Ohio broke up more from internal than external conflicts.[98] Kirtland saw the first schism in the young church between those who viewed Mormonism as part of American religious pluralism and others who envisioned the creation of a separate community both spiritually and temporally.[99] With the religion's growth, its influence over a convert's life grew until all aspects fell

---

94. Flanders, "To Transform History," 113.

95. Lauritz G. Peterson, "The Kirtland Temple," *Brigham Young University Studies* 12 (Summer 1972): 403-404; Thomas G. Alexander, "Between Revivalism and the Social Gospel: The Latter-day Saint Social Advisory Committee, 1916-1922," *Brigham Young University Studies* 23 (Winter 1983): 23.

96. Backman, *The Heavens Resound*, 132-33.

97. Kenney, *Wilford Woodruff's Journal*, 1:122, 17 Jan. 1837. R. Kent Fielding contends Mormon economic success at Kirtland was an illusion with the gathering of Saints to Ohio generating economic activity which "merely created a city without providing a[n economic] reason for its existence." See Fielding, "The Mormon Economy in Kirtland, Ohio," *Utah Historical Quarterly* 27 (Oct. 1959): 343.

98. Winn, *Exiles in a Land of Liberty*, 63-71.

99. Klaus J. Hansen, *Mormonism and the American Experience* (Chicago: University of Chicago Press, 1981), 123-36.

under the church's domain. To some faithful members this posed no problem, but to traditional Americans the church's usurpation of individual rights was unacceptable.[100]

Beginning with the conjecture by some that the failure of Zion's Camp was the result of false prophecy, members increasingly questioned Smith's leadership and prophetic ability. This quickly escalated into issues involving infringement of individual church members' rights.[101] Complicated by the intertwining of spiritual and temporal affairs, an environment of mistrust soon developed.[102] The church's ongoing financial difficulty was not resolved by the establishment in Kirtland of a general store, a sawmill, or tannery, all of which only floundered.[103] Through land speculation the church's debts were mounting and leaders decided to pool resources into a chartered bank which could issue paper money and ease their hardship. When the state legislature denied the bank a charter, Smith circumvented legal barriers by forming the "Kirtland Safety Society Anti-Banking Company." He then began to issue notes, script in the form of "mutual stock association" bonds, in hopes that the notes would circulate as currency.[104]

---

100. Marvin S. Hill, *Quest for Refuge*, 60-63.

101. *Messenger and Advocate* 3 (July 1837): 535-41; *Elders' Journal* 1 (July 1838): 33-83; Smith, *History of the Church*, 3:1; Winn, *Exiles in a Land of Liberty*, 107; Gordon D. Pollock, *In Search of Security: The Mormons and the Kingdom of God on Earth, 1830-1844* (New York: Garland Publishing, 1989), 34-35.

102. Smith, *History of the Church*, 2:487-88. See also Hill, "Cultural Crisis in the Mormon Kingdom," 291-94.

103. Faulring, *An American Prophet's Record*, 19-20; *Messenger and Advocate* 2 (Sept. 1836): 379; Smith, *History of the Church*, 2:54.

104. *Messenger and Advocate* 3 (Mar. 1837): 475-77; Smith, *History of the Church*, 2:467-73; Dean A. Dudley, "Bank Born of Revelation: The Kirtland Safety Society Anti-Banking Company," *Journal of Economic History* 30 (Dec. 1970): 848-53; Scott H. Partridge, "The Failure of the Kirtland Safety Society," *Brigham Young University Studies* 12 (Summer 1972): 437-54; Fielding, "The Mormon Economy in Kirtland, Ohio," 831-56; D. Paul Sampson and Larry T. Wimmer, "The Kirtland Safety Society: The Stock Ledger Book and the Bank Failure," *Brigham Young University Studies* 12 (Summer 1972): 427-36; Marvin S. Hill, C. Keith Rooker, and Larry T.

No doubt the faithful believed a bank sponsored by the Lord's mouthpiece must succeed and become, as Wilford Woodruff hoped, "the greatest of all institutions on EARTH."[105] Had not Joseph Smith been blessed by prophecy "that in a short time the Lord would arrange his providences in a merciful manner and send us assistance to deliver us from debt and bondage[?]"[106] When an inflated Kirtland economy, based solely on paper money, began to spiral out of control, speculation, debt, and the bank's failure devastated the city's fortune. The Kirtland Safety Society's collapse fed disillusionment with Smith's leadership, and in the summer of 1837 Smith was arrested numerous times on debt default charges.[107] Faced with massive rebellion and threat of further arrests, in January 1838 Smith and Sidney Rigdon fled their Ohio creditors for Far West, Missouri. The Kirtland temple, printing press, and other church property were left to the dissenters.[108]

Wimmer, "The Kirtland Economy Revisited: A Market Critique of Sectarian Economics," *Brigham Young University Studies* 17 (Summer 1977): 391-475; Dale W. Adams, "Chartering the Kirtland Bank," *Brigham Young University Studies* 23 (Fall 1983): 467-82; Van Wagoner, *Sidney Rigdon*, 182-87.

105. Kenney, *Wilford Woodruff's Journal*, 1:120, 6 Jan. 1837. See also ibid., 1:134, 6 Apr. 1837; *Messenger and Advocate* 3 (Jan. 1837): 443; Van Wagoner, *Sidney Rigdon*, 184.

106. Faulring, *An American Prophet's Record*, 30-31, 30 Nov. 1834. See also Jessee, *The Personal Writings of Joseph Smith*, 137, 30 Nov. 1834; Hill, "Cultural Crisis in the Mormon Kingdom: A Reconsideration of the Causes of Kirtland Dissent," 289-90.

107. See Hill, Wimmer, and Rooker, "The Kirtland Economy Revisited," 420-23, which lists seventeen separate instances where Smith is listed as defendant. See also Kenney, *Wilford Woodruff's Journal*, 1:147, 28 May 1837; ibid., 1:124-25, 19 Feb. 1837; Smith, *History of the Church*, 2:487-93; Hill, *Joseph Smith: The First Mormon*, 213. Brigham Young would subsequently place the blame for the financial disaster on Sidney Rigdon. See Van Wagoner, *Sidney Rigdon*, 182-83. Years later church leaders maintained it was unscrupulous apostates' actions which led to the bank's failure. See George A. Smith, *Journal of Discourses*, 11:11, 15 Nov. 1864.

108. Faulring, *An American Prophet's Record*, 192-93; Smith, *History of the Church*, 3:1-2; Karl Keller, ed., "'I Never Knew a Time When I Did Not

When hundreds of Saints followed, Kirtland, as a gathering place, was finished.[109]

But the same themes—isolationism and separatism—condemned the Saints in Far West.[110] Through continued migration nearly 5,000 Mormons lived in Caldwell County, and from there the Missouri Saints had expanded into three other counties, Daviess, Carroll, and Ray, with a total Mormon population of nearly 15,000.[111] Two thousand farms had sprung up over the four-county region and the Saints began to realize their societal hope.[112] But as their phenomenal growth persisted, they soon threatened to dominate all western Missouri. When Smith relocated from Ohio, renewed anti-Mormonism arose.[113]

By 1838 Mormon defense mechanisms had been honed by harassment and flight. For nearly a decade a millennial vision had been central to Mormon theology, with the gathering out of Babylon a common theme. In the safety of their own society, they hoped to assemble the righteous and await the destruction of the wicked.[114]

Know Joseph Smith': A Son's Record of the Life and Testimony of Sidney Rigdon," *Dialogue: A Journal of Mormon Thought* 1 (Winter 1966): 28-30; Eliza R. Snow Smith, *Biography and Family Record of Lorenzo Snow* (Salt Lake City: Deseret News Co., 1884), 20-24; McKiernan and Launius, *The Book of John Whitmer*, 159; *The Reed Peck Manuscript*, 5; Van Wagoner, *Sidney Rigdon*, 203-204; Max H. Parkin, "Kirtland, a Stronghold for the Kingdom," *The Restoration Movement*, 88.

109. Davis Bitton, "The Waning of Mormon Kirtland," *Brigham Young University Studies* 12 (Summer 1972): 455-64.

110. See the continued command to gather with the Saints at Far West as "peace shall soon be taken from the earth," in *Elders' Journal* 1 (Nov. 1837): 28.

111. Wayne J. Lewis, "Mormon Land Ownership as a Factor in Evaluating the Extent of Mormon Settlements and Influence in Missouri, 1831-1841," M.A. thesis, Brigham Young University, 1981, 72-74.

112. Allen and Leonard, *The Story of the Latter-day Saints*, 107.

113. Stephen C. LeSueur, *The 1838 Mormon War in Missouri* (Columbia: University of Missouri Press, 1987), 28, 246.

114. Dean C. Jessee and David J. Whittaker, "The Last Months of Mormonism in Missouri: The Albert Perry Rockwood Journal," *Brigham*

But previous persecution now moved the Saints to a militant defense against further abuse, and a willingness to resist force with force.[115] Renewing a heritage of militancy that was initiated with Zion's Camp, in June 1838 a clandestine vigilante band was formed, known as the Sons of Dan or "Danites." Their purpose was to provide security from outside aggression and internal dissent, "to be the means, in the hands of God, of bringing forth the millennial kingdom."[116]

Although they were gathering "for safety against the day of wrath which Is to be poured out without mixture upon this generation," the Saints were no longer willing to wait for judgement on the wicked.[117] As James Davidson points out, at times like those "the temptation [grows] to bring down judgement future and apply it to the present."[118] From this point on, any who discredited Smith's leadership was harassed and either withdrew or was excommunicated from the church. This included a number of prominent church leaders such as John and David Whitmer, William McLellin, Martin Harris, Frederick G. Williams, Oliver Cowdery, Orson

---

Young University Studies 28 (Winter 1988): 5-41.

115. Smith, *History of the Church*, 2:432.

116. Sampson Avard, in Van Wagoner, *Sidney Rigdon*, 251; Faulring, *An American Prophet's Record*, 198, 22 July 1838; McKiernan and Launius, *The Book of John Whitmer*, 163-66; David Whitmer, *An Address to All Believers in Christ* (Richmond, MO: n.p., 1887), 27-28; Stephen C. LeSueur, "The Danites Reconsidered: Were They Vigilantes or Just the Mormon Version of the Elks Club?" *John Whitmer Historical Association Journal* 14 (1994): 35-51; Leland H. Gentry, "The Danite Band of 1838," *Brigham Young University Studies* 14 (Summer 1974): 421-50; LeSueur, *The 1838 Mormon War in Missouri*, 43-47; Hansen, *Quest for Empire*, 49; Launius, *Zion's Camp*, 171; D. Michael Quinn, *The Mormon Hierarchy: Origins of Power* (Salt Lake City: Signature Books, 1994), 93-99.

117. Faulring, *An American Prophet's Record*, 193. See ibid., 210, 1 Sept. 1838, where Smith asserts the purpose of the gathering is so that "the brethren may be together in the hour of the coming of the Son of Man."

118. James West Davidson, *The Logic of Millennial Thought: Eighteenth-Century New England* (New Haven, CT: Yale University Press, 1977), 294; Grant Underwood, "Millenarianism and the Early Mormon Mind," *Journal of Mormon History* 9 (1982): 48.

Hyde, and William W. Phelps.[119] But purging dissenters only intensified the church's separateness, moving its members farther away from the cultural mainstream.[120]

The Saints' prosperity in northwestern Missouri had led to confidence and a sense of security. New opposition now fed their mindset, with Mormons believing they would soon be led to victory.[121] When threatened again with mob violence, church orator Sidney Rigdon defiantly challenged the Missourians.[122] With militant, millennial zeal, he declared:

> We take God and all the holy angels to witness this day, that we warn all men in the name of Jesus Christ, to come on us no more forever. For from this hour, we will bear it no more, our rights shall no more be trampled on with impunity. The man or the set of men, who attempts it, does it at the expense of their lives. And that mob that comes on us to disturb us; it shall be between us and them a war of extermination, for we will follow them till the last drop of their blood is spilled, or else they will have to exterminate us, for we will carry the seat of war to their own houses, and their own families, and one party or the other shall be utterly destroyed.[123]

Rigdon's sentiments were not aberration, and the following month Smith declared publicly that "we are absolutely determined no longer

119. Faulring, *An American Prophet's Record*, 187; Kenney, *Wilford Woodruff's Journal*, 1:339-40, 25-26 June 1839; Kenneth W. Godfrey, "Causes of Mormon Non-Mormon Conflict in Hancock County, Illinois, 1839-1846," Ph.D. diss., Brigham Young University, 1967, 11; Backman, *The Heavens Resound*, 328; Van Wagoner, *Sidney Rigdon*, 187, 214-15; Hill, *Quest for Refuge*, 63, 74-76, 96.

120. Winn, *Exiles in a Land of Liberty*, 128.

121. See David Patten's remarks in *Elders' Journal* 1 (May 1838): 42; Hill, *Quest for Refuge*, 77-79.

122. Van Wagoner, *Sidney Rigdon*, 220-22.

123. Peter Crawley, "Two Rare Missouri Documents," *Brigham Young University Studies* 14 (Summer 1974): 527; Pratt, *Autobiography of Parley Parker Pratt*, 173. Publication of Rigdon's address by a Liberty, Missouri, newspaper is documented in Faulring, *An American Prophet's Record*, 199, 1-3 Aug. 1838.

to bear [mobbings], come life or come death, for to be mobbed any more without taking vengeance, we will not."[124]

Smith's and Rigdon's remarks enraged an already aroused Missourian contempt which soon erupted into open warfare.[125] With the sanction of Governor Lilburn W. Boggs's infamous October 1838 extermination order, a flurry of violence ravaged the countryside. When senior church leaders surrendered and were held under guard, rather than continue in armed resistance, the church agreed to leave the state.[126] Summarizing the paradox of Mormon expulsion from Missouri, Grant Underwood concluded: "Never again in the nineteenth century would the Saints return en masse to their Missouri Zion, the site originally and ironically designated for their 'defense and refuge.'"[127]

With hopes of grandeur, Mormons moved to Missouri believing they were to abide in harmony on the land of their inheritance. Although only a wilderness, Missouri would soon blossom to "become the joy of the world," with the Saints to "assist in enlarging her borders; and stretching forth the curtains of her habitations."[128] "They are gathering from the North, and from the South, from the East, and from [the] West unto Zion," Smith noted. These events

---

124. *Elders' Journal* 1 (Aug. 1838): 54. See also Faulring, *An American Prophet's Record*, 210-11, 1 Sept. 1838; F. Mark McKiernan, "Mormonism on the Defensive: Far West, 1838-1839," in *The Restoration Movement*, 120.

125. In later years, when trying to discredit Rigdon, church leaders admitted Rigdon's public remarks at Far West outraged the Missourians. See *Times and Seasons* 5 (1 Oct. 1844): 667; 5 (15 Sept. 1844): 651; 5 (1 Nov. 1844): 698. See also Gentry, "The Danite Band of 1838," 423-24; Stephen C. LeSueur, "'High Treason and Murder': The Examination of Mormon Prisoners at Richmond Missouri, in November 1838," *Brigham Young University Studies* 26 (Spring 1986): 2-30; Walker, "Sheaves, Bucklers and the State," 44; Hill, *Quest for Refuge*, 79.

126. Pratt, *Autobiography of Parley Parker Pratt*, 186; Smith, *History of the Church*, 4:34, 3:202; *The Reed Peck Manuscript*, 27; LeSueur, *The 1838 Mormon War in Missouri*, 131.

127. Underwood, *The Millenarian World of Early Mormonism*, 34.

128. "The Gathering," *The Evening and Morning Star* 1 (Nov. 1832).

were but preparatory to the Second Coming.[129] But their millennial dream turned into a nightmare. Four times in less than a decade they were driven from their sanctuaries. When the Saints were asked once again to sacrifice their homes, apocalyptic imagery provided strength and encouragement in the face of despair.[130] Only within millenarian theology, where good will ultimately triumph over evil, could the Saints finally take refuge.

---

129. Faulring, *An American Prophet's Record*, 193.

130. Stephen J. Stein, "Signs of the Times: The Theological Foundations of Early Mormon Apocalyptic," *Sunstone* 8 (Jan.-Apr. 1983): 65.

CHAPTER SIX

MORMON NAUVOO:
SEPARATISM DEFINES A CITY

Driven from its promised land, the LDS church maintained the gathering "must take place before the Lord comes to 'take vengeance upon the ungodly.'"[1] In July 1839 Joseph Smith was still warning the faithful that they may be called to prepare for the Second Coming "before some of us leave this stage of action."[2] But in reality expulsion from Missouri dampened their immediate chiliastic hope.[3] Attempting to understand previous disappointments in achieving a millennial deliverance, Smith blamed the loss of their "promised land," Zion's Camp, and other failures on a lack of righteousness and unity. They "must needs be chastened, and tried" in all things, they were told, that they may

1. *Times and Season* 2 (Jan. 1841): 276.

2. Joseph Smith, *History of the Church of Jesus Christ of Latter-day Saints*, 7 vols., 2nd ed. rev., introduction and notes by B.H. Roberts (Salt Lake City: Deseret Book Co., 1974-76), 3:387; see also ibid., 3:390, for "signs" of the Second Coming.

3. John Taylor, *Journal of Discourses*, 26 vols. (Liverpool, Eng.: F.D. Richards, 1855-86), 23:12, 9 Nov. 1881; Louis G. Reinwand, "An Interpretive Study of Mormon Millennialism During the Nineteenth Century with Emphasis on Millennial Developments in Utah," M.A. thesis, Brigham Young University, 1971, 64; Keith E. Norman, "How Long, O Lord? The Delay of the Parousia in Mormonism," *Sunstone* (Jan.-Apr. 1983): 51.

become more righteous before the Savior's return.[4] Greater efforts would need to be made.[5]

A cloud of despair hung over the new religion. With their prophet behind bars and thousands of members scattered across eastern Missouri then driven across a frozen Mississippi River, the Saints' thoughts moved to heaven, believing only divine intervention could save them.[6]

From his Liberty, Missouri, jail cell, Joseph Smith pled with the Lord to shorten the time until the Son of Man would liberate the Saints.[7] Smith would later travel to Washington, D.C., in a futile attempt to secure federal assistance in obtaining compensation for the loss of Mormon property in Missouri. The government's failure to redress the Saints' plight in Missouri now made the nation complicit in crimes against the Mormons, and the judgements of God would soon go forth against the corrupt officials.[8] If the

---

4. *Times and Seasons* 1 (Jan. 1840): 39.

5. Although in 1838 members had been castigated and some even excommunicated for selling their Missouri property, in 1839 Smith began advising Mormons to dispose of their Missouri land holdings. In 1841 the previous command to build a city and temple in Missouri was rescinded by revelation. See Dean C. Jessee, comp. and ed., *The Personal Writings of Joseph Smith* (Salt Lake City: Deseret Book Co., 1984), 310; Smith, *History of the Church*, 3:3-5, 274. For Smith's comments on the feasibility of the Lord revoking a command, see Scott G. Kenney, ed., *Wilford Woodruff's Journal, 1833-1898*, 9 vols. (Midvale, UT: Signature Books, 1983-85), 2:143, 19 Dec. 1841; *Times and Seasons* 2 (1 June 1841): 427; Dan Vogel, *Religious Seekers and the Advent of Mormonism* (Salt Lake City: Signature Books, 1988), 201.

6. Grant Underwood, "Millenarianism and the Early Mormon Mind," *Journal of Mormon History* 9 (1982): 46; Dean C. Jessee, "'Walls, Grates and Screeking Iron Doors': The Prison Experience of Mormon Leaders in Missouri, 1838-1839," in *New Views of Mormon History*, eds. Davis Bitton and Maureen Ursenbach Beecher (Salt Lake City: University of Utah Press, 1987), 19-42. See also *Times and Seasons* 2 (1 Apr. 1841): 373-74.

7. Smith, *History of the Church*, 3:291-92. See *Times and Seasons* 2 (15 June 1841): 445, where William Smith pleads to the Lord to hasten his return. See also Joseph Smith, in *Journal of Discourses*, 6:239, 2 June 1839.

8. *Times and Seasons* 1 (15 Mar. 1840): 74; Smith, *History of the Church*,

United States did not return to righteousness, God would destroy his once-favored nation.[9]

Illinois was initially seen as a temporary place of refuge and, for a while, Joseph Smith may even have doubted the policy of "gathering" which had led to much of the Saints' troubles.[10] A year later Smith broadened the Mormon kingdom's concept of gathering to include "all N[orth] & S[outh] America," and in fact "any place where the Saints gather is Zion."[11] But in April 1839 separatist worries were

---

4:89.

9. Smith, *History of the Church*, 4:145. See also ibid., 6:116; Kenneth H. Winn, *Exiles in a Land of Liberty: Mormons in America, 1830-1846* (Chapel Hill: University of North Carolina Press, 1989), 155-56.

10. Joseph Smith to the Church at Quincy, Illinois, 20 Mar. 1839, in Smith, *History of the Church*, 3:301. See also ibid., 3:260-61; Dean C. Jessee and David J. Whittaker, "The Last Months of Mormonism in Missouri: The Albert Perry Rockwood Journal," *Brigham Young University Studies* 28 (Winter 1988): 34; Brigham Young, *Journal of Discourses*, 11:17, 11 Dec. 1864; Kenneth W. Godfrey, "Causes of Mormon Non-Mormon Conflict in Hancock County, Illinois, 1839-1846," Ph.D. diss., Brigham Young University, 1967, 112; Richard S. Van Wagoner, *Sidney Rigdon: A Portrait of Religious Excess* (Salt Lake City: Signature Books, 1994), 262.

11. Dean C. Jessee, "Joseph Smith's 19 July 1840 Discourse," *Brigham Young University Studies* 19 (Spring 1979): 392. As early as 1839 a shifting concept of gathering to the stakes of Zion was preached by Smith. See Willard Richards Pocket Companion, Aug. 1839, in Andrew F. Ehat and Lyndon W. Cook, *The Words of Joseph Smith* (1980; reprint, Orem, UT: Grandin Book Co., 1991), 11; Smith, *History of the Church*, 3:390; ibid., 6:318-19, 321. To emphasize the new definition's significance, Parley Pratt dramatically announced the change in a letter to his brother with seven exclamation points. See James B. Allen, Ronald K. Esplin, and David J. Whittaker, *Men with a Mission: 1837-1841, The Quorum of the Twelve Apostles in the British Isles* (Salt Lake City: Deseret Book Co., 1992), 87; Grant Underwood, *The Millenarian World of Early Mormonism* (Urbana: University of Illinois Press, 1993), 34. Pratt's disappointment with unfulfilled prophesies regarding Missouri is seen in his query to Joseph Smith, "When Will the *'purchased possession'* be Redeemed and the temple and city commence in Jackson Co. Mo." P[arley]. P. Pratt to Brother Smith, 4 Dec. 1841, in David H. Pratt, "Oh! Brother Joseph," *Brigham Young University Studies* 27 (Winter 1987): 130,

absent when the Saints purchased the swamp-land village of Commerce, re-named Nauvoo, on a bend of the Mississippi River.[12]

In Kirtland Smith's desire to command in all things, temporal and spiritual, led to the apostasy of many including Oliver Cowdery. In Missouri the independent, capitalistic, competitive values of the established citizens ran counter to the Mormon ideal of a cohesive unit. In Nauvoo Smith realized that to establish a separate kingdom of God on earth political independence would be necessary. The Saints' Missouri experience colored their subsequent emotions and decisions, and it was at this point that Mormonism crossed a pivotal point. Treating all obstacles as further examples of the devil's resourcefulness, and seeing the world as marshalling Satan's forces to fight the people of God, they became in Illinois more separatist, more hostile to outsiders, solidifying their identity as a peculiar people, the chosen new Israel.[13]

In Nauvoo Smith attempted to isolate his movement based on self-preservation instincts and the Mormon Missouri experience.[14] Latter-day Saint beliefs, ideals, activities, and ambitions had led to

---

emphasis in original. As early as 1832 William W. Phelps had indicated Zion may include the area from the Mississippi River to the Rocky Mountains. See "The Far West," *Evening and Morning Star* 1 (Oct. 1832).

12. Smith, *History of the Church*, 3:265-76, 3:298, 3:341-42; 3:391; B[righam]. H. Roberts, *A Comprehensive History of the Church of Jesus Christ of Latter-day Saints*, 6 vols. (1930; reprint, Provo, UT: Brigham Young University Press, 1965), 2:9-10. Smith later disbanded all stakes except Nauvoo and on the opposite shore of the Mississippi in Lee County, Iowa. See Smith, *History of the Church*, 4:362.

13. Thomas Ford, *A History of Illinois*, 2 vols. (1854; reprint, Chicago: Lakeside Press, 1945-46), 2:42; Michael Walzer, *The Revolution of the Saints: A Study in the Origins of Radical Politics* (Cambridge, MA: Harvard University Press, 1965), 3; Winn, *Exiles in a Land of Liberty*, 153-56; Grant Underwood, "Early Mormon Millennialism: Another Look," M.A. thesis, Brigham Young University, 1981, 87; Robert Flanders, "Dream and Nightmare: Nauvoo Revisited," in *The Restoration Movement: Essays in Mormon History*, rev. ed., eds. F. Mark McKiernan, Alma R. Blair, and Paul M. Edwards (Independence, MO: Herald Publishing House, 1992), 142.

14. Winn, *Exiles in a Land of Liberty*, 158-59.

suspicion and hostility wherever Mormons called home. Disillusioned with their treatment at the hands of Washington politicians, the Saints stiffened their determination to become self-reliant.[15] With the Missouri episode hanging over their consciousness, Joseph Smith realized that a peculiar group like the Mormons could not rely on tolerance for their safety. As Thomas O'Dea stated, "Power meant politics and armed force, and now the Saints went after both."[16]

Resolving to deal with their "enemies" from a position of strength, Smith obtained the Nauvoo city charter which they considered their "Magna Carte," interpreting it as a device to make Nauvoo an independent city-state.[17] "I concocted it for the salvation of the church," Smith said, "on principles so broad, that every honest man might dwell secure under its protective influence."[18] The city's municipal court then proceeded to issue writs of habeas corpus to protect Smith and other church leaders from arrest from neighboring jurisdictions.[19]

The unique aspect of the charter authorized an armed militia, the Nauvoo Legion. This fed anti-Mormons' fear of Mormon militarism.[20] A standing army was seen as a particular anti-republican evil,

15. Smith, *History of the Church*, 4:88-102.

16. Thomas F. O'Dea, *The Mormons* (Chicago: University of Chicago Press, 1957), 51.

17. Mark F. McKiernan and Roger D. Launius, eds., *And Early Latter Day Saint History: The Book of John Whitmer, Kept by Commandment* (Independence, MO: Herald Publishing House, 1980), 172; Thomas Barnes to Miranda Barnes Haskett, 6 Nov. 1897, in William Mulder and A. Russell Mortensen, eds., *Among the Mormons: Historic Accounts by Contemporary Observers* (New York: Alfred A. Knopf, 1967), 147; James L. Kimball, Jr., "The Nauvoo Charter: A Reinterpretation," *Journal of the Illinois State Historical Society* 64 (Spring 1971): 66-78; James L. Kimball, Jr., "A Wall to Defend Zion: The Nauvoo Charter," *Brigham Young University Studies* 15 (Summer 1975): 499-526; Dallin H. Oaks, "The Suppression of the Nauvoo Expositor," *Utah Law Review* 9 (Winter 1965): 878-82.

18. Smith, *History of the Church*, 4:249.

19. Robert Flanders, *Nauvoo: Kingdom on the Mississippi* (Urbana: University of Illinois Press, 1965), 99.

20. Roger D. Launius, "Anti-Mormonism in Illinois: Thomas C.

and although city officials rhetorically downplayed the Mormon military threat, control of their own militia certainly elicited confidence.[21] By 1844 the legion numbered 4,000 men, second only to the U.S. army, uder the control of Lieutenant General Joseph Smith who flaunted his military title and breached the notion of a separation of power by also functioning as mayor and municipal court justice.[22]

At the same time social and theological structures first developed in Missouri and Ohio led to a solid organization of apostles, seventies, and a priesthood of ecclesiastic rulers called by God. Following the Book of Mormon's example of visionary men as prophets, priests, and law-givers, early Latter-day Saints understood Mormonism's theocratic goal.[23] The suffering in Missouri and Illinois provided the unity necessary for the creation of a distinctive Mormon psyche. This self-identification made them more than just a church but in fact a "peculiar people."[24]

Sharp's Unfinished History of the Mormon War, 1845," *Journal of Mormon History* 15 (1989): 29.

21. *Times and Seasons* 2 (15 May 1841): 417-19; ibid., 2 (15 Apr. 1841): 380-83; Flanders, *Nauvoo*, 109; Winn, *Exiles in a Land of Liberty*, 158-62.

22. Smith, *History of the Church*, 4:295-96; Ford, *A History of Illinois*, 2:66-69; Hamilton Gardner, "The Nauvoo Legion, 1840-1845—A Unique Military Organization," *Journal of the Illinois State Historical Society* 55 (Summer 1961): 181-97; Ronald W. Walker, "Sheaves, Bucklers and the State: Mormon Leaders Respond to the Dilemmas of War," *Sunstone* 7 (July-Aug. 1982): 44-45; Godfrey, "Causes of Mormon Non-Mormon Conflict in Hancock County, Illinois," 35; Marvin S. Hill, *Quest for Refuge: The Mormon Flight from American Pluralism* (Salt Lake City: Signature Books, 1989), 112-13; Flanders, *Nauvoo*, 98.

23. Kenney, *Wilford Woodruff's Journal*, 1:127-28, 2 Apr. 1837; Richard L. Bushman, "The Book of Mormon and the American Revolution," *Brigham Young University Studies* 17 (Autumn 1976): 14-20; Marvin S. Hill, "Quest for Refuge: An Hypothesis as to the Social Origins and Nature of the Mormon Political Kingdom," *Journal of Mormon History* 2 (1975): 12; O'Dea, *The Mormons*, 34-35; D. Michael Quinn, *The Mormon Hierarchy: Origins of Power* (Salt Lake City: Signature Books, 1994), 80.

24. Val Dan MacMurray and Perry H. Cunningham, "Mormons and Gentiles: A Study in Conflict and Persistence," in *Ethnic Conflicts and Power:*

In Nauvoo Mormonism's authoritative structure was reinforced by merging public office, priesthood positions, and the military organization of the Nauvoo Legion. By interlocking political, social, economic, and religious hierarchies, every member of God's kingdom could achieve rank and position. A man whose attempt at success in Jacksonian America had failed could find it in the Mormon kingdom where an oligarchy of church leaders commanded the city's legal apparatus.[25] By combining civic, political, and church offices, Mormons in Nauvoo hoped to create a true theocracy in preparation for the Millennium.

But the Mormon centralized power structure was pragmatic as well, and increased members' hope for this world as well as for the world to come. What Smith's religion offered was opportunity for those previously left out of the larger society. Priesthood hierarchy provided a ladder for those on the bottom rung to ascend, and God's kingdom furnished sanctuary and security from the uncertainty of the outside world.[26] In their religious domain they attempted to create a power structure in which a community, an empire, could be built. By combining religious and secular goals, Mormons hoped both to realize the ante-bellum American Dream and prepare for Christ's coming reign.[27] As one scholar has concluded, "[N]o nineteenth century American movement had a more total view of the new world, and none was more disciplined."[28]

Early Mormonism's total theology accentuated Smith's prophetic role which reigned supreme. No longer bound by precedent, as a seer he was to break from the past, to stand apart from society and bring

---

A Cross-National Perspective, eds. Donald E. Gelfand and Russell D. Lee (New York: John Wiley and Sons, 1973), 212-15; O'Dea, *The Mormons,* 75; Quinn, *The Mormon Hierarchy: Origins of Power,* 105-10.

25. Flanders, *Nauvoo,* 103.

26. Flanders, "Dream and Nightmare," 152; Hill, *Quest for Refuge,* 36.

27. Klaus J. Hansen, "Mormonism and American Culture: Some Tentative Hypotheses," in *The Restoration Movement,* 11-20; Gordon D. Pollock, *In Search of Security: The Mormons and the Kingdom of God on Earth, 1830-1844* (New York: Garland Publishing, 1989), 230-31.

28. Hansen, "Mormonism and American Culture," 18.

about change, with his theology evolving in accordance to divine will.[29] Among his followers, the highest esteem was held for those with proven loyalty to religious superiors. It was "the duty of all men to obey the leaders of the church, and ... no man could commit sin so long as he acted in the way that he was directed by his Church superiors," the Saints were taught.[30]

Because restored religion was not confined to mere scripture, sacred precepts expanded through the heavenly power behind religious creed. In his revelatory calling, Smith enlarged the sacred canon, and the literalism of the early Saints, and their connection to the Old Testament and Ancient Israel, came to fruition in Illinois.[31] Already their unique interpretation of Isaiah 2:3, which held that Zion and Jerusalem were two places, and the gathering was to separate them physically from traditional Protestantism.[32] By exalting the Old Testament to equality with the New, Mormonism's biblical literalism led to doctrinal innovations. In Nauvoo Smith introduced and expanded unique theological tenets such as the temple ceremony, priesthood offices, patriarchal blessings, baptism for the dead, and plural marriage, all principles the Saints believed were to be restored in the last days.[33] As a recent work has concluded, Mormon theology exalted "the particular rites and ordinances that would bring heaven to earth, collapse both primordium and millennium into their own time and space, and tie the Saints to God's work in all time past. This

---

29. J[ohn]. F. C. Harrison, *The Second Coming: Popular Millenarianism, 1780-1850* (New Brunswick, NJ: Rutgers University Press, 1979), 12.

30. John D. Lee, *Mormonism Unveiled* (St. Louis: Bryan, Brand and Co., 1877), 287.

31. *Millennial Star* 10 (Feb. 1841): 258-59; Richard T. Hughes and C. Leonard Allen, *Illusions of Innocence: Protestant Primitivism in America, 1630-1875* (Chicago: University of Chicago Press, 1988), 141.

32. Underwood, *The Millenarian World of Early Mormonism*, 62-65; *Evening and Morning Star* 1 (May 1833); 2 (Mar. 1834): 141.

33. The first public sermon on the doctrine of baptism for the dead is found in *Times and Seasons* 2 (15 Apr. 1841): 387. See also Hill, *Quest for Refuge*, 51; Underwood, *The Millenarian World of Early Mormonism*, 69-71.

perspective ultimately provided the theological basis for the political rule of the Saints."[34]

It was polygamy, in Nauvoo, which some have held "more than any other Mormon doctrine, set the saints apart from the world and made them a peculiar people." Its attempted abandonment of certain social inhibitions became possible only in the Saints' separate political kingdom in Illinois.[35] But polygamy did more than differentiate the Saints from mainstream America. It strengthened Mormon cultural bonds by uniting members, particularly the church hierarchy, through familial ties. The prophet's scribe William Clayton amplified the importance of the new doctrine to Smith and his associates:

> During the last year of his life we were scarcely ever together, alone, but he [Smith] was talking on the subject, and explaining that doctrine and principles connected with it. ... From him I learned that the doctrine of plural and celestial marriage is the most holy and important doctrine ever revealed to man on the earth, and that without obedience to that principle no man can ever attain to the fullness of exaltation in celestial glory.[36]

Polygamy's sexual experimentation also allowed women, on the low rung of society, to obtain status and security by being connected to the upper echelons of church leadership.[37] As women became more closely associated with the prophet as a wife or the wife of an

---

34. Hughes and Allen, *Illusions of Innocence*, 149.

35. "William Clayton's Testimony," in George D. Smith, ed., *An Intimate Chronicle: The Journals of William Clayton* (Salt Lake City: Signature Books in association with Smith Research Associates, 1991), 559; Harrison, *The Second Coming*, 187-88; Sarah S. Scott to My dear Father and Mother, 6 Feb. 1845, in Mulder and Mortensen, *Among the Mormons*, 154; Van Wagoner, *Sidney Rigdon*, 352; Klaus J. Hansen, *Quest for Empire: The Political Kingdom of God and the Council of Fifty in Mormon History* (Lansing: Michigan State University, 1970), 54.

36. Andrew Jensen, *Historical Record* 6 (July 1887): 226, in Van Wagoner, *Sidney Rigdon*, 293.

37. Marvin S. Hill, "The 'Prophet Puzzle' Assembled; or, How to Treat Our Historical Diplopia Toward Joseph Smith," *Journal of Mormon History* 3 (1976): 104.

associate, they increased their own personal security. Kenelm Burridge contends, "[O]n the whole ... the sexual attractiveness of male prophets is to be accounted for less in the amatory skills of the prophet, and more in the conditions of being a woman."[38]

The Saints' religious separatism found physical expression in the Nauvoo temple which symbolized Mormon solidarity. Here the ceremonies introduced in Kirtland were expanded, and the semi-secret rites further isolated the Saints both religiously and psychologically from the outside community. The temple's clandestine nature also increased member loyalty by making one a "privileged holder of holy mysteries" and reinforced adherence to priesthood authority and dictum.[39] When the principle of plurality was tied, in the temple, to eternal celestial glory, Mormon theology came full circle. From this Nauvoo temple doctrine emerged the associated principles of eternal expansion of familial ties, first by expanding families backward through time and saving kindred dead, then forward to the Millennium where polygamy would yield its eternal increase.[40]

Although he believed in isolationism, in preparing for Christ's return, Joseph Smith still planned to use, when possible, American political institutions.[41] Even if prophecies predicted destruction prior to the Second Coming, Smith maintained that some good could occur through the ballot box. As Edward Pessen suggests, perhaps "sin," at least partially, "was to be defeated by majority

---

38. Kenelm Burridge, *New Heaven, New Earth: A Study of Millenarian Activities* (New York: Schocken Books, 1969), 161.

39. O'Dea, *The Mormons*, 59.

40. Andrew F. Ehat, ed., "'They Might Have Known that He Was Not a Fallen Prophet'—The Nauvoo Journal of Joseph Fielding," *Brigham Young University Studies* 19 (Winter 1979): 154; *Millennial Star* 23 (16 Feb. 1841): 102; Smith, *History of the Church*, 5:148-53; 4:231; Orson Pratt, *Journal of Discourses*, 1:161-65, 29 Aug. 1852; *Times and Season* 2 (1 June 1841): 424-27; Thomas G. Alexander, "Between Revivalism and the Social Gospel: The Latter-day Saint Social Advisory Committee, 1916-1922," *Brigham Young University Studies* 23 (Winter 1983): 23.

41. Ernest Lee Tuveson, *Redeemer Nation: The Idea of America's Millennial Role* (Chicago: University of Chicago Press, 1968), 185.

vote."[42] Consequently, convinced that government entities would not protect his people from outside aggression, Smith sought to maximize Mormon politic influence.[43]

Whether good or bad, both Mormons and non-Mormons viewed Nauvoo as kingdom building, and anti-Mormon animosities grew when Mormon solidarity was seen as holding the balance of power between the two political parties.[44] Understanding the hostility that his followers created outside Nauvoo, Smith publicly announced that "he did not wish to have any political influence."[45] But he continued to urge the Saints "to use their political franchise to the best of their knowledge."[46] Almost immediately the Mormons displayed their ability to unite politically and their willingness to vote as a block. In response both Illinois Democrats and Whigs solicited Mormon political support.[47]

The benefits of the Saints' political opportunism was short-lived. Although philosophically aligned with the Democrats, Smith initially rejected the party following Martin Van Buren's cool reception to Mormon appeals for redress. Subsequently finding a powerful political ally in Judge Stephen A. Douglas, a Democrat, the Saints attempted to woo favors from all sides.[48] But soon, due to Mormon vacillation and shifting loyalties, both Whigs and Democrats concluded the Saints were politically unreliable. The Saints' alienation of both parties led to the demise of influence in each, further escalating Mormon isolation.[49] As Marvin Hill has concluded, "In selling the

42. Edward Pessen, *Jacksonian America: Society, Personality, and Politics* (Homewood, IL: Dorsey Press, 1969), 80.

43. Hill, "Quest for Refuge," 16.

44. Winn, *Exiles in a Land of Liberty*, 163, 181; Flanders, "Dream and Nightmare," 147-48.

45. *Times and Seasons* 1 (Apr. 1840): 94.

46. Smith, *History of the Church*, 5:232, 259. See also Hill, *Quest for Refuge*, 108-109, 125.

47. Ford, *A History of Illinois*, 2:60-62; Hill, *Quest for Refuge*, 106-107.

48. Smith, *History of the Church*, 4:479-80; Ford, *A History of Illinois*, 2:68-72.

49. Ford, *A History of Illinois*, 2:144-54; Flanders, *Nauvoo*, 217-40; Hill,

Mormon vote for favors and attempted security to two different parties, Smith caused both parties to distrust him. The consequence was a still greater feeling of alienation between Mormons and their neighbors."[50] By 1841 an anti-Mormon party had developed in Hancock County with a slate of candidates determined to counter Mormon block voting.

In the face of political animosity, the Mormon millennial world view remained intact. "There seems to be Power or Influence exerted against every thing the Saints take in hand to do," Joseph Fielding commiserated, and once again a siege mentality developed where all "gentiles" became the enemy.[51] At Nauvoo Mormon dualism reached new heights with both leaders and laymen pleading for divine liberation: "The brethren united in solemn prayer that God ... would deliver His anointed, His people, from all the vile designs of Governor Boggs, and the powers of the State of Missouri, and of Governor Carlin and the authorities of Illinois, and of all Presidents, Governors, Judges, Legislators and all in authority."[52] Although Satan had fought the people of God throughout history, in the latter days all persecution would converge on the Saints; opposition merely underscored the restored gospel's distinctiveness.[53]

Some writers maintain that Mormon millenarian theology evolved, viewing the migration from Ohio to Missouri to Illinois as evidence that Mormons concentrated more on a place than a time.[54]

Quest for Refuge, 120-22.

50. Hill, *Quest for Refuge,* 133. See also Robert Flanders, "The Kingdom of God in Illinois: Politics in Utopia," *Dialogue: A Journal of Mormon Thought* 5 (Spring 1970): 31.

51. Ehat, "'They Might Have Known that He Was Not a Fallen Prophet,'" 143. See also p. 148.

52. Smith, *History of the Church,* 5:45.

53. *Times and Seasons* 3 (15 Oct. 1842): 951-52.

54. William Mulder, "Mormonism's 'Gathering': An American Doctrine with a Difference," *Church History* 23 (Sept. 1954): 252; Ernest R. Sandeen, *The Roots of Fundamentalism: British and American Millenarianism, 1800-1930* (Chicago: University of Chicago Press, 1970), 48; Norman, "How Long, O Lord?" 51; Flanders, "Dream and Nightmare," 151.

In Nauvoo Joseph Smith may have prolonged his predicted apocalyptic end of the world. Due to the intensity of millennial anticipation, in April 1843 Smith publicly warned followers to resist falling prey to the emotion of Parousia expectation epitomized by William Miller whose initial ominous day of judgement had recently failed to occur.[55] At this point Smith prophesied "in the name of the Lord God, and let it be written—the son of man will not come in the clouds of heaven till I am eighty-five years old."[56] Smith's 1843 prophecy

---

55. Kenney, *Wilford Woodruff's Journal*, 2:365-66, 10 Mar. 1844; Smith, *History of the Church*, 5:326. Based on Jewish calendars, the year 1843 suggested two dates (21 March or 3 April) which Millerites believed would usher in Christ's return. When the expected return did not occur in 1843, the so-called first disappointment, the date for the Second Advent was recalculated to 22 October 1844. See Jonathan Butler, "From Millerism to Seventh-Day Adventism: 'Boundlessness to Consolidation,'" *Church History* 55 (Mar. 1986): 55; Michael Barkun, *Crucible of the Millennium: The Burned-Over District of New York in the 1840s* (Syracuse: Syracuse University Press, 1986), 31-46; Harrison, *The Second Coming*, 193-95. Mormons and Millerites, as apocalyptic, proselyting, and millennial groups, had numerous confrontations. See Grant Underwood, "Apocalyptic Adversaries: Mormonism Meets Millerism," *John Whitmer Historical Association Journal* 7 (1987): 53-61. John Taylor, "Millerism," *Times and Seasons* 4 (15 Feb. 1843): 103-105, criticized "the false foundation upon which Mr. Miller rests his fabric," and declared it "exposed in all its naked deformity."

56. Smith, *History of the Church*, 5:336; Scott H. Faulring, ed., *An American Prophet's Record: The Diaries and Journals of Joseph Smith* (1987; reprint, Salt Lake City: Signature Books in association with Smith Research Associates, 1989), 343, 6 Apr. 1843; Ehat and Cook, *The Words of Joseph Smith*, 179, 6 Apr. 1843. Smith had made the same prophecy four days earlier at a conference in Ramus, Illinois. See Faulring, *An American Prophet's Record*, 340, 2 Apr. 1843; Smith, *An Intimate Chronicle*, 95, 2 Apr. 1843. Clayton recorded the prophecy to state that Smith would be eighty-four years old. Saints deduced Smith would turn eighty-five on 23 December 1890, thus making 1890-91 the appointed time. See "James Burgess Notebook," in Ehat and Cook, *The Words of Joseph Smith*, 334, 10 Mar. 1844; Frankin D. Richards, "Scriptural Items," ibid., 181, 6 Apr. 1843; "Joseph Smith Diary," by Willard Richards, ibid., 179-80, 6 Apr. 1843.

merely substantiated a previous 1835 prophecy in which Smith proclaimed, "Even fifty-six years shall wind up the scene."[57]

Although Smith's statements appeared to push the Millennium
to the end of the century, the Saints' thirst for a divine deliverance
refused to be quenched, and from the pulpit church leaders continued to proclaim that there were still "those of the rising generation who shall not taste death till Christ comes."[58] "I prophesy, in
the name of the Lord God of Israel," Smith declared, "anguish and
wrath and tribulation and the withdrawing of the Spirit of God
from the earth await this generation, until they are visited with
utter desolation."[59] The extended timetable would simply provide
time for the Mormon kingdom to reach its apex prior to Christ's
return.[60]

As tensions grew in 1843-44, Mormon millenarian hope intensified to where "every mob, riot, and national division echoed the hoof
beats of the four horsemen."[61] The powers exercised by Nauvoo
officials under the auspices of their city charter became a political
liability with a significant amount of pressure bearing on politicians
to rescind the legal barriers encircling Nauvoo. In early 1843 a repeal
of the city charter was narrowly defeated in the state legislature and

---

57. The "eighty-five year" prophecy appeared in canon form for the
first time in the *Doctrine and Covenants'* 1876 edition. The fifty-six-year
prophecy is found in Smith, *History of the Church*, 2:182. Richard Lloyd
Anderson has explained that Smith's fifty-six-year prophecy was intended to
be "merely [Smith's] opinion" rather than prophetic revelation. See
Anderson, "Joseph Smith and the Millenarian Time Table," *Brigham Young
University Studies* 3 (1961): 57. Whether or not Joseph Smith's two millennial
proclamations were indeed revelation is immaterial. What is important is that
in the late nineteenth century the Saints believed them to be prophetic
declarations and acted on that belief. See also Jessee, "Joseph Smith's 19 July
1840 Discourse," 393, where Smith declares the Millennium is at least forty
years away.

58. Smith, *History of the Church*, 5:336.

59. Ibid., 6:58.

60. Ibid., 6:254.

61. Winn, *Exiles in a Land of Liberty*, 184.

Nauvoo's legal independence became a rallying cry for both sides.[62] In June Smith declared,

> If our enemies are determined to oppress us & deprive us of our rights & privileges as they have done & if the Authorities that be on earth will not assist us in our rights nor give us that protection which the Laws & Constitution of the United States & of this State garrentees unto us: then we will claim them from higher power from heaven & from God Almighty.[63]

Responding to anti-Mormon sentiments, by mid-1843 Smith's rhetoric became more belligerent, more militaristic. Insinuating an appeal to arms, he proclaimed, "If I [am] under the necessity of giving up our chart[er]ed rights, privileges & freedom ... I will do it at the point of the Bayonet & Sword."[64]

Earlier the apostolic missionary force had been called to return "immediately home for our personal Safety, as great Judgements are nigh in this land even at the Door."[65] And speaking to Stephen A. Douglas, Joseph Smith had chided the United States for refusing to redress the Saints' Missouri injustices and predicted that "in a few years the government will be utterly overthrown and wasted."[66] In the same vein, on 16 December 1843 Smith declared to the Nauvoo City Council, "I prophecy by virtue of the Holy Priesthood vested in me [and] in the name of Jesus Christ that if Congress will not hear our petition and grant us protection they shall be broken up as a government and God shall damn them. There shall nothing be left of them, not even a grease spot."[67]

Smith then began a candidacy for the presidency of the United

---

62. Kimball, "The Nauvoo Charter," 66-78; Godfrey, "Causes of Mormon Non-Mormon Conflict in Hancock County, Illinois," 133-53; Hill, *Quest for Refuge*, 123-25; Flanders, *Nauvoo*, 285.

63. Kenney, *Wilford Woodruff's Journal*, 2:249, 30 June 1843.

64. Ibid., 2:251, 30 June 1843.

65. Ibid., 2:47, 15 Feb. 1841. See also 2:62-63, 15 Mar. 1841; 2:118, 22 Aug. 1841.

66. Smith, *History of the Church*, 5:394.

67. In Quinn, *The Mormon Hierarchy: Origins of Power*, 641.

States. He justified this as a last-ditch hope to save the union.[68] "If I ever get into the Presidential chair," he said, "I will protect the people in their rights and liberties."[69] "The plans of the greatest politicians, the wisest senators, and the most profound statesmen" would all come to naught. "It has been the design of Jehovah, from the commencement of the world, and is his purpose now, to regulate the affairs of the world in his own time; to stand as the head of the universe, and take the reigns of government into his own hands."[70]

After years of persecution the Saints had lost hope that America would repent. Anarchy was expected soon to engulf the nation with only the Saints able to offer a solution based on true principles of virtue and freedom. When the world headed into chaos prior to the Millennium, the righteous would flock to the Mormon theocracy. Mormons would not redeem the promised land of America by sword but merely be there to pick up the pieces as the Almighty slew the unrighteous.[71]

If elected, Smith intended to combine state and religion and give certainty to the nation much as he had done for the church and as God had done in the Old Testament.[72] The "Church must not triumph over [the] State," he declared, "but actually swallow it up like Moses' rod swallowed up the rods of the Egyptians."[73] Smith counted

---

68. Smith's presidential platform is given in Smith, *History of the Church*, 6:197-209.

69. Faulring, *An American Prophet's Record*, 443, 28 Jan. 1844; *Times and Seasons* 5 (1 June 1844): 556-57. Smith's presidential candidacy was publicly announced in ibid., 5 (15 Feb. 1844): 441. See also Smith, *History of the Church*, 6:188.

70. *Times and Seasons* 3 (15 July 1842): 855-56. See also Sidney Rigdon's 5 April 1844 conference address in Smith, *History of the Church*, 6:292.

71. Winn, *Exiles in a Land of Liberty*, 190-92.

72. Kenney, *Wilford Woodruff's Journal*, 2:378, 6 Apr. 1844; Smith, *History of the Church*, 6:322; Robert Flanders, "To Transfer History: Early Mormon Culture and the Concept of Time and Space," *Church History* 40 (Mar. 1971): 115-16; Winn, *Exiles in a Land of Liberty*, 199-204.

73. *Times and Seasons* 5 (15 Mar. 1844): 477.

on the Lord to turn the hearts of the people as his means of winning the presidency.[74] He then petitioned Congress to portion off Nauvoo as a separate federal district with Smith commanding the Nauvoo Legion, converted to federal troops, to defend the city.[75]

In the spring of 1844 Smith formally organized a theocratic assembly termed the "Council of Fifty" to govern the Saints until the resurrection. Its stated purpose was "to organize the political kingdom of God in preparation for the second coming of Christ."[76] The council was the beginning of the hoped-for world government headquartered in Nauvoo which would "become the greatest city in the whole world."[77] With political separation from mainstream America complete, Joseph Smith was anointed, ordained, and crowned "King on earth."[78]

Outside Illinois Mormons taught the new religion's elementary

---

74. Kenney, *Wilford Woodruff's Journal*, 2:357-59, 7 Mar. 1844; Flanders, *Nauvoo*, 301.

75. Smith, *History of the Church*, 6:130-32.

76. Kenney, *Wilford Woodruff's Journal*, 2:366, 11 Mar. 1844; Smith, *An Intimate Chronicle*, 159, 10 Mar. 1845; *Church History in the Fullness of Times* (Salt Lake City: Church of Jesus Christ of Latter-day Saints, 1989), 270.

77. Jessee, "Joseph Smith's 19 July 1840 Discourse," 393; Robert Flanders, "The Kingdom of God in Illinois: Politics in Utopia," *Dialogue: A Journal of Mormon Thought* 5 (Spring 1970): 26-36; Winn, *Exiles in a Land of Liberty*, 194-96; Hansen, *Quest for Empire*, 11, 60-61; Andrew F. Ehat, "Joseph Smith's Introduction of Temple Ordinances and the 1844 Mormon Succession Question," M.A. thesis, Brigham Young University, 1981, 156-57. Smith was also entertaining the possibility of a Mormon kingdom in Texas, Oregon, or California. See Faulring, *An American Prophet's Record*, 447, 20 Feb. 1844.

78. George Miller, in Godfrey, "Causes of Mormon Non-Mormon Conflict in Hancock County, Illinois," 64; Ford, *A History of Illinois*, 2:155-57; Hansen, *Quest for Empire*, 73; D. Michael Quinn, "The Council of Fifty and Its Members, 1844-1945," *Brigham Young University Studies* 20 (Winter 1980): 163-97; Andrew F. Ehat, "'It Seems Like Heaven on Earth': Joseph Smith and the Constitution of the Kingdom of God," *Brigham Young University Studies* 20 (Spring 1980): 253-79; Hill, *Quest for Refuge*, 140-41; Quinn, The *Mormon Hierarchy: Origins of Power*, 124; Flanders, *Nauvoo*, 292.

tenets. Only in the safety of refuge at Nauvoo could the fullness of Mormonism, including polygamy, theocracy, and the political kingdom of God, be revealed.[79] Here, in their pursuit of a new social order, the early Saints challenged economics (capitalism), politics (democracy), and religious (new scripture and priesthood) norms of society, directly assaulting the basic American belief system. As such, overt empire building was not necessary for violent conflict.[80] The *St. Louis New Era* identified the Saints' clannishness and theocratic isolationalism as the root cause of Mormon conflict in general. When they moved to Illinois, "instead of trying to form a component part of the community, ... [the Mormons] set themselves up as a separate people, peculiar for holiness and the favor of heaven, and ... branded all others as Gentiles. This array and separation on their part, soon caused a counter array on the part of all other citizens."[81]

As knowledge of the church hierarchy's secret polygamous unions became more difficult to hide, internal dissent and external anti-Mormon forces converged.[82] Prominent members, including First Presidency counselor William Law, rejected Smith's rule and established an independent press in Nauvoo which advocated repealing the Nauvoo charter. When these dissidents laid before the public Smith's polygamy doctrine, alluded to his coronation, and pronounced their refusal to "acknowledge any man as king or law-

---

79. Sarah S. Scott to My dear Father and Mother, 6 Feb. 1845, in Mulder and Mortensen, *Among the Mormons*, 154; Ford, *A History of Illinois*, 2:219-21; Winn, *Exiles in a Land of Liberty*, 223; R. Laurence Moore, *Religious Outsiders and the Making of Americans* (New York: Oxford University Press, 1986), 36; Leonard J. Arrington and Davis Bitton, *The Mormon Experience: A History of the Latter-day Saints*, 2d ed. (Urbana: University of Illinois Press, 1992), 69; Hansen, *Quest for Empire*, 54.

80. Hill, "The 'Prophet Puzzle' Assembled," 103-104.

81. In Winn, *Exiles in a Land of Liberty*, 221. See also Ford, *A History of Illinois*, 2:42; Godfrey, "Causes of Mormon Non-Mormon Conflict in Hancock County, Illinois," 199-201.

82. Smith, *History of the Church*, 6:210.

giver to the church," internal and outside factions, with no appetite for retreat, intersected.[83]

The "spiritual wife" issue created both internal solidarity among Mormons and served as a rallying point for anti-Mormons declaring their moral indignation at such lawlessness. Mormonism's hidden polygamy became a symbol of the Mormon-gentile struggle and solidified anti-Mormon cohesiveness behind a shield of ethical wrath.[84] Some members involved in the secret practice of polygamy were subsequently initiated into a newly established "Holy Order" that expanded the temple ritual. This only further isolated Smith and other church leaders from non-Mormons and the general membership of their own church who knew nothing of Smith's polygamy and elite temple rites.[85]

---

83. *Nauvoo Expositor* 1 (7 June 1844); Richard S. Van Wagoner, *Mormon Polygamy: A History* (Salt Lake City: Signature Books, 1989), 63-65; Hansen, *Quest for Empire*, 158.

84. Paul Wilbur Tappan, "Mormon-Gentile Conflict: A Study of the Influence of Public Opinion on In-Group Versus Out-Group Interaction with Special Reference to Polygamy," Ph.D. diss., University of Wisconsin, 1939, 420. See also Danel W. Bachman, "A Study of the Mormon Practice of Plural Marriage Before the Death of Joseph Smith," M.A. thesis, Purdue University, 1975, 261-97; Van Wagoner, *Mormon Polygamy*, 63-72; Godfrey, "Causes of Mormon Non-Mormon Conflict in Hancock County, Illinois," 111. The first major public exposure of Smith's secret polygamy doctrine was initially published in serial form in the Illinois press, and is found in John C. Bennett, *The History of the Saints, or an Exposé of Joe Smith and Mormonism* (Boston: Leland and Whiting, 1842).

85. D. Michael Quinn, "Latter-day Saints Prayer Circle," *Brigham Young University Studies* 19 (Fall 1978): 79-105; Quinn, *The Mormon Hierarchy: Origins of Power*, 113-17; David John Buerger, "The Second Anointing in Latter-day Saint Theology and Practice," *Dialogue: A Journal of Mormon Thought* 16 (Spring 1983): 16-22; George D. Smith, "Nauvoo Roots of Mormon Polygamy, 1841-46: A Preliminary Demographic Report," *Dialogue: A Journal of Mormon Thought* 27 (Spring 1994): 1-72. The secret practice of polygamy and the duplicity surrounding it are expanded in D. Michael Quinn, "LDS Church Authority and New Plural Marriages, 1890-1904," *Dialogue: A Journal of Mormon Thought* 18 (Spring 1985): 19-23; Van Wagoner, *Mormon Polygamy*, 19-62; Bachman, "The Study of the Mormon Practice of Plural Marriage,"

As the "Prophet," Smith had always been at the center of Mormon controversy. At Nauvoo, in his multiple roles of mayor, lieutenant-general of the Nauvoo Legion, municipal court justice, and president of the church, he was seen by his enemies as a theocratic dictator.[86] First from non-Mormons outside Nauvoo, then from fellow Mormons who focussed on his plural wife doctrine, Smith's detractors labeled him a fallen if not false prophet, and demanded that he "acknowledge publicly that he had taught and practiced the doctrine of plurality of wives ... and that he should own the whole system (revelation and all) to be from Hell."[87] Less than two months after his murder, Smith's widow, an admitted foe of polygamy, confided to William Clayton that she believed it was these "secret things which had cost Joseph and Hyrum [Smith] their lives."[88] When Smith repeatedly called out the Nauvoo Legion in response to armed aggression against the city, any hope of a Mormon-non-Mormon middle ground disintegrated.[89]

Vigilantism was not a novel approach to justice on the American frontier.[90] Previous calls to arms had been rhetorically justified by both sides, but particularly by an anti-Mormon sense of legal impotence. "When a Government ceases to afford protection," they held, "the citizens of course fall back upon their original inherent right to self-defense."[91] Although destroying a newspaper was not a unique

---

176-217.

86. Ehat, "'They Might Have Known that He Was Not a Fallen Prophet,'" 154; *Times and Seasons* 4 (15 Feb. 1843): 99-100; Smith, *History of the Church*, 6:3; William Mulder, *The Mormons in American History* (1957; reprint, Salt Lake City: University of Utah Press, 1981), 28.

87. William Law Diary, 13 May 1844, in Lyndon W. Cook, "William Law, Nauvoo Dissenter," *Brigham Young University Studies* 22 (Winter 1982): 68. See Smith, *History of the Church*, 5:510-12, for Smith's admission, as early as July 1843, that internal dissent was once again raising its head in the church. See also Flanders, *Nauvoo*, 243.

88. Smith, *An Intimate Chronicle*, 144, 15 Aug. 1844.

89. Smith, *History of the Church*, 6:113, 119-21, 153.

90. Ford, *A History of Illinois*, 2:42.

91. See "Preamble and Resolution" (anti-Mormon meeting at Carth-

event, when enacted by Mormons in Nauvoo and viewed as an ecclesiastical rather than a civil act, it played into the hands of their enemies.[92] Smith's order as mayor to destroy the *Nauvoo Expositor* led to his arrest, and once in the custody of bitter anti-Mormons who became judge, jury, and executioners, his murder, if not predictable, was not inconceivable.[93]

The death of their beloved prophet amounted to the ultimate sacrifice required of God's people and created a leadership vacuum and an eschatological crisis.[94] With the Millennium's imminence, the Saints had not contemplated the need for a successor.[95] In the language of an 1837 revelation, Christ had vested in Smith "keys which ... shall not be taken from him till I come."[96] As Apos-

age, Illinois), 6 Sept. 1843, in Smith, *History of the Church*, 6:4-8.

92. Ford, *A History of Illinois*, 2:162; Dallin H. Oaks and Marvin S. Hill, *Carthage Conspiracy: The Trial of the Accused Assassins of Joseph Smith* (1975; reprint, Urbana: University of Illinois Press, 1979), 6-29. Dallin Oaks affirms that "there was no legal justification in 1844 for the destruction of the *Expositor* press as a nuisance." See Dallin H. Oaks, "The Suppression of the *Nauvoo Expositor*," *Utah Law Review* 9 (Winter 1965): 891.

93. Faulring, *An American Prophet's Record*, 490, 11 June 1844; Smith, *History of the Church*, 6:432-52; Keith Huntress, "The Murder of Joseph Smith," in *Mormonism and American Culture*, eds. Marvin S. Hill and James B. Allen (New York: Harper and Row, 1972), 77; Flanders, "Dream and Nightmare," 157-59; Flanders, *Nauvoo*, 306-307; Roger D. Launius, "The Murders in Carthage: Non-Mormon Reports of the Assassination of the Smith Brothers," *John Whitmer Historical Association Journal* 15 (1995): 17-34.

94. *Times and Seasons* 5 (15 Dec. 1844): 743-44; Linda King Newel and Valeen Tippetts Avery, *Mormon Enigma: Emma Hale Smith, Prophet's Wife, "Elect Lady," Polygamy's Foe, 1804-1879* (Garden City, NY: Doubleday and Co., 1984), 197-202; Hill, *Quest for Refuge*, 154-55; D. Michael Quinn, "Joseph Smith III's Blessing and the Mormons of Utah," *Dialogue: A Journal of Mormon Thought* 15 (Summer 1982): 80; Richard S. Van Wagoner, "The Making of a Mormon Myth: The 1844 Transfiguration of Brigham Young," *Dialogue: A Journal of Mormon Thought* 28 (Winter 1995): 1-24.

95. Sarah Scott to Calvin and Abigail Hall, 22 July 1844, in Mulder and Mortensen, *Among the Mormons*, 152-53; Flanders, *Nauvoo*, 311; Hansen, *Quest for Empire*, 106; Norman, "How Long, O Lord?" 52.

96. Smith, *History of the Church*, 2:500.

tle Erastus Snow related, most early Mormons "supposed that our Prophet was going to continue with us, to lead us on until the coming of the Savior."[97] Brigham Young's "Epistle of the Twelve," published in the Mormon press, attempted to placate the church. "You are now without a prophet present with you in the flesh to guide you," said Young, "but you are not without apostles, who hold the keys of power to seal on earth that which shall be sealed in heaven, and to preside over all the affairs of the church in all the world."[98]

The reality of a delayed parousia forced the former apocalyptics to focus on an extended timetable.[99] Yet even with Smith's death, the issues which created Mormon society's incompatibility with their neighbors persisted, and the prospect of a peaceful "Zion" within the borders of Babylon remained an impossibility.[100] Those who united under Brigham Young's leadership were forced to turn inward as a defense mechanism.[101] Climaxing with Smith's murder, persecution created a tightly woven, cohesive sect with a group consciousness that reaffirmed its own system and identity. As such, church leaders hurried completion of the Nauvoo temple so that large numbers of members could receive their sacred ordinances.[102] Whereas separatist doctrines and practices had created Mormon-gentile boundaries leading to violence, in leaving Nauvoo Mormons became a more distinct people possibly evolving into a novel culture.[103]

---

97. *Deseret Evening News,* 9 Oct. 1882, in Quinn, *The Mormon Hierarchy: Origins of Power,* 144.

98. *Times and Seasons* 5 (15 Aug. 1844): 618.

99. Underwood, *The Millenarian World of Early Mormonism,* 14.

100. O'Dea, *The Mormons,* 73-75; Hill, *Quest for Refuge,* 167-68.

101. The twelve apostles' leadership was officially sustained by a majority of church members in the April 1845 general conference. See *Times and Seasons* 6 (15 Apr. 1845): 869-70.

102. *Times and Seasons* 6 (1 Nov. 1845): 1017-19; 6 (15 July 1845): 971; 6 (1 Aug. 1845): 987; Smith, *History of the Church,* 7:479-80; Hill, *Quest for Refuge,* 173.

103. MacMurray and Cunningham, "Mormons and Gentiles," 215-16;

Following the death of the Mormon prophet, a lull in anti-Mormon persecution proved temporary. By the fall of 1844 a renewed effort to drive the church from the state ensued. In January 1845 the state legislature revoked Nauvoo's charter, thus removing the last remnant of Mormon independence.[104] Finally, when it became obvious that Mormonism's fundamental differences would never allow the church to co-exist side-by-side with mainstream America, Governor Thomas Ford and Brigham Young agreed on a planned Mormon departure.[105]

Due to the Saints' fierce millennialism, the new outbreak of anti-Mormonism in 1845 was seen as further persecution. Although denouncing violence, the Saints took it as another "sign of the times." With the loss of the Nauvoo charter and continued violence due to impotent protection from the state, the last year and a half at Nauvoo witnessed a new round of Mormon-anti-American rhetorical conflict. Predicting the demise of the American constitutional system, church leaders' rebukes fell "upon their enemies, upon the country, upon government, [and] upon all public officers."[106] Apostle Orson Pratt proclaimed,

It is with the greatest joy that I forsake this Republic; and all the Saints have abundant reasons to rejoice that they are counted worthy to be cast out as exiles from this wicked nation ... If our heavenly father will preserve us, and deliver us out of the hands of the blood thirsty christians of these United States, and not suffer any more of us to [be] martyred to gratify holy piety, I for one shall be very thankful.[107]

But for Mormons the prophesied end of the United States heralded

---

Jan Shipps, *Mormonism: The Story of a New Religious Tradition* (Urbana: University of Illinois Press, 1985), 59-60.

104. Flanders, *Nauvoo*, 322-24.

105. Kenney, *Wilford Woodruff's Journal*, 2:616, 18 Nov. 1845; Ford, *A History of Illinois*, 2:301-302; Klaus J. Hansen, *Mormonism and the American Experience* (Chicago: University of Chicago Press, 1981), 139.

106. Ford, *A History of Illinois*, 2:224.

107. *Times and Seasons* 6 (1 Dec. 1845): 1042-43.

a new world, and this millennial hope gave them the strength to endure their current hardship. The abandonment of Nauvoo, the once great Mormon bastion and site of their majestic temple, further isolated an already alienated people.[108] "The State of Illinois And the whole United States have filled up their Cup of Iniquity," wrote Apostle Wilford Woodruff,

> And well may the Saints go out of her midst As did Lot out of Sodom for her Judgement and destruction is equally sure. The Saints having built the Temple of the Lord & the City of Joseph Are now about to be drove out of it by the American Nation. ... The Bible & Book of Mormon Doctrins & Covenants are fast fulfilling upon the heads of this generation.[109]

Explaining the forced exodus as part of God's plan, Brigham Young declared "a new epoch, not only in the history of the church but of this nation" had arrived.[110] As the last days approached, turmoil and persecution meant God's words were about to be fulfilled, deliverance of the Saints was nigh.[111] "There is nothing but Mormonism that will save this generation from wickedness and ruin. Now mark it; [if] fifty years find this nation prosperous without Mormonism, Joseph Smith was a false prophet, and there is no God."[112]

Although Young steadily re-channeled apocalyptic energies toward the new religion's literal survival, the hope of a millennial deliverance persisted.[113] In January 1846 Apostle Heber C. Kimball prayed in the Nauvoo temple that the twelve apostles, their wives, and all of the Saints might live to "see three score years and ten, and behold the kingdom of God established in the earth."[114] God

---

108. Flanders, *Nauvoo*, 209.

109. Kenney, *Wilford Woodruff's Journal*, 2:616-17, 18 Nov. 1845.

110. Smith, *History of the Church*, 7:478.

111. *Times and Seasons* 6 (1 Aug. 1845): 983.

112. *Nauvoo Neighbor*, 11 Dec. 1844, in Winn, *Exiles in a Land of Liberty*, 234.

113. John Gager, *Kingdom and Community: The Social World of Early Christianity* (Englewood Cliffs, NJ: Prentice-Hall, 1975), 67.

114. Smith, *History of the Church*, 7:560.

still promised, even as the Saints left the United States for the desert, that "my arm is stretched out in the last days, to save my people Israel."[115]

Fleeing Babylon, Young led his people out of captivity and away from violence, fulfilling the Lord's promise to remove "the fullness of the gospel" from the midst of they who rejected him (3 Ne. 16:10). By driving the church into the wilderness, the gentiles "turned the last key which seals their Condemnation," said Apostle Wilford Woodruff. "*Wo, Wo, Wo* is their DOOM."[116] But the struggle with American society not only compelled the Saints to leave the United States, it created a "peculiar people" who now became a nation, like Israel of old, identified as God's chosen in the latter-days, part of his divine plan and sacred history.[117] The forced exodus now pointed them to the West where they would be led to a new promised land, a place prepared for their safety and refuge. Here, separated from a corrupt gentile society, they would patiently await Christ's call to usher in his millennial reign.

By gathering in separate communities, the Saints not only symbolized but actuated their withdrawal from the secular world.[118] Mormons saw their trail of persecution—Missouri, Ohio, and Illinois—as following an ancient pattern of the wicked persecuting the Saints

---

115. *Doctrine and Covenants of the Church of Jesus Christ of Latter-day Saints* (Salt Lake City: Church of Jesus Christ of Latter-day Saints, 1981), 136:22.

116. Kenney, *Wilford Woodruff's Journal*, 3:378, 18 Oct. 1848, emphasis in original.

117. Winn, *Exiles in a Land of Liberty*, 78, 236; Ephraim Edward Ericksen, *The Psychological and Ethical Aspects of Mormon Group Life* (1922; reprint, University of Utah Press, 1975), 29-31. Patricia Nelson Limerick contends that while membership in the Mormon church, with its own economic, social, and familiar patterns, laid the foundation for the creation of a new culture or subculture, the forced exodus created a "seperate peoplehood" leading to a unique Mormon "ethnicity." See Limerick, "Peace Initiative: Using the Mormons to Rethink Culture and Ethnicity in American History," *Journal of Mormon History* 21 (Fall 1995): 17-19.

118. MacMurray and Cunningham, "Mormons and Gentiles," 206.

of God. Their temporary achievements in Kirtland, Jackson County, Far West, and Nauvoo were preludes to the building of God's kingdom on earth.[119]

Mormonism's aspirations, founded on millenarian literalism and cultivated by expansionist intent, were based on a vision of theocratic bliss. Although the Mormon ideal of social, economic, religious, and political spheres under one leader ran counter to American ideals, it was the political/military aspect of their anti-pluralism which led to the greatest non-Mormon concerns. The idea of an exclusive body of religious zealots, trained and armed, with apocalyptic conviction and its own beliefs and ethics, brought fear to the hearts of outsiders.[120]

The desire for unity arose from early Mormonism's millennial expectations. The increased need for protection and autonomy under their own sovereign rule was reinforced by ongoing persecutions which became self-fulfilling prophecies.[121] In Nauvoo Smith's demand for independence and control propelled him to the position of prophet, judge, mayor, and military commander. As the peril increased, he tightened the reins of command. Mormon-intimidating rhetoric, backed by political solidarity, fed both internal dissent and external threat.[122] When anti-Mormon forces murdered Joseph Smith and drove the church from Illinois, the Saints' millennial expectations were confirmed. Rejected by the nation, they were now content to leave Babylon to God's judgement.

---

119. *Times and Seasons* 2 (15 Sep. 1841): 546.

120. Nathan O. Hatch, "Mormon and Methodist: Popular Religion in the Crucible of the Free Market," *Journal of Mormon History* 20 (Spring 1994): 40.

121. Hill, *Quest for Refuge*, xiv.

122. O'Dea, *The Mormons*, 113.

1. Joseph Smith, Mormonism's founding prophet.

2. Stained-glass representation of Joseph Smith's first vision experience which initiated Mormonism's millennial world view. The resurrected Christ proclaimed to Smith, "[L]o I come quickly ... in the glory of my Father." (*Joseph Smith's First Vision,* from the Adams Ward meeting house, Los Angeles, California; maker unknown, 1913; copyright The Church of Jesus Christ of Latter-day Saints; used by permission.)

3. The angel Moroni delivering to Joseph Smith the plates from which the Book of Mormon was derived. Moroni warned Smith, "[B]ehold the day cometh that shall burn as an oven, and all the proud, yea, and all that do wickedly shall burn as stubble." *(The Angel Moroni delivering the plates of the Book of Mormon to Joseph Smith, Jr.,* by C. C. A. Christensen, 1886; copyright The Church of Jesus Christ of Latter-day Saints; used by permission.)

4. The Book of Mormon, first published in 1830. To Joseph Smith and his followers, its purpose was "to be united with the Bible for the accomplishment of the purposes of God in the last days."

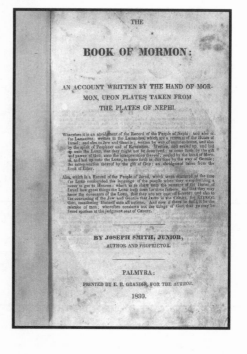

5. The Book of Commandments, the first published compilation of Joseph Smith's revelations, included a number of pronouncements which centered on the Second Advent, the coming Millennium, and the building up of the New Jerusalem.

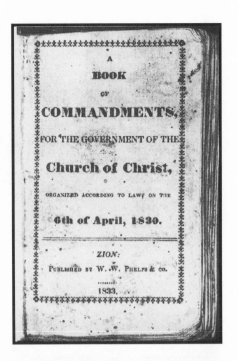

6. The Kirtland temple, ca. 1907. Early Mormons viewed the move to Kirtland, Ohio, as the beginning of the long-awaited gathering of Israel, signaling Christ's return. The temple ceremony, initiated at Kirtland, linked the Saints to the spirit world and supported their continued belief in an imminent millennium.

7. (*above*) Lieutenant-General Joseph Smith addressing the Nauvoo Legion. At Nauvoo Smith combined in one man the roles of prophet, mayor, commander of the armed forces, and municipal judge, merging public, military, and priesthood leadership positions. (*General Joseph Smith addressing the Nauvoo Legion,* by Robert Campbell, 1845; copyright The Church of Jesus Christ of Latter-day Saints; used by permission.)

8. (*left*) An 1844 flyer publicizing Joseph Smith's candidacy for the presidency of the United States which he considered a last-ditch effort to save the Union. The "church must not triumph over [the] state," he declared, "but actually swallow it up like Moses' rod swallowed up the rods of the Egyptians."

9. LDS church president Brigham Young. After the removal west, under Young's leadership a preoccupation with the destruction of the world and the coming of Christ remained a major theme in Mormon thought.

10. The First Presidency and Council of Twelve Apostles, 1884-85. Rather than give up the institution of polygamy, many church leaders went into hiding. Church president John Taylor died while in exile on the "underground." (Courtesy Utah State Historical Society; used by permission; all rights reserved.)

11. First Presidency counselor George Q. Cannon (center) and other polygamists, including Apostle Francis M. Lyman (second from right), incarcerated in 1889 for their plural unions. (Courtesy Utah State Historical Society; used by permission; all rights reserved.)

12. The First Presidency of the LDS church, 1889-98: *(left to right)* George Q. Cannon, Wilford Woodruff, and Joseph F. Smith.

14. The First Presidency and Council of the Twelve at the end of the nineteenth century (September 1898). Back row, left to right: Anthon H. Lund (1844-1921), John W. Taylor (1858-1916), John Henry Smith (1848-1911), Heber J. Grant (1856-1945), Marriner W. Merrill (1832-1906). Middle row: Brigham Young, Jr. (1836-1903), First Counselor George Q. Cannon (1827-1901), President Lorenzo Snow (1814-1901), Second Counselor Joseph F. Smith (1838-1918), Franklin D. Richards (1821-99). Front row: Matthias F. Cowley (1858-1940), Abraham Owen Woodruff (1872-1904). (Courtesy Utah State Historical Society; used by permission; all rights reserved.)

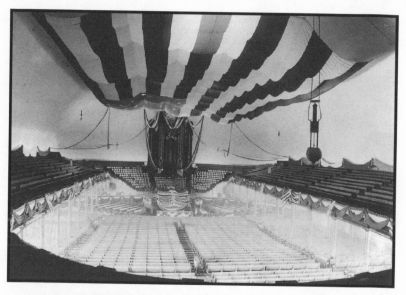

13. The American flag drapes seats in the Salt Lake Tabernacle in 1896 in celebration of Utah's statehood. The abandonment of polygamy, church control over political and economic institutions, and the immediacy of a millennial peace were all casualties of assimilation into the dominant American culture. As such, the Millennium became a fixture event rather than an imminent reality.

CHAPTER SEVEN

MORMONS VERSUS THE UNITED STATES: THE UTAH WAR AND CIVIL WAR PERIODS

Following earlier patterns, the cyclical nature of Mormon millennial expectations continued after Nauvoo.[1] The Saints believed calamity and destruction were necessary prior to the peace offered by the Millennium. The intensity of millennial hope increased with rumors of war and worldwide natural disasters, as well as in proportion to the perceived pressures on the church.[2] As conditions became difficult, church members' thoughts would turn towards heaven for relief. They viewed persecution as proof that the day of the Lord was at hand and looked for Christ's return.[3]

Mormonism's revolt against America's unwritten denominational

---

1. Therald N. Jensen, "Mormon Theory of Church and State," Ph.D. diss., University of Chicago, 1938, 67-68; Louis G. Reinwand, "An Interpretive Study of Mormon Millennialism During the Nineteenth Century with Emphasis on Millennial Developments in Utah," M.A. thesis, Brigham Young University, 1971, 11; and Klaus J. Hansen, *Quest for Empire: The Political Kingdom of God and the Council of Fifty in Mormon History* (Lansing: Michigan State University Press, 1970), 22.

2. Thomas G. Alexander, "Wilford Woodruff and the Changing Nature of Mormon Religious Experience," *Church History* 45 (Mar. 1976): 65.

3. John M. Werly, "Premillennialism and the Paranoid Style," *American Studies* 18 (Spring 1977): 40.

compact (voluntarism and pluralism) was only able to survive because, at the time, the nation had geographical space to accommodate social and political dissenters.[4] In the West Brigham Young's goal was to create a city on a hill in the wilderness of the Great Basin, a place where the chosen of God would grow and eventually overcome America both spiritually and physically.[5]

Although forced to battle the desert elements, politically the church's first ten years in Utah Territory remained relatively peaceful. Physically separated from non-Mormon society, Young was able to implement Mormonism's total theology to a greater extent than ever could have occurred in locales close to mainstream American culture.[6] To the Saints in transplanted Zion, Utah Territory provided a sanctuary from Babylon under the guidance of God's modern mouthpiece. Mormons believed that the Almighty had held this place in reserve for a society set on ushering in the Millennium.[7]

---

4. D. W. Meinig, "The Mormon Nation and the American Empire," *Journal of Mormon History* 22 (Spring 1996): 41-45.

5. "Theocracy—God's Solution of the Social Problem," *Millennial Star* 18 (23 Feb. 1856): 113-19; "The Kingdom of God," ibid., 16 (1 Apr. 1854): 193; John Taylor, *Journal of Discourses*, 26 vols. (Liverpool, Eng.: F.D. Richards, 1855-86), 1:225-30, 8 Apr. 1853; Alfred Cordon, ibid., 2:39, 6 Apr. 1853; Heber C. Kimball, ibid., 6:133, 20 Dec. 1857; Heber C. Kimball, ibid., 4:340, 7 June 1857; Orson Pratt, ibid., 2:60-61, 7 Oct. 1854; Parley P. Pratt, ibid., 1:172-85, 30 Jan. 1853; Juanita Brooks, *On the Mormon Frontier: The Diary of Hosea Stout, 1844-1861*, 2 vols. (Salt Lake City: University of Utah Press, 1964), 2:435, 11 Apr. 1852; "Record of Andrew Jackson Allen," TS, Utah State Historical Society, Salt Lake City, 15, 23 July 1857; Klaus J. Hansen, "Mormonism and American Culture: Some Tentative Hypotheses," in *The Restoration Movement: Essays in Mormon History*, rev. ed., eds. F. Mark McKiernan, Alma R. Blair, and Paul M. Edwards (Independence, MO: Herald Publishing House, 1992), 21.

6. Richard F. Burton, *The City of the Saints*, ed. Fawn M. Brodie (1861, reprint; New York: Alfred A. Knopf, 1963), 334; Andrew Love Neff, *History of Utah, 1847-1869* (Salt Lake City: Deseret News Press, 1940), 107-12.

7. Richard D. Poll and William P. MacKinnon, "Causes of the Utah War Reconsidered," *Journal of Mormon History* 20 (Fall 1994): 16; Eugene E. Campbell, "Pioneers and Patriotism: Conflicting Loyalties," in *New Views of*

A preoccupation with the destruction of the world and the coming of Christ remained a major theme in Mormon thought after the removal west. The Saints were warned that it would come sooner than they expected, that the necessary events would follow in rapid order, and the Lord would cut his work short.[8] Those elders accustomed to looking at sunsets and into the heavens for some special sign could dispense with their anxiety now, said First Presidency member Jedediah M. Grant. The predicted events were rushing on with such speed "as to exceed even our most sanguine expectations."[9] Children were told they would live to raise the dead, and that in no more than fifty years worthy Saints would be borne aloft to meet Christ.[10] Apostle George A. Smith warned the world that "the day of the Lord is near ... and we should watch for the coming of the Son of Man."[11]

As in previous times the gathering of the elect was preached as an overriding theological tenet, with Utah now set apart as the place for God's chosen.[12] Wallace Stegner has pointed out that "crossing the Plains to Zion in the Valleys of the Mountains was not merely a

Mormon History, eds. Davis Bitton and Maureen Ursenbach Beecher (Salt Lake City: University of Utah Press, 1987), 311-12.

8. Heber C. Kimball, *Journal of Discourses,* 1:36, 11 July 1852; Orson Pratt, ibid., 3:17-18, 20 May 1855; Charles W. Penrose, "The Second Advent," *Millennial Star* 21 (10 Sept. 1859): 581-84.

9. Jedediah M. Grant, *Journal of Discourses,* 2:145, 2 Apr. 1854.

10. Lorenzo D. Young, *Journal of Discourses,* 6:212; 13 Dec. 1857; "Address By President Heber C. Kimball," *Millennial Star* 14 (25 Dec. 1852): 693. See also Orson Hyde, *Journal of Discourses,* 5:141, n.d.; Heber C. Kimball, ibid., 5:254, 20 Sept. 1857; Orson Pratt, ibid., 6:202, 24 Jan. 1858; "Pestilence and Plague," *Deseret News,* 9 Feb. 1854.

11. George A. Smith, *Journal of Discourses,* 2:333-34, 24 June 1855. See also Heber C. Kimball, ibid., 1:35, 11 July 1852; Scott G. Kenney, ed., *Wilford Woodruff's Journal, 1833-1898,* 9 vols. (Midvale, UT: Signature Books, 1983-85), 4:269, 6 May 1854; 4:375, 30 Dec. 1855.

12. "The Righteous Gather: The Wicked Perish, *Millennial Star* 28 (16 June 1866): 377-79; "Emigration," ibid., 14 (2 Oct. 1852): 597-600; "Come out of her, My People," ibid., 17 (16 June 1855): 369-71; Orson Pratt, *The Seer* 2 (Feb. 1854): 215; Orson Pratt, "Preparations For The Second Advent," ibid., 2 (Aug. 1854): 319.

journey but a rite of passage, the final, devoted, enduring act that brought one into the kingdom."[13] "The gathering of Israel," Brigham Young said, "is so important a part of the great work in which we are engaged that it occupies much of our thoughts, and we are ever anxious to afford it all just facilities and influence, even to the risk of infringing upon other requirements."[14] Orson Spencer described Utah as "the resting place of Israel for the last days ... and the ultimate joy of the whole earth is the state of Zion established in the mountains."[15] Young restricted certain religious ceremonies to Utah, believing that to do otherwise "would destroy the object of the gathering." One criterion to receive the church's highest ordinance, called the "second anointing," was to have "gathered with the body of the church" as part of the Mormon empire building effort.[16]

Across the Atlantic Mormonism's predominant missionary message continued to include hope of an imminent millennium.[17] But in Europe the first step in preparing for Christ's return was to get to Zion (America). As one writer affirms, for Mormons "crossing the ocean became an act of obedience to the command to come out of Babylon" and join the Saints awaiting Christ's return.[18] To facilitate

---

13. Wallace Stegner, *The Gathering of Zion: The Story of the Mormon Trail* (1964; reprint, Lincoln: University of Nebraska Press, 1992), 1. See also Jan Shipps, *Mormonism: The Story of a New Religious Tradition* (Urbana: University of Illinois Press, 1985), 122; "War and Peace," *Millennial Star* 14 (9 Oct. 1852): 520-22.

14. Brigham Young to Amasa Lyman, 15 Nov. 1861, in Leonard J. Arrington, *Brigham Young: American Moses* (New York: Alfred A. Knopf, 1985), 284.

15. In W[alter]. H. G. Armytage, *Heavens Below: Utopian Experiments in England, 1560-1960* (Toronto: Toronto University Press, 1961), 264. See also Orson Pratt, *The Seer* 1 (Nov. 1853): 161.

16. Kenney, *Wilford Woodruff's Journal*, 6:307-308, 6 Dec. 1866; David John Buerger, *The Mysteries of Godliness: A History of Mormon Temple Worship* (San Francisco: Smith Research Associates, 1994), 99, 119.

17. Douglas James Davies, *Mormon Spirituality: Latter-Day Saints in Wales and Zion* (Nottingham, Eng.: University of Nottingham, 1987), 14; Arrington, *Brigham Young*, 282; Orson Pratt, *The Seer* 1 (Nov. 1853): 166.

18. W[illiam]. H. Oliver, *Prophets and Millennialists* (Auckland, New

relocation in 1849 Brigham Young initiated the Perpetual Emigration Fund. Its purpose was to raise capital and supervise European migration to America where the truthfulness of the American Constitution could be better taught in Utah Mormonism.[19] Spouting emigration rhetoric, the *Millennial Star* declared, "Every particle of our means which we use in Babylon is a loss to ourselves ... Every Saint who does not come *home* [Utah] will be afflicted by the Devil."[20]

Under Young's theocracy the results obtained in the Great Basin confirmed the Saints' confidence and conviction that God would soon beckon his people to prepare for Christ's return. Construction of a temple in the West was required to build the kingdom in preparation for the Lord. When its cornerstones were laid, Brigham Young told the Saints a temple must be erected so that when Christ "shall again appear, he may have a place where he can lay his head."[21] Although the Millennium had yet to arrive, its promise had not gone completely unfulfilled for the Saints had much to show for their endeavors.

But Latter-day Saint success in making the desert "blossom as a rose" also affirmed Mormon leaders' belief that the general membership had fallen into complacency, more interested in material than spiritual things. Attributing crop failures, grasshopper plagues, and natural disasters to an absence of faith, and believing the Saints' lack of outside persecution had allowed their commitment to soften, in 1856-57 Brigham Young instituted a "Reformation," hoping to instill the spiritual strength held by the Saints during their hardship days of Ohio, Missouri, and Illinois.[22]

Zealand: Auckland University Press, 1978), 221.

19. James B. Allen and Glen M. Leonard, *The Story of the Latter-day Saints* (Salt Lake City: Deseret Book Co., 1976), 282-83; Leonard J. Arrington and Davis Bitton, *The Mormon Experience: A History of the Latter-day Saints*, 2d ed. (Urbana: University of Illinois Press, 1992), 130-32.

20. *Millennial Star* 14 (1852): 20, in Armytage, *Heavens Below*, 265. See also the poem "Farewell to England" in *Millennial Star* 18 (21 June 1856): 400.

21. Young, *Journal of Discourses*, 2:33, 6 Apr. 1853; Reinwand, "An Interpretive Study of Mormon Millennialism," 78-82.

22. Thomas G. Alexander, "Wilford Woodruff and the Mormon

Described by one writer as a "fanatical spiritualism that burned across the Basin with religious fury," the Mormon Reformation was based on a millennial world view, its purpose to lay the foundation for divine changes with eternal consequences.[23] Isolated in the West, Brigham Young hoped to encourage the perfecting of his people. If members would cease to do evil, they could bind Satan and help hasten the Millennium.[24] Apostle Lorenzo Snow held the reformation's importance was to obtain the "spiritual energy" necessary "to pass the fiery ordeal ... we feel is fast approaching."[25] Apostle Wilford Woodruff believed its purpose was to equip members "for the great things of God which are coming upon the Earth & upon this people ... for destruction is nigh."[26]

"Repent, reform, and renew your covenants; is the cry of God," exhorted the *Deseret News*.[27] Young's thunderous counselor, Jedediah M. Grant, weary of expounding reformation fervor in the face of lackadaisical efforts, demanded further evidence of members' commitment through mass rebaptism and reconfirmation. Led by Young and many members of the church's hierarchy, these acts represented

---

Reformation of 1855-57," *Dialogue: A Journal of Mormon Thought* 25 (Summer 1992): 25-26; Paul H. Peterson, "The Mormon Reformation of 1856-1857: The Rhetoric and the Reality," *Journal of Mormon History* 15 (1989): 61-64; Nels Anderson, *Desert Saints: The Mormon Frontier in Utah* (1942; reprint, Chicago: University of Chicago Press, 1966), 151-53.

23. Donald R. Moorman, *Camp Floyd and the Mormons: The Utah War* (Salt Lake City: University of Utah Press, 1992), 123; Peterson, "The Mormon Reformation," 60, 75; Hubert Howe Bancroft, *History of Utah: 1540-1886* (San Francisco: The History Co., 1889), 540-41.

24. Gene A. Sessions, *Mormon Thunder: A Documentary History of Jedediah Morgan Grant* (Urbana: University of Illinois Press, 1982), 229; Eugene E. Campbell, *Establishing Zion: The Mormon Church in the American West, 1847-1869* (Salt Lake City: Signature Books, 1988), 181-82.

25. Lorenzo Snow, *Journal of Discourses*, 4:154, 4 Jan. 1857.

26. Kenney, *Wilford Woodruff's Journal*, 4:502-503, 7 Dec. 1856. See also Alexander, "Wilford Woodruff and the Mormon Reformation of 1855-57," 27-31.

27. *Deseret News*, 5 Nov. 1856, in Peterson, "The Mormon Reformation," 64.

outward signs of renewed dedication to gospel ideals.[28] An increase in plural marriages accompanied the reformation's show of faith and devotion, along with initiation of a "home missionary" program and an attempt to reinstitute a limited version of the law of consecration.[29]

The push to demonstrate religious commitment by taking additional plural wives created unique problems including competition for brides and a rush into marriages which soon ended in divorce.[30] Apostle Wilford Woodruff reported nearly "all are trying to get wives, until there is hardly a girl 14 years old in Utah, but what is married or just going to be."[31] One Fillmore, Utah, member commiserated over the marriage possibilities in his home town, reporting, "[T]here were 56 single men besides all the married ones that were anxious to get more wives, and only four single women. Now sir, would it not be a good policy for me to go on a mission to the states or England if you thought best. I know of some good women in the states of my own baptizing that might be got, besides many more."[32]

But the reformation's demand for proof of spiritual devotion led to excesses and bolstered Mormon stereotypes.[33] Rumors of polyga-

---

28. Sessions, *Mormon Thunder*, 207; Peterson, "The Mormon Reformation," 66-68; Campbell, *Establishing Zion*, 184-88.

29. Peterson, "The Mormon Reformation," 61, 71; Leonard J. Arrington, Feramorz Y. Fox, and Dean L. May, *Building the City of God: Community & Cooperation Among the Mormons* (Salt Lake City: Deseret Book Co., 1976), 63-78.

30. Eugene E. Campbell and Bruce L. Campbell, "Divorce among Mormon Polygamists: Extent and Explanations," *Utah Historical Quarterly* 46 (Winter 1978): 4-23. A 65-percent increase in new plural marriages occurred in 1856-57. See Stanley S. Ivins, "Notes on Polygamy," *Western Humanities Review* 10 (Summer 1956): 231.

31. Wilford Woodruff to George A. Smith, 1 Apr. 1857, Journal History, LDS church archives, in Richard S. Van Wagoner, *Mormon Polygamy: A History* (Salt Lake City: Signature Books, 1989), 92.

32. In Campbell, *Establishing Zion*, 197.

33. Gustive O. Larson, "The Mormon Reformation," *Utah Historical Quarterly* 26 (Jan. 1958): 47; Alexander, "Wilford Woodruff and the Mormon Reformation of 1855-57," 36; Peterson, "The Mormon Reformation," 59,

mous harems and exotic doctrines such as "blood atonement," imple-
mented by Mormon "Danite" vigilante bands, depicted Mormon
society as uncivilized, and Americans demanded that lawless Utah be
brought under subjugation. The eastern press was convinced that the
Mormon practice of preaching to Native Americans and bringing
hordes of foreign converts to the West was to establish a religious
empire set on despotic domination and possibly complete separation
from the Union.[34] Writing from his mission headquarters in New
York, Apostle Parley Pratt lamented that "the whole country is being
overwhelmed with the most abominable lying, mockery, and hatred
of the Saints."[35] Upon receipt of mail from the East, prominent
Mormon Hosea Stout reported, "[T]he spirit of the people & rulers
of the Nation seem to be hostile and surley towards the Mormons."[36]
When only days later these accounts were read from the Salt Lake
Tabernacle pulpit, Stout concluded, "[I]t appears that there is now
through out the U.S. the most bitter, revengeful, and mobocratic
feeling against us that has ever been manifested."[37]

But the major irritant continued to be Young and the shadow
leadership resting with the Mormon hierarchy who effectively governed the territory regardless of which officials the federal government commissioned.[38] Young defiantly declared, "I am and will be

---

66-67; B[righam]. H. Roberts, *A Comprehensive History of the Church of Jesus
Christ of Latter-day Saints*, 6 vols. (1930; reprint, Provo, UT: Brigham Young
University Press, 1965), 4:126-30, 242-44; Campbell, *Establishing Zion*, 199.

34. Norman F. Furniss, *The Mormon Conflict, 1850-1859* (New Haven,
CT: Yale University Press, 1960), 84; Thomas F. O'Dea, *The Mormons*
(Chicago: University of Chicago Press, 1957), 101; Orson Pratt, "Latter-Day
Zion," *The Seer* 2 (May 1854): 270.

35. Parley P. Pratt, *Autobiography of Parley Parker Pratt* (1938; reprint,
Salt Lake City: Deseret Book Co., 1979), 444.

36. Brooks, *On the Mormon Frontier: The Diary of Hosea Stout*, 2:627, 29
May 1857.

37. Ibid., 2:628, 14 June 1857. See also Kenney, *Wilford Woodruff's
Journal*, 5:54, 31 May 1857; 5:58, 14 June 1857.

38. Furniss, *The Mormon Conflict*, 18-20; Juanita Brooks, *The Mountain
Meadows Massacre* (1950; reprint, Norman: University of Oklahoma, 1991),

Governor, and no power can hinder it until the Lord Almighty says, 'Brigham, you need not be Governor any longer.'"[39] Motivated by federal appointees' complaints and reports throughout the 1850s of Young's theocratic fanaticism and polygamy, newly elected president James Buchanan decided a show of authority was needed to demonstrate federal sovereignty over Utah. Buchanan authorized a military campaign to escort Young's replacement as governor into the territory.[40] A *New York Times* editor succinctly described the expedition's goal, concluding, "the Government had a clear choice whether to subdue the Saints then [1857] while they were still relatively weak, or wait till they could support their inevitable demand for political sovereignty with a perilously swollen population."[41]

Steeped in reformation zeal, word of General Albert Sydney Johnston's army's westward march to put down the Utah Mormon rebellion and install a gentile governor was seen by the Saints as a step towards ushering in the Millennium. "The greater [the army's] numbers," preached Apostle Orson Hyde in October 1857, "the greater and more complete its overthrow, ... If the Red Sea be not the trap in which the enemy will be caught," he predicted, "there

---

18; Shirley Greenwood Jones, "Brigham Young's Rhetoric: A Critical and Cultural Analysis of Key Sermons in Five Rhetorical Events," Ph.D. diss., University of Utah, 1992, 207-208.

39. Young, *Journal of Discourses*, 1:187, 19 June 1853. See also Heber C. Kimball, ibid., 5:160-64, 30 Aug. 1857; "Church and Kingdom of God," *Millennial Star* 20 (6 Mar. 1858): 145-48.

40. Richard D. Poll, *Quixotic Mediator: Thomas L. Kane and the Utah War* (Ogden, UT: Weber State College Press, 1985), 3; Everett L. Cooley, "Carpetbag Rule—Territorial Government in Utah," *Utah Historical Quarterly* 26 (Apr. 1959): 107-29; Leonard J. Arrington, *Great Basin Kingdom: An Economic History of the Latter-day Saints, 1830-1900* (1958; reprint, Lincoln: University of Nebraska Press, 1966), 174; Furniss, *The Mormon Conflict*, 29, 59-66; Moorman, *Camp Floyd and the Mormons*, 11-16; William P. MacKinnon, "125 Years of Conspiracy Theories: Origins of the Utah Expedition of 1857-58," *Utah Historical Quarterly* 52 (Summer 1984): 212-30; Campbell, *Establishing Zion*, 233-34.

41. *New York Times*, 30 Mar. 1857, in Furniss, *The Mormon Conflict*, 87.

will be a snow of hail storm, a whirlwind, an earthquake, fire from above or from beneath, or the sword of the Lord and of Brigham."[42] Apostle Orson Pratt, believing that the signs of the last days were everywhere visible, declared that the time had arrived when "the mother of abominations was to gather together and fight against the Saints."[43] Young assured his people that government persecution would only "hasten the work" of the Lord.[44] Johnston's army was but the beginning of the collapse of American sovereignty and would allow the Saints to become an independent nation.

It was millennialism which convinced church leaders not to relinquish the valley to an incoming foe.[45] Upon word of the approaching troops, Young stockpiled arms and ammunition, recalled missionaries and outpost settlements, proclaimed marshal law, and initiated a guerrilla campaign against the approaching "invaders." His actions signaled that truly monumental events were about to ensue.[46] The Mormon leadership's inflammatory rhetoric invoked zealous response from members, with past sufferings, government sanctioned

---

42. Orson Hyde Sermon, 7 Oct. 1857, Journal History, in Peterson, "The Mormon Reformation," 78.

43. Pratt, *Journal of Discourses*, 6:202, 24 Jan 1858. See also "Government," *Millennial Star* 19 (19 Dec. 1857): 804.

44. "Record of Andrew Jackson Allen," 14 Mar. 1858. See also Young, *Journal of Discourses*, 5:98, 2 Aug. 1857.

45. Mormon apocalyptic sentiments have been recognized in Arrington and Bitton, *The Mormon Experience*, 169; Poll and MacKinnon, "Causes of the Utah War Reconsidered," 36-38; Poll, *Quixotic Mediator*, 8; Campbell, *Establishing Zion*, 238-39; Reinwand, "An Interpretive Study of Mormon Millennialism," 102; Eugene E. Campbell, "Pioneers and Patriotism: Conflicting Loyalties," in *New Views of Mormon History*, eds. Davis Bitton and Maureen Ursenbach Beecher (Salt Lake City: University of Utah Press, 1987), 312-13.

46. Everett L. Cooley, ed., *Diary of Brigham Young, 1857* (Salt Lake City: Tanner Trust Fund, 1980), 56-57, 4-8 Aug. 1857; 68, 29 Aug. 1857; 80, 14-15 Sept. 1857; Poll and MacKinnon, "Causes of the Utah War Reconsidered," 18; Reinwand, "An Interpretive Study of Mormon Millennialism," 98-99; Arrington, *Brigham Young*, 253-55.

mob violence, burnings, and expulsion from Missouri and Illinois all relived.[47] Apostle John Taylor vowed never again "to bow to the cruelty of Mobs, even when the mob have the name of being legalized by the nation."[48] All believed that soon the Lord would smite down their enemies. Surely deliverance was nigh.[49]

The Utah War intensified the reformation's religious fervor, deepening the Saints' belief in an impending conflict with Christ soon to usher in his millennial reign.[50] Bishop Lorenzo D. Young confessed he had "long prayed that the Lord Almighty would destroy the nation that gave me birth."[51] "I have been looking for the time of deliverance" recorded Apostle Charles C. Rich, "but did not expect it so soon."[52] Apostle Wilford Woodruff warned a congregation that President Buchanan had no idea what he was up against, and prophesied the government was "turning the last key to rend the nation asunder."[53] In 1858 Apostle Orson Pratt told the Saints, "The American continent never was designed for such a corrupt Government ... After they should become ripened in iniquity, it was not intended

47. Brooks, *The Mountain Meadows Massacre*, 22; Jones, "Brigham Young's Rhetoric," 218-19.

48. John Taylor, *Deseret News,* 23 Sept. 1857.

49. Cooley, *Diary of Brigham Young 1857,* 58, 11 Aug. 1857.

50. Kenney, *Wilford Woodruff's Journal,* 5:230, 1 Nov. 1858. For examples of church leaders expounding millennial warning during the Utah War period, see Brigham Young, *Journal of Discourses,* 4:371, 28 June 1857; Young, ibid., 12:119, 17 Aug. 1857; Heber C. Kimball, ibid., 5:218, 6 Sept. 1856; Jedediah M. Grant, ibid., 2:148, 2 Apr. 1854; Wilford Woodruff, ibid., 6:121, 6 Dec. 1857; Lorenzo D. Young, ibid., 6:225, 25 Oct. 1857.

51. Young, *Journal of Discourses,* 6:225, 25 Oct. 1857. See also Jules Remy and Julius Brenchley, *A Journey to Great-Salt-Lake City* ..., 2 vols. (London: W. Jeffs, 1861), 1:142-43, 2:249-52.

52. Rich Diary, TS, Lee Library, Brigham Young University, 7 Oct. 1857, in Reinwand, "An Interpretive Study of Mormon Millennialism," 95.

53. Woodruff, *Journal of Discourses,* 6:121, 6 Dec. 1857; Kenney, *Wilford Woodruff's Journal,* 5:126-31, 2 Dec. 1857. For additional declarations that God would fight the Saints' battles, see Brigham Young, *Journal of Discourses,* 5:340, 18 Oct. 1857; Brigham Young, ibid., 5:171, 30 Aug. 1857; Brigham Young, ibid., 5:293, 4 Oct. 1857; George A. Smith, ibid., 5:168, 30 Aug. 1857.

they should continue. The Lord has designed another thing, and for this reason we are here in these mountains."[54]

By sealing Utah's borders and mobilizing the territorial militia against the U.S. army, Young may have committed an act of treason, and in fact his actions were so labeled in a letter to Young from incoming governor Alfred Cumming.[55]

When the Mormon prophet refused to investigate and admit Mormon complicity in the September 1857 slaughter of the Fancher party at Mountain Meadows, public opinion concluded Utah Mormonism was an empire answering to none but itself.[56] Mormon defiance angered and antagonized the American people and government and military leaders whose resolve stiffened to subdue the rebels.[57] "They have with meditation," concluded General Johnston,

---

54. Pratt, *Journal of Discourses*, 6:204, 24 Jan. 1858. For examples of church leaders prophesying that Utah would be a place of refuge from the world, see Brigham Young, *Journal of Discourses*, 10:38-39, 9 Mar. 1862; Brigham Young, ibid., 4:342-44, 7 June 1857; Brigham Young, ibid., 8:356, 3 Mar. 1861; Brigham Young, ibid., 10:294, 15 May 1864; George A. Smith, ibid., 3:289, 6 Apr. 1856; John Taylor, ibid., 20:135-36, 1 Dec. 1878; John Taylor, ibid., 21:255, 21 Mar. 1880; John Taylor, ibid., 20:266-67, 2 Mar. 1879; John Taylor, ibid., 21:8, 31 Aug. 1879; Orson Pratt, ibid., 3:302, 6 Apr. 1856; Orson Hyde, ibid., 20:99-100, 3 Nov. 1878; George Q. Cannon, ibid., 14:31, 8 Jan. 1871; George Q. Cannon, ibid., 22:179, 12 June 1881; George Q. Cannon, ibid., 23:105, 20 Nov. 1881; Franklin D. Richards, ibid., 24:282, 6 Oct. 1883; Moses Thatcher, ibid., 26:334, 8 Oct. 1855; George Q. Cannon, "Remarks By President George Q. Cannon," *Deseret News* 17 (26 July 1884): 1.

55. Cumming to The People of Utah Territory, 21 Nov. 1858, in Brooks, *On the Mormon Frontier*, 2:646, 29 Nov. 1857; Furniss, *The Mormon Conflict*, 166. While waiting out the winter near Fort Bridger, a civilian grand jury under the jurisdiction of newly appointed territorial chief justice Delana R. Eckels indicted Brigham Young, Daniel Wells, Lot Smith, and other Mormons for treason. See Furniss, 167. Two versions of Young's proclamation are found in Cooley, *Diary of Brigham Young*, 82-83.

56. Kenney, *Wilford Woodruff's Journal*, 5:131, 4 Dec. 1857; Brooks, *The Mountain Meadows Massacre*, 144-47; Moorman, *Camp Floyd and the Mormons*, 138-42.

57. Poll and MacKinnon, "Causes of the Utah War Reconsidered,"

"placed themselves in rebellion against the Union, and entertain the insane design of establishing a form of government thoroughly despotic, and utterly repugnant to our institutions ... I have ordered that wherever they are met in arms, they be treated as enemies."[58]

Young initiated scorched-earth tactics, burning food, army supply wagons, and freight trains, torching miles of grassland forage, and capturing 1,400 of the expedition's 2,000 head of cattle, forcing the detachment to "whole up" for the winter in present-day Wyoming. But it was one thing to strand a floundering detachment on the high plains. It would be a different problem to keep a resupplied army led by a trained veteran general from occupying the territory the following spring.[59] Delaying Johnston's entrance into the Salt Lake Valley allowed time for Young to pursue alternative responses. He hoped that by slowing the troops' arrival a peaceful settlement could be negotiated.[60]

With the Missouri and Illinois experience overshadowing Mormon consciousness, Young had three options: stand and fight, allow the troops to enter Utah and occupy the territory, or flee America leaving behind ten years of sweat and toil.[61] Adopting a siege mentality, Young followed an isolationist strategy, negotiating his way out of armed conflict while seeking to maintain a separate sanctuary. This was illustrated by his sending 30,000 "refuges" south, in essence moving the entire church away from Johnston's

---

23-25, 40.

58. In Furniss, *The Mormon Conflict*, 116. For church leaders' declarations that the thread between Utah and the national government had been cut and "no officer appointed by government ... should come and rule over us from this time forth," see Brooks, *On the Mormon Frontier*, 2:636, 6 Sept. 1857; Jessie Bigler Martin Diary, Special Collections, Lee Library, 13 Sept. 1857; John Pulsipher Journal, TS, Utah State Historical Society, Salt Lake City, 6-7 Oct. 1857; *Deseret News,* 12 Aug. 1857.

59. Moorman, *Camp Floyd and the Mormons*, 30.

60. Brooks, *On the Mormon Frontier*, 2:654, 18 Mar. 1858; Furniss, *The Mormon Conflict*, 123; Campbell, *Establishing Zion*, 241-42; Cooley, *Diary of Brigham Young*, 85-86n83.

61. Moorman, *Camp Floyd and the Mormons*, 18-20.

troops.[62] As a last resort Young organized an exploration party to investigate the unchartered White Mountain region to the southwest should the Saints require a new place of refuge.[63]

With the quiet assistance of Thomas L. Kane, a peaceful settlement of the crisis was found with Young accepting the new governor, Alfred Cumming, and establishment of a military post away from major Mormon settlements in exchange for pardons for individuals involved in the confrontation.[64] Although considered a successful public relations strategy, the "move south" proved not only disruptive but financially devastating to Utah Mormons, many members leaving their homes not from a sense of duty but by mandate from the church hierarchy.[65] As Leonard Arrington pointed out, the sacrifice of property, particularly at Carson Valley and San Bernardino, cost the church millions of dollars and further depleted scarce capital and weakened member morale.[66] As with much of his charismatic leadership, Young's tactics were practical but decisions were based on religious convictions and in this case on chiliastic expectations.[67]

---

62. Richard D. Poll, "The Move South," *Brigham Young University Studies* 29 (Fall 1989): 65-88.

63. Clifford L. Stott, *Search for Sanctuary: Brigham Young and the White Mountain Expedition* (Salt Lake City: University of Utah Press, 1984), 29, 47-84; Arrington, *Great Basin Kingdom*, 184-85. See also Brigham Young, *Journal of Discourses*, 5:336-43, 18 Oct. 1857.

64. Poll, *Quixotic Mediator*, 13, 18; Richard D. Poll, "Thomas L. Kane and the Utah War," *Utah Historical Quarterly* 61 (Spring 1993): 112-35; Furniss, *The Mormon Conflict*, 176-82; Moorman, *Camp Floyd and the Mormons*, 30-42; Campbell, *Establishing Zion*, 244-45; Arrington, *Brigham Young*, 261-63.

65. Furniss, *The Mormon Conflict*, 188; Poll, "The Move South," 78. On church leadership discussion of the public relations benefit of Mormon flight into the wilderness, see Brooks, *On the Mormon Frontier*, 2:654, 18 Mar. 1858. See also Cooley, *Diary of Brigham Young*, 60-61n61; Neff, *History of Utah*, 499-502.

66. Arrington, *Great Basin Kingdom*, 177-78, 188-94; Poll, "The Move South," 84. The financial loss at the San Bernardino colony is detailed in Edward Leo Lyman, *San Bernardino: The Rise and Fall of a California Community* (Salt Lake City: Signature Books, 1996), 371-422.

67. Poll and MacKinnon, "Causes of the Utah War Reconsidered," 41.

When Johnston's army passed through a deserted Salt Lake City and founded Camp Floyd west of the Jordon River, Mormon fear of mobocracy sanctioned by government institutions subsided. Perhaps by the late 1850s Mormons could live amidst U.S. institutions. Once the immediate crisis dissipated, church leaders' millennial rhetoric declined, no longer inflammatory or prophesying God's intervention. No doubt the confidence shown by earlier millennial predictions was shaken as the Saints' prophesied cataclysmic victory failed to produce the consumption of their enemies. The permanence of Johnston's army at Camp Floyd remained an enduring legacy of federal sovereignty over the Great Basin.[68]

Thomas B. H. Stenhouse, president of the church's Eastern States mission, summarized Latter-day Saint millennial disappointment:

> For years previous, the people had been taught to look forward to the time when "the kingdom" should throw off its allegiance to all earthly power, and now [1857] they naturally concluded that "the long-expected blessed day" had arrived, when they beheld on the one side of the mountains the national army advancing to their homes, and on the other side the Prophet with the armies of Israel determined to dispute their entrance into the valleys.[69]

When the anticipated "final" conflict failed to materialize, the Saints were asked once again to delay their deliverance, postponing victory for Israel sometime into the future.[70]

Mormon apocalyptic anticipations, rekindled during the Utah War, were a mere prelude to church leader declarations during the American Civil War. In the Far West, away from the battle lines, the South's secession brought a renewed round of millennial intensity

---

68. Moorman, *Camp Floyd and the Mormons*, 81.

69. Stenhouse, *The Rocky Mountain Saints* (New York: D. Appletone and Co., 1873), 375; Ronald W. Walker, "The Stenhouses and the Making of a Mormon Image," *Journal of Mormon History* 1 (1974): 53.

70. One enthusiastic Mormon refused to relent in his apocalyptic hopes and attempted to establish his own millenarian movement within thirty miles of Salt Lake City. See C. LeRoy Anderson, *Joseph Morris and the Saga of the Morrisites* (1981; reprint, Logan: Utah State University Press, 1988).

predicting the nation's collapse and destruction. Here the prophecy made by Joseph Smith that the final upheaval would commence in South Carolina, that it would involve the slave issue, that it would pit the north against the south and spread throughout the earth until all nations were destroyed seemed to find stunning fulfillment.[71] The excitement felt in connection with the Civil War is difficult to describe.[72] Surely, they believed, the end was now in sight.[73]

---

71. *The Pearl of Great Price: Being a Choice Selection from the Revelations, Translations, and Narrations of Joseph Smith* (Liverpool, Eng.: F.D. Richards, 1851), 35; *Doctrine and Covenants*, 1981 ed., 87, 130:12-13; Robert Glass Cleland and Juanita Brooks, eds., *A Mormon Chronicle: The Diaries of John D. Lee, 1848-1876*, 2 vols. (Salt Lake City: University of Utah Press, 1983), 1:255-56, 20 May 1860; Diary of William McIntosh, TS, Special Collections, Lee Library, 81, 10 June 1861; "The 'Times' on the American War," *Millennial Star* (11 July 1863): 441-42; Brigham Young, *Journal of Discourses*, 9:367, 31 Aug. 1862; Brigham Young, ibid., 8:195, 7 Oct. 1860; Brigham Young, ibid., 9:367-68, 31 Aug. 1862; E[verette]. B. Long, *The Saints and the Union: Utah Territory During the Civil War* (Urbana: University of Illinois Press, 1981), 25-26; Neff, *History of Utah*, 619-20.

72. For contemporary non-Mormon sources crediting Joseph Smith's prophecy with predicting the war, see *Philadelphia Sunday Mercury* 11 (5 May 1861). The article was reprinted in the *Royal Leamington Spa Courier* (England), 1 June 1861; "A Remarkable Revelation—Was Joseph Smith A True Prophet," *The New York Bee*, in "Opinions of the Press," *Millennial Star* (25 May 1861): 330-31; "Opinions of the Press," ibid. (29 June 1861): 404. See also Boyd L. Eddins, "The Mormons and the Civil War," M.S. thesis, Utah State University, 1966, iv.

73. Kenney, *Wilford Woodruff's Journal*, 5:526, 30 Dec. 1860; 5:527-29, 31 Dec. 1860; Stenhouse, *The Rocky Mountain Saints*, 420-21. See also the following examples: "Review Of Past And Present Events," *Millennial Star* 23 (1 Jan. 1861): 34; "Civil War In America—Its Importance As A Warning To The Saints," ibid., 23 (11 May 1861): 297-300; "Blindness of the World to the Signs of the Times," ibid., (21 June 1862): 393-96; "The Fulfillment of Prophecy," ibid., 24 (23 Aug. 1862): 529-33; "Emancipation Of The Slaves—The Prophet Joseph's Plan—Results Of Its Rejection," ibid., 25 (14 Feb. 1863): 97-101; "Minutes Of A District Conference," ibid., 26 (13 Aug. 1864): 517-18; Charles W. Penrose, "A Universal Kingdom," ibid., 27 (30 Sept. 1865): 608-12; Wilford Woodruff, *Journal of Discourses*, 10:13, 27 July

Nationally the concept of Americans as a chosen people came to full development just prior to 1860.[74] To some the Civil War fit into the pattern of apocalyptic history, the next step towards millennial peace. They saw antebellum abolitionism as one way of hastening the Millennium. But in many respects the war shocked postmillennial America. While writers and orators used apocalyptic rhetoric to portray the struggle as an "Armageddon of the Republic," once the Civil War began many questioned whether, through internal discord, the nation may have forfeited its divine providence. Whereas optimism had previously permeated the country's religious culture, feeding on the "redeemer nation" myth, abolitionists wondered for years if America could fulfill its destiny while maintaining the evils of slavery. Admitting godly purpose, Abraham Lincoln confessed the war must last "until all the wealth piled by the bondman's two hundred and fifty years of unrequited toil shall be sunk, and until every drop of blood drawn with the lash shall be paid by another drawn with the sword."[75] Even America's so-called righteousness was not enough to allow it to escape desolating wars that many believed would only affect other nations.[76]

1862; Heber C. Kimball, ibid., 10:46, 4 May 1862; Orson Hyde, ibid., 10:376, 18 Dec. 1864; John Taylor, ibid., 11:26, 11 Dec. 1864.

74. Klaus J. Hansen, "The Millennium, the West, and Race in the Antebellum American Mind," *Western Historical Quarterly* 3 (Oct. 1972): 385.

75. Abraham Lincoln, "Second Inaugural Address," 4 Mar. 1865, in James D. Richardson, comp., *Messages and Papers of the Presidents*, 20 vols. (New York: Bureau of National Literature, 1917), 7:3478. See also Walter E. Wiest, "Lincoln's Political Ethic: An Alternative to American Millennialism," *American Journal of Theology and Philosophy* 4 (Sept. 1983): 125.

76. James H. Moorhead, *American Apocalypse: Yankee Protestants and the Civil War, 1860-1869* (New Haven, CT: Yale University Press, 1978), 42-81; Ernest Lee Tuveson, *Redeemer Nation: The Idea of America's Millennial Role* (Chicago: University of Chicago Press, 1968), 137-96; Ernest R. Sandeen, *The Roots of Fundamentalism: British and American Millenarianism, 1800-1930* (Chicago: University of Chicago Press, 1970), 42-58, 94-101; James H. Moorhead, "Between Progress and Apocalypse: A Reassessment of Millennialism in American Religious Thought, 1800-1880," *Journal of American History* 71 (Dec. 1984): 524-35; Dietrich G. Buss, "Meeting of Heaven and Earth: A Survey and Analysis of the Literature on Millennialism

Yet Mormons accepted the Civil War with no great surprise.[77] As the Book of Mormon made clear (2 Ne. 26:15), two great pre-Columbian civilizations had already been "brought down low in the dust" on this continent with only a "miserable few" remnants yet bearing "the marks of the curse, of God upon them."[78] Unless the present generation hastily repented, it would experience the same fate.[79] Brigham Young warned the Saints to lay up grain, for people would soon be flocking to Utah for peace and sustenance.[80] No doubt "the time is close at hand," wrote Charles Penrose, and events are about to "follow each other in rapid succession."[81]

Prior to the war, Utah Mormons had no national vote and held no particular allegiance. Although Stephen A. Douglas's popular sovereignty doctrine found support among the Saints, his attacks against the church in 1857, including his charge that Utah Mormons were attempting to subvert the U.S. government, negated any chance of Utah's affiliation with national Democrats.[82] Obviously Mormons

---

in America, 1965-1985," *Fides et Historia* 20 (Jan. 1988): 14; Barkun, *Crucible of the Millennium*, 28-29; Ronald D. Rietveld, "The American Civil War: Millennial Hope, Political Chaos, and a Two-Sided 'Just War,'" in *The Wars of America: Christian Views*, ed. Ronald A. Wells (Grand Rapids, MI: William B. Eerdmans Publishing Co., 1981), 67-90.

77. Eddins, "The Mormons and the Civil War," 9.

78. Wilford Woodruff, *Journal of Discourses*, 11:248, 22 Oct. 1865.

79. Kenney, *Wilford Woodruff's Journal*, 5:616, 31 Dec. 1861; 6:305, 17 Dec. 1866; Brigham Young, *Journal of Discourses*, 8:123, 15 July 1860; George A. Smith, ibid., 9:69, 10 Mar. 1861; Orson Pratt, *The Seer* 2 (Feb. 1854): 215. For an example, see Albert P. Rockwood's dream, with interpretation by Wilford Woodruff, in Journal History, 26 Feb. 1861.

80. "Record of Andrew Jackson Allen," 49-50, 19 Dec. 1860, 1 Feb 1861. See also Heber C. Kimball, *Journal of Discourses*, 5:218, 6 Sept. 1856; Heber C. Kimball, ibid., 5:255, 20 Sept. 1857; Heber C. Kimball, ibid., 9:134-35, 12 May 1861; George A. Smith, ibid., 3:289, 6 Aug. 1856; *Millennial Star* 22 (16 June 1860): 378.

81. Charles W. Penrose, "The Second Advent," *Millennial Star* 21 (10 Sept. 1859): 584.

82. Kenney, *Wilford Woodruff's Journal*, 5:87, 30 Aug. 1857; George U. Hubbard, "Abraham Lincoln As Seen By The Mormons," *Utah Historical*

could not align themselves with the Republican party whose first platform in 1856 included a proclamation to outlaw the "barbarism" of polygamy.[83]

By the time events of 1860 climaxed, the past experiences of the Utah War and the Mountain Meadows massacre had already placed a great deal of mistrust between Mormons and the federal government. In a final attempt to decrease Mormon power in the West, just days before leaving office, President Buchanan siphoned off a large portion of western Utah Territory by creating the new Territory of Nevada.[84] Understanding that the Saints' sympathies may lie with the southern states, when forced to abandon Camp Floyd for eastern military positions the army destroyed surplus ammunition rather than allow it to fall into Mormon hands.[85]

The church hierarchy held that Utah was not involved in the crisis between the North and South, and wanted to be left alone to pursue their religious kingdom.[86] "We abide strictly and positively by the Constitution," declared Apostle John Taylor at the 1861 Fourth of July celebration, "we know no north, no south, no east, no west."[87] The national government certainly concurred with the Saints' self-description, enlisting Utah's militia in only one small assignment during

---

Quarterly 31 (Spring 1963): 95-96; Roberts, *A Comprehensive History of the Church*, 4:221-22. For Douglas's denunciation of Utah Mormonism, see Neff, *History of Utah*, 458-60; Vern L. Bullough, "Polygamy: An Issue in the Election of 1860?" *Utah Historical Quarterly* 29 (Apr. 1961): 119-26.

83. Richard D. Poll, "The Mormon Question Enters National Politics, 1850-1856," *Utah Historical Quarterly* 25 (Apr. 1957): 117-31.

84. Long, *The Saints and the Union*, 26.

85. Moorman, *Camp Floyd and the Mormons*, 275; Gustive O. Larson, "Utah and the Civil War," *Utah Historical Quarterly* 33 (Winter 1965): 58-63.

86. Brigham Young, *Journal of Discourses*, 8:172, 16 Sept. 1860; Brigham Young, ibid., 10:250, 6 Oct. 1863; Joshua Williams, *Millennial Star* 23 (30 Nov. 1861): 774-75; A. Karl Larson and Katharine Miles Larson, eds., *Diary of Charles Lowell Walker*, 2 vols. (Logan: Utah State University Press, 1980), 1:102, 1 Jan. 1860; Burton, *The City of the Saints*, 339; Long, *The Saints and the Union*, 8-10.

87. *Deseret News,* 10 July 1861, in Larson, "Utah and the Civil War," 57.

the war and establishing a new military outpost, Camp Douglas, not at the old Camp Floyd site, but on the bench overlooking Salt Lake City where commanding gun positions could overlook the city.[88]

During the Civil War, church leaders disseminated two primary themes: Mormon veneration of the U.S. Constitution with its God-given liberties, and the conviction that neither side in the pending crisis would surface as victor but that the nation would be torn asunder.[89] The Saints would then rise to save true constitutional government and inherit the remains of a shattered nation whose leaders would petition the Mormon hierarchy to take control of the floundering country.[90] "While the waves of commotion are whelming [sic] nearly the whole country," wrote Brigham Young in December 1860, "Utah in her rocky fortress is biding her time to step in and rescue the constitution."[91] Young calculated he would "live to see wickedness swept from the face of the Earth, the Saints possess it for an Everlasting inheritance, and Jesus reign king of

---

88. Journal History, 30 Oct. 1862; Alvin M. Josephy, Jr., *The Civil War in the American West* (1991; reprint, New York: Random House, 1993), 246-55; Larson, "Utah and the Civil War," 59-60; Margaret M. Fisher, comp. and ed., *Utah and the Civil War* (Salt Lake City: Deseret Book Co., 1929); Long, *The Saints and the Union*, 82-93, 107-17; Gaylon L. Caldwell, "'Utah Has Not Seceded': A Footnote to Local History," *Utah Historical Quarterly* 26 (Apr. 1958): 174-75; Campbell, *Establishing Zion*, 293-94; Arrington, *Brigham Young*, 296; Neff, *History of Utah*, 630-31.

89. John Taylor, *Journal of Discourses*, 11:26, 11 Dec. 1864. See also Eddins, "The Mormons and the Civil War," iv, 36-37.

90. "Universal Empire," *Millennial Star* 23 (5 Oct. 1861): 635-38; "The Future Prospects of the Saints," ibid., 26 (14 May 1864): 312-13; "The Impending Cloud," ibid., 22 (4 Feb. 1860): 65-68; "Reign of Terror in America," ibid., 68-69; "Modern Prophecy And Its Fulfillment," ibid., 27 (25 Mar. 1865): 184-90; "Civil War in America—Its Importance as a Warning to the Saints," ibid., (11 May 1861): 299; Heber C. Kimball, *Journal of Discourses*, 5:93, 26 July 1857; Long, *The Saints and the Union*, 20.

91. Young to William H. Hooper, 20 Dec. 1860, Coe Collection, Yale University Library, in Larson, "Utah and the Civil War," 56. See also "Divisions and Revolutions Which Threaten Babylon," *Millennial Star* 23 (2 Nov. 1861): 707-10.

kings."[92] "The day is not far distant," Heber C. Kimball held, when "we will be ruled by those men whom God Almighty appoints."[93]

Predicting dissolution of the Union after Abraham Lincoln's election, the *Deseret News* declared Mormons

> have undeviatingly adhered to the principles of the Constitution, and will venerate them after Congress shall have held its last session, and the United States as a nation shall cease to exist. ... The day is not far distant, when the United States Government will cease to be, and that the Union, about which the politicians have harped and poets sung, will be no more.[94]

God has "commenced to vex the nation," said Brigham Young. "It will not be patched up—it never can come together again ... If our present happy form of government is sustained, which I believe it will be, it will be done by the people I am now looking upon in connection with their brethren and their offspring."[95]

Surely the long-awaited moment was in sight. The beginning conflict would not only kill off the slaves, but lead to the destruction of contending factions.[96] Young concluded, "[T]he [U.S.] Government was the most Corrupt & rotten of any Government in the world & they were ready to be destroyed."[97] Apostle Woodruff predicted the Civil War would destroy both sides, leaving the Saints to see "the Kingdom of God Esstablished upon their ruins."[98] Affirming that God's wrath would be upon America until the "wicked & Corrupt" are destroyed

---

92. Larson and Larson, *Diary of Charles Walker*, 1:225, 27 Apr. 1862. See also "The Consummation Decreed Upon All Nations," *Millennial Star* 25 (4 Apr. 1863): 211-13.

93. Kimball, *Journal of Discourses*, 9:7, 6 Apr. 1861. See also Orson Pratt, "Latter-Day Zion," *The Seer* 2 (May 1854): 268-69.

94. *Deseret News*, 28 Nov. 1860, in Long, *The Saints and the Union*, 13-14.

95. Young, *Journal of Discourses*, 8:324, 10 Feb. 1861.

96. Brigham Young, *Journal of Discourses*, 10:209, 14 June 1863; Brigham Young, ibid., 8:230, 21 Oct. 1860.

97. Kenney, *Wilford Woodruff's Journal*, 5:526-27, 30 Dec. 1860.

98. Ibid., 5:529, 31 Dec. 1860.

and the government turned over to the Saints, Woodruff warned "the Gentiles upon this land [to] prepare to meet their God."[99]

Expecting the government to crumble, in 1862 Young formed an unofficial "ghost" legislature that continued beyond the end of the Civil War.[100] The Mormons were not planning to seize power, but through the priesthood hierarchy they were prepared to take the reins once the existing government was shattered and were separating themselves from society while awaiting destruction of the wicked.[101]

The Civil War was also expected to be the means of cleansing Missouri, preparing the way for the return of the Latter-day Saints "to take possession of the center Stake of Zion."[102] The

---

99. Ibid., 5:617, 31 Dec. 1861; 5:529, 31 Dec. 1860; Journal History, 1 May 1861. The isolationist sentiment of this era is distinctly different from Woodruff's feelings during the Spanish American War when then-church-president Woodruff commented on Utah's need to support the nation against Spain. See ibid., 25 Apr. 1896. See also Alexander, "Wilford Woodruff and the Changing Nature," 69; and Alexander, *Things in Heaven and Earth*, 320-21. For a more complete examination, see D. Michael Quinn, "The Mormon Church and the Spanish-American War: An End to Selective Pacifism," *Pacific Historical Review* 43 (Aug. 1974): 342-46; Ronald W. Walker, "Sheaves, Bucklers and the State: Mormon Leaders Respond to the Dilemmas of War," *Sunstone* 7 (July-Aug. 1982): 43-56.

100. Kenney, *Wilford Woodruff's Journal*, 6:40, 14 Apr. 1862; 6:92, 19 Jan. 1863; Hansen, *Quest for Empire*, 167-68; Larson, "Utah and the Civil War," 61-62; Arrington, *Brigham Young*, 268. See also Journal History, 24 Mar. 1864.

101. Heber C. Kimball, *Journal of Discourses*, 9:7, 6 Apr. 1861; John Taylor, ibid., 9:343, 13 Apr. 1862; Marvin S. Hill, *Quest for Refuge: The Mormon Flight from American Pluralism* (Salt Lake City: Signature Books, 1989), 30.

102. Brigham Young, *Journal of Discourses*, 9:137, 28 July 1861; Brigham Young, ibid., 10:38-39, 9 Mar. 1862; Heber C. Kimball, ibid., 8:108, 1 July 1860; "Civilized Warfare In Missouri," *Millennial Star* 25 (25 July 1863): 470-71; "Civil War in America—Its Importance As A Warning To The Saints," ibid. (11 May 1861): 300; "A Dreary Picture," ibid. (7 Sept. 1861): 581; "News From Home," ibid. (12 Oct. 1861): 662; Orson Hyde, "A Timely Warning from An Apostle of Jesus Christ," ibid. (3 May 1862): 273-75; "History of Brigham Young," ibid., 26 (5 Nov. 1864): 712; Reinwand, "An Interpretive Study of Mormon Millennialism," 120; Campbell, "Pioneers and Patriotism," 318-19.

Lord had led modern Israel to the West to protect them from impending devastation, and the war was God's method of sweeping Missouri clean to pave the way for Mormon repossession.[103] "They are emptying the land of inhabitants, burning the rubbish, and clearing the way for the return of the Saints; and the city of Zion will yet be laid out, and commenced to be built in Jackson County, Missouri, and the temple of the Lord will be erected on that very spot in this generation."[104] Almost every kindred, tongue, and people had, by that time, been given the chance to accept the gospel, said Brigham Young. Young told the Saints that they would soon "go back to Jackson county which [I] Expect will be in 7 years."[105] In 1864 George Q. Cannon declared, "[T]he day is near when a Temple shall be reared in the Center Stake of Zion, and the Lord has said his glory shall rest on that House in this generation in which the revelation was given, which is upwards of thirty years ago."[106]

---

103. H. W. Barnett, "Literal Gathering of the House of Israel," *Millennial Star* 23 (3 Aug. 1861): 484-86; ibid., 22 (27 July 1860): 424-25; "Devastation in Jackson Co. Mo.," *St. Joseph Herald,* 18 Oct. 1863, in Journal History, 18 Oct. 1863; Larson and Larson, *Diary of Charles Walker,* 1:135, 22 Aug. 1860; 1:242-43, 31 Dec. 1863; Kenney, *Wilford Woodruff's Journal,* 6:147, 1 Jan. 1864; Luke William Gallup to Nancy Williams, 2 July 1862, Luke William Gallup Collection, LDS church archives; Cleland and Brooks, *A Mormon Chronicle,* 1:255-56, 20 May 1860; ibid., 1:296-97, 14 Feb. 1861; Isaac Chauncy Haight Journal, TS, LDS church archives, 120, 7 Dec. 1862; George Laub Diaries, TS, Utah State Historical Society, 2, 155-56; Journal History, 1 Jan. 1864; Brigham Young, *Journal of Discourses,* 9:142, 28 July 1861; George A. Smith, ibid., 9:69, 10 Mar. 1861. See also Eddins, "The Mormons and the Civil War," 64-96.

104. *Millennial Star* 27 (1865): 204, in Reinwand, "An Interpretive Study of Mormon Millennialism," 120. See also "The Fulfillment of Prophecy," *Millennial Star* 34 (23 Aug. 1862): 529-33.

105. Kenney, *Wilford Woodruff's Journal,* 6:71, 23 Aug. 1862; Journal History, 22 Aug. 1862; Brigham Young, *Journal of Discourses,* 8:33, 5 Apr. 1860. See also Orson Pratt, "Preparations For The Second Advent," *The Seer* 2 (Aug. 1854): 131; *Times and Seasons* 6 (1 July 1845): 956.

106. Cannon, *Journal of Discourses,* 10:344, 23 Oct. 1864. See also

All agreed the time was short.[107] Apostle Orson Hyde prophesied, "I do believe that God is about to come out of his hiding-place
and to vex the nation according to his word through the martyred
Joseph."[108] "They have made war upon the Saints from the beginning," said Brigham Young, "and now they will have war to the hilt,
until they are used up, root and branch. In the name of Israel's God,
there will not be one of them left upon the earth."[109] In 1860 Hyde
predicted, "Will the nation be broken? ... The signs in the heavens
and upon the earth ... were never more portentous over Jerusalem,
previous to its destruction, than they are now over the United States
of America."[110]

Whereas American Protestantism saw the divided nation's crisis as a just reward for years of slavery, Mormons believed the
war was punishment for the murders of Joseph and Hyrum

"Record of Andrew Jackson Allen," 14 Mar. 1858.

107. "Blindness Of The World To The Signs Of The Times," *Millennial
Star* 24 (21 June 1862): 393-96; "Uneasiness of the Nations of the Earth—Its
Causes," ibid., 39 (27 Sept. 1862): 609-11; G. E. Grove, "The Consumption
Decreed Upon All Nations," ibid., 14 (4 Apr. 1863): 211-12; Ezra T. Benson,
Journal of Discourses, 10:152, 6 Apr. 1863; Orson Pratt, ibid., 8:49, 8 Apr. 1860;
Brigham Young, ibid., 8:134, 29 July 1860.

108. Hyde, *Journal of Discourses*, 6:12-13, n.d. See also "Consequences
of Rejecting the Message of Truth," *Millennial Star* 32 (9 Aug. 1862): 497-99.

109. Young, *Journal of Discourses*, 8:230, 21 Oct. 1860. See also
"Blindness Of The World To The Signs Of The Times," *Millennial Star* 24
(21 June 1862): 393-96.

110. Hyde, *Journal of Discourses*, 8:237, 7 Oct. 1860. Numerous
discourses with similar sentiments can be cited. For a sampling, see Heber
C. Kimball, *Journal of Discourses* 9:55, 14 Apr. 1861; Heber C. Kimball, ibid.,
9:131, 6 Jan. 1861; Brigham Young, ibid., 8:336, 17 Feb. 1861; Brigham
Young, ibid., 9:321, 6 July 1862; Brigham Young, ibid., 9:333, 3 Aug. 1862.
The Mormon press presented the same position. See "The Dark Day of the
United States," *Millennial Star* 22 (28 Jan. 1860): 49-53; "'Civilized' Warfare
in Missouri," ibid., 25 (25 July 1863): 470-71; "A Direful Vengeance And An
Unlooked-for Avenger," ibid., 25 (14 Nov. 1863): 728-29; Joseph G. Romney,
"The Fulfillment of the Purposes of God," ibid., 26 (11 June 1864): 366-71;
"Modern Prophecy And Fulfillment," ibid., 27 (25 Mar. 1865): 184-90.

Smith. Civil War casualties were seen as avenging blood.[111] As early as the 1840s, a widely sung church hymn, "Praise to the Man," predicted that the earth must atone for Joseph Smith's death.[112] Brigham Young chastised America: "[for] the nation that has slain the Prophet of God and cast out his people will have to pay the debt. They will be broken in pieces like a potter's vessel; yea worse, they will be ground to powder."[113] In the Mormon temple early participants were admonished to "pray [to] Almighty God to avenge the blood of the prophets upon *this nation*, and that you will teach the same to your children and your children's children unto the third and fourth generations."[114] First Presidency member George Q. Cannon recalled that in an

---

111. Journal History, 1 Jan. 1864; "Retribution Justice—The Enemies of the Church Guilty of the Crimes Charged on the Saints," *Millennial Star* 23 (23 Nov. 1861): 755-58; "The Dark Day of the United States," ibid., 22 (28 Jan. 1860): 49-53; "A Direful Vengeance And An Unlooked-For Avenger," ibid., 25 (14 Nov. 1863): 728-29; Joseph Romney, "The Fulfillment of the Purposes of God," ibid., 26 (11 June 1864): 366-71; "Consequences of National Sin," ibid., 30 (15 Feb. 1868): 105-108; Orson Hyde, *Journal of Discourses*, 7:51-53, n.d.; Brigham Young, ibid., 12:119, 17 Aug. 1867; Wilford Woodruff, ibid., 10:15, 27 July 1862; Heber C. Kimball, ibid., 10:46, 4 May 1862; Heber C. Kimball, ibid., 8:245, 15 July 1860; Reinwand, "An Interpretive Study of Mormon Millennialism," 117-26.

112. The song was first printed in the *Times and Seasons*, 1 Aug. 1844, and can be found in *Hymns of The Church of Jesus Christ of Latter-Day Saints* (Salt Lake City: Church of Jesus Christ of Latter-Day Saints, 1985), 27. See also "History of Peter Nielson (Autobiography)," translated from the Danish by Orson B. West, TS, LDS church archives, 367-68, for a retrospective entry for the year 1864. See also Long, *The Saints and the Union*, 25; Reinwand, "An Interpretive Study of Mormon Millennialism," 118; Neff, *History of Utah*, 620-22.

113. Young, *Journal of Discourses*, 9:368, 31 Aug. 1862.

114. Walter M. Wolfe, in *Proceeding Before The Committee On Privileges And Elections Of The United States Senate In The Matter Of The Protests Against The Right Of Hon. Reed Smoot, A Senator From The State Of Utah, To Hold His Seat*, 4 vols. (Washington, D.C.: Government Printing Office, 1906), 4:6-7, (emphasis added).

oath he took in the Nauvoo temple he pledged to "avenge the blood of the martyrs."[115]

Utah territorial governor Stephen S. Harding understood Mormon anger at their past treatment at the hands of the government and reported to Secretary of State William H. Seward the LDS belief that, "as the Jewish Nation was cut off and scattered to all parts of the earth, because they rejected the Saviour and crucified him—so the American people ... *for the consenting of the death of the prophet at Carthage, Illinois is to be destroyed.*"[116]

The difficulty, of course, was that instead of giving rise to a holocaust, the war freed the slaves and opposing armies stacked their arms. Even the Emancipation Proclamation was viewed as merely expanding the conflict. The *Millennial Star* editorialized that "it is beyond the power of President Lincoln or any faction in the nation, either North or South, to prescribe a remedy that will heal the fracture or prevent it widening. The decree of the Lord has gone forth respecting this consumation and no power can prevent its complete fulfillment."[117] When cataclysmic destruction failed to occur, the Saints were forced again to look to a future date for millennial relief.[118] Yet even with peace in the East, the Saints were loath to let the conflict go, believing fighting would soon break out again and spread as Joseph's prophecy

---

115. Abraham Hoagland Cannon Diaries, photocopy of MS, Special Collections, Lee Library, 6 Dec. 1889. For a full discussion of the evolution of the retribution oath in the temple endowment ceremony, see David John Buerger, "The Development of the Mormon Temple Endowment Ceremony," *Dialogue: A Journal of Mormon Thought* 20 (Winter 1987): 33-76; Buerger, *The Mysteries of Godliness*, 133-35.

116. Harding to William H. Seward, 30 Aug. 1862, Territorial Papers, Utah Territory, 1860-73, vol. 2:553-54, in Larson, "Utah and the Civil War," 69; emphasis in original. See also Burton, *The City of the Saints*, 276; Brooks, *On the Mormon Frontier*, 2:558, 4 July 1855.

117. "Emancipation of the Slaves—The Prophet Joseph's Plan—Results of Its Rejection," *Millennial Star* 7 (14 Feb. 1863): 98.

118. Reinwand, "An Interpretive Study of Mormon Millennialism," 137.

had decreed.[119] It was but the calm before the storm, a "thin gauge over a burning flame which will eventually burst forth like a mighty volcano."[120] Everything being attempted by Congress would only lead to more war, said Brigham Young.[121]

Soon the "bonds which hold society together" will be destroyed.[122] "There will be one more onset against this people by the Gentiles," declared Heber C. Kimball. "They will make another stroke on us and then there will be such scenes as was never before seen or heard of. The powers of destruction and devastation will be let loose. One scene is passed, but the curtain is about to rise again and oh what will be the next scene."[123] As late as 1866 Utah federal marshal Francis P. Dyer reported that Apostle John Taylor "could not finish" an address "without running on to the one string ... that is the *down fall* of the United States and the building up of *Mormonism.*"[124]

---

119. Eddins, "The Mormons and the Civil War," 122-38.

120. Cleland and Brooks, *A Mormon Chronicle*, 2:117, 1 May 1869; Orson Hyde, *Journal of Discourses*, 11:154, 7 Oct. 1865; Larson and Larson, *Diary of Charles Walker*, 1:249, 7 Aug. 1865; "The New Rebellion And Carnival of Murder," *Millennial Star* 30 (7 Nov. 1868): 710-11; "The Dangerous State of the Country," ibid., 30 (24 Oct. 1868): 684-85.

121. "Corruptions of United States Officials," *Millennial Star* 29 (15 June 1867): 376-78; "Secret Combinations," ibid., 30 (30 May 1868): 344-48; "Cattle Plague in the U.S.," ibid., 30 (19 Sept. 1868): 594-96; Brigham Young, *Journal of Discourses*, 12:120, 17 Aug. 1867. For the continued belief that the prophecies of Joseph Smith would yet be fulfilled, see Brigham Young, ibid., 12:242, 25 July 1868; Brigham Young, ibid., 12:285, 8 Oct. 1868; "'Chain Gang Of States,' Congress Inaugurated A Revolution—A War Of Races In Prospect," *Millennial Star*, 25 (21 Apr. 1866): 246-48.

122. Charles Penrose, "The Impeachment of President Johnson," *Millennial Star* 30 (25 Apr. 1868): 260-63.

123. Journal History, 13 May 1865.

124. Dyer to Addison Pratt, 19 Aug. 1866, in Hansen, *Quest for Empire*, 168-69, emphasis in original. See also "Wars And Rumors Of Wars," *Millennial Star*, 32 (16 Aug. 1870): 520-22; "War," ibid., 34 (10 Sept. 1877): 579-81; "Historical Contrast Betwixt the 27th of June 1844, And the 14th of April 1865," ibid., 27 (1 July 1865): 408-13; "Hand of God Among the Nations," ibid., 30 (5 Sept. 1868): 568-76; "The Famine In India," ibid., 28

But Mormon millennial hope was to be placed on hold and chiliastic expectations reassessed.[125] When Lee surrendered to Grant at Appomattox, the reality was that the Union remained intact.[126] Government authorities had not flocked to Brigham Young to be saved, and the center stake of Zion, Missouri, had not been laid to waste al-

---

(29 Sept. 1866): 615-16; "Political Crisis In America," ibid., 28 (6 Oct. 1866): 628-29; "Prospects of Another American War," ibid., 630-31; "The American Nation's Doom," ibid., 29 (6 Oct. 1866): 633-35; "Testimony of Earthquakes to the Nearness of The Lord's Second Coming," ibid., 31 (13 Feb. 1869): 119; "Remarks By President George Q. Cannon," *Deseret News*, 26 July 1884, 1; George W. Lamb Diary, Huntington Library, San Marino, California, 4 Mar. 1873; "Record of Andrew Jackson Allen," 97-98, 21 Sept. 1873; John Druce to Brigham Young, 3 Feb. 1877, Brigham Young Correspondence, LDS church archives.

125. Pomeroy Tucker, *Origin, Rise, and Progress of Mormonism* ... (New York: D. Appleton and Co., 1867), 220-21. See also Orson Pratt, *Journal of Discourses*, 14:62, 26 Mar. 1871. Prior to the 1921 edition of the *Doctrine and Covenants*, section 87, verse 3, read, "[T]hus wars shall be poured out upon all nations." This provided a causal relationship between the "rebellion of South Carolina," the southern states calling on Great Britain and other nations, and the end of the world. In the early twentieth century World War I was again seen as fulfilling Joseph's prophecy that war would consume the earth. But after the war, a 1921 apostolic revision committee changed the word "thus" to "then," softening the cause-and-effect relationship between American Civil War events and the "consumption decreed" upon all nations. See *Doctrine and Covenants*, 87:3, 6; Robert J. Woodford, "The Historical Development of the Doctrine and Covenants," Ph.D. diss., Brigham Young University, 1974, 1118-19; Anthony A. Hutchinson, "Prophetic Foreknowledge: Hope and Fulfillment in an Inspired Community," *Sunstone* 11 (July 1987): 17. Compare with Wilford Woodruff's linking of Civil War events to Christ's return: "the union has been dissolved[,] ... the spirit of God is being withdrawn from the Nation[,] ... great destruction awaits the Nation[,] ... great Events await all Nations and the way is preparing for the Coming of the Lord Jesus Christ." See Kenney, *Wilford Woodruff's Journal*, 6:147, 1 Jan. 1864.

126. According to Hubert Howe Bancroft, just days before the surrender at Appomattox, Brigham Young predicted that there would be "yet four [more] years of civil war." See Bancroft, *History of Utah: 1540-1886* (San Francisco: The History Co., 1889), 606.

lowing the Saints to redeem the land of their inheritance. With North and South reconciled, and the Saints having failed to acquire national and world domination, Mormons again had to push their hoped-for millennial kingdom into the indefinite future.[127]

127. Long, *The Saints and the Union*, 267; Reinwand, "An Interpretive Study of Mormon Millennialism," 134-37.

CHAPTER EIGHT

MILLENNIALISM AND THE ANTI-POLYGAMY CAMPAIGN

At a special conference in August 1852 the Mormon church formally announced its practice of plural marriage. The general reaction from Americans was indignation and repugnancy. That same year Harriet Beecher Stowe also published *Uncle Tom's Cabin*. The timing emotionally linked the tyranny of slavery to polygamy, a tie that continued throughout the 1850s. Depicting Mormon polygamists as slave holders, abolitionists and reformers carried the image of slave masters over to polygamist husbands.[1] In 1855 and 1856 alone, four anti-Mormon novels were published all using the theme of strong women fighting against cowardly, depraved men.[2]

As part of the pre-Civil War debate, Mormon polygamy be-

---

1. Jessie L. Embry, "The Polygamy Image," *This People*, Fall 1990, 25.

2. Leonard J. Arrington and Jon Haupt, "Intolerable Zion: The Image of Mormonism in Nineteenth Century American Literature," *Western Humanities Review* 22 (Summer 1968): 244-45; Leonard J. Arrington, "Mormonism: Views from Without and Within" *Brigham Young University Studies* 14 (Winter 1974): 144; Neal Lambert, "Saints, Sinners and Scribes: A Look at the Mormons in Fiction," *Utah Historical Quarterly* 36 (Winter 1968): 63; Jan Shipps, "From Satyr to Saint: American Attitudes Toward the Mormons, 1860-1960," paper presented at the 1973 annual meeting of the Organization of American Historians, TS, Utah State Historical Society, Salt Lake City, 18, photocopy in my possession.

came entangled with slavery and the associated questions of territorial and states' rights that linked Mormons and the South in a
common cause.[3] With a direct attack in the 1856 Republican platform, national attention was drawn to ridding the nation of the
"twin relics of barbarism—Polygamy, and Slavery."[4] As such, polygamy became a pawn in the much larger game of sectional politics
as individuals and states determined their allegiance on the controversial issue of what authority Congress could exercise and maintain over U.S. territories.[5] Southerners knew "if we can render polygamy criminal, it may be claimed that we can also render criminal that other 'twin relic of barbarism,' slavery."[6]

During the twenty years from 1871 to 1891, every U.S. president from Ulysses S. Grant to Benjamin Harrison specifically focused on Utah in Congressional addresses,[7] identifying polygamy as
"a remnant of barbarism, repugnant to civilization" and declaring
"the Mormon Church ... offends the moral sense of manhood by
sanctioning polygamy."[8] In his 1884 annual message, Chester A.

---

3. Gustive O. Larson, "Utah and the Civil War," *Utah Historical
Quarterly* 33 (Winter 1965): 63.

4. Platform of the Republican Party, adopted at Philadelphia, 17 June
1856. See Donald Bruce Johnson, ed., *National Party Platforms*, 2 vols.
(Urbana: University of Illinois Press, 1978), 1:27.

5. Orma Linford, "The Mormons and the Law: The Polygamy Cases,"
Utah Law Review 9 (Winter 1964): 312.

6. *Congressional Globe*, 36th Cong., 1st Sess., 1860, p. 1410. For a
detailed study of the background and legislative juxtapositioning over the
slavery and polygamy issues, see Richard D. Poll, "The Twin Relic: A Study
of Mormon Polygamy and the Campaign by the Government of the United
States for Its Abolition, 1852-1890," M.A. thesis, Texas Christian University,
1939, 60-116.

7. James D. Richardson, comp., *Messages and Papers of the Presidents*, 20
vols. (New York: Bureau of National Literature, 1917), Grant—1871: 9:4105;
Hayes—1879: 10:4512, —1880: 10:4557; Garfield—1881: 10:4601; Arthur—
10:1881: 10:4644, —1883: 10:4771, —1884: 10:4837; Cleveland—1885:
10:4946; Harrison—1890: 12:5553.

8. Ulysses S. Grant and James A. Garfield, in Richardson, *Messages and
Papers of the Presidents*, 9:4105, 10:4601.

Arthur recommended that "Congress assume absolute political control of the Territory of Utah."[9] Noting that "the Mormons have given their allegiance to a theocracy," the *New York Times* portrayed church leaders and followers both as scheming, disloyal citizens.[10]

In Utah persecution was a major theme of general conference addresses from 1860 to 1890.[11] Oppression was part of the Plan of Salvation, a refiner's fire to purify the people of God.[12] Oppression also meant the Millennium was near and the Saints were then living in the final stage of history prior to the earth's destruction. That American citizens had turned a deaf ear to their pleas confirmed that the end was in sight: the harsher the persecution, the nearer the Millennium.[13]

Mormon writing and preaching was filled with concern for "last things."[14] "Calamities were thickening in the world," wrote

---

9. Chester A. Arthur, in Richardson, *Messages and Papers of the Presidents*, 10:4837.

10. "A Threat From Mormondom," *New York Times,* 22 June 1875.

11. A. Karl Larson and Katharine Miles Larson, eds., *Diary of Charles Lowell Walker*, 2 vols. (Logan: Utah State University Press, 1980), 1:318, 15 Sept. 1870; Larry M. Logue, *A Sermon in the Desert: Belief and Behavior in Early St. George, Utah* (Urbana: University of Illinois Press, 1988), 33; Gordon Shepherd and Gary Shepherd, *A Kingdom Transformed: Themes in the Development of Mormonism* (Salt Lake City: University of Utah Press, 1984), 76.

12. Larson and Larson, *Diary of Charles Walker*, 1:306, 20 Feb. 1870; Ballard S. Dunn, *The Twin Monsters ...* (New York: James Pott and Co., n.d.), 6; "Report of the Utah Commission," 1887, in *Report of the Secretary of the Interior ...*, 5 vols. (Washington, D.C.: Government Printing Office, 1887), 2:1339.

13. Logue, *A Sermon in the Desert*, 33-34. See also poems by Charles Walker in Larson and Larson, *Diary of Charles Walker*, 2:589, 2 Oct. 1882; 2:774-75, 24 July 1894; Franklin S. Richards to John Taylor, 9 Feb. 1887, photocopy, Franklin S. Richards Correspondence, 1886-90, Utah State Historical Society.

14. Larson and Larson, *Diary of Charles Walker*, 1:388, 15 June 1874; 2:624, 25 Dec. 1883; Robert Glass Cleland and Juanita Brooks, eds., *A Mormon Chronicle: The Diaries of John D. Lee, 1848-1876*, 2 vols. (Salt Lake City:

Charles Walker, the earth's mortal age of six thousand years was nearly over.[15] Many of those then alive were told they would be "quickened," in anticipation of the Parousia, that they would never taste death and would see the dead come forth from their graves and the lost tribes of Israel return from the north.[16]

Congress focused on polygamy in 1862 by passing the Morrill Act to outlaw bigamy.[17] During the congressional debate of the 1860s, many congressmen maintained polygamy "went beyond what was tolerable in America."[18] But problems inherent in enforcing the Morrill Act became readily apparent. Since marriage records were not required to be kept in Utah or many other U.S.

University of Utah Press, 1983), 2:291-92, 29 Aug. 1873; Scott G. Kenney, *Wilford Woodruff's Journal, 1833-1898*, 9 vols. (Midvale, UT: Signature Books, 1983-85), 7:94, 10 Nov. 1872; "Record of Andrew Jackson Allen," TS, Utah State Historical Society, 97-98, 21 Sept. 1873; "Prophetic Warnings," *Deseret News* 17 (11 Aug. 1884): 2; "An Epoch of Commotion," ibid., 17 (24 Apr. 1884): 2; F. D. Richards, *Journal of Discourses*, 26 vols. (Liverpool, Eng.: F.D. Richards, 1855-86), 24:283, 6 Oct. 1883.

15. Larson and Larson, *Diary of Charles Walker*, 1:367, 20 Apr. 1873. See also Orson Pratt, *Journal of Discourses*, 15:263, 29 Dec. 1872; Wilford Woodruff, ibid., 17:247, 9 Oct. 1874; Wilford Woodruff, ibid., 23:331, 10 Dec. 1882; Wilford Woodruff, ibid., 24:53, 27 Jan. 1883; Wilford Woodruff, ibid., 25:10, 6 Jan. 1884; George Teasdale, ibid., 26:54, 11 Jan. 1885; Orson F. Whitney, ibid., 26:200, 19 Apr. 1885.

16. Brigham Young, *Journal of Discourses*, 17:37, 18 Apr. 1874; Wilford Woodruff, ibid., 18:37, 27 June 1875; Anthony Woodward Ivins Diaries, Utah State Historical Society, 1:17-19, 4 Oct. 1871; "Excerpts from a Journal or Sketch of the Life of Joel Hills Johnson," bound printed copy (N.p.: n.p., n.d.), 28-30, Utah State Historical Society; Thomas William Whitaker Journal, 1849-86, photocopy of holograph, Special Collections, Marriott Library, University of Utah, Salt Lake City, Utah, 6 Jan. 1879.

17. Edwin Brown Firmage and Richard Collin Mangrum, *Zion in the Courts: A Legal History of the Church of Jesus Christ of Latter-day Saints, 1830-1900* (Urbana: University of Illinois Press, 1988), 131.

18. James L. Clayton, "The Supreme Court, Polygamy, and Enforcement of Morals in Nineteenth Century America: An Analysis of *Reynolds v. United States,*" *Dialogue: A Journal of Mormon Thought* 12 (Winter 1979): 48.

territories until 1887, proof of multiple marriages demanded under the law was next to impossible to obtain.[19]

Subsiding somewhat during the immediate post-Civil War years, the attack on polygamy once renewed became a major engine for Mormon millennialism. Mormons believed the contest over polygamy represented a "holy war," and defense of the theological tenet re-energized LDS millennial hope.[20] As early as 1860 even non-Mormons had become familiar with the Saints' assertion that Christ would return prior to the turn of the century.[21]

In their redemptive hope, the Saints revisited earlier millennial prophecies, specifically Joseph Smith's identification of 1891 as the year Christ would return to redeem his people.[22] In 1875 Andrew J. Allen reported that elders were preaching that the Savior would come to earth "soon not more than sixteen years according to the revelations Joseph Smith had received."[23] In his 1875 diary Oliver

---

19. Firmage and Mangrum, *Zion in the Courts*, 149-51.

20. John Henry Smith to Joseph Smith III, 21 Apr. 1886, Library-Archives, Reorganized Church of Jesus Christ of Latter Day Saints, Independence, Missouri; Cleland and Brooks, *Diaries of John D. Lee*, 2:235, 18 Apr. 1873; Orson Pratt, "Celestial Marriage," *The Seer* 1 (May 1853): 75; John Thompson, *Mormonism–Increase of the Army ...* (Washington, D.C.: Buell and Blanchard, 1858), 5.

21. Richard F. Burton, *The City of the Saints*, ed. Fawn M. Brodie (1861; reprint, New York: Alfred A. Knopf, 1963), 403; J. H. Beadle, *Life in Utah, or the Mysteries and Crimes of Mormonism* (Toronto: A.H. Hovey, 1872), in Louis G. Reinwand, "An Interpretive Study of Mormon Millennialism During the Nineteenth Century with Emphasis on Millennial Developments in Utah," M.A. thesis, Brigham Young University, 1971, 98.

22. Henry Ballard Diary, TS, Special Collections, Lee Library, Brigham Young University, Provo, Utah, 76, 15 Jan. 1876. See Gordon Shepherd and Gary Shepherd, *A Kingdom Transformed: Themes in the Development of Mormonism* (Salt Lake City: University of Utah Press, 1984), 195-96, which shows that general conference addresses with eschatological themes peaked near the end of the years 1869-89.

23. "Record of Andrew Jackson Allen," TS, Utah State Historical Society, 105, 21 Mar. 1875. See also C. Jacobson Diary, 1876, TS, in Reinwand, "An Interpretive Study of Mormon Millennialism," 145, where

Huntington also recalled Smith's prophecy that "God had revealed to him that the coming of Christ would be within 56 years, which being added to 1835 shows that before 1891 and the 14th of Feb. the Savior of the world would make his appearance again upon the earth and the winding up scene take place."[24]

This revival of Mormon millennialism coincided with an official endorsement of Joseph Smith's prophetic timetable. In 1876 the church published a new edition of the *Doctrine and Covenants* which divided the revelations into numbered verses and added twenty-six new sections. This included the Joseph Smith millennial prophecy, thus canonizing it as scripture.[25] Sold in October 1876 as the first edition published in the United States since the 1846 Nauvoo edition, these revised scriptures offered renewed hope that the Lord would soon appear to aid the Saints in their struggle with the gentiles. Testifying to Smith's prophetic calling, senior church official John Taylor left no doubt that the Saints interpreted literally prophecies uttered from the lips of modern-day prophets: "all that he [God] has said ... through ancient prophets and through Joseph Smith are true, and as sure as God lives they will take place. I will prophecy that they will take place as sure as God lives, and they are approaching very rapidly upon

---

the same fifteen-year time frame is promoted.

24. Oliver B. Huntington Diary, TS, Special Collections, Lee Library, 2:129.

25. Historian Office Journal, 7 July 1874-14 Nov. 1875, p. 70, in Robert J. Woodford, "The Historical Development of the Doctrine and Covenants," Ph.D. diss., Brigham Young University, 1974, 75-76. Editor Orson Pratt included section 130 in the 1876 edition of the *Doctrine and Covenants* under the direction of Brigham Young. See Woodford, "The Historical Development of the Doctrine and Covenants," 1710. This section was first published on 9 July 1856 in the *Deseret News*, and has been in every LDS edition of the *Doctrine and Covenants* since 1876, but is not canonized in RLDS scripture. See Lyndon W. Cook, *The Revelations of the Prophet Joseph Smith: A Historical and Biographical Commentary of the Doctrine and Covenants* (1981; reprint, Salt Lake City: Deseret Book, 1985), 131; Richard P. Howard, *Restoration Scriptures: A Study of Their Textual Development* (Independence, MO: Herald Publishing House, 1969), 229.

us."[26] Reaffirming their faith in modern revelation, George Q. Cannon told the Saints that step by step all of Joseph Smith's prophecies were coming to fruition "just as sure as [if] God [had] spoken it."[27]

Throughout the late 1870s millennialism remained a theme.[28] While attending a conference in Kanab, Utah, L. John Nuttall recorded that Bishop Sixtus E. Johnson retold the account of the Joseph Smith prophecy. Johnson emphasized that if Smith would have lived to be eighty-five, he would have seen the Savior. Johnson "urged the Saints to prepare for the judgements of the Almighty upon the wicked Nations."[29] Tying imminence of the Millennium to the Saints' return to Missouri and the eventual redemption of Zion, Apostle Lorenzo Snow predicted in 1878 that

> the time is speedily coming—we do not want to talk very much though about going to Jackson County, Missouri. ... We are not going tomorrow, nor next day, this week or next week; but we are going, and there are many hundreds and hundreds within the sound of my voice that will live to go back to Jackson County and build a holy temple to the Lord our God.[30]

An increase in Mormon millennial expectation appeared in 1879 in response to the Supreme Court decision in the George Reynolds polygamy case.[31] Reynolds, a secretary to Brigham Young and a

---

26. John Taylor, *Journal of Discourses*, 21:56; 21 Sept. 1878.

27. "Religious Service," *Deseret News* 15 (26 June 1882): 1; "Remarks By President George Q. Cannon," ibid., 17 (26 July 1884).

28. Kenney, *Wilford Woodruff's Journal*, 7:258, 31 Dec. 1875; Wilford Woodruff, *Journal of Discourses*, 19:360-61, 30 June 1878; Wilford Woodruff, ibid., 19:135, 13 Oct. 1877.

29. Leonard John Nuttall Diary, TS, Special Collections, Lee Library, 7 Dec. 1878. Nuttall records Johnson as stating that Smith would have been eighty years old when he would see the Savior.

30. *Millennial Star* 40 (10 Apr. 1878): 64, in Richard S. Van Wagoner, *Sidney Rigdon: A Portrait of Religious Excess* (Salt Lake City: Signature Books, 1994), 153.

31. Reinwand, "An Interpretive Study of Mormon Millennialism," 151. See *Reynolds v. United States*, 98 U.S. 145 (1879); Firmage and Mangrum, *Zion*

prominent polygamist, allowed himself to be used as a test case to challenge the government's anti-polygamy statutes. Initially convicted in 1875 of bigamy under the Morrill Act, Reynolds's case was appealed to the Utah Supreme Court which, in 1876, upheld the lower court's decision. Eventually appealed to the nation's highest tribunal, the U.S. Supreme Court upheld Reynolds's conviction as a legitimate means of prohibiting a practice which threatened the well-being of American social values.[32] Labeling marriage a "sacred obligation," Chief Justice Morrison R. Waite identified polygamy as an evil "which strikes at the foundation of American society." Classified as social corruption, Mormon polygamous behavior fell outside the freedom of religion protection of the First Amendment.[33]

Admitting no illegality, the church hierarchy continued to defend plural marriage as constitutionally protected.[34] The anti-polygamy campaign confirmed the opinion that state officials were indeed their "enemies."[35] From the pulpit church leaders denounced the *Reynolds* decision as an invasion of their right to religious freedom, and prophesied that the wrath of God would fall upon the government officials responsible for the Saints' persecution.[36] In March 1879

in the Courts, 151-59; Linford, "The Mormons and the Law: The Polygamy Cases," 331-41.

32. *Reynolds v. United States*, 98 U.S. 145 (1879); Linford, "The Mormons and the Law: The Polygamy Cases," 341.

33. Firmage and Mangrum, *Zion in the Courts*, 156; B. Carmon Hardy, *Solemn Covenant: The Mormon Polygamous Passage* (Urbana: University of Illinois Press, 1992), 59-60; Clayton, "The Supreme Court, Polygamy, and Enforcement of Morals in Nineteenth Century America," 55.

34. Nels Anderson, *Desert Saints: The Mormon Frontier in Utah* (1942; reprint, Chicago: University of Chicago Press, 1966), 291.

35. Annie Clark Tanner, *A Mormon Mother* (Salt Lake City: Tanner Trust Fund, 1991), 82; John Taylor, 13 Oct. 1882, in James R. Clark, ed., *Messages of the First Presidency of the Church of Jesus Christ of Latter-day Saints, 1833-1964*, 6 vols. (Salt Lake City: Bookcraft, 1965-75), 2:348-49.

36. The most scholarly contemporary reaction to the *Reynolds* decision was George Q. Cannon, *A Review of the Decision of the Supreme Court of the United States in the Case of George Reynolds v. the United States* (Salt Lake City: Deseret News Printing and Publishing Establishment, 1879). A sampling of

Apostle Orson Pratt rhetorically asked, "What about the American nation. That [Civil] war ... was nothing, compared to that which will eventually devastate that country. The time is not very far distant in the future, when the Lord God will lay his hand heavily upon that nation [America]."[37] Apostle Moses Thatcher surmised there was now more freedom in Great Britain than in the United States.[38]

The Saints took the remarks of their leaders to heart. After the Supreme Court decision in the *Reynolds* case, Thomas W. Whitaker confessed in his journal that "The Lord has told us we must obey the law of polygamy and the United States Government say we shall not." Believing the world was fast preparing itself for destruction, he predicted the 1880s would be the "most destructive period of the world's history."[39] Whitaker was not alone. Following the decision a *Millennial Star* editorial titled "The Coming of the Messiah" reiterated Joseph Smith's 1835 prophecy that "fifty-six years should wind up the scene," concluding "this would take us to the year 1891." The article also recounted Smith's second prophecy of seeing the face of the Son of Man should he live to be eighty-five, ascertaining that this "would be in 1890, or on the verge of 1891." Although cautiously reminding readers that Smith gave no specific date, the editorial emphasized that "it is evident that one of the most stupendous occurences,

---

church leaders who declared the *Reynolds* verdict unconstitutional may be found in Lorenzo Snow, *Journal of Discourses*, 20:188, 7 Apr. 1879; Franklin D. Richards, ibid., 23:111, 8 Apr. 1882; John Taylor, ibid., 26:38-39, 14 Dec. 1884; George Q. Cannon, ibid., 26:145, 18 Jan. 1885; "The Reynolds Test Polygamy Case—An Unconstitutional and Oppressive Decision," *Millennial Star* 41 (13 Jan. 1879): 24; Larson and Larson, *Diary of Charles Walker*, 2:513-14, 9-10 Dec. 1880.

37. Pratt, *Journal of Discourses*, 20:151, 9 Mar. 1879. See also L. John Nuttall Diary, 7 Jan. 1879.

38. John Morgan Journals, 1875-92, 10 vols., LDS church archives, Salt Lake City, Utah, 8:158, 7 Oct. 1888.

39. Thomas William Whitaker Journal, Jan. 1879. See also L. John Nuttall Diary, 35, 7 Jan. 1879; Larson and Larson, *Diary of Charles Walker*, 1:474-75, 6 Feb. 1879; George Q. Cannon, *Journal of Discourses*, 23:279, 8 Oct. 1882; Franklin D. Richards, ibid., 20:314-15, 6 Oct. 1879.

relating to the history of this planet, is approaching," and that is "the coming of our Lord and Savior, Jesus Christ, the Redeemer of the world."[40]

Many church leaders and members were convinced that the end of the world was near.[41] In May 1879 Charles Walker recorded that Joseph Smith's contemporary, one O. M. Allen, professed he heard "the prophet Joseph say that those who lived until the year 1881 would see the judgments go forth on the wicked that would make their soul sicken to see and hear of them."[42] That same month Apostle Charles W. Penrose warned the Saints that "the times in which we live ... are just preceding the coming of the Son of man in the clouds of heaven, with power and great glory."[43] In June 1879 Apostle Wilford Woodruff blatantly told the Saints in northern Arizona, "There will be no United States in the Year 1890."[44]

Providing additional encouragement of the Saints' millennial hope, in 1879-1880 the church published a new edition of the *Doctrine and Covenants*, edited by Apostle Orson Pratt and containing footnotes and references for the first time. Canonized at October 1880 general conference, it officially endorsed lay member millennial expectation.[45] Pratt's footnotes for Section 130 highlighted Joseph

---

40. "The Coming of the Messiah," *Millennial Star* 41 (7 Apr. 1879): 216-18.

41. Reinwand, "An Interpretive Study of Mormon Millennialism," 140-41.

42. Larson and Larson, *Diary of Charles Walker*, 1:486, 31 May 1879. Allen's 1881 date may stem from Demick Huntington's recollection that, in surrendering to Illinois officials in 1844, Smith had said, "If they shed my blood it shall shorten this work 10 years. That taken from 1891 would reduce the time to 1881 which is the true time within which the Saviour should come [and] much must be crowded into 6 years." In Oliver B. Huntingon, Diary, TS, Special Collections, Lee Library, 2:129.

43. Charles W. Penrose, *Journal of Discourses*, 20:216, 25 May 1879.

44. Minutes of Eastern Arizona Stake Conferences, 1879-82, 28 June 1879, p. 87, in Charles S. Peterson, *Take Up Your Mission: Mormon Colonizing Along the Little Colorado River, 1870-1900* (Tucson: University of Arizona Press, 1973), 228.

45. The 1879 edition, with footnote references, was first printed and

Smith's 85-year millennial prophecy, adding in the commentary section confirmation of the fateful time frame "near the end of the year 1890." Pratt also cross-referenced the revelation to "See prophecy of Joseph, uttered 14 March 1835 ... 'Even 56 years should wind up the scene.'"[46] To many there was no doubt the Son of Man would make his appearance in 1890-91.[47]

In both public and private remarks church leaders and rank-and-file made clear that intensified persecutions during the 1880s fulfilled the prophesied turbulence prior to a coming apocalypse.[48] Wilford Woodruff in particular believed in the imminence of the cataclysmic end of the world, and his millennial hope developed in conjunction with the increased threat to the Saints. Woodruff's journal records his thoughts during the 1880s, and year after year his conviction that the Millennium was imminent intensified.[49]

---

offered for sale in England in October 1879, and printed for the first time in Utah in 1880. See Woodford, "The Historical Development of the Doctrine and Covenants," 91. For canonization of the new edition of the *Doctrine and Covenants* at general conference in October 1880, see *Deseret News,* 11 Oct. 1880, 2.

46. Woodford, "The Historical Development of the Doctrine and Covenants," 1718. Pratt's extensive footnotes were deleted entirely by a 1921 revising committee. See ibid., 1717. See also Shepherd and Shepherd, *A Kingdom Transformed*, 195-96.

47. Reinwand, "An Interpretive Study of Mormon Millennialism," 143-45, although Reinwand hedges somewhat, claiming that only occasional remarks regarding the Second Coming in 1890 or 1891 "filter[ed] down" from church leaders.

48. In the 1880s the *Deseret News*, edited by Charles W. Penrose, had a periodic column dealing with national and international news. A sampling of the headlines in this column illustrates Penrose's millennialism. Captions commonly used to head these columns were: "Depravity and Disasters," "Death and Disaster," and "The Catalogue of Crime." They can be found in *Deseret News*, 16 June 1884, 1; 20 Feb. 1884, 1; 8 Mar. 1884, 6; 11 Jan. 1884, 1; 21 Oct. 1884, 1; "War and Rumors of War," 9 Feb. 1885, 1; "War Spirit Spreading," 1 Apr. 1885, 2.

49. Kenney, *Wilford Woodruff's Journal*, 8:292-94, 31 Dec. 1884; 8:310, 20 Mar. 1885; 8:336-37, 3 Oct. 1885; 8:343, 12 Nov. 1885; 8:349-50, 20 Dec.

Woodruff's ominous expectations were exemplified by his so-called "Wilderness Revelation" received in January 1880. Its theme was the impending apocalypse, the judgements of God upon the nation, and the Second Coming of Christ.[50] In Woodruff's revelation, the Lord proclaimed:

> The nation is ripened in iniquity ... and I will not stay my hand in judgement upon this nation or the nations of the earth. ... The blood of my servants Joseph and Hyrum ... cries from the ground for vengeance upon the nation which has shed their blood. But their blood shall speedily be avenged and shall cease to cry unto me, for the hour of God's judgement is fully come and shall be poured out without measure upon the wicked. ... prepare ye for the coming of the Son of man, which is nigh at the door. No man knoweth the day nor the hour; but the signs of both heaven and earth indicate His coming, as promised by the mouths of my disciples. The fig trees are leaving and the hour is nigh.[51]

1885; 8:351, 31 Dec. 1885; 8:415, 31 Dec. 1886; 8:474, 31 Dec. 1887; 9:74, 31 Dec. 1889. A recent one-volume condensation of the Woodruff journals reflected the dominance of them in its title: Susan Staker, ed., *Waiting for World's End: The Diaries of Wilford Woodruff* (Salt Lake City: Signature Books, 1993). In contrast, Thomas G. Alexander contends that although Woodruff felt the year 1890 was important, there was no clear indication that Woodruff "actively anticipated" 1890 to usher in the Millennium. Such an interpretation seems to misrepresent Woodruff's own distinctively apocalyptic sentiments. Woodruff's year-end entries were particularly millennial as he both summarized the previous year's events and articulated his predictions (albeit in general terms) for the coming year. See Alexander, "Wilford Woodruff and the Changing Nature of Mormon Religious Experience," *Church History* 45 (Mar. 1976): 66.

50. Alexander, "Wilford Woodruff and the Changing Nature of Mormon Religious Experience," 64-66. For the context surrounding the "Wilderness Revelation," see Kenney, *Wilford Woodruff's Journal*, 7:546-47, 26-28, Jan. 1880. The actual revelation was received on 26 Jan. 1880, see ibid.

51. Woodruff's "Wilderness Revelation" can be found in full in Staker, *Waiting for World's End*, 340-46; and Fred C. Collier, ed., *Unpublished Revelations of the Prophets and Presidents of the Church of Jesus Christ of Latter Day Saints*, 2 vols. (Salt Lake City: Collier's Publishing Co., 1979-93), 1:123-29.

Upon returning to Salt Lake City, Woodruff presented the revelation from the church hierarchy who accepted it as "the word of the Lord." Then, with the presiding authorities of the church gathered in a prayer circle, senior apostle John Taylor, kneeling at the altar and offering prayer for the group, legitimized the church's condemnation of the United States and the current generation. Woodruff's revelation from the Lord symbolized the leaders' solidarity.[52]

Not all general authorities struck an apocalyptic note in their sermons, but Woodruff continued to warn church members of the approaching "hour." At an 1881 conference in Manti he promised "that thousands of the children of the latter day saints would not die but would live to see the Saviour come."[53] The same year at St. George, Utah, Woodruff told the Saints "the coming of the Son of Man was nigh, even at the doors, and that there were thousands living in [the] mountains at [that] time that would see the son of God come and many would not taste death."[54] These pronouncements confirmed members' ongoing gospel discussions, many publicly quoting Joseph Smith "that 56 years should wind up the scene and the Savior should come to his people. It being then Feb. 14th, 1835."[55]

In 1882 an amendment to the Morrill Act, sponsored by Vermont Republican senator George F. Edmunds and later termed the Ed-

---

52. For a description of the presentation of the revelation to the Twelve Apostles, and John Taylor's prayer at the altar, see Thomas G. Alexander, *Things in Heaven and Earth: The Life and Times of Wilford Woodruff, a Mormon Prophet* (Salt Lake City: Signature Books, 1991), 237-39. In the nineteenth century Mormon prayer circles were used as a vehicle for members to covenant to live specific gospel principles to a greater degree. In the church's highest quorums, the First Presidency and the Quorum of Twelve Apostles, administrative and doctrinal matters were discussed and decisions affecting the entire church made while leaders, dressed in temple clothes, met in prayer circles. See D. Michael Quinn, "Latter-day Saint Prayer Circles," *Brigham Young University Studies* 19 (Fall 1978): 103.

53. Larson and Larson, *Diary of Charles Walker*, 2:563-64, 14 Aug. 1881.

54. Ibid., 2:544, 20 Mar. 1881. See also John Taylor, *Journal of Discourses*, 21:253, 21 Mar. 1880.

55. Larson and Larson, *Diary of Charles Walker*, 2:522, 21 Jan. 1881.

munds Act, provided the practical means of prosecuting polygamists
who had eluded arrest under earlier legislation. The federal government's power stemmed from the creation of the new offense of
cohabitation where no proof of marriage was required, and where
any contact between a suspected man and a potential polygamous
wife was seen as sufficient evidence for a conviction.[56]

The precarious position of the church hierarchy was brought to
the forefront by the conviction of Salt Lake City church leader Angus
M. Cannon. Cannon was convicted in a far-reaching decision that
placed a minimal burden on the prosecution. In the case cohabitation
was now defined as providing temporal support, such as food and
shelter, for more than one woman on a regular basis.[57] In specifying
what constituted cohabitation, the courts interpreted the Edmunds
Act to criminalize the appearance of polygamous marriage. The
impetus for conviction under cohabitation as stated by the court was
"not only to punish bigamy and polygamy when direct proof of the
existence of those relations can be made, but to prevent a man from
flaunting in the face of the world the ostentation and opportunities
of a bigamous household."[58]

Most church leaders were polygamists, with the controversial
practice stretching far down into the ranks of local leadership where
most stake presidents, bishops, and counselors also lived this "celestial law." Now forced into hiding by the Edmunds Act during the
period known as "the Raid," the lives of leaders and members alike
underwent tremendous disruption. Men abandoned their farms and
businesses, and plural wives with children went into hiding or moved
continually on the "Underground" to avoid testifying against husbands and fathers.[59]

---

56. Firmage and Mangrum, *Zion in the Courts*, 161.

57. James B. Allen and Glen M. Leonard, *The Story of the Latter-day
Saints* (Salt Lake City: Deseret Book Co., 1976), 392.

58. *Cannon v. United States*, 116 U.S. (1885), *Supreme Court Reporter* (St.
Paul: West Publishing Co., 1886), 287.

59. Kimberly Jensen James, "'Between Two Fires': Women on the
'Underground' of Mormon Polygamy," *Journal of Mormon History* 8 (1986):
49-61; Martha Sonntag Bradley, "'Hide and Seek:' Children on the

The Saints viewed the new legislation as a direct assault not only on polygamy but on Mormonism, designed to "destroy our rights as citizens, to take away from us our liberties under the Constitution and laws, and to obtain the political control of our country."[60] Henry Eyring of St. George fumed that the Edmunds Bill placed them "in a state of bondage[,] ... and completely ruled by our enemies."[61] With tenacity of faith, the Saints interpreted the anti-polygamy crusade as the determining factor separating the righteous from the wicked, representing a "sign of the times," a prelude to the final act of history. That things had now turned against them fit into their millennial scheme.[62]

As in earlier eras, with increased persecution came intensified belief in an imminent millennial salvation.[63] Church members knew the Lord would intercede as soon as he had sufficiently tried the Saints.[64] In 1882 First Presidency member George Q. Cannon warned, "At no period in the history of the children of God in this dispensation have events been of more importance than those which are now taking place in our midst and around us."[65] "The Civil War

---

Underground," *Utah Historical Quarterly* 51 (Spring 1983): 133-53; Jessie L. Embry, *Mormon Polygamous Familes: Life in the Principle* (Salt Lake City: University of Utah Press, 1987), 17-22.

60. Editorial, *Deseret News Semi-Weekly,* 9 Apr. 1886. See also Charles W. Penrose, editorial, *Deseret News,* 15 June 1885; George Q. Cannon, *Journal of Discourses*, 26:145, 18 Jan. 1885.

61. Journal of Henry Eyring, 1835-1902, TS, Special Collections, Lee Library, 63. See also Gibson Condie, "Reminiscence and Diary," LDS church archives, 80.

62. Kenney, *Wilford Woodruff's Journal*, 8:96, 20 Apr. 1882.

63. "Discourse By Apostle F.D. Richards," *Deseret News* 18 (24 Jan. 1885): 1; "Remarks By President George Q. Cannon," ibid., 17 (26 July 1884): 1; "Remarks By Apostle F.D. Richards," ibid., 18 (18 July 1885): 1; *Journal of Jesse Nathaniel Smith* (Salt Lake City: Jesse N. Smith Family Associates, 1953), 288, 16 May 1884.

64. John Willard Young to Susie and Mabel Young, 17 Feb. 1886, John Willard Young Correspondence, LDS church archives; "Discourse By President Joseph F. Smith," *Deseret News* 16 (7 July 1883): 1.

65. George Q. Cannon, *Journal of Discourses*, 23:271, 8 Oct. 1882.

that is past is not the only war that will take place in this land,"
declared Cannon, who described the Edmunds Bill and the policies
of U.S. president Arthur as fulfilling Joseph Smith's prophecies. The
drama of the last days were unfolding as God planned.[66] Cannon
compared the Saints and the United States to the Israelites and
Pharaoh, not only cultivating a sense of severe persecution but also
of expectant deliverance.[67]

As the federal government intensified its attack on God's people,
the church's newspaper and mouthpiece, the *Deseret News*, editorialized on the certain fall of the United States. "Because of her acts she
must pay the penalty," it was said. "Woe is unto her because of the
blood of the Prophets and Saints which has been shed. Woe is unto
her because of unjust legislation. Woe is unto her because of striving
to enforce it."[68] In his last public discourse before going underground, church president John Taylor chastised the nation, declaring,
"You will see trouble, trouble, trouble enough in these United Sates.
And as I have said before I say today, I tell you in the name of God,
Woe! to them that fight against Zion, for God will fight against
them."[69] "Trouble and anxiety and sorrow and judgement will soon
overtake this nation," revealed Taylor, the Lord was about to "take
the matter into His own hands" and "vex" the United States.[70]

It was a scenario that made sense to the troubled Saints, and
members concurred in their leaders' assessment of the church's
situation. "Alas the approach of the Son of God is at hand," wrote
Lorenzo Hatch of Woodruff, Arizona, who described the Edmunds
Act as a precursor to the Millennium. Christ's return, he was certain,

---

66. "Discourse By President George Q. Cannon," *Deseret News* 15 (28
Oct. 1882): 1.

67. "Discourse By President George Q. Cannon," *Deseret News* 18 (13
Dec. 1884): 1.

68. "They Refuse To See," *Deseret News* 28 (6 June 1885): 2.

69. John Taylor, *Journal of Discourses*, 26:156, 1 Feb. 1885. See also
Collier, *Unpublished Revelations*, 1:140.

70. Collier, *Unpublished Revelations*, 1:144; Franklin D. Richards,
Journal of Discourses, 26:102, 18 Jan. 1885; Larson and Larson, *Diary of Charles
Walker*, 2:645, 3 Mar. 1885; L. John Nuttall Diary, 7 Jan. 1879.

was imminent.[71] Charles Walker's seventies quorum in St. George compared the Saints' afflictions in Missouri and Illinois to the current polygamy persecution, foreshadowing "the great things that would transpire before the winding up scene in 1891."[72] Lay members published works demonstrating that the end of the world was at hand.[73] Some Saints, compiling prophecies and predictions, especially Smith's statement that "56 years should wind up the scene," even arrived at an exact date for the event, 14 March 1891.[74]

Throughout the 1880s Mormon millennialism and polygamy cannot be separated. Church leaders continued their attempt to maintain the institution of polygamy by circumventing anti-polygamy laws while awaiting the promised Parousia. Proclaiming that the Saints will not give up "one jot nor tittle" to purchase favor from the United States, John Taylor declared: "I [will] defy the United States [and] obey the will of God."[75] To accomplish their aim, in 1885 Taylor and

---

71. Ruth Savage Hilton, ed., *Lorenzo Hill Hatch Journal* (Provo, UT: n.p., 1958), 125.

72. Larson and Larson, *Diary of Charles Walker*, 2:586, 16 Sept. 1882.

73. See Elder Robert Smith, *Signs of the Times* (Payson, UT: Juvenile Instructor Office, 1887); and W. H. H. Sharp, *Prophetic History and the Fulfillment of Prophecy From 600 Years B.C. to The Year of Our Lord A.D. 1891* (Salt Lake City: Deseret Home Co., 1888). These books were read and discussed by the Saints, Charles L. Walker apparently referring to the latter when he recorded on the final day of 1891: "This is the end of the Great eventful year as some have choosed to call it, and as many have been looking for many years, some ... have even boldly asserted and even prophesied that Christ would come and that the Saints would controll all the Kingdoms of the Earth, and some have written and published Books with diagrams showing the great Image that Daniel refers to, and have calculated as they though to a nicety the Times, time, and half times, etc., etc., etc., and have set forth startling things to come to pass." See Larson and Larson, *Diary of Charles Walker*, 2:731, 31 Dec. 1891.

74. Reinwand, "An Interpretive Study of Mormon Millennialism," 140-42.

75. Samuel W. Taylor, *The Kingdom or Nothing: The Life of John Taylor, Militant Mormon* (New York: Macmillan Publishing Co., 1976), 288. A sampling of sentiments expressing the belief that the church would never

other prominent Mormons, under pursuit as violators of the 1882
Edmunds Act, went "underground," avoiding the law by hiding out
in a series of church members' homes, barns, and other sanctuaries.[76]
That same year the Mormon leadership obtained permission from
the Mexican government to establish colonies across the border.[77] In
September 1886 Taylor commissioned Charles Ora Card to establish
a place of refuge for polygamists in Canada as well.[78]

In the midst of defying the federal government's passing laws
"which are clearly unconstitutional," church leaders continued their
millennial oration.[79] In 1884 and 1885 apostle Erastus Snow told the
Saints to look for some important changes in the world in the next five
to six years, predicting the persecution of the Saints would continue
until the Lord had gathered the grain to himself.[80] Wilford Woodruff

---

give up polygamy includes: "What Shall The Mormon Church Do," *Deseret
News* 12 (6 Sept. 1879): 2; "Honorable George Q. Cannon Interviewed," ibid.,
14 (17 Dec. 1881): 4; "Discourse By President George Q. Cannon," ibid., 17
(8 Dec. 1833): 1; "Expressions From the People," ibid., 18 (24 Mar. 1885): 4;
"Discourse By President George Q. Cannon," ibid., 18 (11 Apr. 1885): 1;
Juvenile Instructor, 1 May 1885; John Taylor, *Journal of Discourses*, 23:68, 9 Apr.
1882; John Taylor, ibid., 26:152-53, 1 Feb. 1885; George Reynolds, ibid.,
26:159-60, 29 Mar. 1885; Orson F. Whitney, ibid., 26:201, 19 Apr. 1885;
Lorenzo Snow, ibid., 26:368, 10 Jan. 1886; Larson and Larson, *Diary of Charles
Walker*, 2:645, 25 Jan. 1885, 2:649, 14 June 1885; Levi Savage, Jr., Diary, TS,
Special Collections, Lee Library, 78, 25 Jan. 1885.

76. Kenney, *Wilford Woodruff's Journal*, 8:333-34, 21 Sept. 1885; 8:351,
31 Dec. 1885; 8:415, 31 Dec. 1886.

77. Hardy, *Solemn Covenant*, 173-78.

78. Donald G. Godfrey and Brigham Y. Card, eds., *The Diaries of
Charles Ora Card: The Canadian Years, 1886-1903* (Salt Lake City: University
of Utah Press, 1993), xxxviii.

79. John Taylor, *Journal of Discourses*, 23:266, 8 Oct. 1882. See also the
Gibson Condie "Reminiscences and Diary" (LDS church archives) where
almost every page for the 1880s recounts disasters throughout the world, as
well as numerous references to the persecution of the Saints by their
"enemies."

80. Larson and Larson, *Diary of Charles Walker*, 2:640, 23 Dec. 1884;
2:656, 1 Nov. 1885.

affirmed that due to the anti-polygamy persecutions the destruction of the United States is "at the door of this generation."[81] Woodruff believed the current tribulations were the last great trial of the Saints forcing them to take a stand one way or the other.[82] Concluding that the government was "at War" with the Saints, he prophesied God would begin to fight the church's enemies, that the signs of the times pointed to the Second Coming.[83] In 1886 Woodruff confided in his journal, "We are in the midst of a national persecution. The United States Government is making war upon the Latter Day Saints... But if the Saints Suffer for their Religion Our Persecutors will Suffer for their sins. Great things await this generation. Behold the signs of the time. Watch for the Coming of the Son of Man."[84]

As the decade progressed, apocalyptic rhetoric increased.[85] In late 1886 Apostle Moses Thatcher told the Saints, "It is my belief that the time of our deliverance will be within five years, the time indicated being February 14, 1891. ... in consequence of the wickedness and corruption of the officers of the nation, the government will pass into the hands of the Saints, and that within five years."[86] At the church's October 1888 general conference Apostle Franklin D. Richards proclaimed many children then alive would witness the redemption of Zion and the Second Coming.[87] Church leaders may

---

81. Kenney, *Wilford Woodruff's Journal*, 8:349, 20 Dec. 1885.

82. Ibid., 8:336-37, 3 Oct. 1885; Levi Mathers Savage Family History Journal, mimeographed copy, Special Collections, Lee Library, 112-13, 14 June 1855.

83. Kenney, *Wilford Woodruff's Journal*, 8:351, 31 Dec. 1885.

84. Ibid., 8:378, 16 Feb. 1886.

85. Thomas William Whitaker Journal, 22-25 Apr. 1886.

86. Abraham Hoagland Cannon Diaries, photocopy of MS, Special Collections, Lee Library, 14 Oct. 1886; "An extract from the Remarks of Apostle Moses Thatcher at Lewiston, Cache Co. Utah Terr[itory] 1886, 6 Nov. 1886," LDS church archives; Arthur Pendry Welchman, "Reminiscences and Diary," LDS church archives, 133, 10 Apr. 1886; *Salt Lake Tribune,* 12 Dec. 1886, in Reinwand, "An Interpretive Study of Mormon Millennialism," 141-42.

87. John Morgan Journals, 6 Oct. 1888, 8:156.

never have named a specific day, but they certainly identified the "generation."

As part of this intense millenarian frame of mind, talk of the return to Missouri revived a "reformation" spirit. Church leaders admonished the Saints to "wake up ... trim our lamps, and be prepared for the coming of the Son of Man."[88] Not only had Jackson County, Missouri, been designated by revelation as a land of promise and the location for the New Jerusalem but the Saints had been told they would possess it and raise a temple there before their generation passed.[89] After their move west, the Saints' hope of returning to reclaim their "inheritance" in Missouri was preached continually. It was expected, especially during dramatic happenings, that the "present" generation would march back across the plains to establish the center stake of Zion, and church leaders continued "proffering [sic] we will soon go to Jackson County in Missouri."[90] Until his death in 1887, John Taylor believed he would die in Jackson County.[91]

This spiritually electric atmosphere with its millennial anticipation explains other events of the time, illustrated by a heightened

---

88. Larson and Larson, *Diary of Charles Walker*, 1:413-14, 11 Aug. 1875; 2:629, 26 Apr. 1884; Winslow Farr Diary, TS, Special Collections, Lee Library, 54, 11 Jan. 1875; Tanner, *A Mormon Mother*, 102; "Life Story of Anson Bowen Call," TS, in possession of B. Carmon Hardy, Orange, California, 2; J. Cecil Alter, ed., "Journal of Leonard E. Harrington," *Utah Historical Quarterly* 8 (Jan. 1940): 49; Wilford Woodruff, *Journal of Discourses*, 21:285, 4 July 1880; John Mills Whitaker Diaries, 3 vols., TS of 7 volume original, Special Collections, Marriott Library, University of Utah, Salt Lake City, Utah, 1:23, 29 June 1884.

89. *Doctrine and Covenants of the Church of the Latter Day Saints: Carefully Selected from the Revelations of God*, comps., Joseph Smith, Junior, Oliver Cowdery, Sidney Rigdon, and Frederick G. Williams (Kirtland, OH: F.G. Williams and Co., 1835), secs. 4 and 97.

90. "Record of Andrew Jackson Allen," 33, 14 Mar. 1858; Elias Smith, *Journal of Discourses*, 6:221, 2 Aug. 1857; Brigham Young, ibid., 10:339, 7 Oct. 1864; George Q. Cannon, ibid., 13:97, 6 Apr. 1869; John Taylor, ibid., 17:66, 7 May 1874; Orson Pratt, ibid., 17:291, 7 Feb. 1875.

91. Reinwand, "An Interpretive Study of Mormon Millennialism," 142.

interest toward converting the Lamanites. The New Jerusalem in Missouri, as it was seen in the 1830s, was to be located on "the borders by the Lamanites."[92] While Mormon attempts to convert Native Americans had never enjoyed dramatic success, it too was looked upon as a necessary step before the Saints could return (3 Ne. 21:23-24).[93] These remnants of Joseph, as American Indians were referred to, were expected to assume a primary role, after their conversion, in building the temple near Independence. It was the eleventh hour, the time of the Lamanites had arrived, and startling developments were expected.[94] It was also said they would act as a shield and protector to the Saints, scourging the gentiles, and church leaders predicted that within five years (as of 1886) these "Lamanites [would] go forth as a battle ax, in fulfilment of prophecy."[95] As the crusade against Mormon polygamy gained momentum, these expectations took on added meaning.[96]

---

92. *A Book of Commandments of the Church of Christ, Organized According to Law, on the 6th of April, 1830* (Zion [Independence], MO: W.W. Phelps and Co., 1833), 68; *Doctrine and Covenants*, 1835 ed., 154; *Evening and Morning Star,* Dec. 1832, 54; Jan. 1833, 62.

93. Orson Pratt, *Journal of Discourses*, 17:301, 7 Feb. 1875.

94. "Movements Among The Indians," *Millennial Star* 1 (Dec. 1874): 760-61; Henry Eyring, "American Indians," *Millennial Star* (19 July 1875): 449-53; Orson Pratt, *Journal of Discourses*, 20:146-47; 9 Mar. 1879.

95. Welchman, "Reminiscence and Diary," 133, 10 Apr. 1886. See also 3 Ne. 21:12-13, 20:16-17; "The Fulfillment of Prophecy," *Millennial Star* 34 (23 Aug. 1862): 531.

96. For a sample of such references, based on the Book of Mormon prophecy at 3 Nephi 20:15-17 and 21:12-13, see Parley P. Pratt, *Mormonism Unveiled* ... (New York: Orson Pratt and Elijah Fordham, 1838), 15; Joseph Smith, *History of the Church of Jesus Christ of Latter-day Saints,* 7 vols., 2d ed. rev., introduction and notes by B. H. Roberts (Salt Lake City: Deseret Book Co., 1974-76), 1:419; Orson Pratt, *Journal of Discourses* 9:178-79, 15 July 1855; Joseph Lee Robinson Journal, mimeographed copy, 13, Utah State Historical Society; Dimick Baker Huntington Journals, 2 vols., LDS church archives, Apr. 1859; Patriarchal Blessings given to Joseph C. Bentley, in "Israel Ivins Bentley," TS, Oral History Interview, by Gordon Irving, May 1973, LDS church archives, 4-5, 9-10, 14-15.

In 1887 Congress increased political, legislative, and judicial pressure on the church through passage of the Edmunds-Tucker Act which dissolved the Corporation of the Church of Jesus Christ of Latter-day Saints as a legal entity. The statute also disfranchised all Utah women, prohibited illegitimate children from inheriting from their fathers, and established the bureaucratic mechanism to escheat to the government all church assets in excess of $50,000 including the Salt Lake City temple block in full.[97] The government's anti-polygamy assault on Mormonism's core institution was on the verge of inflicting its final blow.

Yet while appealing the constitutionality of the Edmunds-Tucker Act, in May 1888 at the dedication of the Manti temple Wilford Woodruff, then senior apostle, instructed other apostles that "we are not going to stop the practice of plural marriage until the coming of the Son of man."[98] Considered by some as "the prophet of the twelve," Apostle John W. Taylor told members in southern Utah they would live to "see the Savior come."[99] As late as November 1889 Woodruff confirmed that "the Lord will never give a revelation to abandon plural marriage," received a new revelation that "the judgements of God, which are to be poured out upon all nations ... are nigh at your doors," promised destruction of the church's opponents, and prophesied the Saints' deliverance from their enemies.[100] Woodruff held fast to his belief, asserted over twenty years earlier, that the

---

97. Firmage and Mangrum, *Zion in the Courts*, 197-202.

98. Heber J. Grant Diary, 17 May 1888, in Jean Bickmore White, ed., *Church, State, and Politics: The Diaries of John Henry Smith* (Salt Lake City: Signature Books in association with Smith Research Associates, 1990), 201n121., 17 May 1888. See also Jean Bickmore White, "The Making of the Convention President: The Political Education of John Henry Smith," *Utah Historical Quarterly* 39 (Fall 1971): 359; Heber J. Grant Journal, 17 May 1888, in D. Michael Quinn, "LDS Church Authority and New Plural Marriages, 1890-1904," *Dialogue: A Journal of Mormon Thought* 18 (Spring 1985): 34.

99. Larson and Larson, *Diary of Charles Walker*, 2:704, 16-17 Dec. 1888; "Biographical Record of Martha [Cragun] Cox," LDS church archives, 141.

100. Kenney, *Wilford Woodruff's Journal*, 9:67-69, 24 Nov. 1889; L. John Nuttall Diary, 24 Nov. 1889; Clark, *Messages of the First Presidency*, 3:171-76.

cities of Albany, Boston, and New York would be destroyed. He then predicted the nation would call upon a future church president to "take the Presidency of the United States to save the Constitution," and that these events would be fulfilled prior to "thirty years hence."[101] In his position as church president, Woodruff continued to tell members that "many" living in 1889 would while "in the flesh" see Christ come in clouds of glory.[102]

As 1890 commenced, events began to whirl out of the church's control. In February gentiles wrestled political control out of Mormon hands in the Salt Lake City municipal elections.[103] Later that same month the U.S. Supreme Court upheld the Idaho Test Oath decision to disfranchise all Mormons, even non-polygamists.[104] On 19 May 1890, in a five-to-four decision, the Supreme Court declared the provisions of the Edmunds-Tucker Act constitutional. The decision allowed for seizure of all church property in excess of $50,000 and redistribution of the funds to finance public non-Mormon schools, leaving open the possibility that the church's temples would be confiscated.[105] Then in the summer of 1890 the Cullom-Struble

---

101. Kenney, *Wilford Woodruff's Journal*, 6:422, 22 Aug. 1868. See also Van Wagoner, *Sidney Rigdon*, 153; Orson Pratt, *Journal of Discourses*, 20:152, 9 Mar. 1879.

102. Wilford Woodruff, "Remarks," at Tooele Stake Conference, 29 July 1889, in Brian H. Stuy, ed., *Collected Discourses*, 5 vols. (Sandy, UT: B.H.S. Publishing, 1987-92), 1:325.

103. Thomas G. Alexander and James B. Allen, *Mormons & Gentiles: A History of Salt Lake City* (Boulder, CO: Pruett Publishing Co., 1984), 100.

104. The Idaho Test Oath, originally passed in February 1885, amended Idaho territorial election laws to exclude any member of an organization which endorsed polygamy (the Mormon church) from voting or holding public position. See Grenville H. Gibbs, "Mormonism in Idaho Politics, 1880-1890," *Utah Historical Quarterly* 21 (Oct. 1953): 295-96; Merle W. Wells, *Anti-Mormonism in Idaho, 1872-92* (Provo, UT: Brigham Young University Press, 1978), 57-61.

105. Leonard J. Arrington and Davis Bitton, *The Mormon Experience: A History of the Latter-day Saints*, 2d ed. (Urbana: University of Illinois Press, 1992), 234.

bill, applying the same Idaho test-oath standards to all U.S. territories including Utah, began to move through Congress.[106]

The year 1890 also saw the culmination of the Native American Ghost Dance movement. This, coinciding with the calamities facing the church, prompted many members to associate the visions of the Messiah declared by Indians with Christ's millennial reign. The Ghost Dance predicted that the Messiah would return in 1890, and the agitation precipitated the infamous Indian massacre at Wounded Knee, South Dakota, in December 1890.[107]

Senior church leaders, including now church president Wilford Woodruff and second counselor in the First Presidency Joseph F. Smith, assigned religious significance to the timing of the Ghost Dance manifestations.[108] Smith announced that the heavenly visitors reported by the Indians were "probably one or more of the Three Nephites" from the Book of Mormon whom Christ allowed to remain on the earth until his coming, "disciples who tarried, whose mission

---

106. Edward Leo Lyman, *Political Deliverance: The Mormon Quest for Utah Statehood* (Urbana: University of Illinois Press, 1986), 126-33.

107. Henry F. Dobyns and Robert C. Euler, *The Ghost Dance of 1889 Among the Pai Indians of Northwestern Arizona* (Prescott, AZ: Prescott College Press, 1967), vii-viii; Dee Alexander Brown, *Bury My Heart at Wounded Knee: An Indian History of the American West* (New York: Holt, Rinehart and Winston, 1971); James Mooney, *The Ghost-Dance Religion and the Sioux Outbreak of 1890* (Chicago: University of Chicago Press, 1965), originally published as part 2 of the *Fourteenth Annual Report of the Bureau of Ethnology to the Secretary of the Smithsonian Institution, 1892-93* (Washington, D.C.: Government Printing Office, 1896), 789-91; Gregory E. Smoak, "Mormons and the Ghost Dance of 1890," *South Dakota History* 16 (Fall 1986): 290-91.

108. Wilford Woodruff-John King correspondence cited in Lawrence G. Coates, "The Mormons and the Ghost Dance," *Dialogue: A Journal of Mormon Thought* 18 (Winter 1985): 107. One writer claims the unique doctrines taught by the church (sacred scripture written by the Indians' ancestors, the promise of Indians rising once again to greatness, Christ previously ministering to the people with a promise to return to usher in the Millennium) led Mormon-converted Indians to be the Indian Messiah Wovoka's "easiest and most enthusiastic converts." See Paul Bailey, *Wovoka, The Indian Messiah* (Los Angeles: Westernlore Press, 1957), 121-22.

was to minister to the remnants of their own race. ... It is in perfect harmony with the order of heaven for ministering spirits or messengers from God or Christ to visit the Lamanites."[109] Responding to the Indian messianic rumors in August 1890, Apostle Anthon H. Lund stated at the San Pete Stake conference, "We need not say—'our Lord delayeth his coming!' ... We can be sure it is in the near future, because the Lord told Joseph Smith ... that if he lived to be a certain age, he should see His face, which points to [18]91."[110]

Never faltering in their millennial hope, church leaders continued to assure one another their deliverance was in sight. On 29 May 1890 president of the Quorum of Twelve Apostles Lorenzo Snow prophesied at a meeting of the Twelve: "[Y]ou brethren will live to behold the savior, you shall not die, death shall have no power over you. You have a great work to perform ... Be faithful and you shall never taste death."[111] Apostle Brigham Young, Jr., recorded the impact of this prophecy: "His words penetrated to the marrow surely God is with us."[112] In August 1890, during a meeting of the Twelve, Snow laid his hands on Abraham H. Cannon's head to give him an apostolic blessing and confirmed that he would "live to see the Savior, [and] the triumph of Zion."[113] As late as September 1890, John Morgan, one of the Seven Presidents of the Seventy, reported a widespread belief that "missions would necesarily be short; that the end is very near and the Elders about to be called home."[114]

---

109. Joseph F. Smith, "The Messiah Craze," *The Young Woman's Journal* 2 (Feb 1891): 268-71, in Coates, "The Mormons and the Ghost Dance," 109-10.

110. *The County Register,* 28 Aug. 1890, in Coates, "The Mormons and the Ghost Dance," 107.

111. Brigham Young [Jr.] Journals, 1862-1902, LDS church archives, 29 May 1890. See also 6 Aug. 1890, where Snow makes a similar prediction. Journal notations and quotations provided by B. Carmon Hardy.

112. Ibid., 29 May 1890.

113. Abraham H. Cannon Diaries, 6 Aug. 1890.

114. In William G. Hartley, "The Seventies in the 1880s: Revelations and Reorganizing," *Dialogue: A Journal of Mormon Thought* 16 (Spring 1983): 83.

Then, for the "Temporal Salvation of the Church," on 24 September 1890 Woodruff issued the Manifesto publicly abandoning polygamy.[115] Although the intent of the Manifesto was ambiguous, it seems clear the document was a temporary solution to solve an immediate crisis, deflecting pressure long enough for Utah to gain statehood or for Christ's return, whichever came first.[116] Years later Franklin S. Richards, the church's general legal counsel, stated that "the imminent danger of these bill [Cullom-Struble] passing Congress was the immediate cause of the issuance of the Manifesto."[117] One church publication boasted that the Manifesto had been given to "subvert the cunning of the devil" and buy time for the Saints, perhaps fulfilling Brigham Young's reported declaration that "we shall pull the wool over the eyes of the American people and make them swallow Mormonism, polygamy and all."[118]

---

115. Kenney, *Wilford Woodruff's Journal*, 9:112-16, 25 Sept. 1890.

116. Jan Shipps, "In the Presence of the Past: Continuity and Change in Twentieth-Century Mormonism," in *After 150 Years: The Latter-day Saints in Sesquicentennial Perspective*, eds. Thomas G. Alexander and Jessie Embry (Provo, UT: Charles Redd Center for Western Studies, 1983), 10. Debate continues on the initial meaning of the Manifesto. While some historians have called it "a revelation" (Thomas G. Alexander, "The Odyssey of a Latter-day Prophet: Wilford Woodruff and the Manifesto of 1890," *Journal of Mormon History* 17 [1991]: 171), and "not simply a political document" (Allen and Leonard, *The Story of the Latter-day Saints*, 413), others consider its issuance a delaying tactic. See Hardy, *Solemn Covenant*, 55, chap. 4 in its entirety and specifically pp. 129-31; Lyman, *Political Deliverance*, 134; Hansen, *Quest for Empire*, 177. See discussion in Quinn, "LDS Church Authority and New Plural Marriages, 1890-1904," 9-11.

117. See "Address Delivered by President Franklin S. Richards to the High Priest Quorum of Ensign Stake," 13 Nov. 1932, LDS church archives, in Ken Driggs, "'Lawyers of Their Own to Defend Them': The Legal Career of Franklin Snyder Richards," *Journal of Mormon History* 21 (Fall 1995): 106. See also Frank J. Cannon and Harvey J. O'Higgins, *Under the Prophet in Utah* (Boston: C.M. Clark Publishing, 1911), 102-105.

118. "The Manifesto," *Millennial Star* 52 (24 Nov. 1890): 744; Brigham Young, quoted in *Proceedings Before The Committee On Privileges And Elections Of The United States Senate In The Matter Of The Protests Against The Right Of*

Having been taught "no principle or Revelation that God ever gave to his people was to be laid on the shelf as a thing of the past," Mormons had believed for half a century that the "celestial law" of plural marriage was crucial to their cosmology.[119] Despite official claims that the voting "was unanimous,"[120] at least some voted against the Manifesto and perhaps a majority abstained. The church membership was unprepared and shocked by this change.[121] When the Manifesto was presented for a sustaining vote in the October 1890 general conference, many supported it only reluctantly, some believing the reversal of the church's stand on polygamy a sure sign that the Millennium was nigh.[122] Apostle Moses Thatcher gave private support for the Manifesto at the 30 September to 1 October 1890 meetings of the apostles based on his faith that the Millennium would occur within months.[123] No doubt Thatcher and others held fast to Wilford Woodruff's declaration that "we won't quit practising Plural Marriage until Christ shall come."[124]

In an attempt to reassure the Saints and decrease apocalyptic concern, no fewer than seven church authorities spoke on the Second

---

Hon. Reed Smoot, A Senator From Utah, To Hold His Seat, 4 vols. (Washington, D.C.: Government Printing Office, 1906), 1:15. See also Ambrose B. Carlton, *The Wonderlands of the Wild West, with Sketches of the Mormons* (N.p.: n.p., 1891), 321.

119. John Henry Smith, in Larson and Larson, *Diary of Charles Walker*, 2:716, 16 Sept. 1890.

120. *Doctrine and Covenants*, Official Declaration—1, 292.

121. Ronald W. Walker, "B. H. Roberts and the Woodruff Manifesto," *Brigham Young University Studies* 22 (Summer 1982): 363-66; Abraham H. Cannon Diaries, 26 Sept. 1890; Hardy, *Solemn Covenant*, 135; Quinn, "LDS Church Authority and New Plural Marriages, 1890-1904," 48-49.

122. Quinn, "LDS Church Authority and New Plural Marriages, 1890-1904," 47-49; Kenneth W. Godfrey, "The Coming of the Manifesto," *Dialogue: A Journal of Mormon Thought* 3 (Autumn 1970): 20-24.

123. Thatcher, in Heber J. Grant Journal, 30 Sept. 1890-1 Oct. 1890, in Quinn, "LDS Church Authority and New Plural Marriages, 1890-1904," 47.

124. White, *Church, State, nd Politics*, 201, 17 May 1888. See also White, "The Making of the Convention President," 359.

Coming during the same October 1890 general conference in which the Manifesto was adopted. Some advised the Saints not to expect Christ's advent in 1891.[125] Gibson Condie recorded in his journal, "Some of the speakers referred to the year 1891, as a great many of the saints have an Idea that the Lord was to come and reign on earth."[126] George Q. Cannon told members that there was "too much agitation" associated with the 1891 prophecy, "no man knoweth the day nor the hour."[127]

Nevertheless, in cryptic tones other church leaders continued to supply the Saints with millennial hope. During the same conference Apostle Franklin D. Richards merely referred with interest to the millennial prophecy, while Apostle Francis M. Lyman told the Saints to "pray twice a day" to "be prepared for what is to come in 1891."[128] Apostle Moses Thatcher warned members to "prepare themselves for 1891" as "the day of calamity is approaching. It is at the doors."[129]

---

125. Church authorities who referred to the year 1891 in connection with the "coming of the Son of Man" reference include B. H. Roberts, Moses Thatcher, Francis M. Lyman, Franklin D. Richards, Heber J. Grant, George Q. Cannon, and Wilford Woodruff.

126. Gibson Condie, "Reminiscences and Diary," 107.

127. Stuy, *Collected Discourses*, 2:121; Marriner Wood Merrill Diaries, 1887-1906, LDS church archives, 1:72, 5 Oct. 1890 (citation provided by B. Carmon Hardy). See also "General Conference," *Deseret Evening News*, 4 Oct. 1890; "General Conference," ibid., 6 Oct. 1890, 4; "The Mormon Conference," *Salt Lake Tribune*, 5 Oct. 1890, 4; "Second Day's Conference," ibid., 6 Oct. 1890.

128. Stuy, *Collected Discourses*, 2:110.

129. "General Conference," *Deseret Evening News*, 6 Oct. 1890, 2; Stuy, *Collected Discourses*, 2:107; *Salt Lake Tribune*, 5 Oct. 1890. Thomas Alexander discounts the influence of Thatcher's belief in the imminence of the Millennium, arguing that by 1889 Thatcher was out of harmony with church leaders. See Alexander, "Wilford Woodruff and the Changing Nature of Mormon Religious Experience," 66. Thatcher's difficulties with George Q. Cannon started in 1887 over control of stock in the Bullion Beck silver mine. The Thatcher-Cannon conflict troubled all members of the Quorum of the Twelve Apostles and First Presidency and in mid-1890 Joseph F. Smith was asked to step in and mediate the controversy to keep it out of the public

Perhaps most telling, after the Manifesto's presentation at general conference, Woodruff promised members:

> I will say to the Latter-day Saints, as an Elder in Israel and as an Apostle of the Lord Jesus Christ, we are approaching some of the most tremendous judgements God ever poured out upon the world. You watch the signs of the times, the signs of the coming of the Son of Man. They are beginning to be made manifest both in heaven and earth. ... We are approaching these things. All that the Latter-day Saints have to do is to be quiet, careful and wise before the Lord, watch the signs of the times, and be true and faithful; and when you get through you will understand many things that you do not today.[130]

As the anti-Mormon *Salt Lake Tribune* reported, the leaders' references to "1891 as an Epoch in Church History," followed by George Q. Cannon's denunciation, merely underscored the intensity of the general membership's millennial expectation.[131]

As 1891 began, many Saints still anticipated the coming of the Lord. On 1 January 1891 President Wilford Woodruff recorded in his journal: "This is New Years day And the year that has been looked upon by many as one of the most important years of the world."[132] Charles Walker reiterated the same sentiment: "Some say and have written that great things are to happen this year ...

---

courts. Thatcher later incurred the wrath of fellow church leaders by not acquiescing to their wishes within the realm of Utah Republican-Democratic politics, and in November 1896 he was dropped from the Quorum of the Twelve Apostles. See Edward Leo Lyman, "The Alienation of an Apostle from His Quorum: The Moses Thatcher Case," *Dialogue: A Journal of Mormon Thought* 18 (Summer 1985): 67-91.

130. Stuy, *Collected Discourses*, 2:136; Carlton, *The Wonderlands of the Wild West*, 321.

131. "The Mormon Conference," *Salt Lake Tribune*, 5 Oct. 1890, 4; "Second Days Conference," ibid., Oct. 1890, 4. See also Keith E. Norman, "How Long, O Lord? The Delay of the Parousia in Mormonism," *Sunstone* 8 (Jan.-Apr. 1983): 53; Allen and Leonard, *The Story of the Latter-day Saints*, 413.

132. Kenney, *Wilford Woodruff's Journal*, 9:133, 1 Jan. 1891.

some even declare that Christ will come and the Millennial Reign inaugurated."[133]

But by then, politically, the Manifesto had already achieved its desired effect. Three weeks after its issuance, district attorney Charles S. Varian told the First Presidency that he favored reversing anti-polygamy legislation, and soon Congress tabled the Cullom-Struble bill.[134] Church leaders privately expressed their belief that congressional anti-polygamy legislation had stalled due to Woodruff's Manifesto.[135] In 1891 the tide began to turn as the U.S. Supreme Court decided to allow children born of polygamous marriages to inherit from their fathers' estates.[136] Non-Mormon federal appointees Judge Charles S. Zane and Utah territorial governor Arthur L. Thomas endorsed a polygamist amnesty petition which was sent to President Benjamin Harrison in late 1891.[137] With relief, church leaders began to feel that the government's hand, "extended to crush us," had been averted. As the year progressed, and the trials and tribulations of the previous year waned, millennial anticipations, and a hoped for divine intervention to save the church from its enemies, diminished. In mid-1892 church leaders asked the Saints to express prayers of gratitude for their deliverance "from the evil which environed [us] and which threatened [our] overthrow," admonishing members to remember how their fate had changed over the past two years.[138] The church began to accept the role, although forced upon it, of assimilation into a gentile world.

---

133. Larson and Larson, *Diary of Charles Walker*, 2:721, 3 Jan. 1891.

134. White, *Church, State, and Politics*, 243, 14 Oct. 1890.

135. Abraham H. Cannon Diaries, 2 Oct., 22 Oct. 1890; Richard D. Poll, "The Legislative Antipolygamy Campaign," *Brigham Young University Studies* 26 (Fall 1986): 119; E. Leo Lyman, "The Political Background of the Woodruff Manifesto," *Dialogue: A Journal of Mormon Thought* 24 (Fall 1991): 38; Lyman, *Political Deliverance*, 185.

136. Hardy, *Solemn Covenant*, 152.

137. White, *Church, State, and Politics*, 264-66, 18-22 Dec. 1891. The amnesty petition, along with Zane's and Thomas's favorable recommendations, is found in "Amnesty," *Contributor* 13 (Feb. 1892): 196-97.

138. Lyman, *Political Deliverance*, 120.

To preserve the church as an institution, successive church presidents Wilford Woodruff, Lorenzo Snow, and Joseph F. Smith increasingly followed a course of accommodation. The abandonment of plural marriage, economic individualism, and political diversity were increasingly accepted as part of the Mormon way. With the "official" passing of polygamy, and the political goal of statehood, millennialism and the immediacy of a kingdom-saving millennial event declined in importance. Historians have described this transitional period as "creative adjustment," "a new era of cooperation and understanding."[139] During these years church leaders came out of hiding, and President Harrison granted amnesty to individuals subject to polygamy-cohabitation laws. Amnesty was further broadened by President Grover Cleveland and polygamists were no longer sent to prison. Between the years 1894 and 1896 church property was returned, thus removing the risk of losing their sacred temples, and finally statehood was granted. These events prepared the church for transition from the nineteenth to the twentieth century.[140]

Polygamy, more than any other issue, identified the Saints as a distinctive group apart from the American mainstream. Mormons had struggled against a hostile America and attempted to nullify its laws as best as they could, creating a separate society, all in preparation for Christ's coming kingdom. Since polygamy was illegal, it could only be legally practiced in a separate politically-independent kingdom. Thus the deferral of its public announcement until the Saints were in Utah. For Latter-day Saints, polygamy served as a rallying point, identifying them as a peculiar people, separate from cultural America, and tied them irrevocably to Mormonism. As Klaus Hansen and Carmon Hardy have pointed out, it was polygamy that "more

---

139. Arrington and Bitton, *The Mormon Experience*, 234; Allen and Leonard, *The Story of the Latter-day Saints*, 416.

140. Arrington and Bitton, *The Mormon Experience*, 242-43; Hardy, *Solemn Covenant*, 152; Orma Linford, "The Mormons and the Law: The Polygamy Cases," *Utah Law Review* 9 (Summer 1965): 584-85. The amnesty proclamations are found in Richardson, *Messages and Papers of the Presidents*, Harrison—1893, 7:5803-5804; Cleveland—1894, 8:5942-43.

than any other Mormon institution came to symbolize the new heaven and new earth."[141]

Yet, in the eyes of the nation, polygamy represented the most visible threat to American society. Spurred on by millennialism, a cycle ensued as the Saints trusted in the Almighty and became socially entrenched against the larger society, which in turn led to a sharper contrast. The Saints believed God allowed persecution to permit the gentiles to show their true colors prior to their annihilation. Anti-Mormon sentiment and persecution only reinforced an us-versus-them mentality. As God's family, the Saints' struggle against persecutions would be short-lived and soon end in their triumph over the world.[142]

Although the hierarchy attempted to present a united front, discrepancies between stated and implied understandings of the Manifesto and the doctrine of the Second Coming betray behind-the-scenes tension. Church leaders split between those publicly condemning plural marriage while privately practicing it and those insisting, "We will sacrifice no principle to save property or life itself." During the 1890s the quorum remained divided not only over polygamy and eschatology, but also over politics.[143]

Until the 1880s, Mormon society acted as it willed, defying the government's attempt to force it to conform with American values.

---

141. Klaus J. Hansen, *Mormonism and the American Experience* (Chicago: University of Chicago Press, 1981), 165, 157; Hardy, *Solemn Covenant*, 56-60. This is also recognized in Harold Bloom, *The American Religion: The Emergence of the Post-Christian Nation* (New York: Simon and Schuster, 1992), 70.

142. Logue, *A Sermon in the Desert*, 35.

143. Abraham H. Cannon, Diaries, 1 Oct. 1890; Walker, "B. H. Roberts and the Woodruff Manifesto," 363-66; Brigham Young, Jr., in Davis Bitton, "The Ordeal of Brigham Young, Jr.," in *The Ritualization of Mormon History and Other Essays* (Urbana: University of Illinois Press, 1994), 132. Brigham Young, Jr., in ibid., specifically identified a generation gap between the older apostles and "the younger men of the Quorum." On the political partisanship of the 1890s, see D. Michael Quinn, "The Mormon Hierarchy, 1832-1932: An American Elite," Ph.D. diss., Yale University, 1976, 234-38; Lyman, *Political Deliverance*, 166-81.

The shock waves of the anti-polygamy raids led to the 1890 Manifesto, but also removed a cornerstone of Mormon culture. Polygamy, long considered a holy obligation, was no longer deemed necessary for salvation. Although some believed, as Charles Walker reported, that leaders had reneged on the revelation on plural marriage, with the ending of polygamy the Millennium became a future event rather than an imminent reality.[144]

Plural marriage had not only been a way of separating the Saints from the world, but a means of hastening the Parousia. Anti-polygamy persecution was the necessary accumulation of fury prior to the end of the world, and increased government persecution provided hope that the Millennium was indeed imminent.[145] As Larry Logue has pointed out, the cessation of polygamy ended the Saints' ability to "provoke non-Mormons' rage with the church's blessing."[146] The passing of polygamy compelled Mormons to abandon the best method of separating themselves from the world, eventually leading to the demise of a millennial world view as the overriding LDS cosmology.[147] With the postponing of millennial deliverance, the "theocratic and separatist aspects" of Mormonism became a casualty of assimilation into the mainstream of American society.[148]

---

144. Larson and Larson, *Diary of Charles Walker*, 2:728, 20 Oct. 1891. See also Logue, *A Sermon in the Desert*, 117.

145. *Millennial Star* 49 (1887): 295-96.

146. Logue, *A Sermon in the Desert*, 119.

147. Ibid., 119-20.

148. Thomas F. O'Dea, *The Mormons* (Chicago: University of Chicago Press, 1957), 171; Richard D. Poll, "The Americanism of Utah," *Utah Historical Quarterly* 44 (Winter 1976): 89.

CHAPTER NINE

THE DECLINE OF MILLENNIALISM

When exactly did belief in the immediacy of a millennial deliverance expire in Mormon thought? Pinpointing a time frame, just as identifying a date for the "final" passing of polygamy, is problematic.[1] Certainly expectation that "the End is not far off" persisted well into the 1890s, with natural disasters and calamities still viewed as signs that the Creator would soon "avenge the blood of the Prophets & Saints & fulfill the Testimony of the Prophets & Apostles upon this Nation."[2] Some held God was already fighting the Saints' battles as witnessed by the

---

1. On the continuance of polygamy after the Manifesto, see B. Carmon Hardy, *Solemn Covenant: The Mormon Polygamous Passage* (Urbana: University of Illinois Press, 1992), 167-335; D. Michael Quinn, "LDS Church Authority and New Plural Marriages, 1890-1904," *Dialogue: A Journal of Mormon History* 18 (Spring 1985): 49-105; Kenneth L. Cannon II, "After the Manifesto: Mormon Polygamy 1890-1906," *Sunstone* 8 (Jan.-Apr. 1983): 27-35; Victor W. Jorgensen and B. Carmon Hardy, "The Taylor-Cowley Affair and the Watershed of Mormon History," *Utah Historical Quarterly* 48 (Winter 1980): 4-36; and Richard S. Van Wagoner, *Mormon Polygamy: A History* (Salt Lake City: Signature Books, 1989), 143-76.

2. A. Karl Larson and Katharine Miles Larson, eds., *Diary of Charles Lowell Walker*, 2 vols. (Logan: Utah State University Press, 1980), 2:801, 27 Sept. 1895; 2:821, 13 July 1896; Scott G. Kenney, *Wilford Woodruff's Journal, 1833-1898*, 9 vols. (Midvale, UT: Signature Books, 1983-85), 9:300, 1 May 1894. See also Larson and Larson, *Diary of Charles Walker*, 2:835, 26 Feb. 1897; 2:842, 30 Apr. 1897.

213

fact that "prosecutions on the marriage question are almost out of date and a thing of the past."[3]

From the pulpit leaders continued to express chiliastic expectations.[4] In 1892 President Wilford Woodruff counseled St. George, Utah, members that the dispensation "was to be cut short" with little time for preparation "before the coming of the Son of Man and the ushering in of the great millennium."[5] When he dedicated the Salt Lake temple the next year, Woodruff prophesied that the "millennium is near at hand" and that the temple would receive Christ at his return after the preparation and perfection of the Saints.[6] Upon its completion, members beheld "power and manifestations of the goodness of God," George Q. Cannon announced, "such as they have never before experienced."[7] During the temple's dedication, Woodruff reported that Isaiah of the Old Testament, numerous Book of Mormon prophets, deceased latter-day prophets Joseph Smith, Brigham Young, John Taylor, as well as Christ himself, all walked the temple halls. Leaders were told that "our enemies would never [again] have so much power over us as they have had" in the past.[8]

At local church conferences bishops and patriarchs persisted in saying that the Millennium was approaching, prophesying "that some

---

3. Levi Mathers Savage Family History Journal, mimeographed copy, Special Collections, Lee Library, Brigham Young Univesity, Provo, Utah, 48, 1 Jan. 1895. See also Larson and Larson, *Diary of Charles Walker*, 2:815, 13 Apr. 1896.

4. Ambrose B. Carlton, *The Wonderlands of the Wild West, with Sketches of the Mormons* (N.p.: n.p., 1891), 321.

5. Larson and Larson, *Diary of Charles Walker*, 2:742, 13 June 1892.

6. Brian H. Stuy, ed., *Collected Discourses*, 5 vols. (Sandy, UT: B.H.S. Publishing, 1987-92), 3:275.

7. In Richard Neitzel Holzapfel, "A Time of Dedication: How history records the unique events of the temple's dedication," *This People* 14 (Spring 1993): 25.

8. Abraham Hoagland Cannon Diaries, photocopy of MS, Special Collections, Lee Library, 18 May 1893; Stuy, *Collected Discourses*, 3:274-75; Cheri Loveless, "The House of the Lord," *This People* 14 (Spring 1993): 22.

present would live to see the Son of Man come in His Glory."[9]
Longtime member Charles Walker expected the final three years of
the century to be more eventful than any previous decades, "for the
time of His coming draws nigh."[10] Perhaps because the nation had
not been destroyed in the Civil War, because the prophecies had not
been entirely fulfilled in the generations up to the turn of the century,
leaders felt they must be ever nearer to the final events. Thus they
continued in their apocalyptic pronouncements.

Clinging to faith in the inevitability of events prophesied for
so long, many Saints began to question their own worthiness. As
in a previous era when members were told they had been expelled
from Missouri because of their own unrighteousness, God's law of
plural marriage was now withdrawn and perhaps Christ's return
would have to await a more righteous generation.[11] "There would
have been no manifesto," declared Apostle Matthias Cowley, "if we
had obey[ed] ... the command [of] God [for he] would fight our
battles for us."[12]

For many, Utah's obtaining statehood through accommodation
was a setback in their attempt to come out of Babylon. To those
members, the Manifesto represented the surrender of a holy prin-

---

9. Anthony Woodward Ivins Diaries, Utah State Historical Society, Salt
Lake City, "Diary, Feb. 2, 1902-April 7, 1902," 9 Mar. 1902; David Fisk Stout
Diaries, LDS church archives, Salt Lake City, Utah, 13:41, 9 Feb. 1902.

10. Larson and Larson, *Diary of Charles Walker*, 2:831, 30 Dec. 1896.

11. John Mills Whitaker Diaries, 3 vols., TS, Special Collections,
Marriott Library, University of Utah, Salt Lake City, 1:281, 9 Apr. 1893; Stuy,
Collected Discourses, 3:280; "Remarks Made by President George Q. Cannon,"
Deseret News, 14 Nov. 1891; Brigham Young, in F. D. Richards, *Journal of
Discourses, Pearson's Magazine* 24 (Oct. 1910): 451; B. Carmon Hardy,
"Self-Blame and the Manifesto," *Dialogue: A Journal of Mormon Thought* 24
(Fall 1991): 43-57; Kimball Young, *Isn't One Wife Enough?* (New York: Henry
Holt and Co., 1954), 411.

12. Matthias S. Cowley, 28 Jun. 1901, quoted in *Proceeding Before The
Committee on Privileges And Elections Of The United States Senate In The Matter
Of The Protests Against The Right Of Hon. Reed Smoot, A Senator From The State
Of Utah, To Hold His Seat*, 4 vols. (Washington, D.C.: Government Printing
Office, 1906), 1:8.

ciple merely to escape the consequences of the government's anti-polygamy campaign.[13] Although Woodruff had earlier said "it would seem proper for us to bend our faith" since "[s]tatehood seems to promise the readiest solution [to] ... the great problem of the day," the Manifesto's "bending" became complete reversal, if not repudiation.[14] With theocracy and polygamy intertwined, the decline in the idea of a separate religious kingdom led to a decrease in Mormon millennialism.[15] The Woodruff Manifesto of 1890, followed by the political-theological accommodation necessary for statehood, forced the Saints to rethink their millennial timetable. The theocratic and separatist aspects of Mormonism were necessarily postponed.[16]

Yet as the decade progressed, Wilford Woodruff's faith in his patriarchal blessing that he would see Christ's return persisted. He now believed that the day had arrived for angels to descend "in their hands sharp Sicles ... sent forth to Visit the Earth ... to poor [sic] out the Judgements of God upon the wicked and will Continue untill the scene is wound up."[17] Well into the late 1890s, Woodruff maintained

---

13. David M. Reay and Londa Lee Skousen Reay, comps., *Selected Manifestations* ..., (Oakland, CA: Published by the Authors, 1985), 131; William E. Berrett and Alma P. Burton, *Readings in L.D.S. Church History*, 5 vols. (Salt Lake City: Deseret Book Co., 1958), 3:108; Gustive O. Larson, *The "Americanization" of Utah for Statehood* (San Marino, CA: Huntington Library, 1971), 272.

14. Wilford Woodruff to William Atkin, 18 Mar. 1889, Special Collections, Merrill Library, Utah State University, Logan, Utah.

15. Klaus J. Hansen, *Quest for Empire: The Political Kingdom of God and the Council of Fifty in Mormon History* (Lansing: Michigan State University Press, 1970), 23; Klaus J. Hansen, *Mormonism and the American Experience* (Chicago: University of Chicago Press, 1981), 145.

16. Richard D. Poll, "The Americanism of Utah," *Utah Historical Quarterly* 44 (Winter 1976): 86-89; Thomas F. O'Dea, *The Mormons* (Chicago: University of Chicago Press, 1957), 171, 117.

17. Kenney, *Wilford Woodruff's Journal*, 9:307, 24 June 1894; "Discourse," *Deseret Evening News* 31 (7 May 1898): 9. See also Kenney, *Wilford Woodruff's Journal*, 1:118-19, 3 Jan. 1837, where Woodruff was also promised that he would "return & stand upon Mount Zion in the flesh even in Jackson

that "many in the flesh at the time would see the savior," although at times his sermons softened, predicting that "*children* [then] living would live to see the Saviour."[18]

After Woodruff's death in 1898, new church president Lorenzo Snow carried belief in an imminent millennium into the twentieth century. In October 1900 he announced to the First Presidency and twelve apostles that "Christ will come before long," and while blessing Apostle Rudger Clawson's son, Snow petitioned God that the child "may live until Thy Son shall come in His glory among the children of men."[19]

As the latter-day prophet, Snow continued to preach that the redemption of Zion was at hand and church members would soon return to Missouri. In November 1900 he told the Saints, "There are many here now under the sound of my voice, probably a majority who will have to go back to Jackson county and assist in building the temple."[20] At a reception for missionaries, Snow testified: "I know that Jesus lives. Many of you who are here tonight will see him, ... When you return to Jackson County and engage in building the temple there, you will see Jesus and be associated with him."[21] He told another group the hour was fast approaching when a large number of them would return to Jackson County. He reported setting aside church monies to assist in constructing the temple in Missouri, believing the "time

County Missouri at the Cumming of Christ."

18. "Ninety Years of Age," *Deseret News Semi-weekly*, 2 (Mar. 1897): 6; Larson and Larson, *Diary of Charles Walker*, 2:868, 9 Apr. 1898 (emphasis added); Stuy, *Collected Discourses*, 3:424.

19. Stan Larson, ed., *A Ministry of Meetings: The Apostolic Diaries of Rudger Clawson* (Salt Lake City: Signature Books in association with Smith Research Associates, 1993), 217, 4 Oct. 1900, hereafter referred to as *Rudger Clawson Diary*. A copy of the blessing is found in ibid., 233-34, 2 Jan. 1901.

20. Lorenzo Snow, 7 Nov. 1900, in Thomas G. Alexander, *Mormonism in Transition: A History of the Latter-day Saints, 1890-1930* (Urbana: University of Illinois Press, 1986), 288-89.

21. Larson, *Rudger Clawson Diary*, 286, 20 June 1901. See also *Deseret News*, 15 June 1901.

has come to commence to redeem the Land of Zion."[22] Snow viewed tithing as a precursor to carrying the gospel to the world for the last time and as a step toward the Millennium. The funds would allow the Saints to redeem Zion and purchase the Jackson County temple site.[23] He promised church leaders in 1899: "If you live 10 or 15 yrs more or less perhaps Less, we are going back to Jackson Co."[24] Apostles Brigham Young, Jr., and Matthias Cowley also emphasized the nearness of Zion's redemption. Cowley declared that "the day is not far distant when the Lord will clean out Jackson County," and advised fellow leaders to prepare to build up the center stake.[25]

But following Snow's death in 1901, his successor, Joseph F. Smith, instituted a policy of assimilation rather than separation. One explanation may be the "changing of the guard." The church hierarchy now consisted primarily of younger general authorities, men who had no personal association with Joseph Smith and the millennial world view so profound and so often professed in the early church. Between 1897 and 1907, the church replaced eleven new apostles, two members of the First Council of the Seventy, and four new members of the Presiding Bishopric. Thus out of the new general

---

22. Larson, *Rudger Clawson Diary*, 215, 4 Oct. 1900; Journal History, 29 May and 15 Sept. 1900, in Alexander, *Mormonism in Transition*, 289. See also the pledge of $100 to assist in the redemption of land in Jackson County, Missouri, in George C. Naegle to Anthony W. Ivins, 1 Sept. 1903, Ivins Collection, box 10, folder 5, Utah State Historical Society; Hardy, *Solemn Covenant*, 188-89.

23. Larson, *Rudger Clawson Diary*, 150, 7 Apr. 1900; 71-72, 2 July 1899; 216-17, 4 Oct. 1900; 153, 9 Apr. 1900; 269, 8 Apr. 1901; 270, 11 Apr. 1901; Anthony Woodward Ivins Diaries, 2:68, 2 July 1899.

24. Donald G. Godfrey and Brigham Y. Card, eds., *The Diaries of Charles Ora Card: The Canadian Years, 1886-1903* (Salt Lake City: University of Utah Press, 1993), 504, 2 July 1899. See also ibid., 449, 6 Apr. 1898; ibid., 568, 7 Oct. 1900; Larson, *Rudger Clawson Diary*, 71-72, 2 July 1899.

25. Larson, *Rudger Clawson Diary*, 78, 11 July 1899; Winslow Farr Diary, TS, Special Collections, Lee Library, 242-43.

authorities, only Charles W. Penrose was born before the Saints' arrival in Utah.[26]

In 1903 Benjamin F. Johnson, a friend of Joseph Smith, expressed his disappointment in the delay of the Millennium. "We were," he said, "over seventy years ago taught by our leaders to believe that the coming of Christ and the millennial reign was much nearer than we believe it to be now."[27] Wilford Woodruff and Lorenzo Snow were the last of the first generation of Mormon leaders. With Snow's death, the church found itself with a prophet who had not known Joseph Smith as an adult.[28]

Church leaders became more indefinite in their millennial rhetoric, speaking generally of the redemption of Zion but only after the Saints first learned to keep the commandments.[29] Some began to speak of Christ's advent as a private return with the Savior making himself known to church leaders to provide instruction.[30] While millennialism remained a doctrine, leaders and members no longer showed the emotional outbursts characteristic of the nineteenth-century church. Rather their preaching was characterized by a calm, expectant mood, anticipating Christ's coming but not emphasizing its immediacy.[31]

In moving to the Great Basin, the Saints had attempted to create a literal kingdom of God, a sacred place for God's chosen people.

---

26. James B. Allen and Glen M. Leonard, *The Story of the Latter-day Saints* (Salt Lake City: Deseret Book Co., 1976), 436; Larson, *The "Americanization" of Utah for Statehood*, 272-73.

27. Benjamin F. Johnson to George S. Gibbs, 1903, in Hansen, *Quest for Empire*, 19; *Benjamin F. Johnson's Letter to Elder George F. Gibbs* (Salt Lake City: Collier's Publishing Co., 1992), 29.

28. Leonard J. Arrington and Davis Bitton, *The Mormon Experience: A History of the Latter-day Saints*, 2nd ed. (Urbana: University of Illinois Press, 1992), 244.

29. Larson, *Rudger Clawson Diary*, 310, 22 Aug. 1901.

30. Ibid., 134, 11 Jan. 1900; 217, 4 Oct. 1900.

31. Louis G. Reinwand, "An Interpretive Study of Mormon Millennialism During the Nineteenth Century with Emphasis on Millennial Developments in Utah," M.A. thesis, Brigham Young University, 1971, 159.

With their intense belief in the immediacy of the Millennium, they planned to usher in the end of time. Social, economic, and political institutions (including polygamy) were expected to remain until the world's end. But by the end of the nineteenth century, American society had made it clear there was no place for a separate, anti-pluralistic Mormon kingdom within the larger structure of American pluralism.[32]

With the 1890 Manifesto and its aftermath, Mormonism was forced to pass through a "psychic watershed," announcing that the old system would pass away to a new order, thereby allowing for the survival of the institutional church.[33] A shared apocalyptic vision had isolated Mormons from the outside community, millennial expectations giving members the fortitude to persevere. Urgently engaged in the Lord's work, they had been counseled to watch for the "signs of the times," anticipating the Bridegroom's return.[34] But when the church was no longer able to shield members from political subordination and cultural disintegration, a resynthesis of beliefs and values was necessary.[35] With the realization that the Millennium had been delayed, the Saints would have to find a way to accommodate the world while continuing to await its inevitable end.[36]

---

32. Hansen, *Mormonism and the American Experience*, xvi; Jan Shipps, "Utah Comes of Age Politically: A Study of the State's Politics in the Early Years of the Twentieth Century," *Utah Historical Quarterly* 35 (Spring 1967): 95.

33. Thomas G. Alexander, "The Odyssey of a Latter-day Prophet: Wilford Woodruff and the Manifesto of 1890," *Journal of Mormon History* 17 (1991): 71; Jan Shipps, "In the Presence of the Past: Continuity and Change in Twentieth-Century Mormonism," in *After 150 Years: The Latter-day Saints in Sesquicentennial Perspective*, eds. Thomas G. Alexander and Jessie Embry (Provo, UT: Charles Redd Center for Western Studies, 1983), 11, 20-22.

34. Glen M. Leonard, "Early Saints and the Millennium," *Ensign* 9 (Aug. 1979): 47; Susan Peterson, "The Great and Dreadful Day: Mormon Folklore of the Apocalypse," *Utah Historical Quarterly* 44 (Fall 1976): 366-70.

35. Michael Barkun, *Disaster and the Millennium* (New Haven, CT: Yale University Press, 1974), 39.

36. Shipps, "In the Presence of the Past," 26.

In many respects the church was faced with having to search for a new way to understand reality, a new paradigm. Such paradigm shifts "are seldom completed by a single man and never overnight."[37] The previous world view had allowed Mormonism to maintain a non-pluralistic community with the integration of politics, economy, and religion, including polygamy, separate from the gentile world. A new Mormon paradigm was now necessary to allow for assimilation into American culture, saving the institutional structure of the church while maintaining the essential religious characteristics that allowed the Latter-day Saints to consider themselves God's chosen people. Polygamy, church control over state and economic institutions, and the immediacy of a millennial peace were all casualties of assimilation.[38]

Some view the early 1890s as the watershed years of Mormon history. In hindsight one can see in the late 1880s and early 1890s a convergence of numerous events, culminating in the 1890 Manifesto and its aftermath, that changed the direction of the church forever. These changes, if not all immediate and planned, have become enduring, carrying Mormonism into the twentieth century and beyond.[39]

One hundred years ago, apocalyptic hope filled the air. Millennialism, so fixed in the minds of Mormonism's first generation, played a major role in shaping the Mormon psyche, heightening tensions that alienated the Saints from the larger community. Only when they realized that Christ's return would not deliver them from their enemies did accommodation gain acceptance; and even then, a generation of Saints had to pass away before the expectation of an immediate apocalyptic solution finally subsided.

---

37. Thomas S. Kuhn, *The Structure of Scientific Revolutions*, 2nd ed. (Chicago: University of Chicago Press, 1970), 7.

38. Alexander, *Mormonism in Transition*, 14; Mark P. Leone, *Roots of Modern Mormonism* (Cambridge, MA: Harvard University Press, 1979), 167.

39. Keith E. Norman, "How Long, O Lord? The Delay of the Parousia in Mormonism," *Sunstone* 8 (Jan.-Apr. 1983): 54; Harold Bloom, *The American Religion: The Emergence of the Post-Christian Nation* (New York: Simon and Schuster, 1992), 86.

CHAPTER TEN

CONCLUSION

Within the nineteenth-century debate between optimistic post-millennialists urging patience and effort in their quest for millennial peace and pessimistic premillennialists awaiting a savior from on high to deliver society from sin, the question became which view carried the greater legitimacy. As John Updike suggests, "What matters in a myth, a belief, is ... Does it enable us to live, to keep going? ... The crucial question isn't Can you prove it? but Does it give us a handle on the reality that otherwise would overwhelm us?"[1] In the midst of this controversy early Latter-day Saints used their eschatology to make sense of the world.

From the Saints' earliest days, apocalyptic fervor accompanied their quest for salvation. The intensity and essentiality of early Mormon belief in an imminent millennium must be examined by anyone who wants to understand the early Mormon mind and how their cosmology influenced Mormon-gentile interaction. Initiated with Joseph Smith's earliest religious experiences, Mormon passage through linear time in search of the Millennium fed the Saints' hunger for divine intervention. Persecutions in New York, Ohio, Missouri, and Illinois were viewed in strictly religious terms and merely confirmed the Saints' belief that the refiner's fire of purification was about to bear fruit. The suffering of the Saints and the events of the day were but part of God's eternal plan, with Mormons soon to inherit "a new heaven and new earth."

---

1. Updike, *The Coup* (New York: Alfred A. Knopf, 1978), 139-41.

Born in an age of uncertainty, Mormonism's "totalist" creed exerted a powerful attraction.[2] Yet Americans were expected to be loyal to the greater "civil religion." Theological peculiarities could only be accommodated as long as the group stayed within the bounds of accepted standards.[3] Like most of the new nation's attributes, religious pluralism was the American way of doing things because it worked.[4] But when a group diverged too radically from societal norms, persecution could result. From its genesis, friction between Mormonism's separatist doctrines and practices and nineteenth-century America ruled the lives of Latter-day Saints.[5]

The institutional church's intent was to develop distinctions necessary to identify Saints from gentiles, just as God had kept Abraham's chosen seed separate from the rest of society.[6] As Laurence Moore has pointed out, in many ways "Mormons were different because they said they were different and because their claims, fre-

---

2. E. R. Dodds, *Pagan and Christian in an Age of Anxiety* (Cambridge, Eng.: Cambridge University Press, 1965), 133.

3. Lawrence Foster, "Cults in Conflict: New Religious Movements and the Mainstream Religious Tradition in America," in *Uncivil Religion: Interreligious Hostility in America*, eds. Robert N. Bellah and Frederick E. Greenspahn (New York: Crossroad Publishing Co., 1987), 196.

4. William A. Clebsch, *From Sacred to Profane America: The Role of Religion in American History* (New York: Harper and Row Publishers, 1968), 212.

5. Larry M. Logue, *A Sermon in the Desert: Belief and Behavior in Early St. George, Utah* (Urbana: University of Illinois Press, 1988), xii; Thomas G. Alexander, "The Odyssey of a Latter-day Prophet: Wilford Woodruff and the Manifesto of 1890," *Journal of Mormon History* 17 (1991): 182. Illinois governor Thomas Ford recognized this, concluding that Mormonism "surprises the people ... [who] cannot rise above the prejudices excited by such [religious] novelty." See Ford to Brigham Young, 8 Apr. 1845, in Robert Flanders, *Nauvoo: Kingdom on the Mississippi* (Urbana: University of Illinois Press, 1965), 331.

6. Jan Shipps, "In the Presence of the Past: Continuity and Change in Twentieth-Century Mormonism," in *150 Years: The Latter-day Saints in Sesquicentennial Perspective*, eds. Thomas G. Alexander and Jessie Embry (Provo, UT: Charles Redd Center for Western Studies, 1983), 18.

quently advanced in the most obnoxious way possible, prompted others to agree and to treat them as such."[7] Exploiting a "rhetoric of deviance," Mormons emphasized their differences from outsiders whom they considered corrupt, creating a context of Mormon separatism and cultural isolation.[8] Mormons have always held that their "enemies" were in Satan's hands, their history a quest for separation from the wicked world, leading to a series of millennial expectations and disappointments. Although the Saints recognized that their millennial anticipations of the 1830s or 1840s were mistaken, eschatological hopes of an imminent advent refused to fade from Mormon consciousness.[9] As such, throughout the nineteenth century Mormonism continued to be an alien culture searching for security in a hostile environment.

After Joseph Smith's death, those who followed Brigham Young visualized the trek as a literal repetition of Israel's sacred journey under Moses, as authentic as the Hebrews' deliverance from Egypt. Reinforcing a sense of distinctiveness, Young led the Saints away from their persecutors, away from the confusion of religious pluralism, to a place where the elect could be isolated and gathered. Here they would claim their inheritance, the goal to establish a righteous people in a holy land where God's kingdom could be built in preparation for the Parousia.[10] As each new wave of immigrants made the pilgrimage of faith, the thought of new Saints entering Zion rejuve-

---

7. R. Laurence Moore, *Religious Outsiders and the Making of Americans* (New York: Oxford University Press, 1986), 31. See also Dernard DeVoto, *The Year of Decision: 1846* (Boston: Little, Brown and Co., 1943), 79-84.

8. Moore, *Religious Outsiders and the Making of Americans,* 33; Ephraim Edward Ericksen, *The Psychological and Ethical Aspects of Mormon Group Life* (1922; reprint, Salt Lake City: University of Utah Press, 1975), 30.

9. Davis Bitton, "Early Mormon Lifestyles; or the Saints as Human Beings," in *The Restoration Movement: Essays in Mormon History,* rev. ed., eds. F. Mark McKiernan, Alma R. Blair, and Paul M. Edwards (Independence, MO: Herald Publishing House), 288-89.

10. Shipps, "In the Presence of the Past," 19-20; Moore, *Religious Outsiders and the Making of Americans,* 38.

nated the Mormon sense of an extraordinary people arriving at the "place prepared" in the West.[11]

In the Great Basin the Latter-day Saints attempted to remain unspotted from the world through unification of the political, social, and economic aspects of life. Once again their intense millennial hope accompanied LDS cosmology during the reformation and the Utah War. The invasion of federal troops crystallized Mormon suspicion and contempt for "outsiders," creating a garrison mentality of both self-righteousness and separatism.[12] The Saints were sure that U.S. aggression would lead to its destruction and usher in the Millennium with the Messiah's return at the door.

With expectations of the Parousia carrying into the 1860s, Mormons saw the North and South poised to destroy each other, leaving the Saints to establish Christ's kingdom on the scattered ruins. At last God was avenging the murders of Joseph and Hyrum Smith and the persecution of the Saints. When the Civil War ended in a continuance of the Union, the federal government's focus on polygamy fed the next round of millennial anticipation. Surely this intense pressure was a test of the church's fortitude, the bearing of persecution a badge of courage and a sign of members' strength, a prelude to imminent deliverance. Soon the Saints would find their just reward as God's earthly kingdom was approaching.

Preparing a domain where Christ could reign, nineteenth-century Latter-day Saints built their institutions separate from and juxtaposed to gentile society. As a symbol of their separateness, the most obvious practice was polygamy. Therefore plural marriage, as a sign of institutional separateness, had to be defended by polygamists and monogamists alike. External pressure, particularly political pressure from the federal government which climaxed in the anti-polygamy campaign, played such a tremendous role in shaping

---

11. Martin Ridge, "Mormon 'Deliverance' and the Closing of the Frontier," *Journal of Mormon History* 18 (Spring 1992): 143; Ronald K. Esplin, "'A Place Prepared': Joseph, Brigham and the Quest for Promised Refuge in the West," *Journal of Mormon History* 9 (1982): 85-111.

12. Bitton, "Early Mormon Lifestyles," 290.

Mormon pioneer history that its influence cannot be ignored. As such, scholarly consensus points to the 1890 Manifesto as the breaking point between past and present. The federal government had made it clear that internally designated borders could not be tolerated, and the Manifesto broke the boundaries that had separated Mormon from American society. The ending of plural marriage was such a disconcerting development it thrust the Saints into a new cosmology.[13]

Late nineteenth-century church presidents Wilford Woodruff and Lorenzo Snow continued to assure members that they would yet witness the winding-up scene. But in the end the day of harmony and peace destined to encircle the world was not to be. As the century closed, old leaders died, leading to both internal and external pressure for change. Whereas Mormonism had risked annihilation and pushed separatism to the brink, when confrontation with America left no room for compromise many Mormons refused to forfeit all in a fruitless attempt to remain autonomous from the larger society.[14] With separatism and isolation no longer possible or acceptable, church leaders abandoned further risk of organizational destruction.

Due to unfulfilled millennial expectations, the fate of millenarian movements is either failure and collapse or they cease to remain millenarian. In order to survive, the movement must generate rational explanations for the delay of the Millennium and redirect prior millennial desire to new aims. Alternating strategies included reaching out to persuade others of their religion's truthfulness and channeling energies from preparing for the Millennium to developing institutional structures. In so doing they must suppress the memory of their millenarian past and transform former millenarian vigor into other forms of action.[15]

---

13. Shipps, "In the Presence of the Past," 9-12, 23-25.

14. Foster, "Cults in Conflict," 195.

15. John G. Gager, "Early Mormonism and Early Christianity: Some Parallels and Their Consequences for the Study of New Religions," *Journal of Mormon History* 9 (1982): 57; Leon Festinger, Henry W. Riecken, and

Repeatedly, Latter-day Saints had been forced into cognitive dissonance, compelled either to explain away the non-event in spite of prophetic declarations or discard eschatological assumptions. Each disappointment gave rise to a new round of predictions until multiple failures broke the cycle. Under collective stress, the church faced either dissolution or revitalization, and when continuance of an apocalyptic cosmology was no longer feasible, transformation and accommodation became necessary. If they continued in the same mode of thought and behavior, they risked losing continuity, unable to meet the new demands of a changing environment. By changing their world view, they could use new energies and talents to effect a new perception of reality.[16]

The institutions and theology crucial to the early Saints—millennialism, communitarianism, theocracy, polygamy—and which separated Mormons from American culture gave way both culturally and intellectually to the need for survival, the quest for statehood, and accommodation.[17] John Gager contends the countercultural aspects of millenarian movements, such as

> unrestrained prophecy, visions, revelations, and new patterns of sexual activity—including polygamy—are precisely what we would expect of a millenarian lifestyle in nineteenth-century America and precisely what we would expect to disappear in those millenarian movements that survive the initial rush of enthusiasm, that cease to be properly millenarian.[18]

For nineteenth-century Mormons, millennial separatism isolated them from profane Babylon. As Martin Ridge suggests, "[W]ithout

---

Stanley Schachter, *When Prophecy Fails* (Minneapolis: University of Minnesota Press, 1956), 3-32; Klaus J. Hansen, *Quest for Empire: The Political Kingdom of God and the Council of Fifty in Mormon History* (Lansing: Michigan State University Press, 1970), 18-20.

16. Michael Barkun, *Crucible of the Millennium: The Burned-Over District of New York in the 1840s* (Syracuse: Syracuse University Press, 1986), 19, 58-59.

17. Klaus J. Hansen, "Mormonism and American Culture: Some Tentative Hypotheses," in *The Restoration Movement*, 2.

18. Gager, "Early Mormonism and Early Christianity," 58.

'the gathering,' without compelling millennialism, without an overly intrusive temporal kingdom, and especially without polygamy, the church stood at a threshold of a new century."[19] Prior to the Manifesto and Mormon capitulation, the LDS belief system exalted defiance of non-Mormon America.[20] But with Christ's second coming continually delayed, the onslaught of the federal government's legal aggression left church leaders with no option other than religious surrender. Faced with either remaining committed to plural marriage or surviving as an institution, the church chose to survive.[21]

Although what church president Wilford Woodruff hoped for with his Manifesto was an expedient compromise to buy time for chiliastic salvation, when the Advent was delayed, its consequence was the fading of hope in apocalyptic deliverance. With accommodation to the dominant American culture a *fait accompli,* revolutionary millennialism could no longer provide a feasible method of viewing the world, giving birth to a new era of Mormonism. For eighty years Joseph Smith's followers had known the Second Coming was nigh. But at the turn of the twentieth century, the Saints' deliverance remained on the horizon, farther from sight than ever before.

---

19. Ridge, "Mormon 'Deliverance' and the Closing of the Frontier," 151.

20. Logue, *A Sermon in the Desert,* 12.

21. Edwin Brown Firmage and Richard Collin Mangrum, *Zion in the Courts: A Legal History of the Church of Jesus Christ of Latter-day Saints, 1830-1900* (Urbana: University of Illinois Press, 1988), 259. Nevertheless, they surreptitiously continued to authorize new polygamous marriages for the better part of two decades.

BIBLIOGRAPHY

Newspapers

Congressional Globe

Contributor

Deseret Evening News

Deseret News

Deseret News Semi-Weekly

Elders' Journal

Evening and Morning Star

Juvenile Instructor

Messenger and Advocate

Millennial Harbinger

Millennial Star

Nauvoo Expositor

New York Times

Ohio Star

Painesville Telegraph

Philadelphia Sun Mercury

Royal Leamington Spa Courier

Salt Lake Tribune

The Seer

Times and Seasons

Wayne Sentinel

Manuscripts Sources

Allen, Andrew Jackson. "Record of Andrew Jackson Allen." TS. Utah State Historical Society, Salt Lake City, Utah.

Ballard, Henry. Henry Ballard Diary. TS. Special Collections, Lee Library, Brigham Young University, Provo, Utah.

Bentley, Israel Ivins. "Israel Ivins Bentley." TS. Oral History Interview, by Gordon Irving, May 1973, Historical Department of the Church of Jesus Christ of Latter-day Saints, hereafter cited as the LDS Church Archives, Salt Lake City, Utah.

Call, Anson Bowan. "Life Story of Anson Bowan Call." TS. In possession of B. Carmon Hardy, Orange, Calif.

Cannon, Abraham Hoagland. Abraham Hoagland Cannon Diaries. Photocopy of MS. Special Collections, Lee Library, Brigham Young University, Provo, Utah.

Condie, Gibson. "Reminiscence and Diary." LDS Church Archives, Salt Lake City, Utah.

Cox, Martha [Cragun]. "Biographical Record of Martha [Cragun] Cox." LDS Church Archives, Salt Lake City, Utah.

Druce, John. Letter to Brigham Young. 3 Feb. 1877. Brigham Young Correspondence, 36/7, LDS Church Archives, Salt Lake City, Utah.

Eyring, Henry. Journal of Henry Eyring, 1835-1902. TS. Special Collections, Lee Library, Brigham Young University, Provo, Utah.

Farr, Winslow. Winslow Farr Diary. TS. Special Collections, Lee Library, Brigham Young University, Provo, Utah.

Fielding, Robert Kent. "Lamanite Redemption: The Mormon Experience with Indians, 1830-1858, an Overview." Paper presented at the Mormon History Association Convention, May 1994. TS. Photocopy in author's possession.

Gallup, Luke William. Letter to Nancy Williams. 2 July 1862. Luke William Gallup Collection, LDS Church Archives, Salt Lake City, Utah.

Haight, Isaac Chauncy. Isaac Chauncy Haight Journal. TS. LDS Church Archives, Salt Lake City, Utah.

Hendricks, Sarah. TS. Interviewed by James Comish, 26 Jan. 1980, LDS Oral History Project, Charles Redd Center, Brigham Young University, Provo, Utah.

Huntington, Dimick Baker. Dimick Baker Huntington Journals. 2 vols. LDS Church Archives, Salt Lake City, Utah.

Huntington, Oliver B. Oliver B. Huntington Diary. TS. Special Collections, Lee Library, Brigham Young University, Provo, Utah.

Ivins, Anthony Woodward. Anthony Woodward Ivins Diaries. Utah State Historical Society, Salt Lake City, Utah.

Johnson, Joel Hills. "Excerpts from a Journal or Sketch of the Life of Joel

Hills Johnson." Bound copy, N.p.: n.p., n.d., Utah State Historical Society, Salt Lake City, Utah.

"Journal History of The Church of Jesus Christ of Latter-day Saints." LDS Church Archives, Salt Lake City, Utah.

Lamb, George W. George W. Lamb Diary. Huntington Library, San Marino, Calif.

Laub, George. George Laub Diaries. TS. Utah State Historical Society, Salt Lake City, Utah.

Martin, Jessie Bigler. Jessie Bigler Martin Diary. Special Collections, Lee Library, Brigham Young University, Provo, Utah.

McIntosh, William. Diary of William McIntosh. TS. Special Collections, Lee Library, Brigham Young University, Provo, Utah.

Merrill, Marriner Wood. Marriner Wood Merrill Diaries. LDS Church Archives, Salt Lake City, Utah.

Morgan, John. John Morgan Journals, 1875-92. 10 vols. LDS Church Archives, Salt Lake City, Utah.

Naegle, George C. Letter to Anthony W. Ivins. 1 Sept. 1903. Anthony W. Ivins Collection, box 10, folder 5, Utah State Historical Society, Salt Lake City, Utah.

Nielson, Peter. "History of Peter Nielson (Autobiography)." Translated from the Danish by Orson B. West. TS. LDS Church Archives, Salt Lake City, Utah.

Nuttall, Leonard. Leonard John Nuttall Diary. TS. Special Collections, Lee Library, Brigham Young University, Provo, Utah.

Pulsipher, John. John Pulsipher Journal. TS. Utah State Historical Society, Salt Lake City, Utah.

Richards, Franklin S. Letter to John Taylor, 9 Feb. 1887. Photocopy. Franklin S. Richards Correspondence, 1886-90, Utah State Historical Society, Salt Lake City, Utah.

Robinson, Joseph Lee. Joseph Lee Robinson Journal. Mimeograph copy. Utah State Historical Society, Salt Lake City, Utah.

Savage Levi, Jr. Levi Savage, Jr., Diary. TS. Special Collections, Lee Library, Brigham Young University, Provo, Utah.

Savage, Levi Mathers. Levi Mathers Savage Family History Journal. Mimeograph copy. Special Collections, Lee Library, Brigham Young University, Provo, Utah.

Shipps, Jan. "From Satyr to Saint: American Attitudes Toward the Mormons, 1860-1960." Paper presented at the 1973 Annual Meeting of the Organization of American Historians. TS. Utah State Historical Society, Salt Lake City, Utah.

Smith, John Henry. Letter to Joseph Smith III. 21 Apr. 1886. Library-Archives of the Reorganized Church of Jesus Christ of Latter Day Saints, Independence, Mo.

Stout, David Fisk. David Fisk Stout Diaries. LDS Church Archives, Salt Lake City, Utah.

Taylor, William Whittaker. William Whittaker Taylor Journals. LDS Church Archives, Salt Lake City, Utah.

Thatcher, Moses. "An extract from the Remarks of Apostle Moses Thatcher at Lewiston, Cache Co. Utah Terr[itory]. 1886, 6 Nov. 1886." LDS Church Archives, MS 7267, Salt Lake City, Utah.

Welchman, Arthur Pendry. "Reminiscences and Diary." LDS Church Archives, MS 1343, folder 1, Salt Lake City, Utah.

Whitaker, John Mills. John Mills Whitaker Diaries. 3 vols. TS. Transcription of 7 vols., original, Special Collections, Marriott Library, University of Utah, Salt Lake City, Utah.

Whitaker, Thomas William. Thomas William Whitaker Journal, 1849-86. Photocopy of Holograph. Special Collections, Marriott Library, University of Utah, Salt Lake City, Utah.

Woodruff, Wilford. Letter to William Atkin. 18 Mar. 1889. Special Collections, Merrill Library, Utah State University, Logan, Utah.

Young, Brigham, [Jr.]. Brigham Young [,Jr.,] Journals, 1862-1902. LDS Church Archives, Salt Lake City, Utah.

Young, John Willard. Letter to Susie and Mabel Young. 17 Feb. 1886. John Young Correspondence, LDS Church Archives, Salt Lake City, Utah.

Printed Sources

Adams, Dale W. "Chartering the Kirtland Bank." *Brigham Young University Studies* 23 (Fall 1983): 467-82.

Ahlstrom, Sydney E. *A Religious History of the American People.* New Haven: Yale University Press, 1972.

Aho, James A. *The Politics of Righteousness: Idaho Christian Patriotism.* Seattle: University of Washington Press, 1990.

Albanese, Catherine L. "Dominant and Public Center: Reflections on the 'One' Religion of the United States." *American Journal of Theology and Philosophy* 4 (Sept. 1983): 83-96.

Alexander, Thomas G. "Between Revivalism and the Social Gospel: The Latter-day Saint Social Advisory Committee, 1916-1922." *Brigham Young University Studies* 23 (Winter 1983): 19-39.

—. *Mormonism in Transition: A History of the Latter-day Saints, 1890-1930.* Urbana: University of Illinois Press, 1986.

—. "The Odyssey of a Latter-day Prophet: Wilford Woodruff and the Manifesto of 1890." *Journal of Mormon History* 17 (1991): 169-206.

—. *Things in Heaven and Earth: The Life and Times of Wilford Woodruff, a Mormon Prophet.* Salt Lake City: Signature Books, 1991.

—. "'To Maintain Harmony': Adjusting to External and Internal Stress, 1890-1930." *Dialogue: A Journal of Mormon Thought* 15 (Winter 1982): 44-58.

—. "Wilford Woodruff and the Changing Nature of Mormon Religious Experience." *Church History* 45 (Mar. 1976): 56-69.

—. "Wilford Woodruff and the Mormon Reformation of 1855-57." *Dialogue: A Journal of Mormon Thought* 25 (Summer 1992): 25-39.

—, and James B. Allen. *Mormons & Gentiles: A History of Salt Lake City.* Boulder, CO: Pruett Publishing Company, 1984.

—, and Jessie L. Embry, eds. *After 150 Years: The Latter-day Saints in Sesquicentennial Perspective.* Midvale, UT: Charles Redd Center for Western Studies, 1983.

Allen, Edward G. *The Second United Order Among the Mormons,* New York: n.p., 1936.

Allen, James B. "Eight Contemporary Accounts of Joseph Smith's First Vision: What Do We Learn from Them?" *Improvement Era* 73 (Apr. 1970): 4-13.

—. "Emergence of a Fundamental: The Expanding Role of Joseph Smith's First Vision in Mormon Religious Thought." *Journal of Mormon History* (1980): 41-61.

—. "The Significance of Joseph Smith's 'First Vision' in Mormon Thought." *Dialogue: A Journal of Mormon Thought* 1 (Autumn 1966): 29-45.

—. *Trials of Discipleship: The Story of William Clayton, a Mormon.* Urbana: University of Illinois Press, 1987.

—, and Thomas G. Alexander, eds. *Manchester Mormons: The Journal of William Clayton, 1840-1842.* Santa Barbara, CA: Peregrine Smith, 1974.

—, Ronald K. Esplin, and David J. Whittaker. *Men with a Mission, 1837-1841: The Quorum of the Twelve Apostles in the British Isles.* Salt Lake City: Deseret Book Company, 1992.

—, and Glen M. Leonard. *The Story of the Latter-day Saints.* Salt Lake City: Deseret Book Company, 1976.

—, and Malcolm R. Thorp. "The Mission of the Twelve to England, 1840-41: Mormon Apostles and the Working Classes." *Brigham Young University Studies* 15 (Summer 1975): 499-526.

Alter, J. Cecil, ed. "Journal of Leonard E. Harrington." *Utah Historical Quarterly* 8 (Jan. 1940): 2-64.

Anderson, C. LeRoy. *Joseph Morris and the Saga of the Morrisites*. 1981. Reprint. Logan, Utah: Utah State University Press, 1988.

Anderson, Nels. *Desert Saints: The Mormon Frontier in Utah*. 1942. Reprint. Chicago: University of Chicago Press, 1966.

Anderson, Richard Lloyd. "Atchison's Letters and the Causes of Mormon Expulsion from Missouri." *Brigham Young University Studies* 26 (Summer 1986): 3-47.

—. "Circumstantial Confirmation of the First Vision Through Reminiscences." *Brigham Young University Studies* 9 (Spring 1969): 373-404.

—. "Jackson County in Early Mormon Descriptions." *Missouri Historical Review* 65 (Apr. 1971): 270-93.

—. "Joseph Smith and the Millenarian Time Table." *Brigham Young University Studies* 3 (1961): 55-66.

—. "The Mature Joseph Smith and Treasure Searching." *Brigham Young University Studies* 24 (Fall 1984): 489-560.

Anderson, Robert D. "Toward an Introduction to a Psychobiography of Joseph Smith." *Dialogue: A Journal of Mormon Thought* 27 (Fall 1994): 249-72.

Anderson, Rodger I. *Joseph Smith's New York Reputation Reexamined*. Salt Lake City: Signature Books, 1990.

Armytage, W[alter]. H. G. *Heavens Below: Utopian Experiments in England, 1560-1960*. Toronto: Toronto University Press, 1961.

Arrington, Leonard J. *Brigham Young: American Moses*. New York: Alfred A. Knopf, 1985.

—. "Early Mormon Communitarianism: The Law of Consecration and Stewardship." *Western Humanities Review* 7 (Autumn 1953): 341-69.

—. *Great Basin Kingdom: An Economic History of the Latter-Day Saints, 1830-1900*. 1958. Reprint. Lincoln: University of Nebraska Press, 1966.

—. "Mormonism: From Its New York Beginnings." *New York History* 61 (Oct. 1980): 387-410.

—. "Mormonism: Views from Without and Within." *Brigham Young University Studies* 14 (Winter 1974): 140-53.

—, and Davis Bitton. *The Mormon Experience: A History of the Latter-day Saints*. 2nd ed. Urbana: University of Illinois Press, 1992.

—, Feramorz Y. Fox, and Dean L. May. *Building the City of God: Community & Cooperation Among the Mormons*. Salt Lake City: Deseret Book Company, 1976.

—, and Jon Haupt. "Intolerable Zion: The Image of Mormonism in Nineteenth-Century American Literature." *Western Humanities Review* 22 (Summer 1968): 243-60.

—, and D. Michael Quinn. "The Latter-day Saints in the Far West, 1847-1900." In *The Restoration Movement: Essays in Mormon History*. Rev. ed. Eds. F. Mark McKiernan, Alma R. Blair, and Paul M. Edwards. 1973. Reprint. Independence, MO: Herald Publishing House, 1992.

Arthur, David. "Millerism." In *The Rise of Adventism; Religion and Society in Mid-Nineteenth-Century America*. Ed. Edwin S. Gaustad. New York: Harper and Row, 1974.

Backman, Milton V., Jr. "Awakenings in the Burned-over District: New Light on the Historical Setting of the First Vision." *Brigham Young University Studies* 9 (Spring 1969): 301-20.

—. *The Heavens Resound: A History of the Latter-day Saints in Ohio, 1830-1838*. Salt Lake City: Deseret Book Company, 1983.

——. *Joseph Smith's First Vision: The First Vision in Historical Context*. Salt Lake City: Bookcraft, 1971.

Bailey, Paul. *Wovoka, the Indian Messiah*. Los Angeles: Westernlore Press, 1957.

Bailyn, Bernard. "Religion and Revolution: Three Biographical Studies." *Perspectives in American History* 4 (1970): 85-169.

Ban, Joseph D., and Paul R. Dekar, eds. *In the Great Tradition: In Honor of Winthrop S. Hudson, Essays on Pluralism, Voluntarism, and Revivalism*. Valley Forge, PA: Judson Press, 1982.

Bancroft, Hubert Howe. *History of Utah: 1540-1886*. San Francisco: The History Company, 1889.

Banks, Loy Otis. "The Evening and Morning Star." *Missouri Historical Review* 43 (July 1949): 319-33.

Barkun, Michael. *Crucible of the Millennium: The Burned-Over District of New York in the 1840s*. Syracuse: Syracuse University Press, 1986.

—. *Disaster and the Millennium*. New Haven: Yale University Press, 1974.

Barlow, Philip L. *Mormons and the Bible: The Place of the Latter-day Saints in American Religion*. New York: Oxford University Press, 1991.

Barry, Richard. "The Mormon Evasion of Anti-Polygamy Laws." *Pearson's Magazine* 24 (Oct. 1910): 451.

Bates, Irene M. "Patriarchal Blessings and the Routinization of Charisma." *Dialogue: A Journal of Mormon Thought* 26 (Fall 1993): 1-29.

Bellah, Robert N. "Civil Religion in America." *Daedalus* 96 (Winter 1967): 9-21.

—, and Philip E. Hammond, eds. *Varieties of Civil Religion*. San Francisco: Harper and Row, 1980.

Benjamin F. Johnson's Letter to Elder George F. Gibbs. Salt Lake City: Collier's Publishing Co., 1992.

Bennett, John C. *The History of the Saints, or an Exposé of Joe Smith and Mormonism.* Boston: Leland and Whiting, 1842.

Bercovitch, Sacvan. *The American Jeremiad.* Madison: University of Wisconsin Press, 1978.

—. *The Puritan Origins of American Self.* New Haven: Yale University Press, 1975.

Berger, Peter L. *The Sacred Canopy: Elements of a Sociological Theory of Religion.* Garden City, NY: Doubleday and Company, 1967.

Bergera, Gary James. "Secretary to the Senator: Carl A. Badger and the Smoot Hearings." *Sunstone* 8 (Jan.- Apr. 1983): 36-41.

—. "Toward 'Psychologically Informed' Mormon History and Biography." *Sunstone* 15 (Dec. 1991): 27-31.

Berrett, William E., and Alma P. Burton. *Readings in L.D.S. Church History.* 5 vols. Salt Lake City: Deseret Book Company, 1958.

Bitton, Davis. "Early Mormon Lifestyles: or the Saints as Human Beings." In *The Restoration Movement: Essays in Mormon History.* Rev. ed. Eds. F. Mark McKiernan, Alma R. Blair, and Paul M. Edwards. Independence, MO: Herald Publishing House, 1992.

—. "The Ordeal of Brigham Young, Jr." In *The Ritualization of Mormon History and Other Essays.* Urbana: University of Illinois Press, 1994.

—. "The Waning of Mormon Kirtland." *Brigham Young University Studies* 12 (Summer 1972): 455-464.

—, and Maureen Ursenbach Beecher, eds. *New Views of Mormon History: A Collection of Essays in Honor of Leonard J. Arrington.* Salt Lake City: University of Utah Press, 1987.

Blanke, Gustav H., and Karen Lynn. "'God's Base of Operations': Mormon Variations on the American Sense of Mission." *Brigham Young University Studies* 20 (Fall 1979): 83-92.

Block, Ruth H. *Visionary Republic: Millennial Themes in American Thought, 1756-1800.* Cambridge, Eng.: Cambridge University Press, 1985.

Bloom, Harold. *The American Religion: The Emergence of the Post-Christian Nation.* New York: Simon and Schuster, 1992.

Book of Commandments for the Government of the Church of Christ, Organized According to Law, on the 6th of April, 1830. Zion [Independence], Mo.: W. W. Phelps and Co., 1833.

Book of Mormon. 1830. Reprint. Salt Lake City: The Church of Jesus Christ of Latter-day Saints, 1981.

Bradley, Martha Sonntag. "'Hide and Seek:' Children on the Underground." *Utah Historical Quarterly* 51 (Spring 1983): 133-53.

Brauer, Jerald C. "Revivalism and Millenarianism in America." In *In the Great*

Tradition: In Honor of Winthrop S. Hudson, Essays on Pluralism, Voluntarism, and Revivalism. Eds. Joseph D. Ban and Paul R. Dekar. Valley Forge, PA: Judson Press, 1982.

Bringhurst, Newell G. *Saints, Slaves, and Blacks.* Westport, CT: Greenwood Press, 1981.

Brink, T[erry]. L. "Joseph Smith: The Verdict of Depth Psychology." *Journal of Mormon History* 3 (1976): 73-83.

Brodie, Fawn M. *No Man Knows My History: The Life of Joseph Smith the Mormon Prophet.* 2nd enl. rev. ed. New York: Alfred A. Knopf, 1985.

Brooks, Juanita. *The Mountain Meadows Massacre.* 1950. Reprint. Norman: University of Oklahoma Press, 1991.

—, ed. *On the Mormon Frontier: The Diary of Hosea Stout, 1844-1861.* 2 vols. Salt Lake City: University of Utah Press, 1964.

Brown, Dee Alexander. *Bury My Heart at Wounded Knee: An Indian History of the American West.* New York: Holt, Rinehart and Winston, 1971.

Brown, Ira V. "Watchers for the Second Coming: The Millenarian Tradition in America." *Mississippi Valley Historical Review* 39 (Dec. 1952): 441-58.

Buerger, David John. "The Development of the Mormon Temple Endowment Ceremony." *Dialogue: A Journal of Mormon Thought* 20 (Winter 1987): 33-76.

—. *The Mysteries of Godliness: A History of Mormon Temple Worship.* San Francisco: Smith Research Associates, 1994.

—. "The Second Anointing in Latter-day Saint Theology and Practice." *Dialogue: A Journal of Mormon Thought* 16 (Spring 1983): 10-44.

Bullough, Vern L. "Polygamy: An Issue in the Election of 1860." *Utah Historical Quarterly* 29 (Apr. 1961): 119-26.

Burridge, Kenelm. "Millennialisms and the Recreation of History." In *Religion, Rebellion, Revolution.* Ed. Bruce Lincoln. New York: St. Martin's Press, 1985.

—. *New Heaven, New Earth: A Study of Millenarian Activities.* New York: Schocken Books, 1969.

Burton, Richard F. *The City of the Saints.* Ed. Fawn M. Brodie. 1861. Reprint. New York: Alfred A. Knopf, 1963.

Bush, Lester E., Jr. "Mormonism's Negro Doctrine: An Overview." In *Neither White nor Black.* Eds. Lester E. Bush, Jr., and Armand L. Mauss. Midvale, UT: Signature Books, 1984.

—, and Armand L. Mauss, eds. *Neither White nor Black.* Midvale, UT: Signature Books, 1984.

Bushman, Richard L. "The Book of Mormon and the American Revolution." *Brigham Young University Studies,* 17 (Autumn 1976): 3-20.

—. "The Book of Mormon in Early Mormon History." In *New Views of Mormon History*. Eds. Davis Bitton and Maureen Ursenbach Beecher. Salt Lake City: University of Utah Press, 1987.

—. "The First Vision Story Revived." *Dialogue: A Journal of Mormon Thought* 4 (Spring 1969): 82-96.

—. *Joseph Smith and the Beginnings of Mormonism*. Urbana: University of Illinois Press, 1984.

—. "Mormon Persecutions in Missouri, 1833." *Brigham Young University Studies* 3 (Autumn 1960): 11-20.

Buss, Dietrich G. "Meeting of Heaven and Earth: A Survey and Analysis of the Literature on Millennialism in America, 1965-1985." *Fides et Historia* 20 (Jan. 1988): 5-28.

Butler, John M. "Adventism and the American Experience." In *Rise of Adventism: Religion and Society in Mid-Nineteenth-Century America*. Ed. Edwin S. Gaustad. New York: Harper and Row, 1974.

Butler, Jon. *Awash in a Sea of Faith: Christianizing the American People*. Cambridge, MA: Harvard University Press, 1990.

Butler, Jonathan. "From Millerism to Seventh-day Adventism: 'Boundlessness to Consolidation.'" *Church History* 55 (Mar. 1986): 50-64.

Caldwell, Gaylon L. "'Utah Has Not Seceded': A Footnote to Local History." *Utah Historical Quarterly* 26 (Apr. 1958): 171-75.

Campbell, Eugene, E. *Establishing Zion: The Mormon Church in the American West, 1847-1869*. Salt Lake City: Signature Books, 1988.

—. "Pioneers and Patriotism: Conflicting Loyalties." In *New Views of Mormon History*. Eds. Davis Bitton and Maureen Ursenbach Beecher. Salt Lake City: University of Utah Press, 1987.

—, and Bruce L. Campbell. "Divorce among Mormon Polygamists: Extent and Explanations." *Utah Historical Quarterly* 46 (Winter 1978): 4-23.

Cannon, Donald Q., and Lyndon W. Cook, eds. *Far West Record: Minutes of the Church of Jesus Christ of Latter-day Saints, 1830-1844*. Salt Lake City: Deseret Book Company, 1983.

Cannon, Frank J., and Harvey J. O'Higgins. *Under the Prophet in Utah*. Boston: C. M. Clark Publishing, 1911.

Cannon, George Q. *A Review of the Decision of the Supreme Court of the United States in the Case of George Reynolds v. the United States*. Salt Lake City: Deseret News Printing and Publishing Establishment, 1879.

Cannon, Kenneth L. II. "After the Manifesto: Mormon Polygamy, 1890-1906." *Sunstone* 8 (Jan.-Apr. 1983): 27-35.

Cannon, M. Hanlin. "Migration of English Mormons to America." *American Historical Review* 52 (Apr. 1947): 436-55.

Hudson, Essays on Pluralism, Voluntarism, and Revivalism. Eds. Joseph D. Ban and Paul R. Dekar. Valley Forge, PA: Judson Press, 1982.

De Pillis, Mario S. "The Quest for Religious Authority and the Rise of Mormonism." *Dialogue: A Journal of Mormon Thought* (Mar. 1966): 68-88.

De Voto, Bernard. "The Centennial of Mormonism." *American Mercury* 19 (Jan. 1930): 1-13.

—. *The Year of Decision: 1846.* Boston: Little, Brown and Company, 1943.

Divett, Robert T. "His Chastening Rod: Cholera Epidemics and the Mormons." *Dialogue: A Journal of Mormon Thought* 12 (Fall 1979): 6-15.

Dobyns, Henry F., and Robert C. Euler. *The Ghost Dance of 1889 Among the Pai Indians of Northwestern Arizona.* Prescott, AZ: Prescott College Press, 1967.

Doctrine and Covenants of the Church of Jesus Christ of Latter-day Saints. Salt Lake City: The Church of Jesus Christ of Latter-day Saints, 1981.

Doctrine and Covenants of the Church of Jesus Christ of Latter-day Saints: Carefully Selected from the Revelations of God. 2nd ed. Nauvoo, IL: John Taylor, 1844.

Doctrine and Covenants of the Church of the Latter Day Saints: Carefully Selected from the Revelations of God. Comps. Joseph Smith, Junior, Oliver Cowdery, Sidney Rigdon, and Frederick G. Williams. Kirtland, OH: F. G. Williams and Co., 1835.

Dodds, E[ric]. R. *Pagan and Christian in an Age of Anxiety.* Cambridge, Eng.: Cambridge University Press, 1965.

Douglas, Mary. *Natural Symbols: Explorations in Cosmology.* London: Cresset Press, 1970.

Driggs, Ken. "'Lawyers of Their Own to Defend Them': The Legal Career of Franklin Snyder Richards." *Journal of Mormon History* 21 (Fall 1995): 84-125.

Dudley, Dean A. "Bank Born of Revelation: The Kirtland Safety Society Anti-Banking Company." *Journal of Economic History* 30 (Dec. 1970): 848-853.

Dudley, Guilford III. *Religion on Trial: Mircea Eliade & His Critics.* Philadelphia: Temple University Press, 1977.

Dunn, Ballard S. *The Twin Monsters* ... New York: James Pott and Co., n.d.

Edwards, Paul M. "The Secular Smiths." *Journal of Mormon History* 4 (1977): 3-17.

Ehat, Andrew F. "'It Seems Like Heaven on Earth': Joseph Smith and the Constitution of the Kingdom of God." *Brigham Young University Studies* 20 (Spring 1980): 253-79.

—. ed. "'They Might Have Known That He Was Not a Fallen Prophet'—The

Nauvoo Journal of Joseph Fielding." *Brigham Young University Studies* 19 (Winter 1979): 133-66.

—, and Lyndon W. Cook. *The Words of Joseph Smith: The Contemporary Accounts of the Nauvoo Discourses of the Prophet Joseph.* 1980. Reprint. Orem, UT: Grandin Book Company, 1991.

Eliade, Mircea. *The Sacred and the Profane.* 1957. Reprint. New York: Harcourt, Brace and Company, 1959.

—. "The Sacred in the Secular World." *Cultural Hermeneutics* 1 (1973): 101-13.

Elliot, David R. "The Devil and William Aberhart: The Nature and Function of His Eschatology." *Studies in Religion* 9 (1980): 325-37.

Ellis, Richard E. *The Union at Risk: Jacksonian Democracy, States' Rights and the Nullification Crisis.* New York: Oxford University Press, 1987.

Ellsworth, S. George. "Utah's Struggle for Statehood." *Utah Historical Quarterly* 31 (Winter 1963): 60-69.

Embry, Jessie L. *Mormon Polygamous Families: Life in the Principle.* Salt Lake City: University of Utah Press, 1987.

—. "The Polygamy Image." *This People* (Fall 1990): 24-27.

Endy, Melvin B., Jr. "Just War, Holy War, and Millennialism in Revolutionary America." *William and Mary Quarterly* 42 (Jan 1985): 3-25.

Ericksen, Ephraim Edward. *The Psychological and Ethical Aspects of Mormon Group Life.* 1922. Reprint. Salt Lake City: University of Utah Press, 1975.

Erickson, Kai. *Wayward Puritans: A Study in Sociological Deviance.* New York: John Wiley, 1966.

Ernst, Eldon G. "Beyond the Protestant Era in American Religious Historiography." In *In the Great Tradition: In Honor of Winthrop S. Hudson, Essays on Pluralism, Voluntarism, and Revivalism.* Eds. Joseph D. Ban and Paul R. Dekar. Valley Forge, PA: Judson Press, 1982.

Esplin, Ronald K. "'A Place Prepared': Joseph, Brigham and the Quest for Promised Refuge in the West." *Journal of Mormon History* 9 (1982): 85-111.

Evanoff, Alexander. "The Turner Thesis and Mormon Beginnings in New York and Utah." *Utah Historical Quarterly* 33 (Spring 1965): 157-73.

Evans, John Henry. *Joseph Smith: An American Prophet.* 1933. Reprint. Salt Lake City: Deseret Book Company, 1989.

Faulring, Scott H., ed. *An American Prophet's Record: The Diaries and Journals of Joseph Smith.* 1987. Reprint. Salt Lake City: Signature Books, 1989.

Festinger, Leon, Henry W. Riecken, and Stanley Schachter. *When Prophecy Fails.* Minneapolis: University of Minnesota Press, 1956.

Fielding, R. Kent. "The Mormon Economy in Kirtland, Ohio." *Utah Historical Quarterly* 27 (Oct. 1959): 331-56.

Findlay, James F., Jr. *Dwight L. Moody: American Evangelist, 1837-1899*. Chicago: University of Chicago Press, 1969.

Firmage, Edwin Brown, and Richard Collin Mangrum. *Zion in the Courts: A Legal History of the Church of Jesus Christ of Latter-day Saints, 1830-1900*. Urbana: University of Illinois Press, 1988.

Firth, Katherine R. *The Apocalyptic Tradition in Reformation Britain, 1530-1645*. Oxford: Oxford University Press, 1979.

Fisher, Margaret M., comp. and ed. *Utah and the Civil War*. N.p.: Deseret Book Company, 1929.

Flanders, Robert. "Dream and Nightmare: Nauvoo Revisited." In *The Restoration Movement: Essays in Mormon History*. Rev. ed. Eds. F. Mark McKiernan, Alma R. Blair, and Paul M. Edwards. Independence, MO: Herald Publishing House, 1992.

—. "The Kingdom of God in Illinois: Politics in Utopia." *Dialogue: A Journal of Mormon Thought* 5 (Spring 1970): 26-36.

—. *Nauvoo: Kingdom on the Mississippi*. Urbana: University of Illinois Press, 1965.

—. "To Transform History: Early Mormon Culture and the Concept of Time and Space." *Church History* 40 (Mar. 1971): 108-17.

Ford, Thomas. *A History of Illinois*. 2 vols. 1854. Reprint. Chicago: Lakeside Press, 1945-46.

Foster, Lawrence. "Cults in Conflict: New Religious Movements and the Mainstream Religious Tradition in America." In *Uncivil Religion: Interreligious Hostility in America*. Eds. Robert N. Bellah and Frederick E. Greenspahn. New York: Crossroad Publishing Company, 1987.

—. "First Visions: Personal Observations on Joseph Smith's Religious Experience." *Sunstone* 8 (Sept.-Oct. 1983): 39-43.

—. "The Psychology of Religious Genius: Joseph Smith and the Origins of New Religious Movements." *Dialogue: A Journal of Mormon Thought* 26 (Winter 1993): 1-22.

—. *Religion and Sexuality: The Shakers, the Mormons, and the Oneida Community*. 1981. Reprint. Urbana: University of Illinois Press, 1984.

Freehling, William W. *Prelude to Civil War: The Nullification Controversy in South Carolina, 1816-1836*. New York: Harper and Row, 1965.

Furniss, Norman F. *The Mormon Conflict, 1850-1859*. New Haven: Yale University Press, 1960.

Gabriel, Ralph H. "Evangelical Religion and Popular Romanticism in Nineteenth-Century America." *Church History* 19 (Mar. 1950): 34-47.

Gager, John G. "Early Mormonism and Early Christianity: Some Parallels and

Their Consequences for the Study of New Religions." *Journal of Mormon History* 9 (1982): 53-60.

—. *Kingdom and Community: The Social World of Early Christianity*. Englewood Cliffs, NJ: Prentice-Hall, 1975.

Gardner, Hamilton. "The Nauvoo Legion, 1840-1845—A Unique Military Organization." *Journal of the Illinois State Historical Society* 55 (Summer 1961): 181-97.

Garvey, Kevin. "The Prophet from Palmyra: Joseph Smith and the Rise of Mormonism." In *Psychodynamic Perspectives on Religion, Sect and Cult*. Ed. David A. Halperin. Boston: John Wright PSG, 1983.

Gaustad, Edwin S. "The Great Tradition and 'The Coercion of Voluntarism.'" In *In the Great Tradition: In Honor of Winthrop S. Hudson, Essays on Pluralism, Voluntarism, and Revivalism*. Eds. Joseph D. Ban and Paul R. Dekar. Valley Forge, PA: Judson Press, 1982.

—. *The Rise of Adventism: Religion and Society in Mid-Nineteenth-Century America*. New York: Harper and Row 1974.

Gentry, Leland H. "The Danite Band of 1838." *Brigham Young University Studies* 14 (Summer 1974): 421-450.

Gibbs, Grenville H. "Mormonism in Idaho Politics, 1880-1890." *Utah Historical Quarterly* 21 (Oct. 1953): 285-305.

Godfrey, Donald G., and Brigham Y. Card, eds. *The Diaries of Charles Ora Card: The Canadian Years, 1886-1903*. Salt Lake City: University of Utah Press, 1993.

Godfrey, Kenneth W. "The Coming of the Manifesto." *Dialogue: A Journal of Mormon Thought* 3 (Autumn 1970): 11-25.

Goen, C. C. "Jonathan Edwards: A New Departure in Eschatology." *Church History* 28 (Mar. 1959): 25-40.

Grant, H. Roger. "Missouri's Utopian Communities." *Missouri Historical Review* 56 (Oct. 1971): 20-48.

Griffith, Howard. "Eschatology Begins with Creation." *Westminister Theological Journal* 49 (Fall 1987): 387-96.

Grugel, Lee E. *Society and Religion During the Age of Industrialization: Christianity in Victorian England*. Washington, D. C.: University Press of America, 1979.

Hallman, Joseph M. "God and the End of Civilization." *American Journal of Theology & Philosophy* 4 (Sept. 1983): 110-15.

Handy, Robert T. *A Christian America: Protestant Hope and Historical Realities*. New York: Oxford University Press, 1971.

Hansen, Klaus J. "The Metamorphosis of the Kingdom of God: Toward a Reinterpretation of Mormon History." *Dialogue: A Journal of Mormon Thought* 1 (Autumn 1966), 63-83.

—. "The Millennium, the West, and Race in the Antebellum American Mind." *Western Historical Quarterly* 3 (Oct. 1972): 373-90.

—. "Mormonism and American Culture: Some Tentative Hypotheses." In *The Restoration Movement: Essays in Mormon History*. Rev. ed. Eds. F. Mark McKiernan, Alma R. Blair, and Paul M. Edwards. Independence, MO: Herald Publishing House, 1992.

—. *Mormonism and the American Experience*. Chicago: University of Chicago Press, 1981.

—. *Quest for Empire: The Political Kingdom of God and the Council of Fifty in Mormon History*. N.p.: Michigan State University Press, 1970.

Hanson, Paul D. *The Dawn of Apocalyptic*. Philadelphia: Fortress Press, 1975.

Hardy, B. Carmon. "Self-Blame and the Manifesto." *Dialogue: A Journal of Mormon Thought* 24 (Fall 1991): 43-57.

—. *Solemn Covenant: The Mormon Polygamous Passage*. Urbana: University of Illinois Press, 1992.

Harrison, J[ohn]. F. C. *The Second Coming: Popular Millenarianism, 1780-1850*. New Brunswick, NJ: Rutgers University Press, 1979.

Hartley, William G. "The Seventies in the 1880s: Revelations and Reorganizing." *Dialogue: A Journal of Mormon Thought* 16 (Spring 1983): 62-88.

Hatch, Nathan O. "The Christian Movement and the Demand for a Theology of the People." *Journal of American History* 67 (Dec. 1980): 546-61.

—. *The Democratization of American Christianity*. New Haven: Yale University Press, 1989.

—. "Millennialism and Popular Religion in the Early Republic." In *The Evangelical Tradition in America*. Ed. Leonard I. Sweet. Macon, Ga.: Mercer University Press, 1984.

—. "Mormon and Methodist: Popular Religion in the Crucible of the Free Market." *Journal of Mormon History* 20 (Spring 1994): 24-44.

—. *The Sacred Cause of Liberty: Republican Thought and the Millennium in Revolutionary New England*. New Haven: Yale University Press, 1977.

—, and Mark A. Noll, eds. *The Bible in America: Essays in Cultural History*. New York: Oxford University Press, 1982.

Heimert, Alan. *Religion and the American Mind: From the Great Awakening to the Revolution*. Cambridge, MA: Harvard University Press, 1966.

Hill, Donna. *Joseph Smith: The First Mormon*. Midvale, UT: Signature Books, 1977.

Hill, Marvin S. "Cultural Crisis in the Mormon Kingdom: A Reconsideration of the Causes of Kirtland Dissent." *Church History* 49 (Sept. 1980): 286-97.

—. "Money-Digging Folklore and the Beginnings of Mormonism: An Interpretive Suggestion." *Brigham Young University Studies* 24 (Fall 1984): 473-488.

—. "Positivism or Subjectivism? Some Reflections on a Mormon Historical Dilemma." *Journal of Mormon History* 20 (Spring 1994): 1-23.

—. "The 'Prophet Puzzle' Assembled; or, How to Treat Our Historical Diplopia toward Joseph Smith." *Journal of Mormon History* 3 (1976): 101-105.

—. "Quest for Refuge: An Hypothesis as to the Social Origins and Nature of the Mormon Political Kingdom." *Journal of Mormon History* 2 (1975): 3-20.

—. *Quest for Refuge: The Mormon Flight from American Pluralism.* Salt Lake City: Signature Books, 1989.

—. "The Rise of Mormonism in the Burned-over District: Another View." *New York History* 61 (Oct. 1980): 411-430.

—. "Secular or Sectarian History? A Critique of *No Man Knows My History.*" *Church History* 33 (Mar. 1974): 78-96.

—. "The Shaping of the Mormon Mind in New England and New York." *Brigham Young University Studies* 9 (Spring 1969): 351-72.

—, and James B. Allen, eds. *Mormonism and American Culture.* New York: Harper and Row, 1972.

—, C. Keith Rooker, and Larry T. Wimmer. "The Kirtland Economy Revisited: A Market Critique of Sectarian Economics." *Brigham Young University Studies* 17 (Summer 1977): 391-475.

Hilton, Ruth Savage, ed. *Lorenzo Hill Hatch Journal.* Provo, UT: n.p., 1958.

Holzapfel, Richard Neitzel. "A Time of Dedication: How history records the unique events of the temple's dedication." *This People* 14 (Spring 1993): 25-26.

Howard, Richard P. "Christmas Day, 1832: Joseph Smith Responds to the Nullification Crisis." *Saints Herald* 116 (May 1969): 54.

—. *Restoration Scriptures: A Study of Their Textual Development.* Independence, MO: Herald Publishing House, 1969.

Howe, E[ber]. D. *Mormonism Unvailed: or A Faithful Account of that Singular Imposition and Delusion, from Its Rise to the Present Time.* Painesville, OH: E. D. Howe, 1834.

Hubbard, George U. "Abraham Lincoln as Seen by the Mormons." *Utah Historical Quarterly* 31 (Spring 1963): 91-108.

Hughes, Richard T. "The Apocalyptic Origins of the Churches of Christ and the Triumph of Modernism." *Religion and American Culture: A Journal of Interpretation* 2 (Summer 1992): 181-214.

—. "From Primitive Church to Civil Religion: The Millennial Odyssey of

Alexander Campbell." *Journal of the American Academy of Religion* 44 (Mar. 1976): 87-103.

—. and C. Leonard Allen. *Illusions of Innocence: Protestant Primitivism in America, 1630-1875*. Chicago: University of Chicago Press, 1988.

Huntress, Keith. "The Murder of Joseph Smith." In *Mormonism and American Culture*. Eds. Marvin S. Hill and James B. Allen. New York: Harper and Row, 1972.

Hutchinson, Anthony A. "Prophetic Foreknowledge: Hope and Fulfillment in an Inspired Community." *Sunstone* 11 (July 1987).

Hymns of The Church of Jesus Christ of Latter-day Saints. Salt Lake City: The Church of Jesus Christ of Latter-day Saints, 1985.

Irving, Gordon. "The Mormons and the Bible in the 1830's." *Brigham Young University Studies* 13 (Summer 1973): 473-488.

Ivins, Stanley S. "Notes on Polygamy." *Western Humanities Review* 10 (Summer 1956): 229-39.

Jackson, Richard H. "The Mormon Village: Genesis and Antecedents of the City of Zion Plan." *Brigham Young University* 17 (Winter 1977): 223-40.

James, Kimberly Jensen. "'Between Two Fires': Women on the 'Underground' of Mormon Polygamy." *Journal of Mormon History* 8 (1986): 49-61.

Jennings, Warren A. "The Army of Israel Marches into Missouri." *Missouri Historical Review* 62 (Jan. 1968): 107-35.

—. "The City in the Garden: Social Conflict in Jackson County, Missouri." In *The Restoration Movement: Essays in Mormon History*. Rev. ed. Eds. F. Mark McKiernan, Alma R. Blair, and Paul M. Edwards. Independence, MO: Herald Publishing House, 1992.

—. "Factors in the Destruction of the Mormon Press in Missouri, 1833." *Utah Historical Quarterly* 35 (Winter 1967): 57-76.

—. "Isaac McCoy and the Mormons." *Missouri Historical Review* 61 (Oct. 1966): 62-82.

Jensen, Richard L. "C. C. A. Christensen on Art." *Brigham Young University Studies* 23 (Fall 1983): 401-416.

—, and Malcolm R. Thorp. *Mormons in Early Victorian Britain*. Salt Lake City: University of Utah Press, 1989.

Jessee, Dean C. "Early Accounts of Joseph Smith's First Vision." *Brigham Young University Studies* 9 (Spring 1969): 275-94.

—. "Joseph Smith's 19 July 1840 Discourse." *Brigham Young University Studies* 19 (Spring 1979): 390-94.

—. "'Walls, Grates and Screeking Iron Doors': The Prison Experience of Mormon Leaders in Missouri, 1838-1839." In *New Views of Mormon*

History. Eds. Davis Bitton and Maureen Ursenbach Beecher. Salt Lake City: University of Utah Press, 1987.

—. ed. *The Papers of Joseph Smith*. 2 vols. Salt Lake City: Deseret Book Company, 1989-92.

—. comp. and ed. *The Personal Writings of Joseph Smith*. Salt Lake City: Deseret Book Company, 1984.

—, and David J. Whittaker. "The Last Months of Mormonism in Missouri: The Albert Perry Rockwood Journal." *Brigham Young University Studies* 28 (Winter 1988): 5-41.

Johnson, Benjamin F. *My Life's Review*. Independence, MO: Zion's Printing and Publishing Co., 1947.

Johnson, Clark V., ed. *Mormon Redress Petitions: Documents of the 1833-1838 Missouri Conflict*. Salt Lake City: Bookcraft, 1992.

Johnson, Donald Bruce, ed. *National Party Platforms*. 2 vols. Urbana: University of Illinois Press, 1978.

Johnson, Paul E. *A Shopkeeper's Millennium: Society and Revivals in Rochester, New York, 1815-1837*. New York: Hill and Wang, 1978.

Jorgensen, Danny L. "Dissent and Schism in the Early Church: Explaining Mormon Fissiparousness." *Dialogue: A Journal of Mormon Thought* 28 (Fall 1995): 15-39.

Jorgensen, Victor W., and B. Carmon Hardy. "The Taylor-Cowley Affair and the Watershed of Mormon History." *Utah Historical Quarterly* 48 (Winter 1980): 4-36.

Josephy, Alvin M., Jr. *The Civil War in the American West*. 1991. Reprint. New York: Random House, 1993.

Journal of Discourses. 26 vols. Liverpool, England: F.D. Richards, 1855-86.

Journal of Jesse Nathaniel Smith. Salt Lake City: Jessie N. Smith Family Associates, 1953.

Keller, Karl, ed. "'I Never Knew a Time When I Did Not Know Joseph Smith': A Son's Record of the Life and Testimony of Sidney Rigdon." *Dialogue: A Journal of Mormon Thought* 1 (Winter 1966): 15-42.

Kenney, Scott G., ed. *Wilford Woodruff's Journal, 1833-1898*. 9 vols. Midvale, UT: Signature Books, 1983-85.

Kern, Louis J. *An Ordered Love: Sex Roles and Sexuality in Victorian Utopias–The Shakers, the Mormons, and the Oneida Community*. Chapel Hill: University of North Carolina Press, 1981.

Kimball, James L., Jr. "The Nauvoo Charter: A Reinterpretation." *Journal of the Illinois State Historical Society* 64 (Spring 1971): 66-78.

—. "A Wall to Defend Zion: The Nauvoo Charter." *Brigham Young University Studies* 15 (Summer 1975): 499-526.

Kimball, Stanley B. *On the Potter's Wheel: The Diaries of Heber C. Kimball.* Salt Lake City: Signature Books in association with Smith Research Associates, 1987.

Kirkham, Francis W. *A New Witness for Christ in America.* 2 vols. 1942. Reprint. Salt Lake City: Utah Printing Co., 1967.

Kuhn, Thomas S. *The Structure of Scientific Revolutions.* 2nd ed. Chicago: University of Chicago Press, 1970.

Lambert, Neal. "Saints, Sinners and Scribes: A Look at the Mormons in Fiction." *Utah Historical Quarterly* 36 (Winter 1968): 63-76.

Landes, Richard. "Lest the Millennium be Fulfilled: Apocalyptic Expectations and the Pattern of Western Chronography, 100-800 CE." In *The Use and Abuse of Eschatology in the Middle Ages.* Eds. Werner Verbeke, Daniel Verhelst, and Andries Welkenhuysen. Leuven, Belg.: Leuven University Press, 1988.

Larson, A. Karl, and Katharine Miles Larson, eds. *Diary of Charles Lowell Walker.* 2 vols. Logan: Utah State University Press, 1980.

Larson, Gustive O. *The "Americanization" of Utah for Statehood.* San Marino, Calif.: Huntington Library, 1971.

—. "The Mormon Reformation." *Utah Historical Quarterly* 26 (Jan. 1958): 45-63.

—. "Utah and the Civil War." *Utah Historical Quarterly* 33 (Winter 1965): 55-77.

Larson, Stan, ed. *A Ministry of Meetings: The Apostolic Diaries of Rudger Clawson.* Salt Lake City: Signature Books in association with Smith Research Associates, 1993.

Launius, Roger D. "Anti-Mormonism in Illinois: Thomas C. Sharp's Unfinished History of the Mormon War, 1845." *Journal of Mormon History* 15 (1989): 27-45.

—. "Mormon Memory, Mormon Myth, and Mormon History." *Journal of Mormon History* 21 (Spring 1995): 1-24.

—. "The Murders in Carthage: Non-Mormon Reports of the Assassination of the Smith Brothers." *John Whitmer Historical Association Journal* 15 (1995): 17-34.

—. *Zion's Camp: Expedition to Missouri, 1834.* Independence, MO: Herald Publishing House, 1984.

Lee, John D. *Mormonism Unveiled.* St. Louis: Bryan, Brand and Company, 1877.

Legg, Phillip R. *Oliver Cowdery: The Elusive Second Elder of the Restoration.* Independence, MO: Herald Publishing House, 1989.

Leonard, Glen M. "Early Saints and the Millennium." *Ensign* 9 (Aug. 1979): 43-47.

Leone, Mark P. *Roots of Modern Mormonism*. Cambridge, MA: Harvard University Press, 1979.

Lester, Hiram J. "Alexander Campbell's Millennial Program." *Discipliana* 48 (Fall 1988): 35-39.

LeSueur, Stephen C. "The Danites Reconsidered: Were They Vigilantes or Just the Mormon Version of the Elks Club?" *John Whitmer Historical Association Journal* 14 (1994): 35-51.

—. *The 1838 Mormon War in Missouri*. Columbia: University of Missouri Press, 1987.

—. "'High Treason and Murder': The Examination of Mormon Prisoners at Richmond, Missouri, in November 1838." *Brigham Young University Studies* 26 (Spring 1986): 2-30.

Lichtman, Allan J., and Valeri French. *Historians and the Living Past*. Arlington Heights, IL: Harlan Davidson, 1978.

Limerick, Patricia Nelson. "Peace Initiative: Using the Mormons to Rethink Ethnicity in American Life." *Journal of Mormon History* 21 (Fall 1995): 1-29.

Linder, Robert D., and Richard Pierard. *Twilight of the Saints: Biblical Christianity and Civil Religion in America*. Downers Grove, IL: Inter-varsity Press, 1978.

Linford, Orma. "The Mormons and the Law: The Polygamy Cases." *Utah Law Review* 9 (Winter 1964): 308-70.

—. "The Mormons and the Law: The Polygamy Cases." *Utah Law Review* 9 (Summer 1965): 543-591.

Linn, William Alexander. *The Story of the Mormons*. 1902. Reprint. New York: Russell and Russell, 1963.

Lofland, John. *Doomsday Cult*. Englewood Cliffs, NJ: Prentice-Hall, 1966.

Logue, Larry M. *A Sermon in the Desert: Belief and Behavior in Early St. George, Utah*. Urbana: University of Illinois Press, 1988.

Long, E[verette]. B. *The Saints and the Union: Utah Territory During the Civil War*. Urbana: University of Illinois Press, 1981.

Loveless, Cheri. "The House of the Lord." *This People* 14 (Spring 1993): 20-23.

Loy, R. Philip. "Saints or Scoundrels: Images of Mormons in Literature and Film about the American West." *Journal of the American Studies Association of Texas* 21 (Oct. 1990): 57-74.

Lyman, Edward Leo. "The Alienation of an Apostle from His Quorum: The Moses Thatcher Case." *Dialogue: A Journal of Mormon Thought* 18 (Summer 1985): 67-91.

—. "The Political Background of the Woodruff Manifesto." *Dialogue: A Journal of Mormon Thought* 24 (Fall 1991): 21-39.

—. *Political Deliverance: The Mormon Quest for Utah Statehood.* Urbana: University of Illinois Press, 1986.

—. *San Bernardino: The Rise and Fall of a California Community.* Salt Lake City: Signature Books, 1996.

MacKinnon, William P. "125 Years of Conspiracy Theories: Origins of the Utah Expedition of 1857-58." *Utah Historical Quarterly* 52 (Summer 1984): 212-30.

Maclear, J. F. "New England and the Fifth Monarchy: The Quest for the Millennium in Early American Puritanism." *William and Mary Quarterly* 32 (Apr. 1975): 222-60.

—. "The Republic and the Millennium." In *The Religion of the Republic.* Ed. Elwyn A. Smith. Philadelphia: Fortress Press, 1971.

MacMurray, Val Dan, and Perry H. Cunningham. "Mormons and Gentiles: A Study in Conflict and Persistence." In *Ethnic Conflicts and Power: A Cross-National Perspective.* Eds. Donald E. Gelfand and Russell D. Lee. New York: John Wiley and Sons, 1973.

Marini, Stephen A. *Radical Sects of Revolutionary New England.* Cambridge, MA: Harvard University Press, 1982.

Marquardt, H. Michael, and Wesley P. Walters. *Inventing Mormonism: Tradition and the Historical Record.* San Francisco: Smith Research Association, 1994.

Marsden, George M. "Everyone One's Own Interpreter? The Bible, Science, and Authority in Mid-Nineteenth-Century America." In *The Bible in America: Essays in Cultural History.* Eds. Nathan O. Hatch and Mark A. Noll. New York: Oxford University Press, 1982.

—. *Fundamentalism and American Culture: The Shaping of Twentieth-Century Evangelicalism: 1870-1925.* New York: Oxford University Press, 1980.

Marty, Martin E. *Righteous Empire: The Protestant Experience in America.* New York: Dial Press, 1970.

—. Foreword to *Mormonism and the American Experience,* by Klaus J. Hansen. Chicago: University of Chicago Press, 1981.

McDermott, Gerald Robert. "Civil Religion in the American Revolutionary Period: An Historiographic Analysis." *Christian Scholar's Review* 18 (1989): 346-62.

McKiernan, F. Mark. "Mormonism on the Defensive: Far West 1838-1839." In *The Restoration Movement: Essays in Mormon History.* Rev. ed. Eds. F. Mark McKiernan, Alma R. Blair, and Paul M. Edwards. Independence, MO: Herald Publishing House, 1992.

—. and Roger D. Launius, eds. *An Early Latter Day Saint History: The Book of*

John Whitmer, Kept by Commandment. Independence, MO: Herald Publishing House, 1980.

—, Alma P. Blair, and Paul M. Edwards, eds. *The Restoration Movement: Essays in Mormon History*. Rev. ed. Independence, MO: Herald Publishing House, 1992.

McLaughlin, William G. "Religious Freedom and Popular Sovereignty: A Change in the Flow of God's Power, 1730-1830." In *In the Great Tradition: In Honor of Winthrop S. Hudson, Essays on Pluralism, Voluntarism, and Revivalism*. Eds. Joseph D. Ban and Paul R. Dekar. Valley Forge, PA: Judson Press, 1982.

—. *Revivals, Awakenings, and Reform*. Chicago: University of Chicago Press, 1978.

—. ed. *The American Evangelicals, 1800-1900: An Anthology*. New York: Harper Torchbooks, 1968.

McNeill, William H. *Mythhistory and Other Essays*. Chicago: University of Chicago Press, 1986.

Mead, Sidney E. *The Lively Experiment: The Shaping of American Christianity in America*. New York: Harper and Row, 1963.

—. "The Nation with the Soul of a Church." *Church History* 36 (Sept. 1967): 262-83.

—. *The Nation with the Soul of a Church*. New York: Harper and Row, 1975.

—. *The Old Religion in the Brave New World: Reflections on the Relation between Christendom and the Republic*. Berkeley: University of California Press, 1977.

Meinig, D. W. "The Mormon Nation and the American Empire." *Journal of Mormon History* 22 (Spring 1996): 33-51.

Meyers, Marvin. *The Jacksonian Persuasion*. Stanford, CA: Stanford University Press, 1957.

Middlekauff, Robert. *The Mathers: Three Generations of Puritan Intellectuals, 1596-1728*. New York: Oxford University Press, 1971.

Miller, Perry. "The End of the World." *William and Mary Quarterly* 8 (Apr. 1951): 171-91.

—. *The Life of the Mind in America: From the Revolution to the Civil War*. New York: Hardcourt, Brace and World, 1965.

—. "The Old Testament in Colonial America." In *Historical Viewpoints*. Ed. John A. Garraty. New York: Harper and Row, 1970.

Miller, Perry G. E. "The Contribution of the Protestant Churches to Religious Liberty in Colonial America." *Church History* 4 (Mar. 1935): 57-66.

Moench, Melodie. "Nineteenth-Century Mormons: The New Israel." *Dialogue: A Journal of Mormon Thought* 12 (Spring 1979): 42-56.

Mooney, James. *The Ghost-Dance Religion and the Sioux Outbreak of 1890.* Chicago: University of Chicago Press, 1965. Originally published as part 2 of the *Fourteenth Annual Report of the Bureau of Ethnology to the Secretary of the Smithsonian Institution, 1892-93.* Washington, D. C.: Government Printing Office, 1896.

Moore, R. Laurence. *Religious Outsiders and the Making of Americans.* New York: Oxford University Press, 1986.

Moorhead, James H. *American Apocalypse: Yankee Protestants and the Civil War, 1860-1869.* New Haven: Yale University Press, 1978.

—. "Between Progress and Apocalypse: A Reassessment of Millennialism in American Religious Thought, 1800-1880." *Journal of American History* 71 (Dec. 1984): 524-42.

—. "Searching for the Millennium in America." *Princeton Seminary Bulletin* 8 (1987): 17-33.

—. "Social Reform and the Divided Conscience of Antebellum Protestantism." *Church History* 48 (Dec. 1979): 416-30.

Moorman, Donald R. *Camp Floyd and the Mormons: The Utah War.* Salt Lake City: University of Utah Press, 1992.

Mortimer, William James. "Patriarchal Blessings." In *Encyclopedia of Mormonism.* 5 vols. Ed. Daniel H. Ludlow. New York: Macmillan Publishing Company, 1992.

Mouly, Ruth, and Roland Robertson. "Zionism in American Pre-millenarian Fundamentalism." *American Journal of Theology and Philosophy* 4 (Sept. 1983): 96-109.

Mulder, William. "Mormonism's 'Gathering': An American Doctrine with a Difference." *Church History* 23 (Sept. 1954): 248-64.

—. *The Mormons in American History.* 1955. Reprint. Salt Lake City: University of Utah Press, 1981.

—, and A. Russell Mortensen, eds. *Among the Mormons: Historic Accounts by Contemporary Observers.* New York: Alfred A. Knopf, 1967.

Neff, Andrew Love. *History of Utah, 1847-1869.* Salt Lake City: Deseret News Press, 1940.

Newell, Linda King, and Valeen Tippetts Avery. *Mormon Enigma: Emma Hale Smith, Prophet's Wife, "Elect Lady," Polygamy's Foe, 1804-1879.* Garden City, NY: Doubleday and Company, 1984.

Noll, Mark A. "From the Great Awakening to the War for Independence: Christian Values in the American Revolution." *Christian Scholar's Review* 12 (1983): 99-110.

Norman, Keith E. "How Long, O Lord? The Delay of the Parousia in Mormonism." *Sunstone* 8 (Jan.-Apr. 1983): 49-58.

Novick, Peter. *That Noble Dream: The "Objectivity Question" and the American Historical Profession*. Cambridge, Eng.: Cambridge University Press, 1988.

Oaks, Dallin H. "The Suppression of the Nauvoo Expositor." *Utah Law Review* 9 (Winter 1965): 862-903.

—, and Marvin S. Hill. *Carthage Conspiracy: The Trial of the Accused Assassins of Joseph Smith*. 1975. Reprint. Urbana: University of Illinois Press, 1979.

O'Dea, Thomas F. "Mormonism and the Avoidance of Sectarian Stagnation Study of Church, Sect, and Incipient Nationality." *American Journal of Sociology* 60 (Nov. 1954): 285-93.

—. *The Mormons*. Chicago: University of Chicago Press, 1957.

Oliver, W[illiam]. H. *Prophets and Millennialists*. Auckland, NZ: Auckland University Press, 1978.

Olsen, Steven L. "Joseph Smith and the Structure of Mormon Identity." *Dialogue: A Journal of Mormon Thought* 14 (Autumn 1981): 89-99.

—. "Zion: The Structure of a Theological Revolution." *Sunstone* 6 (Nov.-Dec. 1981): 21-26.

Olson, Earl E. "The Chronology of the Ohio Revelations." *Brigham Young University Studies* 11 (Summer 1971): 329-49.

Olson, Theodore. *Millennialism, Utopianism, and Progress*. Toronto: University of Toronto Press, 1982.

Ostler, Blake T. "The Book of Mormon as a Modern Expansion of an Ancient Source." *Dialogue: A Journal of Mormon Thought* 20 (Spring 1987): 66-123.

Parkin, Max H. "Kirtland, a Stronghold for the Kingdom." In *The Restoration Movement: Essays in Mormon History*. Rev. ed. Eds. F. Mark McKiernan, Alma R. Blair, and Paul M. Edwards. Independence, Mo.: Herald Publishing House, 1992.

—. "Mormon Political Involvement in Ohio." *Brigham Young University Studies* 9 (Summer 1969).

Parrish, Alan K. "Beginnings of the Millennial Star: Journal of the Mission to Great Britain." In *Regional Studies in Latter-day Saint Church History: British Isles*. Ed. Donald Q. Cannon. Provo, UT: Brigham Young University, 1990.

Partridge, Scott H. "The Failure of the Kirtland Safety Society." *Brigham Young University Studies* 12 (Summer 1972): 437-454.

Paul, William W. "Time and Historical Significance." In *Interpretation and History*. Eds. R. Laird Harris, Swee-Hwa Quek, and J. Robert Vannoy. Singapore: Christian Life Publishers, 1986.

The Pearl of Great Price: Being a Choice Selection from the Revelations, Translations, and Narrations of Joseph Smith. Liverpool, Eng.: F. D. Richards, 1851.

Pessen, Edward. *Jacksonian America: Society, Personality, and Politics.* Homewood, IL: Dorsey Press, 1969.

Peterson, Charles S. *Take Up Your Mission: Mormon Colonizing along the Little Colorado River, 1870-1900.* Tucson: University of Arizona Press, 1973.

Peterson, Lauritz G. "The Kirtland Temple." *Brigham Young University Studies* 12 (Summer 1972): 400-409.

Peterson, Paul H. "The Mormon Reformation of 1856-1857: The Rhetoric and the Reality." *Journal of Mormon History* 15 (1989): 59-87.

Peterson, Susan. "The Great and Dreadful Day: Mormon Folklore of the Apocalypse." *Utah Historical Quarterly* 44 (Fall 1976): 365-78.

Poll, Richard D. "The Americanism of Utah." *Utah Historical Quarterly* 44 (Winter 1976): 76-93.

—. "A Kingdom to Come." Review of *Quest for Empire: The Political Kingdom of God and the Council of Fifty in Mormon History,* by Klaus J. Hansen. *Dialogue: A Journal of Mormon Thought* 2 (Autumn 1967): 135-40.

—. "The Legislative Anti-polygamy Campaign." *Brigham Young University Studies* 26 (Fall 1986): 107-21.

—. "The Mormon Question Enters National Politics, 1850-1856." *Utah Historical Quarterly* 25 (Apr. 1957): 117-31.

—. "The Move South." *Brigham Young University Studies* 29 (Fall 1989): 65-88.

—. *Quixotic Mediator: Thomas L. Kane and the Utah War.* Ogden, Utah: Weber State College Press, 1985.

—. "Thomas L. Kane and the Utah War." *Utah Historical Quarterly* 61 (Spring 1993): 111-35.

—, and William P. MacKinnon. "Causes of the Utah War Reconsidered." *Journal of Mormon History* 20 (Fall 1994): 116-44.

Pollock, Gordon D. *In Search of Security: The Mormons and the Kingdom of God on Earth, 1830-1844.* New York: Garland Publishing, 1989.

Pratt, David H. "Oh! Brother Joseph." *Brigham Young University Studies* 27 (Winter 1987): 127-31.

Pratt, Parley P. *Autobiography of Parley Parker Pratt.* 1938 Reprint. Salt Lake City: Deseret Book Company, 1979.

—. *Mormonism Unveiled ...* New York: Orson Pratt and Elijah Fordham, 1838.

—. *A Voice of Warning ...* New York: W. Sanford, 1837.

Prince, Gregory A. *Power from on High: The Development of Mormon Priesthood.* Salt Lake City: Signature Books, 1995.

Proceedings Before The Committee On Privileges And Elections Of The United States Senate In The Matter Of The Protests Against The Right Of Hon. Reed Smoot, A Senator From The State Of Utah, To Hold His Seat. 4 vols. Washington, D. C.: Government Printing Office, 1906.

Quinn, D. Michael. "The Council of Fifty and Its Members, 1844-1945." *Brigham Young University Studies* 20 (Winter 1980): 163-97.

—. *Early Mormonism and the Magic World View*. Salt Lake City: Signature Books, 1987.

—. "The Evolution of the Presiding Quorums of the LDS Church." *Journal of Mormon History* 1 (1974): 21-38.

—. *J. Reuben Clark: The Church Years*. Provo, UT: Brigham Young University Press, 1983.

—. "Joseph Smith III's Blessing and the Mormons of Utah." *Dialogue: A Journal of Mormon Thought* 15 (Summer 1982): 69-90.

—. "Latter-day Saint Prayer Circles." *Brigham Young University Studies* 19 (Fall 1978): 79-105.

—. "LDS Church Authority and New Plural Marriages, 1890-1904." *Dialogue: A Journal of Mormon Thought* 18 (Spring 1985): 9-105.

—. "The Mormon Church and the Spanish-American War: An End to Selective Pacifism." *Pacific Historical Review* 43 (Aug. 1974): 342-66.

—. *The Mormon Hierarchy: Origins of Power*. Salt Lake City: Signature Books, 1994.

—. "The Mormon Succession Crisis of 1844." *Brigham Young University Studies* 16 (Winter 1976): 187-223.

Ratner, Lorman. *Antimasonry: The Crusade and the Party*. Englewood Cliffs, N.J.: Prentice-Hall, 1969.

Reay, David M., and Londa Lee Skousen Reay, comps. *Selected Manifestations* ... Oakland: Published by the Authors, 1985.

The Reed Peck Manuscript. Salt Lake City: Utah Lighthouse Ministry, n.d.

Reid, W. Stanford. "The Kingdom of God: The Key to History." *Fides et Historia* 13 (Spring-Summer 1981): 6-15.

Remini, Robert V. *The Life of Andrew Jackson*. 1988. Reprint. New York: Penguin Books, 1990.

Remy, Jules, and Julius Brenchley. *A Journey to Great Salt Lake City* ... 2 vols. London: W. Jeffs, 1861.

"Report of the Utah Commission." 1887. In *Report of the Secretary of the Interior* ... 5 vols. Washington, D. C.: Government Printing Office, 1887.

Richardson, James D., comp. *Messages and Papers of the Presidents*. 20 vols. New York: Bureau of National Literature, 1917.

Richardson, Robert, ed. *Memoirs of Alexander Campbell*. 2 vols. 1868-1870. Reprint. Cincinnati: Standard Publishing Co., 1913.

Ridge, Martin. "Mormon 'Deliverance' and the Closing of the Frontier." *Journal of Mormon History* 18 (Spring 1992): 137-52.

Rietveld, Ronald D. "The American Civil War: Millennial Hope, Political

Chaos, and a Two-Sided 'Just War.'" In *The Wars of America: Christian Views*. Ed. Ronald A. Wells. Grand Rapids: William B. Eerdmans Publishing Company, 1981.

Riley, Isaac Woodbridge. *The Founder of Mormonism: A Psychological Study of Joseph Smith, Jr.* New York: Dodd, Mead, 1902.

Roberts, B[righam]. H. *A Comprehensive History of The Church of Jesus Christ of Latter-day Saints*. 6 vols. 1930. Reprint. Provo UT: Brigham Young University Press, 1965.

Romig, Ronald E. "The Lamanite Mission." *John Whitmer Historical Association Journal* 14 (1994): 25-33.

Rowe, David. "A New Perspective on the Burned-over District: Millerites in Upstate New York." *Church History* 47 (Dec. 1978): 408-420.

Salt Lake School of the Prophets Minute Book, 1883. Palm Desert, CA: n.p., 1981.

Sampson, D. Paul, and Larry T. Wimmer. "The Kirtland Safety Society: The Stock Ledger Book and the Bank Failure." *Brigham Young University Studies* 12 (Summer 1972): 427-436.

Sandeen, Ernest R. "The 'Little Tradition' and the Form of Modern Millenarianism." *Annual Review of the Social Sciences of Religion* 4 (1980): 165-81.

—. *The Roots of Fundamentalism: British and American Millenarianism, 1800-1930*. Chicago: University of Chicago Press, 1970.

Sanford, Charles L., ed. *Quest for America, 1810-1824*. New York: New York University Press, 1964.

Schmithals, Walter. *The Apocalyptic Movement: Introduction and Interpretation*. Trans. John E. Steely. Nashville: Abingdon Press, 1975.

Schwartz, Hillel. "The End of the Beginning: Millenarian Studies, 1967-1975." *Religious Studies Review* 2 (July 1976): 1-15.

—. *The French Prophets: The History of a Millenarian Group in Eighteenth-Century England*. Berkeley: University of California Press, 1980.

Sehr, Timothy. "John Elliott Millennialist Missionary." *Historian* 46 (Feb. 1984): 187-203.

Sessions, Gene A. *Mormon Thunder: A Documentary History of Jedediah Morgan Grant*. Urbana: University of Illinois Press, 1982.

Sharp, W[illiam]. H. H. *Prophetic History and the Fulfillment of Prophecy from 600 Years B. C. to the Year of Our Lord A. D. 1891*. Salt Lake City: Deseret Home Co., 1888.

Shepherd, Gordon, and Gary Shepherd. *A Kingdom Transformed: Themes in the Development of Mormonism*. Salt Lake City: University of Utah Press, 1984.

Shepherd, William H., Jr. "Revelation and the Hermeneutics of Dispensation-alism." *Anglican Theological Review* 71 (Summer 1989): 281-99.

Shipps, Jan. "In the Presence of the Past: Continuity and Change in Twenti-eth-Century Mormonism." In *After 150 Years: The Latter-day Saints in Sesquicentennial Perspective*. Eds. Thomas G. Alexander and Jessie Embry. Midvale, UT: Charles Redd Center for Western Studies, 1983.

—. *Mormonism: The Story of a New Religious Tradition*. Urbana: University of Illinois Press, 1985.

—. "The Principle Revoked: A Closer Look at the Demise of Plural Marriage." *Journal of Mormon History* 11 (1984): 65-77.

—. "The Prophet Puzzle: Suggestions Leading Toward a More Comprehen-sive Interpretation of Joseph Smith." *Journal of Mormon History* 1 (1974): 3-20.

—. "Utah Comes of Age Politically: A Study of the State's Politics in the Early Years of the Twentieth Century." *Utah Historical Quarterly* 35 (Spring 1967): 91-111.

—, and John W. Welch, eds. *The Journals of William E. McLellin, 1831-1836*. Provo, UT: *BYU Studies*, 1994.

Smith, David E. "Millenarian Scholarship in America." *American Quarterly* 17 (Fall 1965): 535-49.

Smith, Elder Robert. *Signs of the Times*. Payson, UT: Juvenile Instructor Office, 1887.

Smith, Eliza R. Snow. *Biography and Family Record of Lorenzo Snow*. Salt Lake City: Deseret News Company, 1884.

Smith, Elwyn A., ed. *The Religion of the Republic*. Philadelphia: Fortress Press, 1971.

Smith, George D. "Nauvoo Roots of Mormon Polygamy, 1841-46: A Prelimi-nary Demographic Report." *Dialogue: A Journal of Mormon Thought* 27 (Spring 1994): 1-72.

—. ed. *An Intimate Chronicle: The Journals of William Clayton*. Salt Lake City: Signature Books in association with Smith Research Associates, 1991.

Smith, Joseph. *History of The Church of Jesus Christ of Latter-Day Saints*. 7 vols. 2nd ed. Revised. Introduction and notes by B. H. Roberts. Salt Lake City: Deseret Book Company, 1974-76.

Smith, Lucy. *Biographical Sketches of Joseph Smith the Prophet and His Progenitors for Many Generations*. 1912. Reprint. Independence, MO: Herald Publish-ing House, 1969.

Smith, Melvin T. "Faithful History: Hazards and Limitations." *Journal of Mormon History* 9 (1982): 61-69.

Smith, Robert W., and Elizabeth A. *The Last Days*. N.p.: Pyramid Press, 1943.

Smith, Timothy L. "The Book of Mormon in a Biblical Culture." *Journal of Mormon History* 7 (1980): 3-21.

—. *Revivalism and Social Reform: Protestantism on the Eve of the Civil War*. New York: Abingdon Press, 1957.

Smoak, Gregory E. "Mormons and the Ghost Dance of 1890." *South Dakota History* 16 (Fall 1986): 269-94.

Staker, Susan, ed. *Waiting for World's End: The Diaries of Wilford Woodruff*. Salt Lake City: Signature Books, 1993.

Stegner, Wallace. *The Gathering of Zion: The Story of the Mormon Trail*. 1964. Reprint. Lincoln: University of Nebraska Press, 1992.

Stein, Stephen J. "A Notebook on the Apocalypse by Jonathan Edwards." *William and Mary Quarterly* 29 (Oct. 1972): 623-634.

—. "Signs of the Times: The Theological Foundations of Early Mormon Apocalyptic." *Sunstone* 8 (Jan-Apr. 1983): 59-65.

Stenhouse, Thomas B. H. *The Rocky Mountain Saints*. New York: D. Appletone and Co., 1873.

Stott, Clifford L. *Search for Sanctuary: Brigham Young and the White Mountain Expedition*. Salt Lake City: University of Utah Press, 1984.

Stuy, Brian H., ed. *Collected Discourses*. 5 vols. Sandy, UT: B. H. S. Publishing, 1987-92.

Supreme Court Reporter. St. Paul: West Publishing Company, 1886.

Sweet, Leonard I. "The Evangelical Tradition in America." In *The Evangelical Tradition in America*. Ed. Leonard I. Sweet. Macon, GA: Mercer University Press, 1984.

—. "Millennialism in America: Recent Studies." *Theological Studies* 40 (Sept. 1979): 510-31.

Sweet, William Warren. *Religion in the Development of American Culture, 1765-1840*. 1952. Reprint. Gloucester, MA: Peter Smith, 1963.

—. *Revivalism in America: Its Origin, Growth and Decline*. 1944. Reprint. Gloucester, MA: Peter Smith, 1965.

Tanner, Annie Clark. *A Mormon Mother*. Salt Lake City: Tanner Trust Fund, 1991.

Taylor, Alan. "The Early Republic's Supernatural Economy: Treasure Seeking in the American Northeast, 1780-1830." *American Quarterly* 38 (Spring 1986): 6-34.

Taylor, John. *The Government of God*. Liverpool, Eng.: S. W. Richards, n.d.

Taylor, Samuel W. *The Kingdom or Nothing: The Life of John Taylor, Militant Mormon*. New York: Macmillan Publishing Co., 1976.

Thomas, Mark D. "Scholarship and the Book of Mormon." In *The Word of*

God: Essays on Mormon Scripture. Ed. Dan Vogel. Salt Lake City: Signature Books, 1990.

Thompson, John. *Mormonism–Increase of the Army* ... Washington, D. C.: Buell and Blanchard, 1858.

Thorp, Malcolm R. "The Religious Backgrounds of Mormon Converts in Britain, 1837-52." *Journal of Mormon History* 4 (1977): 51-66.

—. Review of *The Second Coming: Popular Millenarianism, 1780-1850*, by J. F. C. Harrison. *Brigham Young University Studies* 21 (Fall 1981): 534-536.

Thrupp, Sylvia L., ed. *Millennial Dreams in Action*. The Hague: Mouton and Co., 1962.

Toon, Peter. *Puritans, the Millennium and Future Israel: Puritan Eschatology, 1600-1660*. Cambridge, Eng.: James Clark, 1970.

Toqueville, Alexis de. *Democracy in America*. 2 vols. Ed. Phillip Bradley. 1835. Reprint. New York: Vintage Books, 1945.

Tucker, Pomeroy. *Origin, Rise, and Progress of Mormonism* ... New York: D. Appleton and Co., 1867.

Tullidge, Edward Wheelock. *History of Salt Lake City*. Salt Lake City: n.p., 1886.

Turner, Rodney. "Franklin D. Richards and the Pearl of Great Price." In *Regional Studies in Latter-day Saint Church History: British Isles*. Ed. Donald Q. Cannon. Provo, UT: Brigham Young University, 1990.

Tuveson, Ernest Lee. *Millennium and Utopia: A Study in the Background of the Idea of Progress*. 1949. Reprint. New York: Harper and Row, 1964.

—. *Redeemer Nation: The Idea of America's Millennial Role*. Chicago: University of Chicago Press, 1968.

Underwood, Grant. "Apocalyptic Adversaries: Mormonism Meets Millerism." *John Whitmer Historical Association Journal* 7 (1987): 53-61.

—. "Book of Mormon Usage in Early LDS Theology." *Dialogue: A Journal of Mormon Thought* 17 (Autumn 1984): 35-74.

—. "Early Mormon Millennialism: Another Look." *Church History* (June 1985): 215-29.

—. "Early Mormon Perceptions of Contemporary America: 1830-1846." *Brigham Young University Studies* 26 (Summer 1986): 49-61.

—. *The Millenarian World of Early Mormonism*. Urbana: University of Illinois, 1993.

—. "Millenarianism and the Early Mormon Mind." *Journal of Mormon History* 9 (1982): 41-51.

—. "The Religious Milieu of English Mormonism." In *Mormons in Early Victorian Britain*. Eds. Richard L. Jensen and Malcolm R. Thorp. Salt Lake City: University of Utah Press, 1989.

—. "Re-Visioning Mormon History." *Pacific Historical Review* 55 (Aug. 1986): 403-426.

—. "'Saved or Damned': Tracing a Persistent Protestantism in Early Mormon Thought." *Brigham Young University Studies* 25 (Summer 1985): 85-103.

—. "Seminal Versus Sesquicentennial Saints: A Look at Mormon Millennialism." *Dialogue: A Journal of Mormon Thought* 14 (Spring 1981): 32-44.

Updike, John. *The Coup.* New York: Alfred A. Knopf, 1978.

Van Wagoner, Richard S. "The Making of a Mormon Myth: The 1844 Transfiguration of Brigham Young." *Dialogue: A Journal of Mormon Thought* 28 (Winter 1995): 1-24.

—. *Mormon Polygamy: A History.* Salt Lake City: Signature Books, 1989.

—. *Sidney Rigdon: A Portrait of Religious Excess.* Salt Lake City: Signature Books, 1994.

—, and Steve Walker. "Joseph Smith: 'The Gift of Seeing.'" *Dialogue: A Journal of Mormon Thought* 15 (Summer 1982): 49-68.

Vaughn, William Preston. *The Anti-masonic Party in the United States, 1826-1843.* Lexington: University Press of Kentucky, 1983.

Vogel, Dan. *Indian Origins and the Book of Mormon.* Salt Lake City: Signature Books, 1986.

—. "The Locations of Joseph Smith's Early Treasure Quests." *Dialogue: A Journal of Mormon Thought* 27 (Fall 1994): 197-231.

—. "Mormonism's 'Anti-Masonick Bible.'" *John Whitmer Historical Association Journal* 9 (1989): 17-30.

—. *Religious Seekers and the Advent of Mormonism.* Salt Lake City: Signature Books, 1988.

—. ed. *The Word of God: Essays on Mormon Scripture.* Salt Lake City: Signature Books, 1990.

Walker, Ronald W. "B. H. Roberts and the Woodruff Manifesto." *Brigham Young University Studies* 22 (Summer 1982): 363-66.

—. "The Persisting Idea of American Treasure Hunting." *Brigham Young University Studies* 24 (Fall 1984): 429-59.

—. "Seeking the 'Remnant': The Native American During the Joseph Smith Period." *Journal of Mormon History* 19 (Spring 1933): 1-33.

—. "Sheaves, Bucklers and the State: Mormon Leaders Respond to the Dilemmas of War." *Sunstone* 7 (July-Aug. 1982): 43-56.

—. "The Stenhouses and the Making of a Mormon Image." *Journal of Mormon History* 1 (1974): 51-72.

Wallis, Wilber B. "Reflections on the History of Pre-millennial Thought." In *Interpretation and History.* Eds. R. Laird Harris, Swee-Hwa Quek, and J. Robert Vannoy. Singapore: Christian Life Publishers, 1986.

Walters, Wesley P. "New Light on Mormon Origins from Palmyra Revival." *Dialogue: A Journal of Mormon Thought* 4 (Spring 1969): 60-81.

Walzer, Michael. *The Revolution of the Saints: A Study in the Origins of Radical Politics.* Cambridge, MA: Harvard University Press, 1965.

Watson, Elden J., ed. *The Orson Pratt Journals.* Salt Lake City: Elden Jay Watson, 1975.

Weber, Eugene. *A Modern History of Europe.* New York: W. W. Norton and Company, 1971.

Weber, Max. *Economy and Society.* 3 vols. New York: Bedminister Press, 1968.

—. *The Sociology of Religion.* Trans. Ephraim Fischoff. Boston: Beacon Press, 1963.

Weber, Timothy P. *Living in the Shadow of the Second Coming: American Pre-millennialism, 1875-1925.* New York: Oxford University Press, 1979.

—. "Pre-millennialism and the Branches of Evangelicalism." In *The Variety of American Evangelicalism.* Eds. Donald W. Dayton and Robert K. Johnston. Knoxville: University of Tennessee Press, 1991.

Wells, Merle W. *Anti-Mormonism in Idaho, 1872-92.* Provo, UT: Brigham Young University Press, 1978.

Wells, Ronald A. *The Wars of America: Christian Views.* Grand Rapids: William B. Eerdmans Publishing Company, 1981.

Werly, John M. "Pre-millennialism and the Paranoid Style." *American Studies* 18 (Spring 1977): 39-55.

Whitcomb, John C. "C. H. Spurgeon, Biblical Inerrancy and Pre-millennialism." Review of *Lamplighter and Son*, by Craig Skinner. *Grace Theological Journal* 7 (Fall 1986): 229-34.

White, Jean Bickmore. "The Making of the Convention President: The Political Education of John Henry Smith." *Utah Historical Quarterly* 39 (Fall 1971): 350-69.

—. ed. *Church, State, and Politics: The Diaries of John Henry Smith.* Salt Lake City: Signature Books in association with Smith Research Associates, 1990.

Whitmer, David. *An Address to All Believers in Christ.* Richmond, MO: n.p., 1887.

Wiest, Walter E. "Lincoln's Political Ethic: An Alternative to American Millennialism." *American Journal of Theology and Philosophy* 4 (Sept. 1983): 116-26.

Wilcox, Alanson. *A History of the Disciples of Christ in Ohio.* Cincinnati: Standard Publishing, 1918.

Wilson, Bryan R. "An Analysis of Sect Development." *American Sociological Review* 24 (Feb. 1959): 3-15.

—. *Magic and the Millennium: A Sociological Study of Religious Movements of*

Protest Among Tribal and Third-World Peoples. London: Heineman Education Books, 1973.

Wilson, John F. "Comment on 'Two Roads to the Millennium.'" *Church History* 32 (Sept. 1963): 339-43.

—. "Some Comparative Perspectives on the Early Mormon Movement and the Church-State Question, 1830-1845." *Journal of Mormon History* 8 (1981): 63-77.

—. "The Status of Civil Religion in America." In *The Religion of the Republic.* Ed. Elwyn Smith. Philadelphia: Fortress Press, 1971.

Winn, Kenneth H. *Exiles in a Land of Liberty: Mormons in America, 1830-1846.* Chapel Hill: University of North Carolina Press, 1989.

Wolfinger, Henry J. "An Irrepressible Conflict." Review of *The "Americanization" of Utah for Statehood,* by Gustive O. Larson. *Dialogue: A Journal of Mormon Thought* 6 (Autumn-Winter 1971): 124-31.

—. "A Reexamination of the Woodruff Manifesto in Light of Utah Constitutional History." *Utah Historical Quarterly* 39 (Fall 1971): 328-49.

Wood, Gordon S. "Evangelical America and Early Mormonism." *New York History* 61 (Oct. 1980): 359-86.

Young, Kimball. *Isn't One Wife Enough?* New York: Henry Holt and Company, 1954.

Zamora, Lois Parkinson, ed. *The Apocalyptic Vision in America: Interdisciplinary Essays on Myth and Culture.* Bowling Green, Ohio: Bowling Green University Popular Press, 1982.

Theses And Dissertations

Bachman, Danel W. "A Study of the Mormon Practice of Plural Marriage Before the Death of Joseph Smith." Master's thesis, Purdue University, 1975.

Chadwick, Effie Marion. "Extent to Which Early Mormon Beliefs and Practices Reflected the Environment of That People." Master's thesis, Brigham Young University, 1940.

Collette, D. Brent. "In Search of Zion: A Description of Early Mormon Millennial Utopianism as Revealed Through the Life of Edward Partridge." Master's thesis, Brigham Young University, 1977.

Eddins, Boyd L. "The Mormons and the Civil War." Master's thesis, Utah State University, 1966.

Ehat, Andrew F. "Joseph Smith's Introduction of Temple Ordinances and the 1844 Mormon Succession Question." Master's thesis, Brigham Young University, 1981.

Fielding, Robert Kent. "The Growth of the Mormon Church in Kirtland, Ohio." Ph.D. diss., Indiana University, 1957.

Gentry, Leland H. "A History of the Latter-day Saints in Northern Missouri from 1836-1839." Ph.D. diss., Brigham Young University, 1965.

Godfrey, Kenneth W. "Causes of Mormon Non-Mormon Conflict in Hancock County, Illinois, 1839-1846." Ph.D. diss., Brigham Young University, 1967.

Higdon, Barbara McFarlane. "The Role of Preaching in the Early Latter Day Saint Church, 1830-1846." Ph.D. diss., University of Missouri, 1961.

Hill, Marvin S. "The Role of Christian Primitivism in the Origin and Development of the Mormon Kingdom, 1830-1844." Ph.D. diss., University of Chicago, 1968.

Jensen, Therald N. "Mormon Theory of Church and State." Ph.D. diss., University of Chicago, 1938.

Jones, Shirley Greenwood. "Brigham Young's Rhetoric: A Critical and Cultural Analysis of Key Sermons in Five Rhetorical Events." Ph.D. diss., University of Utah, 1992.

Lewis, Wayne J. "Mormon Land Ownership as a Factor in Evaluating the Extent of Mormon Settlements and Influence in Missouri, 1831-1841." Master's thesis, Brigham Young University, 1981.

Parkin, Max H. "The Nature and Cause of Internal and External Conflict of the Mormons in Ohio Between 1830 and 1838." Master's thesis, Brigham Young University, 1966.

Poll, Richard D. "The Twin Relic: A Study of Mormon Polygamy and the Campaign by the Government of the United States for Its Abolition, 1852-1890." Master's thesis, Texas Christian University, 1939.

Quinn, D. Michael. "The Mormon Hierarchy, 1832-1932: An American Elite." Ph.D. diss., Yale University, 1976.

Reinwand, Louis G. "An Interpretive Study of Mormon Millennialism During the Nineteenth Century with Emphasis on Millennial Developments in Utah." Master's thesis, Brigham Young University, 1971.

Robertson, A. Richard. "A Comparative History of the Periodicals of the Church of Jesus Christ of Latter-day Saints." Master's thesis, University of Utah, 1951.

Tappan, Paul Wilbur. "Mormon-Gentile Conflict: A Study of the Influence of Public Opinion on In-Group Versus Out-Group Interaction with Special Reference to Polygamy." Ph.D. diss., University of Wisconsin, 1939.

Underwood, Grant. "Early Mormon Millennialism: Another Look." Master's thesis, Brigham Young University, 1981.

Whittaker, David J. "Early Mormon Pamphleteering." Ph.D. diss., Brigham Young University, 1982.

Woodford, Robert J. "The Historical Development of the Doctrine and Covenants." Ph.D. diss., Brigham Young University, 1974.

Index

Aberhart, William, 30n58

Abraham, chosen seed, 224; lineage, 46

Abrahamic covenant, 96

Ahlstrom, Sydney, 8

Albany, New York, 75; destruction of predicted, 201

Allen, Andrew J., 183

Allen, O. M., 188

America, chosen land, 55, 226; divine mission of, 21, 26; promised land to Nephites and Mormons, 48; redeemer nation, 26; site of City of Zion, 95

amnesty petition, 208-209

Anthon, Charles, 47

anti-Christ, 18

anti-Mormon party, 134

anti-Mormonism, 90, 117, 140, 142-43

anti-polygamy campaign, 5-6, 179-211, 226-29

apocalypse, 15

apocalyptic tradition, 14

apocalypticism, 30, 66

apostles, 128; to witness Christ's return, 112

apostolic Church, 38

Appomattox, 176

Armageddon, 25, 222n30

Army of Israel, 108

Arrington, Leonard, 85

Arthur, Chester, 180-81, 194

Asbury, Francis, 28

Augustine, 20

baptism for the dead, 130

Barlow, Philip, 9

bigamy, 186. See also polygamy

blood atonement, 156

Boggs, Lilburn, 4, 120, 134

Book of Mormon, 31, 96, 128, 166; and Mormon eschatology, 53; answered religious questions, 62; anti-masonic nature of, 56; appealed to religious seekers, 52; associates Indians with lost tribes of Israel, 48; break with Protestantism, 50; coming forth to precede last days, 49; condemnation of Jacksonian America, 53; document of social protest, 54; dualism in, 55; fulfillment of prophecy, 53; identifies Indians as Lamanites, 47, 94; importance of America in, 55, 95; means of preparing for the Millennium, 45; mission to recover lost remnant of Israel, 94; most correct book on earth, 49; prophecies regarding Christ's return, 46; sign that gathering had begun, 94; testified of Joseph Smith's mission, 64; three Nephites, 202; to precede Christ's return, 45, 47

Boston, 75, 201

British Isles, 81

Brown, Ira, 1

Buchanan, James, 157, 167

burned-over district, 28, 34-35

Burridge, Kenelm, 10, 132

Bushman, Richard, 52

Caldwell County, Missouri, 111, 117

Camp Douglas, 168

Camp Floyd, 163, 167-68

Campbell, Alexander, 38, 45, 61-62, 69, 84

Campbellites, 60, 69

Canada, 6, 81, 196

Cannon, Abraham H., 203

Cannon, Angus M., 192

Cannon, George Q., importance of current dispensation, 193-94; Joseph Smith's 1891 prophecy, 206-207; Joseph Smith's prophecies to be fulfilled, 185; oath in Nauvoo temple, 173; Salt Lake temple, 214; temple to be built in center stake, 171

Card, Charles Ora, 196

Carlin, Thomas, 134

Carroll County, Missouri, 117

Carson Valley, Nevada, 162

Carthage, Illinois, 174

Catholic church, 56

Catholicism, enemy to protestantism, 28

celestial law, 205. See also polygamy

celestial marriage, 131. See also polygamy

center stake of Zion, 176, 198, 218

cholera, 109

Christ. See Jesus Christ

Christianity, apocalyptic tradition, 14-15, 19-20; first century, 14; restored through Joseph Smith, 50

Church of the Devil, 20

Church of the Lamb of God, 55

City of God, The, 20

City of Zion, 61, 64, 90, 171; converging point in last days, 97; Independence, Missouri, identified as site of, 99; on the borders of the Lamanites, 95; place of refuge, 91, 97; plot map of, 106n58; purpose of, 97

civil millennialism, 25

civil religion, 26, 224

Civil War, 78-79, 163-77, 215, 226; Joseph Smith prophecy regarding, 75-78, 164; prelude to the apocalypse, 79; to cleanse Missouri, 170

Clawson, Rudger, 217

Clay County, Missouri, 106, 108-109, 111

Clayton, William, 131, 142

Cleveland, Grover, 209

cohabitation, 5-6, 192. See also polygamy

Cohn, Norman, millenarian model, 16-19, 66

Colesville, New York, 86

Colesville Saints, 86, 98-99

Columbia College, 47

Commerce, Illinois, 126

communitarianism, 228. *See also* Law of Consecration

Condie, Gibson, 206

Constitution, 75, 153, 168-69, 201

Cotton, John, 23

Council of Fifty, 139

Cowdery, Oliver, 40, 98, 113, 118, 126; regarding end of world, 71; to locate site for City of Zion, 95

Cowley, Matthias, 215, 218

Cullom-Struble Bill, 201-202, 204, 208

Cumming, Alfred, 160, 162

Daniel, Book of, 14

danites, 118, 156

Darby, John Nelson, 31n58

Davidson, James West, 14, 55, 118

Daviess County, Missouri, 117

democrats, 133-34, 161

Deseret, State of, 6

Deseret News, 154, 169, 194

Disciples of Christ, 45

dispensationalism, 31n58

Doctrine and Covenants, 78, 184, 188

Douglas, Stephen A., 133, 137, 166

dualism, apocalyptic expectations, 57-58; in Nauvoo, 134; in Book of Mormon, 53, 55; in Christian thought, 16; in early Mormonism, 46, 53, 59; Mormons and gentiles, 75; in Kirtland temple dedicatory prayer, 113; premillennialism and, 43; postmillennialism and, 28

Dunklin, Daniel, 107-109

Dyer, Francis P., 175

economics, status of early Mormons, 38n22

Edmunds, George F., 191

Edmunds Act, 191-94, 196; precursor to Millennium, 194

Edmunds-Tucker Act, 200-201

Edwards, Jonathan, 23, 25; postmillennialism of, 24

Elliot, John, 21

Emancipation Proclamation, 174

England, 79, 82

eschatology, 2, 13, 223; Christian, 16; diversity of, 65; Joseph Smith, 45; Mormonism and America, 61; Mormonism and the gathering, 94; Mormon theology, 46; Jonathan Edwards and, 24; premillennial in Book of Mormon, 53

Ether, 95

evangelicalism, 23

Evening and Morning Star, 54, 67-68, 99, 103

extermination order, 4

Eyring, Henry, 193

Fancher party, 160

Far West, Missouri, 4, 111, 116, 117, 148

Fielding, Joseph, 134

Fillmore, Utah, 155

Finney, Charles G., 28, 33

First Council of Seventy, 218

Fishing River, 108-109

Ford, Thomas, 145, 224n5

Fox sisters, 34n6

freemasonry, enemy to protestantism, 28

freemasons, 56

French and Indian War, 25

frontier thesis, 34n6

Gager, John, 228

Garden of Eden, 37

Gathering, Book of Mormon a sign
of, 94; escape from tribulation,
93; importance of Missouri, 97;
Indians at the New Jerusalem,
48; Jews to Jerusalem, 48; Mormon hymns regarding, 69; necessary to precede millennium, 81;
New Jerusalem, 60; premillennial belief regarding, 94; to include North and South America, 125; to prepare for Christ's
return, 53, 71-72, 90, 120-21; to
separate righteous from wicked,
89; Utah, 151-52

gentiles, 7; destruction of, 83

ghost dance, 202-203

gold plates, 51-52

Grant, Jedediah M., 151, 154

Grant, Ulysses S., 176, 180

Great Awakening, 24

Great Britain, 187

Greely, Horace, 106n59

Hancock County, Illinois, 134

Hansen, Klaus, 7, 91, 209-10

Harding, Stephen S., 174

Hardy, Carmon, 209-10

Harmony, Pennsylvania, 39

Harris, Martin, 47, 56, 118; regarding Christ's return, 71

Harrison, Benjamin, 180, 208-209

Hatch, Lorenzo, 194

Hatch, Nathan, 7, 35, 36, 37n21,
54, 63

Hill, Marvin, 38, 133

history, God's role in, 14; methodology of, 9-11; millennial, 16; sacred, 14; teleological, 8

Holy One of Israel, 112

Holy Order, 141

Howard, Richard, 78

Howe, Eber D., 76, 90

Huntington, Demick, 188n42

Huntington, Oliver, 183-84

Hutchinson, Anthony, 79

Hyde, Orson, 79, 80, 118-19, 157,
172

Idaho Test Oath, 201

Independence, Missouri, 67, 98,
100-101, 108; identified as site
of Zion, 99; Indians to assist in
building temple at, 199; Mormon press destroyed at, 105;
gathering place, 99

Indian territory, 98

Indians, 64, 96, 103, 156; a tool to
destroy gentiles, 48, 102, 199; descendants of Book of Mormon
authors, 94; ghost dance movement, 202-203; identified as Lamanites, 47; identified as lost
tribe of Israel, 21n30; included
in restoration of Israel, 82; Mormon alliance with, 104; Mormon
belief regarding origins of, 48;

primary role of, 199; to assist building New Jerusalem, 100

Islam, 8

Israel, 171; Nephites and Lamanites identified as branch of, 46, 47; lost tribes, 21n30, 182; restoration of, 82

Jackson, Andrew, 76, 106n61; Indian relocation by, 48, 96

Jackson County, Missouri, achievements at prelude to God's kingdom on earth, 148; Civil War to clear for Mormon return, 171; gathering at, 4; imminence of Mormon return to, 185, 198, 217-18; identified as in Mormon enemies' hands, 102; importance of in Mormon millennialism, 107-108; Law of Consecration initiated at, 101; Mormons flee from, 106; Mormons forced to gather outside of, 110; Mormon growth in, 104-105; New Jerusalem to be built in, 86; Parley Pratt missionary to, 98; sanctuary for Mormon poor, 101

Jacksonian America, 36, 57, 61, 63, 129; Book of Mormon condemned, 53

Jehovah's Witnesses, 30

Jerusalem, 46, 51, 130; Mormon theology identifies two locations, 47

Jesus Christ, 4, 8, 15, 35, 38; appeared to Joseph Smith, 41-42, 113; appeared to Oliver Cowdery, 113; battle with Satan, 27; early Christian belief regarding return of, 15; imminent return of, 42; Joseph Smith to prepare for, 44; postmillennial role of, 24

Jews, 95; apocalyptic tradition of, 14; conversion prior to winding-up scene, 44, 49; to gather to Jerusalem, 48

John the Baptist, 74

Johnson, Benjamin F., 219

Johnson, Sixtus E., 185

Johnston, Albert Sydney, 157-63

Jordon River, 163

Kanab, Utah, 185

Kane, Thomas L., 162

Kimball, Heber C., 83, 146, 169, 175

Kirtland, Ohio, gathering place, 4, 60, 98, 114; internal dissent in, 108, 111, 114; Law of Consecration initiated at, 84; Lucy Mack leads Saints to, 51; millennialism of Saints at, 101, 106; prophecy on war received at, 75-76; temple, 112-14, 116; temporary achievements at, 148

Kirtland High Council, 109, 111

Kirtland Safety Society Anti-Banking Company, 115-16

Lamanites, 46, 95, 96, 199, 203. *See also* Indians

last days, 21, 44-45, 83, 97; signs of, 82

Law, William, 140

Law of Consecration, 84-85, 87, 99, 155; in Jackson County, Missouri, 101; in Kirtland, Ohio, 84

Lee, Anne, 34n6

Lee, Robert E., 176

Lehi, 51

Leone, Mark, 7

Liberty, Missouri, 107-108, 111, 124

Limerick, Patricia Nelson, 147n117

Lincoln, Abraham, 169, 174

literalism, 64, 130, 148

Liverpool, 83

Logue, Larry, 211

Lund, Anthon H., 203

Lyman, Francis M., 206

Malachi, 72

Manifesto, 6; breaking point be-
    tween Mormon past and future,
    227, 229; diversity of meaning
    of, 210-11; issued by Wilford
    Woodruff, 204-207; millennial-
    ism and, 216, 220-21; political ef-
    fects of, 208

Manti, Utah, 191

Manti temple, 200

Mather, Cotton, 21, 22

Mather, Increase, 21

McLellin, William, 118

McNeill, William, 11

Mead, Sidney, 26

Mede, Joseph, 21n30

Messenger and Advocate, 40

Methodist, 39

Mexico, 6, 196

Middle Ages, 20

millenarian, 42, 65; characteristics
    of early movements, 30; model,
    16-19, 66

millenarianism, 2, 18, 70

Millennial Star, 67-68, 153, 174, 187

millennialism, anti-polygamy cam-
    paign and, 183, 185, 195; apoca-
    lyptic tradition of, 14; diversity
    of meaning of, 8; dualism of, 43;
    enthusiasm of, 11; expounded
    in Mormon newspapers, 67; his-
    toriography of, 1-2; history of,
    13-31; impact on social struc-
    ture, 13; impetus for Mormon
    separatism, 8; in New York, 37;
    leads to anti-Mormonism, 145;
    Manifesto leads to a decline of,
    216, 221, 228; meaning appropri-
    ated by others, 25; radicalism of,
    7-8; revivals and, 35; separatist
    tendencies of, 3; Utah War and,
    158

millennium, Book of Mormon to
    prepare for, 45; calamities neces-
    sary prior to, 149; early Mor-
    mon belief in imminence of, 72;
    eschatology and, 223; gathering
    to prepare for, 93, 98; human ef-
    forts to hasten, 88; human inter-
    vention and, 22; imminence of,
    33; imminence proven false, 18;
    in premillennial thought, 19, 65;
    in postmillennial thought, 65;
    Joseph Smith's revelations con-
    cerning, 58, 61; last stage of his-
    tory of, 15; Law of Consecration
    to prepare for, 84; Manifesto
    and, 207-208, 211, 220; mem-
    bers able to hasten, 154; meta-
    phoric interpretation of, 19-20;
    oppression of Mormons sign of
    imminence of, 181, 185; period
    of peace, 22; preparation for,
    93; ramification of delay of, 226-
    27; signs of, 75, 77, 81; theoc-
    racy in preparation for, 129;
    Utah War precursor to, 157; Wil-

ford Woodruff predicts nearness of, 214

Miller, Perry, 33

Miller, William, 135

Millerism, 29n56

Millerites, 30, 34

Mississippi River, 124, 126

Missouri, 80, 100, 103

Moody, Dwight, L., 30n58

Moore, Laurence, 224-25

Moorhead, James, 1

Morgan, John, 203

Morgan, Joseph, 23

Mormon bible, 45. *See also* Book of Mormon

Mormon Reformation, 153-55

Mormonism, break with traditional christianity, 8, 42; rejection of pluralism, 40; viewed as enemy to protestantism, 28; viewed as un-American, 7

Moroni, 43

Morrill Act, 182, 186, 191

Moses, 138, 225; appeared to Joseph Smith and Oliver Cowdery, 113

Mountain Meadows, 160, 167

Nauvoo, Illinois, 4-5, 123-48; baptism for the dead at, 130; polygamy in, 130-32, 140; temple, 130, 132, 144, 146, 174

Nauvoo Charter, 5, 127, 136, 140, 145

Nauvoo City Council, 137

Nauvoo Expositor, 143

Nauvoo Legion, 127, 129, 139, 142

negroes, 103-105

Nephites, America a promised land to, 48, 74; anti-pluralistic nature of, 54; importance of historicity in Mormon theology, 52-53; previously lived on American continent, 43-44; righteous people, 46; visitation by three who tarried seen as a sign of coming millennium, 202

Nevada Territory, 167

new heaven/new earth, 16, 43, 93, 223

New Israel, 91, 95, 126. *See also* Indians

New Jerusalem, built with assistance of Indians, 100; gathering at, 61, 64, 91, 94, 96; importance of in Mormonism, 110; located on the American continent, 21, 32, 47, 95; place of gathering, 60; revelations concerning, 58, 198; to be built in Independence, Missouri, 86, 99-100

New York City, 75; destruction of predicted, 201

New York Times, 157, 181

Nickerson, Freeman, 75

Noah, 70

Noyes, John, 33

nullification crisis, 76-78

Nuttall, Leonard John, 185

Oaks, Dallin, 143n92

O'Dea, Thomas, 127

Old Testament, 130, 138

Oneida community, 29, 34n6

Origen, 19

Owen, John, 23

Painesville Telegraph, 76

Palestine, 95

Palmyra, New York, 37, 40, 46

patriarchal blessings, 9

patriotic millennialism, 25

Penrose, Charles W., 166, 188, 189n48, 219

perpetual emigration fund, 153

Pessen, Edward, 132

Phelps, William W., anti-Mormons in Missouri and, 107; believed Book of Mormon identified Indians, 48; compared contemporary America to Book of Mormon civilization, 74; deliberates bringing "free people of color" to Missouri, 103; disassociated from Mormon church, 119; editor of *Evening and Morning Star*, 67; expanded location for Zion, 126n11; identified dissolution of South Carolina as a sign of the coming millennium, 77-78; on Mormon communitariansim, 86n80

plural marriage. *See* polygamy

plural wife, 142. *See also* polygamy

Plymouth brethren, 31n58

polygamy, 179-211; and Canada, 6; and Joseph Smith, Jr., 131; and Mexico, 6; in Nauvoo, 130-32, 140; casualty of assimilation, 221, 229; cause of conflict in Utah, 5-6; continuation of after the Manifesto, 213; expected to continue until world's end, 220; increased during Mormon Reformation, 155-56; intertwined with

theocracy, 216; James Buchanan's reaction to, 157; lack of worthiness led to abandonment of, 215; Manifesto, 6, 204-207, 210-11; millennialism and, 226-27; public announcement of, 7, 179, 209; secrecy of, 140-41

popular sovereignty, 161

postmillennialism, and Civil War, 165; and revivialism, 13, 28; definition of, 65; diversity of meaning of, 24n39; emphasis on human effort, 23; in eighteenth century, 22; in nineteenth century, 26; of Augustine, 20; of Jonathan Edwards, 25; optimism of, 223; rejected by Book of Mormon, 47; rejected by Sidney Rigdon, 69

Pratt, Orson, belief regarding Christ's imminent return, 101; believed signs of last days were visible, 158, 159, 187; includes footnotes in Doctrine and Covenants regarding Joseph Smith's millennial prophecy, 188-89; rejects United States, 145

Pratt, Parley P., author of *A Voice of Warning*, 83; editor of *Millennial Star*, 68; letter to Queen Victoria, 83; mission to Jackson County, Missouri, 98; on hostility to Mormonism, 156; prophesied America's destruction, 72, 75; purpose for Book of Mormon, 47-49; reaction to expanded definition of Zion, 125n11, role of Zion's Camp, 107

premillennialism, and Book of Mormon, 47, 53; and puritans, 22; and Sidney Rigdon, 69; characteristics of, 19, 65; diversity of interpretation of, 2, 11, 13, 24n39; in Middle Ages, 20; in early America, 21; in nineteenth century, 29; model of, 16-17; pessimism of, 223

presiding bishopric, 218

primitivism, 61

Puritans, 21, 22, 54, 61, 91

rapture, 31n58

Ray County, Missouri, 117

Reformation, 20

Republican millennialism, 25

Republican platform, 167, 180

response model, 17n16

Revelation, Book of, 14-16, 20, 23

revelation, modern, 8-9, 62

revivals, 13, 35; evangelical nature of, 30; factious nature of, 34; freedom found in, 34; in New York, 28, 33, 37; quest for perfection, 33; sign of postmillennialism, 27

Reynolds, George, 185-87

Rich, Charles, C., 159

Richards, Franklin D., 197, 206

Richards, Franklin S., 204

Ridge, Martin, 228-29

Rigdon, Sidney, 60n113, 87-88, 119-20; communitarianism of, 84; criticism of postmillennialism, 69, 70n15; flees Kirtland, Ohio, 116

Rochester, New York, 28, 77

Salt Lake City, municipal elections of 1890, 201

Salt Lake temple, 153, 200; built to receive Christ, 214

Salt Lake Tribune, 207

San Bernardino, California, 162

Satan, 22, 57; battle with Christ, 27

Saxton, N. C., 77

Schwartz, Hillel, 18

scripture, modern, 8-9, 11

Second Advent, 20, 58, 68

second anointing, 152

Second Coming, Book of Mormon to precede, 47; Boston inhabitants advised to prepare for, 75; City of Zion to be built prior to, 98; Civil War catalyst for, 79; delay of, 20, 229; diversity of meaning in Mormonism, 2; gathering preparatory for, 121; imminence of, 6; in Mormon hymn books, 69; Manifesto and, 210; Mormon eschatology offers answers regarding, 46; Orson Hyde warns England regarding, 81; revelations declare time is at hand, 59; righteous to be gathered in preparation for, 53; Saints warned to prepare for, 123; theme during 1890 general conference, 205-206; Wilford Woodruff predicts nearness of, 190, 197

Second Great Awakening, 27, 30, 34-35, 51; democratic nature of, 29

seekers, 29, 31-32, 37n21, 38, 49; Book of Mormon appealed to, 52

Seward, William H., 174

Sewel, Samuel, 21n30, 23

Shakers, 29-30, 34n6

Shipps, Jan, 8

slavery, catalyst for Second Coming, 79; Civil War and, 169, 172, 174; Joseph Smith's revelations and, 164; linked to polygamy, 179-80; Missourians distrust Mormons regarding, 103; uprising to precede Second Coming, 103n47

Smith, Emma, 142

Smith, George A., 71, 151

Smith, Hyrum, blood cries from the ground, 190; Civil War punishment for death of, 172-73; death of, 5, 142, 226

Smith, Jessie J., 109

Smith, Joseph, Jr., advises Mormons to resist mobs, 119-20; advises Saints in Missouri to maintain possession of land, 106; anointed king, 139-40; anxiety in early years, 38-40; arrested, 116; in Nauvoo, 148; blessed by father, 70; blood cries from the ground, 190; Book of Mormon testifies of mission of, 31, 64; calls Saints to prepare for Second Coming, 123; candidacy for U. S. presidency, 7, 137-38; charismatic seer, 36; chooses apostles and seventies, 109, 112; Civil War prophecy of, 164, 174; Civil War punishment for murder of, 172-73; continuing revelation through, 51; death of, 5, 6, 142-43, 226; desire to establish political kingdom, 7; first vision, 41-43, 53; flees Kirtland, Ohio, 116; instructs Saints to purchase land in Missouri, 110; instrument to prepare for the Millennium, 44; Law of Consecration,

84; Lieutenant-General of Nauvoo Legion, 79, 128, 142; millennial prophecy of, 183-84, 187-89, 191, 195, 203; millennial time-table delayed, 135-36; Mormon millennialism initiated with, 3-4, 223; polygamy of, 131; predicts members will witness Second Coming, 72; prophetic role of, 129; prophecy on war, 75-79, 103n47; receives vision: of Christ, 113; of Moses, 113; reveals location of City of Zion, 95; revelations: on economics, 86; regarding calamities, 70; regarding imminence of Second Coming, 65, 89; regarding Millennium, 61; role as millenarian prophet, 74; supernatural aid in economic pursuits, 36; to prepare way for Christ's return, 74; treasure seeking, 39; true Christianity restored through, 50; use of political institutions, 132; visited by Moroni, 43; visits Salt Lake temple, 214; warns Boston, Albany, and New York City of imminent destruction, 75; Zion's Camp, 107-109

Smith, Joseph, Sr., 36, 38, 70; family's religious differences, 39; patriarchal blessing given to Wilford Woodruff, 73

Smith, Joseph F., 202-203, 209

Smith, Lucy Mack, 51, 60

Snow, Erastus, 144, 196

Snow, Lorenzo, accommodation policy of, 209 219; and Mormon Reformation, 154; belief in imminent millennium, 203, 217-18, 227; predicts return to Jackson County, Missouri, 185

Son of Man, Civil War prelude to return of, 79; church leaders predict return of, 188-91, 197-98, 214-15; Joseph Smith pleads for return of, 124; polygamy to continue until return of, 200; signs of, 151, 207

South Carolina, 76-79, 164

Spencer, Orson, 152

spiritual wife, 141. *See also* polygamy

spiritualists, 34n6

St. George, Utah, 191, 193, 195, 214

St. Louis New Era, 140

Stegner, Wallace, 151

Stenhouse, Thomas B. H., 163

Stout, Hosea, 156

Stowe, Harriet Beecher, 179

Sweet, Leonard, 1, 13

Taylor, John, condemns government officials, 191, 194, 195; identifed Catholic church as Babylon, 56; millennialism of, 72, 80; on Mormons and Civil War, 167, 175; predicts Christ's imminent return, 200; regarding Joseph Smith's prophecies, 184; separatist strategy of, 6, 196; visits Salt Lake temple, 214

temple, 173, 198; at center stake, 171; command to build is rescinded, 124; Jackson County, Missouri, identified as site of, 99; to be built in America, 72; to be constructed in Missouri, 218; to receive Christ, 98

Thatcher, Moses, 187, 197, 206; and Manifesto, 205

theocracy, abandonment of, 228; and millennialism, 91, 216; in

Nauvoo, 128-29, 138, 140; in Utah Territory, 5, 153, 157, 181

Thomas, Arthur L., 208

Timely Warning to the People of England, A, 80

Times and Seasons, 67

Toqueville, Alexis de, 25

Turner, Frederick Jackson, 34n6

Tuveson, Ernest, 2, 14

Uncle Tom's Cabin, 179

underground, 6, 192, 196

Underwood, Grant, 2, 58, 62n124, 94, 120

United Order. *See* Law of Consecration

Updike, John, 223

urim and thummim, 52

Utah Territory, 5-6, 150, 181

Utah War, 159-63, 167, 226

Van Buren, Martin, 133

Varian, Charles S., 208

Vermont, 35

Victoria, Queen, 83

Vogel, Dan, 37

Waite, Morrison R., 186

Walker, Charles, 182, 188, 195, 211, 215

Washington, D. C., 124

Waterloo, New York, 87

Wavoka, 202n108

Weber, Eugene, 9

Western Reserve, 98

Whigs, 133-34

Whitaker, Thomas W., 187

White Mountains, 162

Whitmer, David, 118

Whitmer, John, 72, 104n48, 118

Wilkinson, Jemima, 34n6

Williams, Frederick G., 78, 118

Wilson, Bryan R., 16n16

Wood, Gordon, 2

Woodruff, Arizona, 194

Woodruff, Wilford, accommoda-
    tion policy of, 209; Civil War,
    169, condemns United States,
    80, 146-47; ghost dance move-
    ment, 202; Kirtland Safety Soci-
    ety, 116; Manifesto, 6, 204-207,
    216; Mormon Reformation, 154-
    55; millennialism of, 72, 73, 189;
    part of first generation of Mor-
    mons, 219; patriarchal blessing
    promises his witnessing winding-
    up scene, 73, 216; predicts
    Christ's imminent return, 83,
    188, 191, 196-97, 227, 314;
    prophecy in Manti temple, 200;
    Utah War, 159; wilderness reve-
    lation, 190-91

Wounded Knee, South Dakota, 202

Wyoming, 161

Young, Brigham, abandonment of
    Nauvoo, 145-47; Civil War, 166,
    168, 169; defies U. S. govern-
    ment, 156-58; "Epistle of the
    Twelve," 144; ghost legislature,
    170; importance of gathering,
    152; interview with Horace
    Greely, 106n59; millennialism
    of, 72; Mormon Reformation,
    154; on economics, 85n76; per-
    petual emigration fund, 153; pre-
    dicts destruction of United
    States government, 172-73, 175;
    predicts imminent return to
    Jackson County, Missouri, 171;
    relocates Saints to Utah, 150,
    225; Utah War, 160-62; visits
    Salt Lake temple, 214

Young, Brigham, Jr., 203, 218

Young, Lorenzo D., 159

Zane, Charles S., 208

Zion, center stake, 170-71, 176;
    City of, 4; designated as refuge,
    90; dualism of, 53; eschatologi-
    cal significance of, 110; identi-
    fied as the New Jerusalem, 47,
    96, 130; Indians to gather at, 48;
    in Utah, 151-52; Lamanites gath-
    ered on the borders of, 48; loca-
    · tion identified, 6, 48, 95; Mor-
    mon attempt to redeem, 107;
    Mormons expelled from, 106;
    Mormons to gather at, 53; re-
    demption of, 185, 197, 219;
    Saints told not to abandon land
    in, 105-106, 120; sanctuary from
    Babylon, 150; triumph of, 203

Zion's Camp, 107-10, 115, 118, 123